In Pursuit of Gold

IN PURSUIT OF GOLD

Chinese American Miners and Merchants in the American West

Sue Fawn Chung

UNIVERSITY OF ILLINOIS PRESS
URBANA, CHICAGO, AND SPRINGFIELD

First Illinois paperback, 2014

Manufactured in the United States of America
1 2 3 4 5 C P 5 4 3 2 1
∞ This book is printed on acid-free paper.

The Library of Congress cataloged the cloth edition as follows:
Chung, Sue Fawn
In pursuit of gold : Chinese American miners and
merchants in the American West / Sue Fawn Chung.
p. cm.
Includes bibliographical references and index.
ISBN 978-0-252-03628-6 (acid-free paper)
1. Chinese Americans—Nevada—Elko County—History—
19th century. 2. Gold miners—Nevada—Elko County—
History—19th century. 3. Merchants—Nevada—Elko County—
History—19th century. 4. Mining camps—Nevada—
Elko County—History—19th century. 5. Community life—
Nevada—Elko County—History—19th century. 6. Intercultural
communication—Nevada—Elko County—History—19th century.
7. Elko County (Nev.)—Ethnic relations—History—19th century.
8. Chinese Americans—Oregon—History—19th century.
9. Oregon—Ethnic relations—History—19th century.
10. Chinese Americans—West (U.S.)—History—19th century.
I. Title.
F847.E4C47 2011
979.3'1602—dc22 2010051965

PAPERBACK ISBN 978-0-252-08054-8

This book is dedicated to
Alan, Walter, and Alexander,
and my parents, who have
encouraged my pursuit
of knowledge

Contents

Foreword

ROGER DANIELS

NOT SO MANY years ago historians wrote as if whatever economic contribution Chinese workers might have made to the development of the American West ended with the completion of the transcontinental railroads. That myth was demolished by the 1986 publication of Sucheng Chan's *This Bittersweet Soil: The Chinese in California Agriculture, 1860–1910*, which transformed the nature of Chinese American history by showing that, in addition to being exploited toilers, Chinese had made important entrepreneurial contributions.

The great virtues of Sue Fawn Chung's fine study of a handful of small mining towns in Eastern Oregon and Nevada are that she shows that here, too, the Chinese economic presence was important and enduring, and the way in which she meticulously depicts small multiethnic communities with a very high level of mutual dependence at a time when Chinese were being persecuted severely in most areas of the American West in which they lived.

Sue Fawn, a former student whose varied contributions to Asian American history and culture I have long admired, is superbly equipped to create this study. In addition to the standard tools of the historian, she has a good command of the Chinese language and has participated in archeological digs and worked with anthropologists and historic preservationists. She is able to use the evidence developed in those disciplines as well as the traditional written and printed sources of the historian to craft detailed histories of vanished and largely ignored communities.

The fact that she has tramped over the relatively isolated and rugged terrain in several of the communities she writes about adds a dimension to her narrative. Her purpose is not antiquarian but historical: she provides a new dimension to the traditional picture of the Chinese in the exclusion era and makes meaningful comparisons between the experiences of the folks that she writes about and the more general experience of other Chinese Americans. Her closing summary puts it well: "In general during this early period [the Chinese of these towns] were not driven out [and] in all of the towns, at least one Chinese resident remained there long after mining declined and could not be considered a sojourner."

Acknowledgments

THIS PROJECT WOULD NOT have been possible without the assistance of many people and organizations. Only some are mentioned below.

My interest in Chinese American history began with the planning and execution of my senior honors thesis under Roger Daniels, who introduced me to the leading scholarship in the field at that time and the methodology and approach that I have used. My Chinese history background under David Farquhar, John King Fairbank, Benjamin Schwartz, John Pelzel, and Ezra Vogel was furthered by Joseph Levenson and Frederic E. Wakeman Jr. James Cahill enhanced my knowledge of Chinese art history and helped me develop an interest in photography and the arts.

The U.S. Department of Agriculture Forest Service, Humboldt–Toiyabe National Forest, especially Fred P. Frampton, archaeologist, and Dale Hom, a forest supervisor in the Olympia National Forest, did the initial investigations and sought the funding for the archaeological excavations at Island Mountain that inspired this study. The "Passport in Time" summer volunteer program from 1999 to 2001 provided the workers, including volunteers from the Wing Luke Museum, Seattle, Washington, who were supervised by graduate students working under Donald Hardesty, professor of anthropology, University of Nevada–Reno. Patricia Hunt-Jones, who worked all three summers on the dig, wrote her master's thesis on China Lem's store. Melissa Farnscomb served one summer as the graduate director of the dig and interviewed Della Baker Johns, whose family was close to China Lem. The Johns family kindly sent me photographs of Island Mountain and Gold Creek. Fred Frampton provided me with copies of the Hilda Matthey 1903 photographs. The late Mary and Elmer Rusco of the University of Nevada–Reno, worked on the dig and Mary introduced me to Chinese American historical archaeology. Priscilla Wegars of the University of Idaho–Moscow also served as a consultant on the dig and provided many insights for this project. William Fawcett of the Bureau of Land Management in Elko provided me with Eric Dillingham's report on Tuscarora. Guy Rocha, former Nevada state archivist, and his staff found numerous items on the Chinese in Nevada and solved problems like the records of the payment of poll taxes. The Nevada State Museum staff in Carson City made the artifacts from Tuscarora and Carson City's Zhigongtang available to me. The staff of the Northeastern Nevada Museum in Elko opened their archives to me, and Della John's granddaughter assisted in obtaining information and photographs. David Valentine, an archaeologist formerly with the Bureau of Land Management in Winnemucca, Nevada, assisted in numerous ways and read the first rough draft. Maxine Chan of Seattle, Washington, who lectured on Chinese medicine, foods, and customs, provided insights into the daily lives of the late nineteenth-century Chinese. John Fulton, Judge Lem Tuai, and other people too numerous to mention were extremely helpful, and for this I am very grateful.

Neil Thomsen, former head archivist at the National Archives and Records Administration (NARA), San Bruno, California, helped me locate immigration files, and William Greene and Dan Nealand continued his work for me. Vincent Chin shared his compilations of Chinese partnership records from NARA and Joseph Ellis worked with me at NARA, Washington, D.C., for several years. Roger Daniels introduced me to Marian Smith of the Immigration and Naturalization Service, as it was formerly called. Staff members at NARA in Laguna Nigel, California, and Seattle, Washington, also opened their Chinese immigration files for me.

The staff members of the University of California–Berkeley Bancroft Library and Ethnic Studies Library, and the University of California–San Diego Special Collections that houses the papers from Professor and Mrs. Richard Lingenfelter on mining, were very helpful. Staff members of the recorder's offices in Storey County, Elko County, Washoe County, and Douglas County (all in Nevada) opened their records for me. I also want to thank the staffs at the Family History and Genealogy Library in Salt Lake City, Utah, and Idaho State Library in Boise for their help.

For my research on Oregon, Leslie Hara Shick, who took me to John Day for several days, the Friends of Kam Wah Chung and Company, the Oregon Historical Society, and staff and directors of the Baker and Grant County Libraries, especially Gary Dielman and Perry Stokes, Oregon State Parks, R. Gregory Nokes, Barbara Sidway, and Oregon's First Lady, Mary Oberst, were invaluable in their enthusiasm and guidance. The University of Nevada–Las Vegas, National Forest Service, Nevada Humanities, Elko County Commissioners, and American Council of Learned Societies provided grants that made the research on the American West and nineteenth-century China possible.

University of Illinois Press editors Laurie Matheson and Tad Ringo were very helpful in editing the manuscript.

I also wish to thank my family, especially my husband Alan, and my sons Walter and Alexander, for their support. Alan drove or accompanied me to many remote locations and participated, like Alexander, in the the archaeological excavations at Island Mountain. Walter furnished much needed encouragement at critical times. I am grateful to them.

Introduction

TENS OF THOUSANDS OF Chinese came to the United States in pursuit of gold in the late nineteenth century. A popular late nineteenth-century Cantonese song described how "the Spirit of Money" graced a miner's home so that "in one blink" he had become a rich young man with gold and silver, no longer facing a desperate financial situation.[1] Few Chinese gold seekers were that fortunate however, and most faced many adversities. By examining the miners and merchants living in three small, relatively isolated, predominantly Chinese mining towns and other contemporary mining camps scattered throughout the American West, some insights into their lives has been possible: what their experiences were and how they compared to other Chinese mining communities, what Chinese traditions and practices they preserved, if and how they were financially successful, and what contributions they made to the development of the American West. Despite discriminatory laws and anti-Chinese movements, some merchants and miners flourished, bought and sold land, businesses, and mining claims, and remained in the United States for many decades.

The miners and merchants in the three towns of John Day, Oregon; Tuscarora, Nevada; and Island Mountain, Nevada, were selected for this study because the Chinese were among the early miners there; during the formative years in the history of the towns, they constituted the majority of the town's residents. The towns were established after the initial gold rush, so some of the Chinese miners and merchants had lived in other American mining towns and were probably familiar with some American ways. The three towns were in relatively isolated, mountainous areas having inhospitable weather: snow and cold in the winter, and heat in the summer. The climate and terrain were very different from the tropical, humid, and hilly southeastern China and adjustments to the environment had to be made quickly. The difficulty in reaching these mountainous places by wagon or foot meant that all of the residents became interdependent upon one another and were not caught up in the whirlwind of anti-Chinese rhetoric that was characteristic of larger EuroAmerican dominated mining towns. The influence of "outsiders" often was limited.

The Chinese helped build the towns and irrigation ditches and made the area productive—at first for mining, and later for agricultural production. They paid taxes and other fees that contributed to the funds of local and state governments. They purchased food products and other items from the local community members, especially EuroAmerican store owners and farmers, and supported the freighters who transported goods to and from the mining towns. In general during this early period between 1850 and 1900 they were not driven out of these three towns and they did not have their homes burned, common occurrences elsewhere.

The leaders of the communities, both EuroAmerican and Chinese, were not hostile toward each other and laid a foundation for a more harmonious atmosphere that was not found in most other mining towns during a time of virulent anti-Chinese sentiment. The limited size of the Chinese population permitted a closer examination of these communities over time through census data, archaeological finds, government records, oral interviews, and newspapers. These Chinese taught the other ethnic groups in the community about Chinese culture, foods, and beliefs, and had the opportunity to learn more about America than some of their fellow countrymen. In at least one town, their relationship with Native Americans involved recreational activities and even some marriages. In all of the towns, at least one Chinese resident remained there long after mining declined and could not be considered a "sojourner." In some ways the merchants and miners in these towns were similar to other gold miners and merchants in the Chinese diaspora but in many cases, as discussed in the conclusion, there were differences—so many previously held generalizations are not valid.

When the California gold fields began to be depleted in the mid-1850s, miners searched for new deposits. The two closest, uncharted territories were Oregon to the north and Nevada to the east. Like the EuroAmerican miners, the Chinese explored these areas and in the mid-1850s a substantial number of them began mining outside of California.

The mining communities in California have been studied and have not been considered in depth in this work because in all of the famous towns, the Chinese represented a minority of the population.[2] At the same time it is important to note that California's mining laws and anti-Chinese movements influenced most of the mining communities in the American West.[3] With the mid-1850s gold decline and completion of the first transcontinental railroad in 1869, the California miners, both Chinese and EuroAmerican, moved to Oregon, Nevada, Idaho, Washington, British Columbia, Montana, and elsewhere in search of new sites. EuroAmericans brought with them the prejudice and racism against the Chinese that had developed in California and that contributed to the violence that the Chinese immigrants often encountered.[4]

The Chinese were not unlike other immigrants in their dreams of instant wealth, new opportunities, and a better life. Until the late nineteenth century when gold mining was primarily taken over by large corporations with expensive machinery, the Chinese were involved in ephemeral placer mining, sometimes with the use of hydraulic equipment, throughout the American West, and sometimes into more capital-intensive quartz mining. A few brought with them some prior knowledge of mining techniques. The Chinese immigrants had a reputation of working hard as individuals or in groups, or for mine owners as wage laborers. Their success at making a profit from abandoned claims became legendary in the gold fields. But few have found answers as to how this was possible.

They faced enormous challenges from hostile miners who wrote anti-Chinese regulations to govern their districts and influenced state and federal legislation. When economic depression and high unemployment affected the EuroAmerican miners, they targeted the Chinese as a major cause of their plight because of the low wages paid them. In the 1870s Chinese miners earned $1.30 to $2 per day, with skilled miners earning $3 per day and foremen getting $4 to $10 dollars per day.[5] Ditch diggers, working ten to twelve hours per day, were paid $2.25 to $3 per day. EuroAmerican miners generally earned twice as much, but to compete with the Chinese they sometimes received only $2.75 without board. The low wages gave the Chinese an image of "cheap" workers, but a closer study of payroll records of the period may indicate otherwise when wages were not averaged but viewed in terms of work classification.

The Chinese presence coincided with a growing "color" consciousness that developed prior to and after the Civil War and the founding of labor unions whose leaders found a common enemy of the working man—the Chinese—that expanded union membership, united the new members, and helped them gain the support of aspiring politicians and many newspaper men. In this period of social Darwinism, a belief in the superiority of the white man, the influx of "different looking" new immigrants from eastern Europe, the growing nonmainstream religious groups such as Jews and Mormons, and the development of nativism and racism led to the Chinese becoming a scapegoat in anti-Chinese campaigns that were part of a larger phenomenon.

The miners' relationship to Chinese merchants played an important role in their lives. Sometimes these merchants left fragmentary records in these or other locations that provide information about what probably occurred. The merchants, who usually were literate in Chinese (e.g., could read and write) and who knew some English, often were the leaders of the community and interfaced with the EuroAmerican community leaders. They frequently acted as labor brokers, dealt with the "boss headman" of teams of miners who worked for Chinese owners/investors or EuroAmerican mine owners, and provided goods for both independent and company miners. Most also had non-Chinese customers. The merchant's main profits came from the goods sold to the miners and the monthly credit extended at the general store as was done in China. They ordered goods from China and, as in the case of Lem Hong Ng of Island Mountain, sent items used by the Cantonese to China in a continuing trans-Pacific trade. The cost of transporting goods from China to the Pacific Coast towns and cities was very reasonable because the ships carrying heavy loads like lumber to China did not want to return to the United States empty or with light loads, so items like altars and deities for temples and association headquarters, clothing, foodstuffs, dishware, and wooden rocker boxes used by miners were inexpensively shipped to Chinese American stores. Often goods were sold on credit, which had to be paid in full by Chinese New Year, in keeping with Chinese tradition. Many merchants had some rudimentary knowledge of American laws so they could advise the miners and contact the Chinese associations or EuroAmerican lawyers if there was trouble that had to be solved on the larger scale. They also might pay the taxes and other fees on behalf of the miners, an amount deducted from the miners' wages. They updated the miners on changes in the American laws. Some also participated in mining. They played a critical role in the pursuit of gold.

Because the miners themselves left few written records, a variety of sources and approaches, especially historical, archaeological, and sociological, on the topic have been used. Immigration and business records; census manuscripts (also called population schedules); archaeological site reports; newspaper articles; memoirs; oral histories; local, state, and federal records; laws; and summaries of legal judgments provided the foundation for this study. More often than not, examples of the experiences of the Chinese miners and merchants were selected from documents describing the situation in other locations that were probably similar. Although generalizations can be made, the importance of the individual and his accomplishments has been recognized.

The Bureau of the Census provided basic information. Census summaries and census manuscripts were not always accurate but gave an indication of the number of Chinese in any given location. The number of Chinese miners fluctuated between 1860 and 1880. In 1860 California's Chinese population was 34,933 out of a state total of 379,994; some 24,282 of the Chinese were miners.[6] Miners in Oregon and Nevada were not a significant number until the 1870 census. In 1870 California's Chinese population rose to 49,277 (of which 9,087 were miners) out of a state total of 560,247. Based on tabulations from the census manuscript for 1870 (as opposed to the summaries), economist Ping Chiu counted 14,415 Chinese miners and historian Sucheng Chan tallied a higher figure of 16,000 for California.[7] The count probably did not include the 75 to 150 Chinese who lived and worked in the isolated, mountainous, rich mining community of present-day Hite's Cove, Mariposa County, not far from Yosemite.[8] They were too far away and isolated for the census taker to count. In 1870 Oregon's Chinese population was 3,330 out of a state total of 90,923, of which 1,516 of the Chinese, or 45.5 percent, were miners, mostly concentrated in mountainous eastern Oregon. Oregon's total number of miners was 2,476 so the Chinese represented a large percentage and played a major role in the development of Oregon's early mining history. In 1870 Nevada's Chinese population was 3,123, or 7.3 percent of the total state's population of 42,491, with only 228 Chinese listed as miners. In the 1870s mining was a major occupation for both Oregon and Nevada and continued to be so in the 1880s.

The profile of the overall population changed in between 1880 and 1890, the height of the Chinese population in the American West. California was still the primary place of residence for the Chinese. In 1880 California saw its largest Chinese population growth, an increase from 25,855 (1870) to 75,132.[9] Economic historian Ping Chiu counted 15,055 Chinese as miners.[10] Nevada had a total of 8,241 miners but only 343 Chinese miners (out of a total Chinese population of 5,416 [8.7 percent] of the state's total population of 62,266).[11] The census takers in Nevada were careful about who deserved the coveted title of "miner": a person who worked in a mine, did placer mining, or worked for a mining company full time. Moreover, only one occupation could be listed, so if an individual was only a half-time miner, he was not labeled a miner. If the newspapers and other literature were even somewhat accurate, then these Nevada census figures were far below the actual number of Chinese miners. Just as the Chinese were very visible in Nevada, in 1880 the Chinese population in Oregon grew to 9,510 with 3,965 Chinese miners who worked primarily in eastern Oregon. In comparison, although Idaho had a large Chinese population of 4,274 in 1870, anti-Chinese movements and mining declines saw a substantial drop in the Chinese population from 3,379 to 2,007 between 1880 and 1890. By 1880 the character of the mining industry changed as the majority of miners either worked for EuroAmerican or Chinese mining companies, leaving few of the independent miners of the 1860s and 1870s.

Table 1. Population of Chinese in the United States and the states of California, Oregon, Nevada, and Idaho, 1860–1920*

	United States	California	Oregon	Nevada	Idaho
1860	35,565	34,933	425	23	—
1870	63,199	49,277	3,330	3,162	4,274
1880	105,463	75,132	9,510	5,416	3,379
1890	107,488	72,472	9,540	2,833	2,007
1900	89,863	45,753	10,397	1,352	1,467
1910	71,531	36,248	7,363	927	859
1920	61,639	28,812	3,090	689	585

*United States, Bureau of the Census, *Characteristics of the Population* (title varies), 1870–1890, Washington, D.C. (dates vary).

This study utilized the United States Bureau of the census manuscripts for 1860, 1870, 1880, 1900, 1910, 1920, and 1930 that have been microfilmed by the National Archives and Records Administration (NARA) Service and the Nevada State Historic Preservation Office (SHPO) online database of individuals living in Nevada prior to 1930. The critical 1890 census manuscript for the West was accidentally destroyed in a fire, creating an important gap in information. All scholars have agreed that the census manuscripts provided an inaccurate snapshot of the Chinese individuals in their communities and yet they have been the only indicators of the residents of communities. Census figures differed greatly from the estimates published in the local newspapers and from statistical analyses done by scholars like Sucheng Chan.[12] The 1860 census of Chinese in eastern Washington counted 420 Chinese east of the Cascades while the *Oregonian* (Portland) estimated 1,000 to 1,200 Chinese miners in Oregon, the same general region, in 1857.[13] This kind of difference in figures existed in most locations throughout the American West because it was so difficult to count the Chinese, in part owing to the difficulty in spelling their names or obtaining the other information required for the census. If the census taker could not obtain the data from a Chinese "headman," he often opted not to count the Chinese at all. During the decades before 1880 (and even afterwards in some cases), it was easier to not count them or simply list them as "Chinese" or "Chinaman" with no additional information, as was done, for example, in the case of Nez Perce County, Idaho, in 1870 and the 1875 Nevada state census for Elko County.

The Chinese also were guilty of intentionally avoiding the census taker, who, from their experience in China, was closely allied with or was the same as the tax collector or other government representative. The Chinese had a history of bad experience with poll tax collectors because they could not always determine who was a legitimate poll tax collector and because of the well-known story of how some tax collectors in California had killed resistant Chinese taxpayers. The county assessor's office sent the poll tax collector around and the tax varied between $3 and $4, depending upon the year. In 1872 approximately three hundred Chinese workers in Washoe County who were working on the Virginia and Truckee Railroad paid $1,200 in poll taxes.[14] The *Nevada State Journal* (May 1, 1884) pointed out that the Chinese passed the poll tax receipt around to avoid paying the tax. This was a common practice used throughout the American West. Since all Chinese looked alike according to most EuroAmericans, the Chinese who paid the tax could sell the receipt for half the price to another who would then show the collector that he had already paid and the tax collector was never the wiser. But, as Randall E. Rohe concluded, "The Chinese paid their share of taxes—miner's taxes, property taxes, poll taxes, and other assessments—and they received none of the service their tax money provided."[15] Because the Chinese sometimes avoided both the tax collectors and the census takers, tracing individual male Chinese has been difficult. Once the poll and other taxes were ruled illegal, many of the records of earlier tax collections were not preserved.

Often the Chinese community leader provided the information to the census taker since many Chinese could not speak English, but he might not be concerned about accuracy. The census revealed other invaluable facts, however: occupation, gender, marital status, wealth of individuals in 1870, the ability to read and/or write, and the households, some of which were integrated. The 1880 census manuscript in Oregon and Idaho even identified the miners with their mining companies. The Chinese population dropped as a result of the 1882 Chinese Exclusion Act, the 1892 Geary Act extending the 1882 Chinese Exclusion Act, and subsequent anti-Chinese immigration acts, culminating in the 1924 Immigration Act that essentially closed the door to Chinese immigrants.

One of the few records that provided the "voice" of Chinese miners and merchants was found in the NARA in San Bruno and Laguna Nigel, California; Seattle, Washington; and Washington, D.C. Records from the Immigration and Naturalization Service (INS) have been deposited in these and other NARA locations. San Bruno has Chinese business partnership records, admission and readmission immigration records, duplicate certificates of residence and/or identity, and court records. Laguna Nigel is the depository for Nevada records and has many regional deportation cases. Seattle has files on Chinese individuals in both Oregon and Washington state. Washington,

D.C., has hundreds of thousands of applications for duplicate Certificates of Residence that describe the life of the applicants from their arrival until the date of their application (discussed in chapter 1) in addition to a variety of other types of immigration documents and photographs. Washington, D.C., also has correspondence between the regional immigration bureaus and the central office.

Studying Chinese miners and merchants prior to the mid-1960s was difficult due to the many early misperceptions and biased writings.[16] The early writers were either for or against Chinese immigrants and had backgrounds in missionary work or diplomacy in China or were part of the nascent labor union movement. From the 1890s to 1924 the importance of assimilation and being a part of the "melting pot" dominated the racist thinking of many Americans; many believed that the Chinese did not fit into this category.

In 1865 California Senator John Conness coined the term "sojourner" to refer to the Chinese because he considered them to be only temporary residents who planned to return home, and therefore did not feel any necessity to "melt" into American society. Social scientists, often influenced by Robert Park (1864–1944), a student of Georg Simmel who wrote about transplanted old-world traits, human migration, the marginal man, race relations, assimilation, and different societies, continued to focus on assimilation issues.[17] One of his students, Rose Hum Lee, pioneered a more analytical and yet uniquely biased approach to Chinese American studies as she portrayed a closed, isolated Chinese American community.

The label of sojourner continued for over a century and in 1952, sociologist Paul Siu presented his "Chinese sojourner hypothesis" that influenced later scholars to ignore the adaptations and adjustments the Chinese made during the nineteenth century and, at the same time, neglected to point out that other immigrant groups also shared the attachment to the culture and homeland of their ancestors but could assimilate because they could visibly "pass" in the majority community.[18] Contemporary newspapers and other writings tended to ignore the presence of the Chinese or discussed them in derogatory descriptions. Scholarly literature before the civil rights movement of the 1960s seldom covered the Chinese experiences. Historian Gunther Barth, one of the early scholars focusing on Chinese Americans who studied under Oscar Handlin, implied in his book *Bitter Strength* that though the Chinese were uprooted, they simply wanted to make money and return home, thus refusing involvement in the American society, making assimilation a moot question.[19] Historian Roger Daniels, as well as many others, has questioned the validity of this line of scholarship on assimilation, writing, "The notion that an immigrant could shed his culture the way a snake sheds his skin is nonsense."[20] Along this line, one has to inquire what traditions the Chinese kept and what American values they adopted. Recent scholarship has been less concerned with assimilation and more focused upon what changes were taking place as the Chinese adjusted to America.

By the mid-twentieth century new perspectives and interpretations prevailed. American scholars looked more closely at groups that had not been included in the mainstream of study. Daniels, for example, criticized American historians of immigration for ignoring Asian Americans; gradually, more mainstream historians have included the Asian American experience.[21] Historians of American immigration, such as Marcus Lee Hansen, John Higham, and Oscar Handlin, raised new questions about immigrants, their lifestyles, and experiences and suggested models of behavior.[22] Barth brought new details to Chinese American history but was hampered both by his inability to read Chinese and the European immigrant model that he used. John Bodnar introduced the idea of transplantation of cultural traits and provided a new way of interpreting the Chinese American past. New western historians, most notably Richard White and Patricia Limerick, highlighted the convergence of the diverse peoples of the American West and further stimulated interest in Asian Americans.[23]

Pioneers in the field of academic-based Asian American history, most notably Roger Daniels, Sucheng Chan, Shirley Hune, Shih-shan Henry Tsai, Benson Tong, and Ronald Takaki, laid the groundwork for future work in response to the Asian American movement seeking more accurate information about Asian Americans.[24] Investigations were based on new documents and were more objective in their interpretations. More recently Peter Kwong and Dusanka Miscevic looked more deeply into the "untold story" of the Chinese American community from a national, instead of western, perspective. Community-based historians, like Him Mark Lai and Thomas Chinn, regional historians and writers, including Huping Ling and Marie Rose Wong, and cultural historians, like Shehong Chen, have added to knowledge about Chinese Americans and, along with the other works, dispelled many of the old stereotypes that often shaped the information and analyses of older scholarship.[25] Dissertations and theses focused on specific issues and uncovered new sources. By the late twentieth century scholars in the field of Chinese American studies could work in both Chinese and English language materials, including historians Madeline Hsu and Liping Zhu. Developments in other academic fields provided more insights through the greater accessibility and diversity of source materials. Chinese American history was more objective and reflected what transpired more accurately.

In 1910 anthropologists began to examine the link between history and archaeology, but the field remained in its infancy until the mid-twentieth century. Anthropologists, most notably Clifford Geertz, examined culture, cultural ideals, and symbols to interpret the life and times of peoples. This led to a focus on historic ethnography in anthropology that examined multiethnic relations, cultural preservation, acculturation and assimilation, and history that was related to the artifact assemblages found in a specific archaeological site.[26] The shift in the paradigm of racial dynamics led to a concern not just for the dominant EuroAmerican's interaction with minorities but also to include interactions between minority groups as well as the recognition of cultural diversity and the contributions of minority groups to the larger landscape, culminating in more studies about ethnic groups.[27] The study of overseas Chinese first began to examine the urban areas in the 1970s and 1980s and then considered work camps and more rural locations. The development of historic ethnography (research focusing on the sociocultural aspects of an ethnic group or community) in anthropology and archaeological studies of Chinese American sites have provided other aspects to consider. Advances in scholarship and critical thinking have led to a broadening of perspectives.

Eventually state and federal archaeologists became aware of late nineteenth-century Chinese sites under their supervision. This included John Day, Tuscarora, and Island Mountain. The Bureau of Land Management surveyed Tuscarora, and Oregon State Parks had several archaeological projects involving John Day. The Forest Service sponsored the archaeological digs at Island Mountain, for example, between 1999 and 2001, through their voluntary Passport in Time program. Some of the early volunteers to Island Mountain included members of the Wing Luke Museum in Seattle and a former Chinese American Seattle judge whose family name originally was Wu (Ng or Ing in Cantonese, but Tuai according to American immigration officials). This was the same last name as the leading merchant, China Lem (Lem Hong Ng) of Island Mountain and Doc Ing Hay who played an important role in the development of John Day. Donald Hardesty of the University of Nevada–Reno and his graduate students in archaeology, most notably Melissa Farnscomb and Patricia Hunt-Jones, supervised the volunteers.[28] I served as the historian for the project for three summers and with county, state, federal, and university funding, conducted the research for this work.

The archaeological finds enhanced the few written records available and provided much insight into the Chinese miners and merchants in the mining towns. Historic ethnographers, archaeologists, and historians use much of the same written literature, such as census manuscripts, oral histories, government documents, memoirs, newspapers, geological reports, maps, and other documents. However, archaeologists focus upon the location, types, and quantities of artifacts found at a specific site, and then use documents to give a context to the site. A major objective is to classify the objects uncovered and note the location where the objects were found. For a group like the Chinese who left few written records, the work of archaeologists laid the foundation for studies about the people, their lifestyle, and the community. Fragments of pages of a book published after 1911 was found in Island Mountain, for example, substantiate the assertion that the merchant Lem Hong Ng was literate and demonstrated that he kept abreast of governmental changes in China. This study relied upon several archaeological reports, as noted in the bibliography.

Unfortunately many of the archaeological reports are difficult to access because of the sensitivity of the information, so they are not always in the public realm. The intensity of the study and the cost involved limited which sites have been excavated. Public sites are easier to study than private ones. The government has done only one superficial archaeological study on Tuscarora because most of the town is privately owned, so archaeological knowledge about Tuscarora is not as extensive as that of Island Mountain.[29] The only known archaeological study of Tuscarora had to be obtained directly from the Bureau of Land Management in Elko.

The historian, on the other hand, examines a wider scope of written literature and other materials and places the site and its inhabitants in a broader historical context. The artifacts are of interest for their significance and as a reflection of the community's lifestyle and provide an entry point for study. The historian's research centers upon written materials, government documents, oral histories, and archival materials. The published literature can be found in libraries and archives, especially NARA. County records of land deeds, taxes, and miscellaneous information demonstrated that the Chinese acquired claims through preemption (the earliest one on record in Yuba County, California, in 1856), or purchased mining claims as well as other property and equipment.[30] More often than not, due to a variety of circumstances discussed later, land ownership was not officially recorded. Court cases also have provided information not readily accessible elsewhere. Although some justices tried to treat the Chinese cases fairly, others, like congressmen and later Ninth Circuit justices Joseph McKenna and William W. Morrow, gained political prominence from their anti-Chinese stance and decisions in the late nineteenth century.[31] Themes of gender, power strategies, labor exploitation, imperialism, globalization, and colonialism have been integrated in the study of post-industrial cultures and the social structure and social interaction in mining towns.[32] New, more objective studies resulted.

The recent writings on Chinese miners and merchants are diverse in approach and coverage. Numerous studies focus on the Chinese miners in California. In 1930 Stephen Williams wrote his master's thesis for Stanford University on the Chinese in the California mines; in 1963 Ping Chiu examined Chinese laborers in his classic work, *Chinese Labor in California, 1850–1880*; and Ralph Mann focused his attention on Grass Valley and Nevada City, with their large Chinese population, after the gold rush in his book, *After the Gold Rush*. Other historians incorporated information about the Chinese miners in their studies of mining in the American West. The anti-Chinese movement, especially in the mining towns, was seen in the writings of Elmer Clarence Sandmeyer and Alexander Saxton, and more recently, Jean Pfaelzer.[33] Outside of California, the most notable historian of Chinese miners is Liping Zhu, whose study *A Chinaman's Chance* (focusing on the Chinese in the Boise Basin, Idaho) represented the new generation of scholars utilizing Chinese and American sources. Priscilla Wegars and Darby Stapp focused on the Chinese in Idaho and provided many comparisons for this study. Madeline Hsu's works linking the Chinese in the United States and those in China shed light upon the transnational aspect of their lives. Master's theses by Christopher Edson and Chia-lin Chen on the Chinese in eastern Oregon, along with the archaeological investigations of Laban Richard Steeves and Jeffrey LaLande, described the Chinese in Oregon. These authors and others provided many new insights.

Outside of the United States, the Chinese miners and merchants created communities that were similar to, but not identical with, the isolated American West Chinese towns. Archaeologist Ying-ying Chen looked at the Chinese mining communities in the North Cariboo District in British Columbia between the 1860s and 1940s.[34] A few were predominantly Chinese. For example, in 1877 a Barkerville miner, William Stephenson, his wife, and two sons were "the only white people living in a purely Chinese town."[35] These North Cariboo communities declined beginning in 1911 and therefore correspond in time to many of the mining towns in the American West. Influenced by the growing anti-Chinese sentiments in Victoria and other cities, the Chinese settled in ghettoes and avoided contact with the majority of Canadians—but some interaction did occur. The most active researchers in the field of new Chinese diaspora studies can be found in Australia and New Zealand. Among these scholars, archaeologist Barry McGowan has provided new information about Chinese mining camps in Australia, and Neville Ritchie studied the acculturation, adaptation, and change of the Chinese in southern New Zealand.[36] Almost all of the Chinese miners left no written records and the non-Chinese observers writing at the time did not understand what they saw, so the new generations of archaeologists have assisted in filling in some of the gaps in our knowledge.

In a study of any immigrant group, it is essential to try to understand their motivation for deciding to leave, which often directly related to experiences in their home country, their migration pattern, and the new situation in which they found themselves upon their arrival or in their new place of settlement.

Chapter 1 traces some of the important developments in China and provides a background to the advent of Chinese miners and merchants and the challenges they faced. After arriving in the America West, they adapted some of their traditional methods of operation and established organizations that assisted them. They encountered discriminatory laws, practices, and actions, but despite all of the negativism, they continued to seek that elusive gold.

Chapter 2 begins with an overview of Oregon and then focuses upon eastern Oregon, where the Chinese played a major role in mining until the turn of the twentieth century. The merchants Kam Wah Chung, Doc Ing Hay, and Lung On were prominent individuals in John Day.

Chapter 3 provides an overview of the Nevada experience and looks at the large mining town of Tuscarora that the Chinese helped settle at the conclusion of the construction of the first transcontinental railroad. Two Chinese merchants who headed rival brotherhoods were the leaders of the Chinese community and one, Ah Lee Lake of the Zhigongtang (Chinese Free Masons) remained in the town long after mining had declined and most of the Chinese had left.

Chapter 4 provides a more in-depth study of a small Nevada mining town called Island Mountain and the Chinese miners, merchants, and other residents. Founded by Emanuel Penrod, the town was predominantly Chinese and economic interdependence led to positive social interactions. China Lem (the name given to two brothers who lived there, one after the other) was one of the wealthiest Chinese in Elko County by the turn of the twentieth century.

Even after most of the Chinese had left and his closest Chinese friends who were miners had died, he stayed on.

The study concludes with some comparisons with Idaho (as an area where the Chinese mined but were driven out) and other mining communities in the Chinese diaspora both inside and outside of the United States, showing some similarities and differences that have occurred. It is my hope that some new information and ideas on Chinese miners and merchants will be presented and will inspire further scholarly work.

Note on Transliteration of Names

CHINESE NAMES HAVE BEEN problematic for American historians because there has been no standard method of transliterating the Chinese characters. Emma Woo Louie tried to unravel aspects of the problem in her book, *Chinese American Names: Tradition and Transition.*[1] In the nineteenth century American scholars adopted the British Wade-Giles system of transliteration of Chinese characters for place names and for names of people with last name, then first name hyphenated if there were two characters, thus "Wang Shou-jing" was a typical rendition. The *Hanyu pinyin* (abbreviated *pinyin)* system, adopted by the People's Republic of China and in 1979, by the United States, rendered the same name "Wang Shoujing," eliminating the hyphenated first name. The transliteration system made other changes but the result was a uniform and phonetically correct rendition of the Chinese characters.

The international postal system adopted a variety of spellings for place names; this was further complicated by the problem of having different names for the same place: for example, Peking ("northern capital") became Peiping ("northern peace") when China's capital was moved, and later transliterated Beijing ("northern capital") when the pinyin system was adopted. Kwangtung (postal system) became Guangdong (a more phonetic way of transliterating the name of the province in south China from where most nineteenth-century Chinese immigrants originated), and Fukien became Fujian. The Four Counties/Districts of Guangdong province is *Siyi* instead of *Ssu-yi* (Wade-Giles) or *Sze Yup* (Cantonese) and *Zhongshan* (name changed in honor of Sun Yatsen's style name) is used instead of *Chung-shan* (Wade-Giles) or *Heungshan* (Cantonese original name of Sun Yatsen's birthplace and name of district in the late nineteenth century). Pinyin is used to transliterate place names in this study.

American immigration officials and census takers adopted a random method of transliterating Chinese names. In nineteenth-century Guangdong province, a person had a family name that was usually monosyllabic but in rare instances two syllables, such as Si-ma (often transliterated Ssuma) and Ou-yang (often transliterated Owyang, Oyang, Auyang). The family name (*xing*) or the clan name (*shi)* was followed by the first name that consisted of one or two characters. In numerous cases, the second character of the first name was recorded as one's last name because American officials did not understand the order in which Chinese names are given—therefore Zhao Jinhui (immigration spelling, Chow Gin Huey) became Mr. Zhaojin Hui and all of his children and grandchildren were given the surname of Hui (Huey, their American surname). When another Mr. Chow followed his older brother through the immigration line, he told the official that he was Chow Erh (Chow Number Two) and his last name, and those of his American born descendants, then became Jower. Some, like Shirley Hune, ended up with a family name that does not resemble her Chinese family name. Few Chinese bothered to change their family name legally to the correct spelling, although most second-generation Chinese Americans knew their correct family name.

The transliteration of any part of the Chinese name was done randomly so that the difficult-to-pronounce family name of Ng (Wu in pinyin) could be written Ung, Ing, and Eng, to give a few examples. Dialectic differences in spoken Chinese also led to different spellings of the same family names so that Zhang (pinyin) became Chung, Cheung, and Jung on immigration papers. Transcribing the names varied according to what the official heard as he tried to spell out the name. There are one hundred common Chinese family names, but some Chinese family names in the United States were not among them and were actually "invented" by the American government official or Chinese individual. Kee was not a surname but Kee as a last name can be found in many census manuscripts. Chung Kee (1847–1909) of Hawthorne, Nevada, was born Zhang (family name in pinyin) Gee Wen (Cantonese) in Kaiping, Guangdong province, China; all of his descendants have the surname of Kee.

Chinese merchants often were known by their company name rather than their personal name., For example, Kam Wah Chung, the name of the store in John Day, Oregon, became the name of the individual as far as the EuroAmerican population was concerned. In a similar manner, Non Chong Yee of Carson City was better known by his store's name, Quong Hing (also spelled Kwong Hing and other variations), or his adopted American name, Sam Gibson. Nineteenth-century first-generation Chinese Americans who considered themselves "Americanized Chinese" often took a EuroAmerican name, like Sam Gibson and Joseph Tape (Chinese name, Zhao Qia or Chew Dip in Cantonese) of the famous *Tape v. Hurley* (1885) fame.[2]

Chinese first names were also confusing to Americans. Officials failed to understand that the Chinese had a formal first name (*zi*), which usually included a character common to all members of the same generation, and a style name (*hao*), which also might have a character common to all members of the same generation. Most Chinese were known to other Chinese by their hao. Unbeknownst to American officials, the Chinese also had milk (from childhood), studio, pen, school, married, and nick names. American immigration officials often accounted for the different names in depositions by acknowledging "married names" as the reason for a different first name. Another common mistake was to assign "Ah," a term of familiarity, as a person's first or last name. These individuals cannot be identified as to family names and some, knowing that "Ah" really was not part of their name, signed "Ah" in Chinese because "Ah" agreed with the legal documents that referred to them.

The spelling of the names of the individuals differed from census year to census year, but the pronunciation often remained the same and combined with birth dates and other information, a link could be made from one census to another or from one government document to another despite the different versions of the names.

Chinese women often were dubbed "China Mary" or some similar name that was easy for Americans to pronounce. Married Chinese women usually added "Shee" to their maiden name but this was interpreted as their first name, therefore Mrs. Chan's maiden name was Sun (her maiden name) Shee, thus she was called Sun Shee or Shee Sun by her close friends and children. Chinese women often were not reported to the census takers even if they were wives of prominent individuals; thus, for example, the wife of merchant Non Chong Yee of Carson City, Nevada, who owned and operated two boarding houses in the 1870s, did not make it into the census but was listed in the Carson City tax lists.[3] Her three children, born in Carson City, also were not listed in the census manuscript. However, her husband was the leader of Carson City's Chinatown and paid the poll taxes for some of the Chinese residents as well as acted as the intermediary between the Chinese and EuroAmerican communities, so he and his wife were both known to local officials.

Finally there was the complicated situation of men who established a household of relatives with one woman, who was the first or second wife of the head of the household. All of the men were related despite the different last names in the census and the woman usually "kept house" for everyone but was the mate only to her husband and kept her maiden name. Without insight into the actual situation, these women often were regarded as "prostitutes" when in actuality they were not. In wealthier families, first wives often remained in China to take care of her husband's parents and their children while second wives were allowed to go abroad with their spouses. Some couples had sufficient funds to bring a younger woman, usually single, to assist the wife in household chores, especially if the wife's feet were bound, making it almost impossible to walk the rough mining town roads. This type of servant also was often mistaken for a "prostitute." This profile could be found among Chinese merchants and physicians, but not among miners as a general rule. Often a married woman "kept house" (as the census taker noted) in a household of several men and in many cases, as told to me by first-generation Chinese American women, the household consisted of relatives—hers and his—but often skeptical scholars have regarded these women as "prostitutes" but they really were not.

In this study, individuals connected to Chinese history have their names given in the traditional manner of last name–first name with no comma between the last name and first name, thus Sun Yatsen (as his name has been commonly spelled in the United States). In most cases the pinyin system is used to transliterate their names. Those living in the United States are given in the western manner of first name (usually two characters) and then last name. In most cases, the names are transliterated as they are commonly seen in documents and other sources but reversed in the correct order of last name last if the documents were incorrect. When the Chinese characters are known, the name is given in pinyin with the last name first. A Tuscarora Chinese merchant name was Ah Lee Lake, in pinyin Li (surname) Li (first name), but in some immigration and government documents it is Gee (first name) Lee (surname), and sometimes Lee Gee. Sometimes American government documents listed him as Lee Lake and other times he was Lake Lee or Ah Lake, but to lessen confusion only one version of the name, Ah Lee Lake, was used throughout this study.

Birth and death dates and dates of immigration are given whenever known because this provides the reader with the time period in which the individuals lived. The immigration dates are of interest because they often showed that the individual lived in the United States for more than twenty years and, when living in a multiethnic community, had more time to adjust and adapt to American life.

The names of organizations and associations are given in the American rendition upon first mention with the pinyin and then given in pinyin thereafter unless it is better known by its English name or abbreviation, as in the case of the Chinese Consolidated Benevolent Association (Zhonghua huiguan, Chinese Six Companies) as CCBA.[4] Although the Chee Kung Tong ("Chinese Free Masons") also was a well-known organization in the United States, the various spellings, such as Gee Hing Tong, could make its name confusing so the pinyin Zhigongtang has been used. The same applies to the Binggongtang (Cantonese Bing Kong Tong), another secret fraternal organization claiming ties to international Masonry.

"Chinese American" includes the first generation of Chinese immigrants and "EuroAmerican" designates those of European origins and descent.

In Pursuit of Gold

1 The Coming and Early Challenges

CHINESE MIGRATED TO THE United States for many reasons. Upon arrival, they faced many challenges and established organizations to assist in coping with their new environment while preserving some traditions. The miners left few or no records about their experiences, but several different types of government documents provide some insights. The merchants in the mining towns and camps played an important role; some became very wealthy from their selling of both domestic and imported goods. In western societies they would be considered literate because they knew arithmetic and some reading and writing. (But, since knowledge of the Chinese classics was one of the main hallmarks of a literate man, by traditional Chinese standards they would not be regarded as such.) They became the community leaders in the American West. By the 1860s the anti-Chinese sentiment, with all of its violence and racism, contributed to discriminatory legislation that adversely affected Chinese miners; it did not diminish until the early twentieth century. This in turn contributed to the hostility and violence directed toward the Chinese. Chinese miners and merchants faced these challenges until placer mining for small groups and individual miners began to disappear by the turn of the twentieth century.

The Chinese came hoping to become rich and escape the problems in China. Economic, social, and political dislocations, combined with natural disasters, characterized southeastern China in the mid-nineteenth century. During economic declines, the Chinese in Guangdong and neighboring Guangxi and Fujian provinces had a long tradition of seeking new opportunities overseas. As early as the ninth century, southern Chinese had looked abroad for new economic and political opportunities. In the face of the numerous problems evident after the 1840s, they continued the tradition of outward migration. Although they usually went to Southeast Asia, improvements in transportation and shipping enabled approximately 2.4 million Chinese during the last sixty years of the nineteenth century to travel farther to create a global "overseas Chinese" (*huaqiao*) population.

Numerous American scholars of Chinese history have detailed the reasons for the overseas migration in the 1800s, but the peasants were especially affected.[1] The population of Guangdong almost doubled between 1787 (16 million) and 1850 (28 million), increasing pressure on the arable land and causing farmers, plagued by high rents and taxes, to face starvation.[2] Tenant farming, absentee landlordism, and banditry combined with flooding, famine, and plagues made life unbearable for many peasants. Rich peasant farmers became penniless quickly. Stories of men such as He Wen (1836–1901), who was forced to sell his recently deceased father's prosperous farm land and house and to use part of the funds to start a new life in the United States, were not uncommon as the economic conditions in China worsened.[3] The survival of the nuclear family (*jia*) often meant going abroad.

Specialized occupations suffered. The decline in cottage industries due to cheaper imports, especially cotton cloth, contributed to the exodus of men who had been the cornerstone of village economies. Some found their skills useful in the laundry business overseas. Mining and timber resources were depleted and men with knowledge in these trades sought new opportunities as unemployment rose. Natural calamities also contributed to the outward migration. Disastrous fires in the new treaty port cities often wiped out a family's or clan's wealth. Desperate financial, political, and social problems forced many to leave.

The socioeconomic problems in China fueled political discontent. The Taiping rebels, who arose from Guangxi-Guangdong in 1850 and were not suppressed until 1864, and other anti-Manchu secret society rebels also caused major social, political, and economic chaos. Several known Taiping supporters, including Yet Low and Ah Quin, eventually settled in California and elsewhere and became community leaders.[4] If they had remained in China, they faced the government-mandated death sentence. If they returned to China, they had a price on their heads and were subject to immediate imprisonment and beheading. These men probably played a role in the establishment of secret societies, often called "brotherhoods," such as the Anliangtang (On Leong Tong) and Binggongtang (Bing Kong Tong) in the United States. The Kejia (Cantonese Hakka, "guest people") versus Punti (Han Chinese) warfare (1854–67) and clan rivalries in southern Chinese towns intensified and continued in the United States where they were labeled "tong wars" in the American press.

The weak central government made many of the problems worse. The formerly nomadic Manchus controlled China beginning in 1644, but their military and administrative ineptness were revealed during these troubled decades of the nineteenth century and their Qing dynasty fell in 1911 to Sun Yatsen (1866–1925), who established the Republic of China (1911-present) and was named first provisional president.[5] Like several other Cantonese antigovernment leaders, his supporters founded revolutionary groups among the overseas Chinese and these organizations gave financial support to the aspiring, and later, new republican government. This trend of overseas Chinese support became an important factor in the governance of China in the twentieth century.

The Qing government forbade the Chinese from going abroad until the signing of the Burlingame Treaty between the United States and China in 1868.[6] Thousands had left anyway. In the eighteenth century the Manchus mandated that foreign governments repatriate Chinese traders and other nationals who went abroad so that they could be executed upon their return to China. But after initial passage, enforcement of these laws was largely ignored. The threat of execution officially was removed with the Burlingame Treaty and contributed to the large numbers of Chinese going abroad.

Many men and a few women risked their lives to travel overseas to escape from the oppressive political, social, and economic situation at home and to pursue the elusive gold or employment that promised a better life. Some were adventurers or men with a price on their heads, some wanted to escape an oppressive family situation or wife, some were sent by relatives to establish commercial and other links, some had to earn money to support the extended family or nuclear family in China, and some simply wanted a different lifestyle. Many observed the newly acquired wealth of returned Chinese—the new homes, luxury items, and higher socioeconomic status—and believed they could have the same if they went abroad. By the turn of the twentieth century, returned Chinese communities were built in Guangdong with forts to protect the women and children from bandits and marauders, and many of the homes there were of western architectural design.[7] However, it was a "loss of face" if a "returned" Chinese could not afford luxuries for himself and his family.

There were additional reasons for the massive mid-nineteenth century migration. Yong Chen demonstrated that a decline in subsistence agriculture and change to a market-oriented economy in Xinning (later part of Taishan) County, Guangdong province, and other emigrant communities resulted in the emigration of Chinese who recognized the potential overseas trade in America and who knew about employment opportunities in America.[8] The Chinese merchants from places like Taishan and Zhongshan counties, not far from Macao and Hong Kong, were quick to realize the advantages of expanding

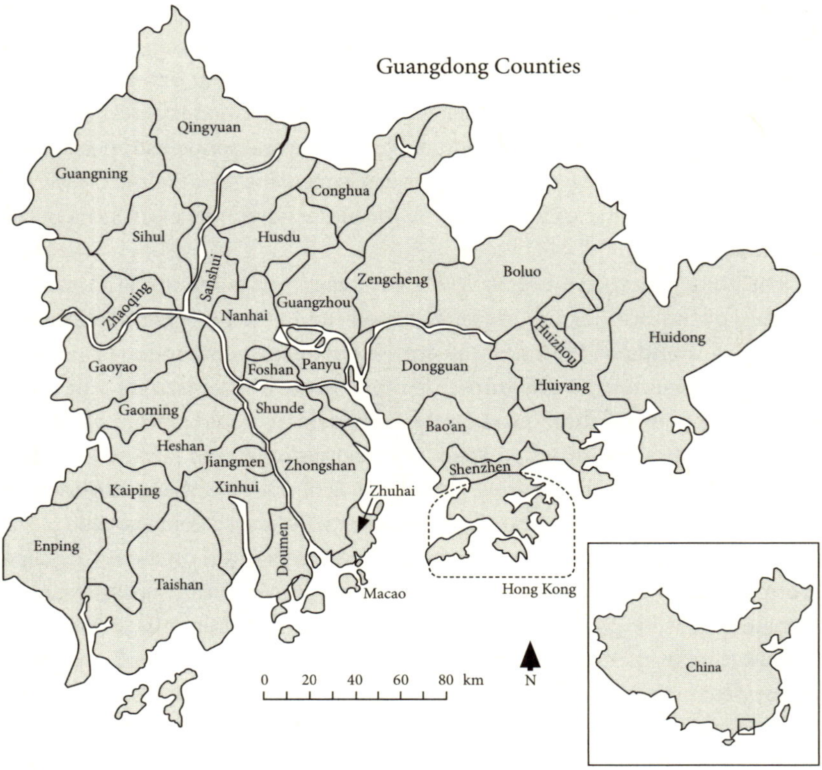

Major Emigration Areas

Siyi	*Sanyi*	*Zhongshan*
(Four Counties/Districts):	*(Three Counties/Districts):*	(formerly called
Taishan (former Xinning)	Nanhai	Xiangshan "Fragrant
Enping	Panyu	Mountain"; includes
Kaiping	Shunde	present-day Zhuhai)
Xinhui		

Map of Guangdong and emigrant counties. An estimated 90 percent of the Chinese emigrants in the United States in the late nineteenth century were born and raised in the Sanyi, Siyi, and Zhongshan Counties of Guangdong.

their companies overseas to make money. They dominated the early group of Chinese immigrants, especially merchants, to the American West and continued to hold important Chinese community positions because they supplied the much needed goods. Living close to Hong Kong, the Zhongshanese had greater opportunities to learn English and western ways before emigrating.

The potential expansion of companies accounted for the migration of Chinese merchants, especially young men, to the American West. They created the "family firm," which took three distinct forms: the nuclear family enterprise, the extended family stores (in-laws, cousins, uncles), and the partnerships.[9] These merchants maintained commercial ties with their homeland and, more often than not, relatives, especially those who provided goods and services. At the same time the merchants in China urged the Qing government to protect Chinese American merchants because they had "intimate relationships with Chinese stores in San Francisco. We are mutually dependent."[10] These were some of the factors in the "push" (reasons for leaving) part of the "push-pull" theory of migration. The attractions were obvious: new economic opportunities, new adventures, and a potentially good lifestyle and future.

Stories of "instant wealth" from mining were a major motivation for going abroad. Some of the Chinese, particularly future small mining company owners, had some prior knowledge about mining. The nineteenth century western assumption that the Chinese had no knowledge or experience was misleading. Success in mining was usually a combination of knowledge, experience, and hard work. Gold existed in almost every province in China, sometimes in metamorphosed pre-Cambrian granite but "usually as placer deposits in stream gravels, to a smaller extent in quartz veins."[11] Although many of the resources had been depleted by the early nineteenth century, gold mining had existed in southeastern China. According to James P. Dorian, even in the twentieth century China was the sixth largest producer of gold in the world; 10 percent of that production was from placer deposits.[12] As early as the eighteenth century, the Chinese began working in the diamond, tin, and gold mines of Southeast Asia; by the early nineteenth century they worked in mines in Borneo, Malaya, Sarawak, Burma, and Vietnam, to name a few.[13] Tin mining, also found in Guangdong and Southeast Asia, used many of the same techniques as placer mining. This may have provided the experience needed for the American gold seekers.

Even women participated in gold mining. Tang dynasty poet Liu Yuxi (772–842) provided this description:

> The sun drives off the mist and shines on the strand,
> Women washing gold from the sand gather at the bend of the river.
> Ornaments for beautiful women and gold seals for lords and kings,
> All come through the efforts of such women [working] with the sand.[14]

Although almost all of the nineteenth-century gold miners were men, Nevada had a female placer miner named Ah Ho (born 1848), who was married and immigrated in 1873.[15] She lived with a large group of Chinese placer miners in Foltz Precinct, Humboldt County, Nevada in 1900. There may have been others who were not enumerated in the census.

Traditional knowledge and beliefs played a role in their approach to mining. The Chinese believed that minerals were the result of a combination of natural forces having yin (female, dark) and yang (male, light) elements in the earth. But the frequent mining of gold "will exhaust the stock, and the yield is likely to be limited when a place has been worked over a period of years."[16] From this they knew that the work did not allow them to settle in one place for very long, so mining usually was done away from home but with regular returns to one's native place. In China, placer gold miners worked seasonally and usually as an adjunct to farming. The practice was continued abroad. In the United States, some, like miners in Hawthorne, Nevada, worked in mining most of the year and agriculture on a part-time basis.[17]

Historian Peter J. Golas and archaeologists Laban Richard Steeves and David Valentine have summarized Chinese historical knowledge and techniques in their studies on traditional Chinese mining, thus providing insight into the miners' working style and occupational organization in China.[18] Ancient texts, often with woodblock print illustrations, described how to observe geological formations that contained gold. Archaeological evidence has shown that the Chinese knew about sluicing for ore separation since the eleventh century to eighth century BC and in textual evidence, about gold mining techniques in the Tang (618–907) and Song (960–1279) dynasties.[19] Undated woodblocks prints showed use of rockers and woven baskets instead of metal pans, extensive irrigation systems, and rock walls to brace sluices. The suggestion that the Chinese used some type of woven mat to isolate smaller gold pieces may explain why the Chinese were able to work abandoned placer sites profitably in the American West. Moreover, the Chinese sent specifications for some of their equipment, such as rockers, to China, had them manufactured there, and then shipped them to sites throughout the American West.[20] Since the fourth century BC, the Chinese use mercury as an amalgam to extract gold and they continued to use this technique in the American West.[21]

Water management was a major concern even in prehistoric times and the use of levees, along with the chain-pump and water-powered wheel pump evolved in the Zhou (1122 or 1027–221 BC), Chin (221–206 BC), and Han (206 BC –220 AD) dynasties for farming, especially rice cultivation. The chain-

Woodblock print from a Chinese agricultural manual circa eighteenth century. The Chinese immigrants brought knowledge of irrigation systems with them to the American west and built numerous wooden waterwheels, ditches, canals, dams, reservoirs, and other irrigation systems, some similar to this woodblock print.

pump and water-powered wheel pump effectively raised the water to the level that was needed for agriculture and mining; the equipment probably was modified in the American West.[22] South China farmers working in groups constructed and maintained irrigation channels in over 50 percent of the farmland, often using a hydraulic system. These skills in irrigation projects served the Chinese well in mining overseas where they were employed to build irrigation ditches, dams, flumes, siphons, channels, and reservoirs for placer mining that often were used later for farming and ranching. The four thousand years of knowledge about mining, smelting, and alloying of gold, copper, tin, and lead, and irrigation methods in China probably contributed to Chinese immigrants' success in mining in the American West.

Other Chinese-innovated mining techniques might have been brought to the American West, but further research is needed in this area. For example, tamped earth dams within a wooden frame and ditch berms were common in China and these water management systems have been found in Chinese mining sites in the American West. At Island Mountain, Nevada, sturdy iron water gates manufactured in San Francisco were used to control the flow of water from the Sunflower Reservoir. Information undoubtedly was transmitted orally or by woodblock prints to those doing construction work who were unable to read. Their success has been showed by the substantial sum in gold and silver sent from the Port of San Francisco to China between 1855 and 1870, totaling $72,581,219.[23]

Archaeologists have found some unique characteristics of Chinese placer mining sites that indicated the transplantation of traditional techniques and practices. One common feature at Chinese placer sites dating from the 1860s and 1870s was neatly stacked piles of rocks, such as seen in Australia; Jackson County, Oregon; and Island Mountain, Nevada. Archaeologist Barry McGowan theorized that the neatly packed mounds or walls of rocks found in Chinese sites, as differentiated from the unstructured tailings found in the majority of EuroAmerican sites, were used to hold sluices or sluice boxes.[24] This was in keeping with traditional practices. The advantage to this technique was that less manpower was required—especially useful in hydraulic sluicing. Chinese mining sites had an abundance of fragments of Chinese imported goods, such as dishware and food containers; evidence of the reuse of cans, other metal artifacts, and different types of containers demonstrated that the Chinese were very frugal; and when pits were involved, smaller holes with closer foot holdings were evident (the Chinese were usually shorter than EuroAmericans).[25] Upon closer examination, bone fragments from food consumed, the combination of goods both of western and Chinese origin, boots with nails in the soles for greater traction, and the layout of the architectural features of the dwellings provided additional information about the lifestyle of Chinese miners.

The organizational and wage system used in China probably was modified somewhat in the American West. In China professional miners scouted the sites for mine owners who eventually organized the workers into squads averaging ten men, headed by a foreman. The foreman was responsible for recruiting workers and for their activities. An overseer was in charge of the business establishments at the mining camp and a tax man collected mining duties on behalf of the authorities and other mining "officials."[26] The mine superintendent served as the liaison between the government and the mine owners. The mine owner provided the land and paid the start-up expenses, such as for buildings and equipment. The headman or manager provided the working capital—usually basic necessities and tools—so that in the American West, this role was linked to the local merchant who imported food products and other goods from China and other locations. In large-scale operations, the work agreement also included medical care. The foreman (or headman, as he often was called) had the same function that he had in China: organize the workers, keep an accounting of who worked and for how long, and transact business matters for those under his supervision.

Workers were often recruited from the agricultural community to work during the off-season. The wages were very low, with skilled workers getting more than unskilled laborers. In the seventeenth century in Yunnan Province in southwestern China, the excavated ore was divided into four equal parts: taxes, expenses, the headman, and the miners. But by the nineteenth century, in another part of China, the headman got 60 percent of the profits and the miners 40 percent.[27] Nevertheless the occupation "was marked by a high degree of egalitarianism" among the workers because of the interdependent living and working conditions of the miners, almost all of whom had left their families in their home base that often was somewhere else in China.[28] Generally the entire workforce came from the same village or clan in China and migrated as a group from one mining site to another. This was seen in their gold mining work in Borneo from the 1760s to 1870s when the Chinese and Kejia, numbering thirty thousand in the 1790s, established "associations" or "unions" in the mining towns and worked under the supervision of the sultans.[29] When the gold played out, the group leader or individuals looked for new gold discoveries elsewhere. When they arrived in the American West, the Chinese miners often used the same or very similar systems of organization, wage scale, and employment conditions in gold mining. Overseas gold miners returning home demonstrated how easy it could be to obtain instant wealth; this encouraged others to travel abroad to work in mining.[30]

Placer mining was hard work. Simply described, a placer site occurs when the particles of gold embedded in rocks and veins in mountains are eroded and redeposited in streams, hillside colluvial deposits, and glacial till with gravel and, in many cases, other minerals.[31] Water was a key component of placer mining since it was needed to loosen and wash these deposits, therefore the construction of ditches, dams, and irrigation systems, often very complex and gravity driven, was a specialty of the Chinese farmer-turned-miner. Mine owners often first hired the Chinese to dig ditches and irrigation systems. Later these irrigation systems aided EuroAmerican

Chinese miners modified the long tom and carried it on the traditional shoulder pole as they moved around in their search for gold in the nineteenth century. Other types of heavy equipment, such as stoves, were also transported in this manner. (Courtesy of Nevada Historical Society, Reno)

farmers and ranchers and thus made a major contribution to the development of frontier America.

The early miners used simple hand tools—mining pans, picks, and shovels. In China the gold miners had made some unique modifications to mining tools but none of these changes seems to have influenced EuroAmerican miners in the American West. Later, other devices and new technologies for placer deposits developed. By 1848 California miners used the cradle, a wooden box that rested on rockers, with a riddle box on top containing an iron sheet with holes in it.[32] The iron sheets frequently have been found in mining sites. The heavier gold and sand were trapped in the cleats of the cradle's floor, and then cleaned to find the gold. Usually at least two men worked this system and could wash an average of three hundred pans a day using the cradle, about three times more than the pan method. By 1850 other equipment was added—but as the equipment became more sophisticated and technologically efficient, more men were needed. Chinese miners liked to use rockers, long toms (a type of sluice), or sluice boxes to separate the lighter sand and gravel from the heavier gold particles. They also used woven cloth to filter the sand and gravel, catching the fine gold in the fabric and then burning the cloth to recover the gold. How similar this equipment was to that used in China has yet to be discovered.

Mining equipment, like rockers, often was special ordered, built in China, and shipped to the Chinese merchants in mining communities in the American West. The Chinese often adapted mining equipment so that it could be easily moved from place to place. For example, the long tom was suspended in two parts at opposite ends of the traditional shoulder pole for transportation from one site to another. They also carried iron stoves with locking devices to connect the two halves for heating and cooking in this manner.[33] They were creative in adapting western equipment and, for example, from an archaeological site in Idaho, they used metal strips from opium tins to hold together a rocker.[34] Throughout Nevada they refashioned tin cans to create a spout for pouring liquids.[35] Frugality and reuse were characteristics of Chinese miners.

Visiting Scotsman John David Borthwick, who traveled in California during the Gold Rush from 1851 to 1854, wrote about his observations of the Chinese miners.[36] He noted that they tended to work in isolated and inaccessible places, pitched their tents next to their diggings, worked in large groups for protection (or smaller ones of three to four men, thus attracting little attention from outsiders), and avoided EuroAmerican towns in an effort to avoid robbery or mob violence that usually occurred when

EuroAmerican miners noted their successes. He correctly observed that some of the Chinese worked in groups that were actually Chinese mining companies, continuing a mining tradition from China. Borthwick was not always accurate in his perceptions about the Chinese, but he is one of the few European writers commenting on aspects about their work and lifestyles in mining during the Gold Rush.

~

At the outset in California various methods were devised in dividing the value of the gold. The profits from mining could be shared equally among the participants, usually two to eight men, on a daily basis or the land was divided according to a contract—but the costs of building the ditch or any irrigation system was divided before the profits were shared.[37] This worked well for groups of sixteen or less. The Chinese tended to favor the equal division system. One story demonstrating this involved a forty-pound nugget that the group of miners chiseled into small pieces to sell along with their gold dust so that each man could receive his fair share as well as not draw unwanted attention to the group and where they were working.[38] But the contract system broke down around 1850 when outsiders entered into the mining sites and miners formed districts with regulations to govern themselves.

~

The major event that drew the Chinese to the American West was the news of the discovery of gold at Sutter's sawmill in California as well as the promise of work publicized by labor contractors. The word spread quickly in South China through a variety of methods. Letters from Chinese in California and the return of financially successful men were the main motivators. For example, in 1847 Chum Ming, a San Francisco merchant from Guangzhou, wrote his friend Chang Yum in the Sanyi (Three Counties) region of the Pearl Delta about the 1848 discovery of gold at Sutter's Mill, thus sparking the Chinese migration, especially from Sanyi, to California.

Labor contractors or agents also tried to attract Chinese to California to fulfill labor demands as industrialization in the American West progressed. Both Chinese and EuroAmerican firms had offices in Hong Kong and Guangzhou for this purpose. Handbills and pamphlets told of the great benefits of going to the American West, such as one in 1848 from a "gold mountain company" recruiting laborers in Guangzhou (Canton) that stated, "American people are living in a very affluent country. We welcome Chinese to our country. We offer you good wages, accommodations, food, and clothes. You are free to

In the northwestern region of North America, Chinese miners migrated to numerous sites, including eastern Oregon, northeastern Nevada, Idaho, Washington, and British Columbia.

send back money to your family and friends."[39] Chinese emigrants believed this type of literature and saw the prosperity of the returned Chinese.

The news attracted some experienced Chinese miners, including those who previously had worked overseas goldfields in places like Borneo, Indonesia, Malaysia, and Australia.[40] As in other locations the overseas Chinese miners organized themselves in groups or companies, often owned or managed by merchants, worked for non-Chinese mine owners under a headman or foreman, or were individual miners working alone or with one to four other people. By 1850 Calaveras County, California, had 139 Chinese miners, 10 merchants, and 1 baker while Sutter County, California, reported 176 Chinese miners and Tuolumne County, California, had 18 Chinese miners and 1 merchant.[41] The Chinese population grew rapidly thereafter.

Little has been written about the Chinese and EuroAmerican labor contractors and recruiters (who were paid by the head) in Hong Kong or had offices in the American West with links to Hong Kong.[42] Cornelius Koopmanschap, Macondray and Company, W.T. Coleman and Company, and Sisson, Wallace, and (later) Crocker were among the most notable West Coast firms with recruiters in China and the American West.[43] Although they were known for their recruiting of railroad laborers, they also sought Chinese workers for other types of industries. George W. Gift (1833–79), following the advice of Koopmanschap, recruited two hundred Chinese to work for the Arkansas Company in New Orleans for four years. (Gift was one of the few EuroAmerican contractors who has been studied.[44] Undoubtedly there were others like him.) Finally, the trans-Pacific shipping companies, most notably the Pacific Mail Steamship Company, often with ship's officers who were EuroAmerican and crews who were Chinese, were involved in the trans-Pacific movement of people, transporting approximately 80,523 Chinese to the American West between 1876 and 1906.[45]

The image of the "American streets paved with gold" began in this period and persisted into the twenty-first century. One of the challenges the Chinese faced was funding the trip across the Pacific Ocean. Businessmen, employment agents, relatives, or friends often advanced money for travel and required repayment in the amount of the loan plus interest.[46] The fare varied from $50 to $200 (the higher fee charged by brokers) going to the United States. But it was always less—from $30 to $50—to return. This made it easier for the Chinese to return to China.

Historian Zo Kil Young, who studied the various means by which the Chinese paid for their passage, asserted that most utilized kinship or regional connections for funding.[47] Lee Chew, writing in 1882, described how his father gave him $100 that enabled him to go to Hong Kong with five other boys from his village; he paid $50 for his passage to San Francisco, had an uncomfortable trip, and reached San Francisco half-starved.[48] He worked as a servant, then a laundryman for a railroad gang, then a miner, and eventually as a general merchant in New York City. Based on a survey of records from the Immigration and Naturalization Service (INS), many Chinese immigrants followed friends and relatives in a process called "chain migration" that was characteristic of other immigrant groups going to the United States.[49] Returned emigrants (*jiuke*, "old guests") often paid the expenses for new emigrants (*xinke*, "new guests") who would take over a thriving business or participate in an employment group for economic benefits to both. Young men were especially excited about the new possibilities overseas and were not hesitant about changing jobs.

The common belief in America, however, was that most of the Chinese immigrants were contract laborers who were similar to indentured servants or slaves. Many of the Chinese miners were individual miners or worked in groups with other Chinese and acquired their travel funding from relatives or associations. EuroAmerican mining companies employed some Chinese miners often through Chinese labor contractors, who were either Chinese merchants or Chinese associations or EuroAmerican firms like Sisson and Wallace (located in Truckee, California; Carlin, Nevada; and other towns along the Central Pacific line). Over 50 percent of the railroad workers for the Central Pacific were recruited from among the Chinese already in the American West.[50] Many of these men had worked in the goldfields and had been discouraged by their meager finds. Sometimes a labor boss or headman accompanied the workers overseas and stayed with them until the repayment was completed. Often relatives traveled together and assisted each other during the long journey and the adjustment to American society. Despite the stereotype that all were "coolie laborers" or "contract laborers" instead of voluntary migrants, there are no figures to determine through what method a Chinese immigrant entered the United States. There also are no figures as to the number who left and later returned to the United States (what is called "circular migration"), but this group had at least some financial success.

When Chinese emigrants arrived in the port cities in the United States, men from their district and/or family associations greeted them and assisted them in finding American boots (one of the first purchases made), housing (usually in the association boarding house), food, and employment opportunities. Although these kinds of associations existed in China, they had expanded their mutual aid and protection functions in the United States because of the anti-Chinese movements, the absence of the nuclear and extended family as found in China, and the need of the newcomers to understand their new environment.

Chinese merchants or other entrepreneurs acted as pivotal leaders in the community. Their acceptance as leaders depended upon a variety of factors: the geographical features of the community; its relationship to nearby urban areas and transportation systems; the character of the community founder or founders and their attitude toward the Chinese; the influx of new EuroAmerican residents who may have brought anti-Chinese attitudes from their previous location; the multiethnic component of the community and the nature of their interaction; the size and economic fluctuations of the community; the local newspaper or regional newspapers that may or may not have reflected national or local stereotypic sentiments; the power and influence of the labor and mining unions or other anti-Chinese organizations; the knowledge of the Chinese merchants in legal matters; their ability to speak English; and the nature of the Chinese community itself and its relationship to the rest of the local community and to China.

Merchant networks played a role in the migration because the merchants served as the labor contractors for mining companies, both Chinese and EuroAmerican, and their stores were the sources of imported and American goods. Men like Gee Hee Chin (Chen Yixi in pinyin, 1844–1929) of Seattle and Jin Mun Moy of San Francisco were both miners and railroad workers before they became merchants and labor contractors.[51] Both men quickly learned that knowing English, American laws, and influential EuroAmericans, including lawyers and sheriffs, were important. Also, merchants were often the mine owners and hired a headman or supervisor who was probably trained in the Sierra Nevada goldfields. The supervisor contracted laborers to go to new mining areas in Oregon and Nevada, for example, and often went with the men, purchasing abandoned claims from EuroAmerican miners, finding or establishing housing for them, dividing the duties so that someone performed the cooking, and assigned the men their work.[52] Labor contractors and employment agents were found in many parts of the American West but decreased in visibility as the Chinese labor pool diminished due to the Chinese exclusion acts and the availability of manual labor types of jobs.

Some miners aspired to be merchants, especially after the passage of the 1882 Chinese Exclusion Act that prohibited laborers from immigrating but allowed students, diplomats, and merchants and their families to immigrate and travel to and from China.[53] Kue Quong Gee, also known as Ngin Pit Gee, immigrated in 1879 and eventually became a miner in Quincy, Plumas County, California. By 1890 he invested in a company in Quincy, then another in La Porte, and finally in a drug store in Oakland so that he could have the ability to travel to and from China. But even with this privilege, he only had funds to make the trip three times prior to 1919 to be with his nuclear and extended family.[54] In 1919 he fulfilled his cherished dream of bringing a son to the United States to carry on his work. These types of long-distance marriages were hard on the husband, wife, and children, and resulted in a lifestyle very different from the traditional Chinese family life. Gee's son, Ton Gee, also known as Hoy Quan Gee, never knew his father when he was growing up and as a young adult, had to make many adjustments to American life quickly in order to take over his father's business. This was a common pattern in the early twentieth century.

Merchants in rural communities often were the only ones who could read and write Chinese and, in many cases, English. Merchants sometimes wrote letters home for the overseas Chinese and were the agents through whom money was sent to China. They also read letters from home for those who could not read. General merchandising stores often served as a social gathering place for those interested in storytelling, gossiping, playing musical instruments, informal gaming, and exchanges and discussions of news and other events. For this reason many Chinese merchants subscribed to Chinatown newspapers, especially ones published in San Francisco. Tea and snacks customarily were served during social exchanges. Often the merchant and his family, if he had one, lived in the back of the store. Since the store was used for communal gatherings, the residences of miners did not need to be large and spacious and often were regarded only as a place to sleep and keep belongings.

Family links were as important as regional or birthplace identities. As Him Mark Lai has shown in his study of Chinese American butchers, clans tried to dominate specific occupations in any given community.[55] Chinese immigrants fought wars over territories and occupations. Merchants also wanted to see clansmen in jobs in their mining areas. Thus the Lee, Ng (Ung), and Yee clans were prominent merchants in Elko, Carlin, and Island Mountain (Elko County, northeastern Nevada), and had a continuous flow of "relatives" brought into the area.[56] Lung On, a merchant in John Day, Oregon, assisted countrymen in attempting to immigrate into the United States. As a general rule, merchants purchased their supplies from wholesalers and middlemen from their native place or from kinsmen.

Chinese merchants also often engaged in mining, thus augmenting their income. In the American West, the mine manager often was a local merchant who raised the funds for the mining operations and acted as the labor contractor and provider of goods for the miners. He also might lease the claim and fund the construction of the ditch system for placering as well as lend his ability to interact with the EuroAmericans. The Chinese miner purchased his basic necessities from the Chinese merchant: pick, shovel, pan, cradle, rocker, and sluice box. He also bought food products, clothing, and other items, many imported from China. Although EuroAmerican merchants also carried these goods, the Chinese workers preferred to do business "the Chinese way" and patronized the Chinese merchants whenever they could. Whether some of the Chinese company-owned stores followed the American tradition of restricting or trying to restrict their workers so that their stores were patronized has not been uncovered, but undoubtedly some of that occurred. In many cases the merchant-labor contractor made his profits from goods sold rather than adding a fee for contracting services.

Some merchant-miners were very successful. Loke Kee of Idaho, for example, reportedly saved nearly $90,000 from mining and operating a general store between 1863 and 1906.[57] The combination of occupations could bring the wealth that was so desired. Jim H. Low (1846–1909) of Winnemucca, Nevada, began as a railroad worker on the Central Pacific, then became involved in mining and merchandising, and achieved financial success by the time of his death in the early twentieth century.[58] Wong Kee, the principal leader of Chinese placer and quartz mining in Spring Valley (also called American Canyon), Nevada, founded in 1881, leased claims and constructed ditches for placering, was involved in quartz mining, and operated a store until 1906 when he left Spring Valley as a man of wealth to reside in nearby Lovelock, Nevada.[59] Part of his fame came from his financial relationship with the famous "Death Valley Scotty," who was associated with the famous Scotty's Castle and owed Wong Kee money.

Miners and merchants also were the most likely to earn sufficient funds to return home to China, to have and raise a family either in the United States or China, and become leaders of the community.[60] At the same time, the last Chinese residents of John Day, Tuscarora, and Island Mountain were miner-merchants—men who had interacted in positive ways with the majority community and stayed long after mining declined. They never saw their wives and families in China in their declining years. They rejected going home and being with their families perhaps because they had adjusted to the American lifestyle.

Although many EuroAmericans believed that the district associations (*huiguan*) were labor contractors for Chinese workers, merchants performed that role as individuals. EuroAmericans generally approached the local storekeeper for workers because he could contact fellow merchants in San Francisco and elsewhere. For example, in 1864 when EuroAmerican mine owners in Oro Fino district, Idaho, needed two hundred Chinese workers, they contacted merchant Shu Lee in nearby Walla Walla, Washington, to find them in San Francisco.[61] Shu Lee undoubtedly turned to his district or lineage association to locate the workers. Although merchants headed the different organizations in the Chinatowns, it usually was not in their capacity as a leader of a district association to perform this task.

Chinese American merchant-led community organizations had roots in traditional China but had more power and duties in the United States.[62] In Ming (1368–1644) China the *huiguan* was a hostel in some provincial cities that provided lodging for travelers from the same native place, or for holding feasts and gatherings of officials from the same native place, and later, in the Qing dynasty (1644–1911) for those from the same native place engaged in the same trade in a rapidly growing marketplace. From this evolved the urban trade associations (*hang*), which served as brokers for goods, set prices for merchandise such as tea and dyed cloth, worked with government officials, hosted operas and other types of entertainment, and provided funerary arrangements and burial grounds for people from the same native place.

In the American West, these organizations were regarded as merchant guilds and labor unions but actually differed from western guilds and unions. In the late eighteenth century the Chinese guilds were called *gongsuo* ("meeting hall") rather than *huiguan* ("clubhouse") and the emphasis was on common trade rather than common geographic birth place. In the early nineteenth century, Chinese craft and service guilds were established in the major urban areas and native place often no longer was a requirement for membership. The guilds mediated disagreements among members and could set wages and regulations for a particular occupation. Nonmembers were forbidden from working in a business under the guidance of the guild. Apprentices also had to join the guild. Guilds also established altars in the headquarters to worship deities from their native place as well as Guan Yu (also known as Guan Gong), the third-century general of the Three Kingdoms period who was known for his loyalty to the previous Han dynasty, has been revered as the "God of Literature" as well as the "God of War," and popularized the concept of a sworn brotherhood. Other deities worshipped might include Caishen ("God of Wealth") and Tianhou ("Empress of Heaven" also known as Mazu), the protectress of seamen on the China coast and travelers abroad. In the United States, these guilds set rules for laundries and restaurants, dividing up the territories or areas of service.[63] Guilds probably established some type of regulation for the Chinese mining companies, but no known records have been uncovered.

The *huiguan* (district associations) were founded to foster comradeship among people from the same place by providing mutual support in social, cultural, religious, and economic ways in both China and the American West. In the late nineteenth century the payment of dues to the association was mandatory for individuals who needed or might need the association's services. This allowed the associations to construct their headquarters, which were often the most permanent and impressive structures in the Chinatowns. The merchant-leaders believed that it was better for miners to work in teams with men from their same district, and in recognition of that, acted as an employment agency by providing information about job openings.[64]

The Gangzhou (Cantonese, Kong Chow) Association provided the blueprint for later ones. In 1849 Yuan Sheng (Norman Assing, a Zhongshan merchant who was fluent in English and entertained EuroAmerican politicians at one of his two restaurants) formed the Chew Yick Association, which later became known as the Kong Chow Association—by 1853 the organization had sufficient funds to build an elaborate temple and meeting house in San Francisco's Chinatown. Thereafter there was confusion in American Chinatowns about the nature of the "joss houses" in Chinatowns. Many joss houses, so named for the incense, or joss, sticks burned on the altars (usually two) in front of the images of the deities or taken from the Portuguese word for "gods," were mistaken for temples when in actuality they were association halls with altars for worship. However the primary purposes for these buildings were for recreation for their members, temporary housing, banquet facilities for Chinese New Year and other celebrations, and a meeting hall for members.

There were several *huiguan* in San Francisco, Chicago, New York, and other major cities having a large Chinese population. At first the largest group of Chinese immigrants came from the Sanyi (Sam Yup, or Three Counties: Nanhai, Panyu, and Shunde; later adding Hua Xian, Sanshui, Sihui, Gaoyao, Gaoming, and Qingyuan) area of southeastern Guangdong, near the provincial capital, Guangzhou. This large commercial city was the only port open to foreign traders prior to the Opium War (1839–42).[65] The inhabitants were more familiar with the world beyond China. They had a tradition of emigration that has been documented as early as 1397, when Liang Daoming, a native of Nanhai, led thousands of Fujianese and Guangdongese to eastern Sumatra. They also understood something about international trade.

In 1851 Sanyi merchants established the second association in San Francisco to assist the newcomers; provide room and board for transients; act as intermediaries between the EuroAmerican and Chinese; provide mutual aid services, such as assistance for the sick in returning to China, provisions for burial, cemetery grounds, and vaults for the deceased; transmit news about trade conditions and the homeland; raise funds for the homeland; and provide general services including giving advice, sending remittances and letters home, and getting medical care in the form of physicians and drugs. The Sanyi *huiguan* also protected the members' civil and legal rights, including representation at governmental institutions, mediation of disputes among members, and certification and preservation of documents and deeds. Like the other associations, they had a rotating credit system to aid in the establishment of businesses and loaned money for the "credit-ticket" system that allowed workers from their native place to immigrate to the United States.[66] Until the mid-twentieth century, membership was not voluntary—the dues provided a financial foundation for buildings, loans, legal expenses, and other activities. Eventually the association provided Chinese language education whenever possible. One could not leave the United States without a certificate issued by his association showing that all debts had been paid. The Sanyi *huiguan* was known to EuroAmericans as the "Canton Company," with its headquarters at Clay and Powell Street in San Francisco.

Other *huiguans* were organized, offering the same services. Later in 1851, the merchants from Siyi (Four Counties, or Sze Yup: Xinhui, Taishan, Kaiping, and Enping), located slightly west of the Pearl River Delta, established the next *huiguan* with functions similar to the earlier ones. Eventually this became the largest of the district associations. These men were small farmers and handicraft workers, some of who found themselves out of business because of foreign imports. The villages in these four districts often consisted of one or two clans and the relationships established through marriages closely connected them.[67] For example, all of the residents of Hock Wan Village were members of the Yee clan. Immigrants from Taishan constituted 45 percent of the Chinese in the American West in 1876 and as many as 50 percent after 1882.

In 1852 the next and third-most influential *huiguan* was founded. Yuan Sheng, Cai Libi, and Liu Zuman of Zhongshan (also known as Xiangshan, located near Macao) established the Yanghe *huiguan* (Cantonese, Yeong Wo), made up of immigrants from Dongguan, Zengchen, and Xin'an (modern Bao'an). The latter locality was the home of Kejia people, a minority group disliked and discriminated against by most of the Guangdong people. The Kejias formed their own Xin'an *huiguan* (Sun On Company) and changed its name several times over the course of the years until it settled upon Renhe *huiguan* (Cantonese, Yan Wo).

In 1853 internal disputes in the Siyi *huiguan* led to the formation of the Ningyung (Ning Yeung) *huiguan*, whose members came from Taishan. This organization became the most powerful in San Francisco's Chinatown until the mid-twentieth century. Another dispute in the Siyi *huiguan* led to the establishment of the Hehe *huiguan* (Hop Wo) in 1862, made up of men from Kaiping and Enping with a few from Taishan. The Yee clan dominated this association. A group of dissidents splintered off and formed the Zhaoqing *huiguan* (Sue Hing) in 1878. Divisions and reuniting occurred in the ensuing years but all of these district associations were under the general umbrella of the Chinese Consolidated Benevolent Association (CCBA, more popularly known as the Chinese Six Companies because of the six original district associations; in Chinese Zhonghua *huiguan*), which acted as the unofficial spokesmen for the Chinese in the United States. The CCBA interacted with EuroAmericans at the federal, state, and local levels and became the most famous of all of the Chinese American organizations.

As disputes among members of the different *huiguan* became more frequent around 1862, an organization called a *gongsuo* (*kongso* or *kongsi*, "meeting hall") was established. Made up of representatives from the different associations, the organization acted as the informal tribunal for the Chinese communities and, as seen in Los Angeles, often even had their own "jail" or other detention center. Because of its role in the response to the 1882 Chinese Exclusion Act and at the urging of the Chinese envoy in Washington, D.C., another name for the CCBA when judicial matters were being decided was the "Zhonghua gongsuo" to indicate a different function.[68]

According to an article in the *San Francisco Bulletin* (November 24, 1865), upon arrival the Chinese immigrant paid his district association $5 to $10 in return for benefits including protection, advice, instructions in respect to mining districts, job opportunities, health care benefits, funeral and burial benefits, temporary housing, and other matters related to his well-being. Upon departure, the individual had to pay an exit fee and inform his district association, the secretary of which informed the other district associations so that all debts, especially to merchants, had been paid. This included receipts for the payment of mining and poll taxes. If the individual could not pay all of his debts, the association covered the amount and then charged the individual's assets on a pro-rata basis. Once this process had been completed, the person received a document indicating that he could return to China. These powers were much more extensive than the functions of the district associations in China and were characteristic of some of the district associations serving overseas Chinese outside of North America.

Since one of the functions of the district associations was to keep a record of their members, American government officials pressured the leaders for a count. The *San Jose Republican* reported on November 27, 1858, the following membership numbers and range of annual dues required from each member: Siyi, 15,700 members with dues ranging from $15 to $20; Yanghe, 18,500 members with dues ranging from $7 to $10; Sanyi, 9, 200 members with dues at $15; Ningyung, 3,600 members with dues at $10; and Renhe, 1,400 members with no dues. On December 6, 1869, the *Oregonian* (Portland) reprinted these figures: Ningyung, 46,867 members, of these 12,262 returned, 3,487 died, and 27,118 remained (10,756 were in California); Yanghe, 28,207 members, of these 4,295 returned, 2,085 died, and 21,820 remained (8,550 in California); Siyi, 19,111 members with 8,015 returned, 1,005 died, and 10,061 remained (6,370 in California); Sanyi, 15,023 members, of these 3,202 returned, 987 died, and 10,834 remained (6,875 in California); Hehe, 25,002 members, of these 4,407 returned, and 18,717 remained (7,780 in California); and Renhe, the smallest group, 4,374 members, of these 1,112 returned, 983 died, and 2,281 remained. The Ningyung reported that 7,000 members went to Nevada, 12,000 to Montana, 10,000 to Idaho, 8,000 to Oregon, and 4,000 to Colorado and Utah. The number of members, all paying regular dues, differentiated the power and prestige of the individual associations. The change within a decade in membership numbers indicated the shifting balance of power. Ningyung, Yanghe, Siyi, and Sanyi became embroiled in a power struggle with each other despite the fact that they were represented in the CCBA. The result was the dominance of Ningyung district association until the mid-twentieth century.

The report was significant because this Chinese "census" was done shortly after the completion of the first transcontinental railroad and during the expansion of gold mining into areas outside of California. The numerical dominance of Ningyung, Yanghe, Siyi, and Hehe was evident and the percentage of returnees was not so high as to justify the appellation of "sojourners." The high number of deaths meant that the district associations and other community organizations had to be concerned with funeral arrangements, cemeteries, burials, and, for the privileged, the transportation of remains to China for reburial in the home village. The Chinese believed that to be buried in the place of one's birth was important for one's spirit as well as one's ancestors.[69]

Another major function of the associations was the preservation of Chinese traditions. An association's headquarters was usually the most impressive building in the community. Many were built according to a standard formula with the social and recreational activities, kitchen, and bunk beds on the first floor and the altar and meeting room on the second floor.[70] In these association halls there were Chinese language newspapers and magazines, some from the home districts for distribution in overseas Chinese communities and some published in the United States. Gambling, food, storytelling, musical performances, and other activities took place, binding the members socially and providing a network (*guanxi*) system. The most important events were the celebration of traditional holidays. Without the nuclear family present, one of the first adjustments that the Chinese made was to celebrate Chinese New Year and other holidays with men from the same district or lineage. During Chinese New Year, instead of the family dinner, the association sponsored a banquet. Instead of giving the traditional candy and lucky money wrapped in red paper to unmarried children who were related, men frequently gave these small gifts to the small number of the Chinese children—and sometimes non-Chinese children—in the community. EuroAmerican scholars and writers often overlooked these subtle adjustments to American life.

The leaders of the district associations and CCBA were active in protecting the rights of Chinese miners. They became important to Chinese miners because Americans mistakenly regarded them as the owners or agents of mining companies. One early example of this was the work of Tang Maozhi.[71] Tang (1828–97, also known as Tingzhi and Ah Chick) was from Zhongshan and had been educated at the Morrison Society School in Hong Kong, where he learned English. This ultimately led to an early career as a court interpreter in Hong Kong. He was dismissed from this position and left for San Francisco in January 1852. He made contacts with EuroAmerican missionaries, including Reverend William Speer, and gained their support in several situations, including the opposition to a California's Tingley bill supporting contract labor. As one of the organizers of the Yanghe *huiguan,* he represented Chinese miners to California Governor John Bigler on several occasions in 1852 (pointing out that the Chinese were willing to pay the Foreign Miners' Tax) and to the California Legislature's Committee on Mines and Mining Interests in 1853 (presenting them with a detailed account of the five *huiguan* and their membership numbers). In 1856 or 1857 Tang returned to China permanently and eventually held positions in Jardine, Matheson, and Company, the China Merchants Steam Navigation Company, and the Kaiping Mines, the latter two playing an important role in the late nineteenth-century modernization of China.

In addition to the *huiguan,* there were clans, surname, or family associations (usually called *fang, gongsuo, gongsi,* or *tang*). Membership was based upon patrilineal kinship or an ancient unity of clans, such as the Longgongtang (Loong Kong Association, or Four Brothers' Association, dating from the Three Kingdoms Period, 222–64). In this system the place of one's birth was not considered. These associations offered similar charitable services to those of the district associations, including the rotating credit system, but provided even more protection to its members whenever outsiders threatened them. They established norms that regulated the group's activities and rotated their leadership. The strength of the clan associations and kinship ties in southeastern China were transplanted to the United States, especially in urban areas but were less powerful in rural America because of the insufficient number of members. In San Francisco, the Li (Lee), Huang (Wong), and Yu or Yi (Yee) family names were the largest and most influential and they sent their members to regions where kinsmen were finding that elusive gold.

The guilds (*gongsuo, hang*) were based upon occupation and had played a role in urban Chinatowns, but in the rural areas, probably only the laundry and restaurant associations provided the Chinatowns with regulations on distances between these occupations and a range of rates for their products or services. There has been no evidence of a gold miners' guild, but a butchers guild existed—certain clans dominated the butcher business whenever they could, so there was a relationship between family associations and guilds. Some EuroAmericans erroneously believed that the guilds were "Chinese labor unions" but the traditions and functions were very different and should not be equated since the guilds represented owners rather than the workers, especially in dealings with government.

The most important Chinese associations in the mining communities were the fraternal organizations and secret societies whose closed membership was based on the nomination for membership by a current member. All of these existed in traditional China but in the United States, they had a more expansive agenda. All had traditional rituals, secret signs or codes, and the same general functions and goals that characterized the district and family associations. Many were short-lived, but the two most influential and continuous ones that rivaled the CCBA in power and influence were the Zhigongtang (Chee Kong Tong, also known as Hee Gong Tong and other variations) and the Binggongtang (Bing Kong Tong). Both organizations claimed links to the international Free Masons, and were commonly found in rural and small-town Chinese America. The organizations had signs, symbols, and rituals similar to the international Free Masons. This may have been due to the branch in Hong Kong or Southeast Asia from which many of the early leaders came. The Zhigongtang was a political organization dedicated to the overthrow of the Manchu government, while the Binggongtang, a splinter group, emphasized gambling, prostitution, and opium sales as a major part of its activities. In places like Singapore, where the other associations did not exist, membership in the Binggongtang was mandatory.[72] Pressure often was placed on the Chinese immigrants to join one of the organizations.

Information about these secret societies has been difficult to obtain but recent scholarship in the field has indicated the general outline of their operations.[73] Whereas the CCBA elected or appointed scholars, often from China, as president, the Zhigongtang was headed by influential community leaders. In Portland and Seattle, for example, Chin Gee Hee, a merchant and labor contractor who began his career as a railroad worker in Nevada and moved up the economic ladder to become a merchant, labor contractor, and ticket agent for the Northern Pacific Railroad and Pacific Steamship Company, was the president of Seattle's Zhigongtang.[74] The leaders were local men who were literate and, more often than not, bilingual and knowledgeable in several Chinese dialects so that they could communicate with the Chinese and EuroAmerican communities. Archaeologists Ying-ying Chen in British Columbia and Florence and Robert Lister in Tucson, Arizona, and sociologist Stanford Lyman uncovered documents about the Zhigongtang, the rules of membership, the oaths, and other artifacts.[75] Often the members constituted a large percentage of the rural Chinese American population. In 1896 in Boise, for example, there were 150 Zhigongtang members, an estimated three-fourths of Boise's Chinese population.[76] The Zhigongtang also admitted EuroAmericans, though few in number, as members.[77]

In the 1890s the competition in power and prestige between the CCBA and the Zhigongtang reached a critical point when the Bureau of Immigration (BI, forerunner of the INS) decided to control the Chinese American population by issuing mandatory Certificates of Identity and Certificates of Residence with the passage of the Geary Act in 1892 that extended the 1882 Chinese Exclusion Act for another ten years. Any Chinese (whether born in China or the United States) found without a certificate of identity or residence (which were originally issued between 1892 and 1893) was subject to deportation or imprisonment and a year of hard labor. The CCBA told its members not to comply with the law and raised $60,000 to hire lawyers and prepare a test case based on the unconstitutionality of the Geary Act because it treated Chinese residents the same as those trying to immigrate and denied them protection under the Bill of Rights.[78]

The Zhigongtang, on the other hand, urged its members to have their pictures taken and apply for the certificates. Because the Zhigongtang complied with the law, it gained greater power in many Chinese communities. The Supreme Court disagreed with the CCBA and, beginning in 1897, their members had to obtain the certificates. But this delayed date indicated to the BI, under the domination of former labor union leaders, that those individuals had been "resisters" to the law. Using the Bureau's police powers, agents checked for the identity papers, arrested individuals, and even tried to conduct a census of individuals with and without certificates during the early twentieth century.[79]

Some of the secret societies traced their origins to related organizations in China and Southeast Asia, particularly the Triads (Sanhehui) and Heaven and Earth Society (Tiandihui). Among these were the Anliangtang (On Leong Tong) and Xieshengtang (Hip Sing Tong), who included in their membership trained fighters and body guards. The leaders often worked with or were labor contractors and therefore were closely connected with the working class. Membership in these fraternities was not exclusively Chinese and an individual could belong to several different categories of organizations, such as a district association, clan association, and secret society.[80] Because the *tang* often became involved in gambling, opium, illegal immigration, and prostitution as part of the activities offered to members and from which much needed revenue was derived, "tong wars" characterized much of the violence within the Chinese communities in the late nineteenth and early twentieth centuries. However, the western presses, which loved to report the sensationalism of such violence, seldom understood the reasons for the wars or the underlying issues. The Chinese were able to avoid going through the American court system to settle many types of disputes because the associations also had judicial functions and tried to solve internal problems.

Unless the Chinese miners in a location came from the same district or belonged to the same lineage, the organization that provided protection, insurance, and burial arrangements was a *tang* that was not necessarily a secret society but a "burial society." Since the names were so confusing, fraternal organizations were mixed up with district associations, family associations, guilds, and other organizations in the American press.

The associations became involved in mining rights of their constituencies and this led to some of the infamous tong wars. For example, in July 1854, the members of the Sanyi, Siyi, and Ningyung associations fought against the Yanghe association, representing immigrants from Zhongshan, in Weaverville, Trinity County, California, in the first known Chinese tong war in California.[81] Weaverville had a bustling Chinatown with four stores, four gambling establishments, and one restaurant. The war in Weaverville left twenty-six dead and sixty wounded. The second famous war took place in September 1856. Continuing the rivalry from their home districts in China, the Sanyi fought against the Kejia over mining rights at Chinese Camp near

Knight's Ferry in Tuolumne County, California. Pitting 1,200 Sanyi members against 900 Kejias, four people died and four were wounded. Eventually these kinds of disputes were resolved within the Chinese community because the EuroAmerican police force did not interfere with internal "Chinese" fights.

Through the rotating credit system and other financial programs, Chinese associations could assist in the investment of mining companies. Prior to 1860, Chinese mining companies were already in existence in California. Sacramento County had several, with assessed value of the mines ranging from $1,725 to $3,600, and per capita income of the partners amounting to $40 to $50 per month, which was slightly less than the $60 for EuroAmerican companies of comparable sizes.[82] The improved mining technology required larger investments of capital, so the Chinese miners banded together to meet the challenge. In Moose Creek, Idaho, the Chinese built ditches and a flume measuring 3,000 feet long and 56 feet high at the cost of $8,000, then added a six-inch wrought-iron-pipe-inverted siphon that was 3,500 feet long—the first such inverted siphon used in Idaho—at the cost of $4,000, and purchased goods from Weiser and Wax's general store totaling $4,000 to $6,000 per annum.[83] In the Pierce Mining District in Idaho, the average cost of the fifty-two claims owned by the Chinese as recorded officially in 1867 was $816.[84] If the average Chinese laborer was earning $1 per working day, this was way beyond his means unless funds were pooled and directed by a manager and/or merchant and/or *tang*.

Spoken Chinese often divided, rather than united, Chinese merchants and miners because the different dialects were mutually unintelligible. A few linguistically talented people could speak and understand several dialects, but the average Chinese could not. Spoken Siyi differed greatly from Sanyi. Zhongshan dialect was closer to Sanyi but unintelligible to those from Siyi. Few could understand Kejia and Fujian dialects. Some Kejias knew other dialects because they had lived in several different counties, so, for example, those who lived in Taishan (where they constituted about one-third of the county's population) usually knew how to speak Siyi dialect.[85] The Kejias also had very different cultural traditions and were, from the perspective of most southern Chinese, physically distinctive. Whenever possible, they established their own segregated residential and work area within or near the main Chinatown.

In addition to differences in the spoken language, each of the regions had different food customs and styles of cooking. Food played an important role in the lives of these immigrants, who often were eating better than their families in China—familiar tastes (even with the same ingredients) made the hardships of life in the American West more bearable. Often, one miner in a group was the cook for the entire group, and miners tended to stay longer if the food was to their liking. Therefore, the Chinese companies and men who worked in small groups usually were from the same district in southeastern China and, more often than not, were related in some way or another, such as through their wives if the last names were not the same. Unfortunately, in most cases the census manuscripts do not reveal these relationships.

One of the keys to a miner's success in the American West was his ability to read, write, and speak English. Not all miners had the opportunity to learn English, but some attended schools in Hong Kong where English was taught or participated in one of the religious-sponsored English-language schools established throughout the American West. Chung Kee Sing, a miner in Iowa Hills, California, had immigrated at the age of 21 in 1882 and could speak and write both languages.[86] He made EuroAmerican friends and thus gained advice and support from them when the need arose. Language skills gave him a great advantage in succeeding in the United States over those who did not know English.

Census manuscript records in Oregon and Idaho indicated there were Chinese mining companies, with an average of ten men, who probably shared the profits. Once the expenses of the mine owner or manager were covered, the profits were divided proportionately according to the amount of contribution, so no set wages were paid.[87] Although some EuroAmericans miners used this system of shared profits, most preferred other types of arrangements in mining. Some Chinese miners adopted the western employment system of paid salaries or division of land with the profits going to the individual, but in the early decades the traditional "shared" method was used. Other Chinese miners worked for a EuroAmerican employer and received a set salary. Because of the changes in mining technology, very few miners could be independent and few worked alone as the decades passed.

In China and the American West, Chinese miners often worked as part-time farmers or gardeners, two occupations that were complimentary due to their seasonal nature. For example, in Hawthorne, Nevada, Chung Kee (1847–1909, who died and was buried in Hawthorne) used the Lucky Boy miners to help him harvest his well-known white asparagus and other vegetables that he sold to famous hotel restaurants in San Francisco and Salt Lake City, as well as nearby locations.[88] Community leaders, like the Leland Stanford family, recognized Chinese talents in growing fresh vegetables and fruits during and after the construction of the Central Pacific Railroad and utilized Chinese horticultural talents on their California ranches.[89] By the 1880s the Chinese had established themselves in truck farming or "gardening" (farming plots of land that were smaller than the EuroAmerican farms) in California, especially in the Sacramento Delta region. This dual occupation complicated the count for the census enumerators, who only wanted to list a primary occupation and did not take into consideration a secondary occupation.

The lure of mining only lasted about fifty years—until the turn of the twentieth century. The number of Chinese miners decreased through the decades because of the decline in new finds, the introduction of new and more expensive technology and equipment, the risk of violence encountered by Chinese miners, the decline in the pool of workers due to exclusion laws, and other economic opportunities that were safer and did not require such hard physical labor. In 1860, approximately 70 percent of the gainfully employed Chinese over age fifteen in California were miners. But this figure dropped to 65 percent in 1870 as the Chinese moved into other occupations, including the fishing, woolen, and cigar making industries; service industries such as restaurants, boarding houses, and laundries; and especially into railroad maintenance.[90] In 1870 in Nevada, 4 percent (126) of all the Chinese in the state worked as miners, but in 1880 only 3 percent (164) were so employed. The growth of industrial and lode mining saw a corresponding decline of individual and small group placer mining.[91] This change prompted many Chinese to seek other types of employment. The transition to service occupations began in the late nineteenth century and lasted through the mid-twentieth century to eventually become the major occupations for Chinese Americans.

Initially Americans could not decide whether the Chinese presence was an asset. However, by the 1860s and1870s, hostility grew and eventually led to the passage of the 1882 Chinese Exclusion Act and later discriminatory federal legislation. Chinese miners reputedly were migrants who longed to return to China rather than become permanent immigrants.[92] Popular and scholarly literature written before the mid-1960s stressed this point. In the 1860s California's Republican Senator John Conness promoted the idea of the Chinese as sojourners based on the fact that few Chinese women were in the United States—and without wives, he believed the Chinese men would not remain in the United States for very long.[93] This belief, combined with racial discrimination, opposition to Chinese non-Christian beliefs and values, and labor competition, contributed to the idea of the undesirability of Chinese living and working in mining communities as well as in other towns and cities in the American West.

The enmity and racism that they experienced caused many Chinese miners and merchants to return to China or to move to remote territories, like Oregon, Nevada, Utah, and Idaho. One might assume that between 1880 and 1900 most of the Chinese miners, especially the "bosses" who made more money, returned to China. Won Woo was an example of a mining boss who did not.[94] Woo was born in 1850 in Guangdong and immigrated in 1874 to work on a railroad construction team. He eventually served for many years as the foreman in the Chinese-owned and -operated quartz mine at Firstborn, near Stockton, Calaveras County, California. Although he lived in Firstborn, he registered in compliance with the 1892 Geary Act using a San Francisco address, probably a business owned by a kinsman or the district association headquarters. (Miners moved around so it was safer to have a more permanent address for legal matters.) In January 1904, when he applied for a duplicate Certificate of Residence because his original one was destroyed in a fire, he stated that all of the men who worked with him at the mine had returned to China. To his knowledge, he was the only one in that company who remained. This suggests two things: that the mine had been very profitable so the miners could return home in semi-retirement, but that Woo preferred living in the United States. His story is one of the few that has been documented. This preference of being a settler and not a soujourner was also exemplified by individuals in John Day, Tuscarora, and Island Mountain.

The greatest adversity Chinese miners and merchants faced upon arriving in the American West was racism that was expressed in erroneous beliefs, hostility, violence, laws, and negative attitudes. Najia Aarim-Heriot discussed the racial anxiety experienced by African Americans as similar to what happened to the Chinese in the era preceding the passage of the 1882 Chinese Exclusion Act.[95] The rapid influx of foreigners to California led to development of nativism by late 1849 to early 1850.[96] In 1849 the first of many anti-Chinese riots occurred in Tuolumne County, California, when a group of EuroAmerican miners drove out approximately sixty Chinese miners who worked for a British mining company.[97] The lawlessness in Tuolumne County continued into the early 1850s as the general population doubled between 1850 (8,351) and 1852 (16,153); the same was true for Calaveras County.[98]

The prevalence of violence in these early mining towns led to vigilante justice, but eventually a formal justice system was established. In 1853 the

Indian "Pijo" was hanged for killing two Chinese miners on Canyon Creek near Indian Valley in Sierra County, California.[99] Native American attacks on Chinese were part of the sensationalism of frontier news. In 1855 the San Francisco Chinese merchants were the first to point out to the American government that the Chinese in the mines were subjected to violence, theft of their property, and quarrels about their shares.[100] In 1858 Mexicans attacked Chinese miners near Downieville, California, killing one and wounding another after robbing them of gold dust valued at $150.[101] For the next three to four decades towns in other states and nearby territories experienced similar population booms and violent acts against the Chinese.

The growing visibility of the Chinese contributed to the "fear of foreigners" that sociologist Georg Simmel and his disciples have described.[102] According to the 1852 California state census, one-tenth of California's population (an estimated 25,000) was Chinese, who settled primarily in San Francisco. Other locations in California with a large Chinese population were Nevada County (3,886, of a total 21,365), Placer County (3,019, of a total 10,784), and Yuba County (2,100, of a total 22,005).[103] Within a few years the Chinese represented the largest number of foreign-born miners (approximately 35 percent) in the seven main mining communities of California—Calaveras, El Dorado, Mariposa, Nevada, Placer, Sierra, and Tuolumne.[104] EuroAmericans were not accustomed to the physical appearance and cultural values and beliefs of these strangers. Resentment against the Chinese grew rapidly and the fear that the locality, state, or region was to be populated by Chinese became widespread. As Philip Choy and others have demonstrated, this was evident in the popular literature of the time and helped to fan the flames of discrimination.[105]

One of the reasons for this distrust of foreigners stemmed from the EuroAmerican miners themselves. Many of the early residents came from the same state or region or were related to one another and "were disposed not only to trust and to associate intimately with men from their own sections of the country, but also to distrust and segregate themselves from natives of other sections."[106] The attitudes they adopted resonated with people from the same place. This kind of "place of origin identity" was found in many mining towns even into the early twentieth century and oddly enough extended to Chinese Americans who migrated and lived near people from "their own region." In addition, some immigrants from Europe experienced harsh discrimination elsewhere in the United States and upon moving to the West, turned around and applied the same prejudice and hostility toward the Chinese, who were now the underdog of the American West.

Although some praiseworthy comments were made about Chinese immigrants, most publicized statements reflected disdain for them. In reference to the Chinese, Alfred T. Jackson, in his diary of a Forty-niner, wrote a remark typical for the time, "They [the Chinese] are not looked upon as human beings and have no rights that a white man is bound to respect."[107] The antipathy and disregard for the rights of these "nonhumans" became widespread and persisted into the late twentieth century.

Mining towns, subjected to the boom and bust atmosphere, often were "enclaves of violence" because of the sudden influx of a transient, ethnically diverse, mostly single male population moving into a town far from an urban center. Usually there were a large number of saloons, gambling establishments, and prostitution houses; the beginnings of a working class that supported unionism and its campaign against "cheap Chinese labor"; and political and newspaper leaders who found that the townspeople could be somewhat united over the issue of the exclusion of Chinese.[108] The population generally lacked social bonds that form the basis of a community. As the decades passed, the violence that should have diminished did not because the anti-Chinese movement became connected to the nascent labor movement. Open hostility was finally abated with the passage of the 1924 Immigration Act that essentially closed the door to Chinese immigration.

Stories of stereotypes and ethnic hostilities and prejudices were commonly found in the early California rural mining towns such as Grass Valley and Nevada City, where the community leadership and newspapers vehemently opposed the increasing number of Chinese immigrants in their midst. As Ralph Mann has demonstrated, Grass Valley and Nevada City, although only four miles apart in the lower foothills of the Sierra Nevada, were very different despite their origins as placer camps.[109] Nevada City developed hydraulic and quartz mining and therefore had a broad-based economy while Grass Valley was a hardrock quartz mining site with over 50 percent of the men engaged in mining.

Like the Irish, the Chinese remained in inferior social positions from the beginning of their presence in the towns. Nevada County, which included Grass Valley and Nevada City, recorded 3,396 Chinese in 1852; between 1850 and 1870 the county collected $103,250 in Foreign Miners Tax almost exclusively from the Chinese.[110] The Chinese moved from place to place but were more attracted to hydraulic mining in Nevada City than quartz mining in Grass Valley. Broken down, Grass Valley had 305 Chinese males and 15 Chinese females in 1860; that number increased to 339 men but decreased to 5 women in 1870. Nevada City showed greater growth with 441 Chinese men and 41 women in 1860, compared to 641 men and 28 women in 1870.[111]

The Chinese established Chinatowns, a smaller one in Grass Valley (where they were excluded from quartz work), and a larger, more diverse one in Nevada City (where they lived separately from the rest of the population). They interacted with some of the EuroAmericans during Chinese New Year celebrations and other traditional Chinese celebrations, as was typical throughout the American West. The Chinese Quarter in Nevada City offered general merchandise as well as the services of doctors, herbalists, barbers, assayers, laundymen, and cooks. There were brothels, gambling halls, opium dens, and boarding houses. Those who were servants usually lived with the EuroAmerican family. As a predominantly male society that gradually evolved into a more permanent living environment, EuroAmericans claimed that the Chinese did not contribute to the stable family-oriented society that new western towns wanted. These accusations were repeated in many locations in the late nineteenth and early twentieth centuries, but in Nevada City the EuroAmericans became more adamant. In June 1880 the city passed an ordinance stating that the Chinese would be removed from the city within sixty days. The CCBA fought against this injustice and, eventually, the Chinese established a new Chinatown further away from the center of town.

The media often helped to fan the flames of anti-Chinese hostility. China's political and economic decline in the late Qing dynasty influenced the negative image of the Chinese projected in the United States.[112] As early as 1850s the local newspapers regarded the Chinese as ignorant, degraded, cowardly, cheap laborers (thus threatening the livelihood of others), racially inferior, amoral, sojourners rather than settlers, and chicken thieves.[113] All Chinese women were assumed to be prostitutes: this belief eventually led to the 1870 California law and 1875 federal Page Law prohibiting the immigration of prostitutes. The immigration procedure required an entering female Chinese to prove that she was not a prostitute and this discouraged Chinese women from trying to immigrate to the United States.[114] Although in proportion to the rest of the population few Chinese were imprisoned, the media often sensationalized any criminal activities: gambling, selling and smoking opium, and prostitution. These negative images were repeated and became the dominant characterization for the Chinese in the late nineteenth-century popular press throughout the American West.[115] The media also supported newly elected Governor John Bigler's 1852 denunciation of the Chinese. An anti-Chinese position was seen as a way to gain political support against an unpopular, alien nonvoting group of immigrants.

One of the major results of this racism was the passage of discriminatory laws. In September 1849 future Californians drafted the state's new constitution. As supporters of free labor, they wanted to protect mining from slave labor. Because they regarded the Chinese as "coolie" (from the Tamil word *keli,* meaning "transient laborer,") or contract laborers (akin to indentured servants), Californians believed that they were not "free labor." In 1852 California State Senator George Tingley introduced a bill that recognized this status by trying to get the state to enforce "coolie" contracts as proof of their servile status, but his bill failed. Meanwhile Senator Paul K. Hubbs proposed a more popularly supported bill to prevent coolie labor from working in the mines.[116] In May 1852, the miners held a convention in Yuba County, California, and passed a resolution denying Chinese the right to hold mining claims and to remain in the area after May 3, 1852.[117] The controversies in the California state legislature were repeated in other gold mining states during the next two decades and the idea of discouraging Chinese from mining took many forms.

The American public did not stop to analyze whether the Chinese "coolies" were really equivalent to African American slaves. Most Chinese laborers traveled to the United States through the credit-ticket system in which the shipping company, labor recruiter, relative, or employer advanced the cost of the ticket for passage and a small stipend that the laborers agreed to pay back—expenses plus interest—through their earnings or through working for an certain employer, which usually took an average of one year or more.[118] Once the debt was settled, theoretically they could change jobs and therefore were "free" from any obligations. However, EuroAmericans did not view the situation this way; rather, they saw the system as a form of slavery. EuroAmerican miners wanted mining open only to free labor. "Coolie labor" became a major political issue as California goldfields were depleted in the mid to late 1850s.

Other discriminatory state and federal laws and anti-Chinese movements affected the miners. The 1850 California Foreign Miners Tax was designed to oust Mexican immigrants from Sonora from mining—but eventually the Chinese were the only foreigners paying the tax because they did not belong to the category of "foreigners intending to be naturalized." The $3 per month fee, which varied from time to time, was in force and affirmed in the California court decision *People v. Naglee* until 1870 when the federal Civil Rights Act voided it as a consequence of the adoption of the Fourteenth Amendment to the Constitution of the United States. But by then the Chinese had paid 25 percent to 50 percent of the state's budget.[119] The mandatory tax effectively discouraged many Chinese miners from continuing this work. Instead, they turned to the service industry—working as servants, boarding house operators, or in restaurants or laundries—as a means of employment.

The success in passing this tax and the revenue it produced for California prompted other states to do the same. For example, in 1865 Idaho debated the issue when $8 per month was proposed as a means to deter the Chinese from mining. But the *Idaho Statesman* (December 26, 1865) concluded that since their presence was "detrimental to the interests of the American laborer, then they should be prohibited altogether." Oregon, Washington, Arizona, and Nevada were among the states levying taxes specifically on the Chinese.

According to Charles McClain, 1855 was the "high water mark" of anti-Chinese sentiment in California.[120] In January of that year, EuroAmerican miners drove the Chinese miners from their claims in Weaverville, California, and passed a resolution to boycott Chinese from working in the mines in Shasta County.[121] This corresponded to the decline in output of gold as miners earned an average of $16 a day in 1849, but only $5 a day from 1852 onwards in California.[122] In the search for gold in neighboring regions, California racist precedents and mining regulations were continued in Oregon, Idaho, Montana, and Nevada. One technique for getting rid of the Chinese was by expulsion. In 1858, when the Chinese were used as strike breakers in a wage dispute between Irish miners and a mine owner, the EuroAmerican residents of Nevada City, California called for expelling the Chinese from their town.[123] They were not successful but other towns (such as Eureka, Humboldt County, California, in 1885) tried this technique and were successful.[124] In the spring of 1869 another strike occurred in Nevada City in which the mine owner used Germans and Chinese as strike breakers against Cornish and Irish miners. This led to increased racial animosity, political awareness and popularization of the anti-Chinese stance, and political activism among EuroAmerican miners.[125]

The Chinese also were not on equal footing with EuroAmericans in the courts. The inability to testify against EuroAmericans in court placed the Chinese in an extremely vulnerable situation. In 1853 George W. Hall was convicted of murdering a Chinese miner in Nevada County and was sentenced to death. His attorney filed an appeal to the California Supreme Court on the grounds that the testimony of the three Chinese witnesses and one EuroAmerican should not be allowed because of an 1850 California law that stated, "No

Black, or Mulatto person, or Indian shall be allowed to give evidence in favor of, or against a White man." In 1854, after a very convoluted rationale that concluded that Chinese were the same as Native Americans because of their shared heritage (which was consistent with census categories), the California Supreme Court in *People v. Hall* ruled that Chinese testimony was inadmissible as evidence against EuroAmericans.[126]

The Chinese reaction to the decision was resentment and one of their advocates, Reverend William Speer of San Francisco, editorialized against it in his Chinese and English language newspaper, *The Oriental*.[127] The long-term effect of the court's decision was hesitancy on the part of the Chinese to use the American judicial system and to rely upon traditional Chinese methods of settling disputes whenever possible. The *People v. Hall* decision, codified in 1863 and extended to civil cases, denied Chinese the right to justice and legal protection for many decades. For example, when the Joint Select Committee of the California Legislature investigated the decision's impact in 1862, they learned that of the eighty-eight Chinese who had been murdered by EuroAmericans, only two had been convicted and hanged.[128] As late as 1903–4, a Nevada jury disregarded the testimony of Chinese eyewitnesses and one EuroAmerican night watchman in the murder of a seventy-year-old Chinese laundryman during an anti-Chinese riot in Tonopah; as a result, all of the arrested laundry union members, including one African American, were freed.[129] This type of decision became common and was repeated throughout the American West. A few justices allowed the Chinese to testify as witnesses but the prevailing attitude was not to allow their testimony in either criminal or civil cases, thus making them vulnerable to many types of abuse without legal protection.

The absence of legal rights was linked to the prevailing view that people of color were inferior and such ideas were reinforced in court decisions.[130] It would not be until the *Baldwin v. Franks* case in 1887 that the U.S. Supreme Court implied to Congress that Congress had the power to legislate to protect the civil rights of foreign residents; however, in the case of the Chinese, about whom the issue was raised, little protection was forthcoming because they were not white and therefore could not become naturalized citizens.[131]

The most significant discriminatory legislation against Chinese miners was the federal Mining Law of 1866 and its successors, the Placer Act of 1870 and the General Mining Law of 1872.[132] There were no rules or regulations when the miners started to flock to Sutter's Mill, but the miners soon realized the need to establish laws to maintain order. This occurred in most of the new mining camps throughout the American West. Originally the Chinese had the same rights as other miners—and technically, all were mining illegally or trespassing on federal land. The Homestead Act of 1862 was created for farming; nevertheless, miners believed that the free land should be extended to them. The federal policy that evolved, in an effort to encourage mining, was to allow miners to work the land. The concept of "free mining" prevailed in the American West—but not for the Chinese. Eventually, the issue was debated in Congress.

For example, in Nevada a debate occurred over the ownership of mining claims. The miners on the newly discovered Comstock Lode recognized the need for codification. In 1859, they issued one of the earliest mining regulations for the Gold Hill Mining District to clarify mining claims (defined as the right to explore for and extract minerals from the land) and to prohibit the Chinese from filing such claims.[133] Other mining districts followed the precedent, often elaborating on the conditions. In March 1860, the EuroAmerican miners in Cottonwood, Siskiyou County, California, stated that because the Chinese had committed thefts in the area, they had two months to leave town and that EuroAmericans would "use force, if necessary, it being our firm determination to remove the evil."[134] In 1861 the Pierce Mining District, Idaho, passed Article 14 stating that "Chinese or Tartars are hereby prohibited from working these mines, under any and all circumstances"—but like Oregon and elsewhere, they had to amend the law in 1864 so that abandoned claims could be sold to the Chinese.[135]

The local regulations on the Comstock were also incorporated into federal law stipulating that aliens ineligible for naturalization, that is, Chinese, could not own a mining claim unless it was owned jointly with a citizen.[136] (The 1790 Naturalization Act specified that only free white persons could be naturalized; when it was amended by the Fourteenth Amendment to include African Americans, the Chinese were excluded.) The national Mining Law of 1866, which focused on placer or gravel claims, was the handiwork of Comstock lawyer and mining investor Senator William Morris Stewart of Nevada, who, in 1865 as a first-term U.S. senator, established the Senate Committee on Mines and Mining. Stewart also authored the subsequent 1872 mining law. Both laws included a provision that a miner must be, or affirm the intention of becoming, a citizen of the United States—this disallowed claims by the Chinese.[137]

However, the Chinese could own unpatented mining claims and protect their rights through adverse proceedings, but they could not obtain a patent. These laws favored companies or large-scale mining and all but eliminated the individual miner in many regions.[138] This probably led to the creation of Chinese mining companies that allowed individuals to pool their money to work claims or for individuals to work for mine owners. Miners who did not patent their claim had to spend $1,000 annually to improve the land since it could not lay dormant.[139] Local rules and regulations were regarded as the law and many districts and towns had the stipulation that the Chinese could not file original claims. Dissatisfaction with the vagueness of the 1866 law led to two additional laws, one in 1870 and another in 1872 that focused upon placer mining. Local codes passed before 1866 were not overturned but advantages were given to large mining companies that had supplanted individual prospectors. Once again it was reaffirmed that aliens who did not intend to become naturalized were forbidden to stake mining claims.

The Chinese found and used loopholes in the system. According to the 1872 mining law once the mining claim had a patent from the government, the owner or owners had the right to sell the same to any person, be he alien or citizen, Chinese or EuroAmerican. In this way Congress hoped that mineral resources might be developed with the use of foreign capital. The law was challenged in the Montana Supreme Court in the case of *The Territory of Montana v. Fouk Lee* (1874).[140] Fouk Lee, an alien, purchased, held, and occupied three thousand feet of placer mining ground from a EuroAmerican named Stearns. Due to the agitation of EuroAmerican miners, the territory of Montana tried to take away Fouk Lee's placering rights and a lower court decided in favor of Montana. The Supreme Court reversed the lower court's decision, ruling that the 1866 mining law did "not prohibit citizens who rightfully acquire[d] this possessory title, from selling and transferring the same to aliens, or to any other persons."[141] This allowed the Chinese to purchase and sell formerly owned EuroAmerican claims.

Nothing was said about selling abandoned claims to noncitizens and it was through this loophole that the Chinese were able to buy mining properties. Oregon and other states changed their local mining regulations when EuroAmericans who had given up on their claims wanted to sell them. Chinese miners became famous for being able to profit from abandoned claims; sometimes their success was due to their ability to bring in water. In Idaho, for example, once the EuroAmerican miners had finished with placer claims at Warren in 1872, the miners reconsidered their earlier prohibition on selling claims to 1,200 Chinese, who then paid as much as $8,000 for claims that later were worth more than $20,000 because of the water the Chinese brought into the area.[142] Their successes sometimes led to EuroAmericans wanting to reclaim the site even though the Chinese owned and registered it or leased it—but, as the *San Francisco Bulletin* (February 5, 1869) commented, the Chinese could be driven off the site when EuroAmericans coveted it.

The situation continued to worsen. An 1889 decision in the Montana Territory had a major impact on Chinese miners. Anti-Chinese supporter Judge Willis Sweet ruled that the Chinese could not legally hold mining ground.[143] This meant that if a EuroAmerican sold or leased an abandoned mining claim to a Chinese person and a U.S. citizen or an alien intending to become a citizen then wanted the claim, the Chinese miner had to abandon his rights to the site. Although some Chinese miners were willing to take their chances, many felt that this ruling was the final blow to their attempts at finding that elusive gold.

As the Chinese population increased, the hostility of many mining communities was expressed in their local and regional newspapers. The public supported discriminatory legislation, often originating in California and then spreading to neighboring states, laws such as those prohibiting Chinese to stake mining claims, to mine in certain localities, and to buy and sell property. Eventually these restrictions were incorporated into federal legislation. At the same time discriminatory taxes were levied against the Chinese, including a $5 per head entrance tax for California; in time, the courts ruled that these taxes were illegal.[144] These laws and taxes were concrete expressions of the racism that prevailed in the American West.

The financial successes of the Chinese also contributed to the animosity toward them. John David Borthwick, after visiting California mines in the 1850s, wrote, "[They worked] in such places as yielded them a dollar or two a day [and thus] were allowed to scratch away unmolested. Had they happened to strike a rich lead, they would have been driven off their claim immediately."[145] As early as 1859, some three hundred to four hundred Chinese worked the North Fork of the American River in California, and eleven Chinese "companies" took out $40,000 worth of gold per week on the Middle Fork.[146] By 1860 California's population was 380,000, which included 34,933 Chinese of whom 24,282 were miners living in the seven main placer mining counties.[147] They worked in mining sites such as Chinese Camp and Dutch Flat, California, which by 1860 had approximately 2,000 Chinese.[148] They were known for working deserted or neglected sites, "content with one to two dollars a day; while the white man starves or moves on disgusted with twice that," observed Samuel Bowles (editor of the Springfield, Massachusetts, *Republican*) when he visited the Pacific states in the 1860s.[149]

Publicity about unusual finds by the Chinese often made the news. The *San Francisco Bulletin* (August 24, 1869) announced that some Chinese miners on South Side, Sierra County, found a gold nugget weighing over nine pounds and valued at $1,600. On April 4, 1876, a story appeared about a Chinese miner's discovery of a $300 lump of gold. Another story circulated about two Chinese miners who never made over $2 a day discovering a 240-pound gold nugget valued at $30,000.[150] Until the late 1870s the Chinese became well known for making a profit on abandoned claims.[151] Local newspapers publicized their activities. Their economic success, physical distinctiveness, and inability to become integrated into the community helped fuel anti-Chinese sentiments.

The decline in new placer sites, as well as Chinese successful endeavors in a depressed economy led to economic competition and ultimately to the intensification of anti-Chinese sentiments. Exaggerated assessments of estimated Chinese placer successes circulated. For example, the *Los Angeles Times* (October 29, 1892) carried a report from U. S. Mint statistician Charles Yale stating that in 1892 California's small placer mines brought in $2,000,000 and the Chinese (who never reported their full earnings) were responsible for $1,200,000 of that amount. Jealousy and hostility naturally arose among EuroAmerican miners. Mining declines contributed to the hostility.

The Chinese often were very frugal and able to save more than the EuroAmerican miners. As Liping Zhu argued, the Chinese miner subsisted on a cheaper but healthier vegetable-and-fruit diet than did EuroAmerican miners and paid less for housing, thus needing no more than $2 per day to survive compared to the EuroAmerican miner who needed $15 per day for food and lodging.[152] The figures may be questionable but in all probability, the Chinese were able to save some money from their wages. They did not spend their money on luxury items or alcoholic beverages and were known for their thrift except when it came to gambling and recreational activities.

By the 1870s anti-Chinese movements expanded. In trying to determine the reasons for the discrimination, sociologists Eric W. Fong and William T. Markham proposed that when the proportion of the minority population is high, the members of the majority are more likely to perceive the minority as a threat.[153] The rapid growth rate of the minority population also leads to more intense conflict. Other factors include occupational segregation, poor economic conditions, and the percentage of minority workers in occupations with strong competition between the two groups, thus resulting in those majority workers becoming active in the conflict and establishing organizations and activities directed against the minority. Urbanization contributes to the conflict because the ethnically diverse populations reside or work in close proximity to each other. While the Fong-Markham theory is useful in understanding the anti-Chinese movement in mining communities, the predicted outcome was not evident, for example, in John Day, Tuscarora, and Island Mountain, where better relationships were more common.

Politicians and labor union organizers rose to prominence using the Chinese issue to gather support for their causes. The easiest criticism was that the Chinese worked for less money and therefore took away jobs that should have been filled by others. An examination of the payroll records of the Tenabo Mill and Mining Company, Cortez, Nevada, in December 1896 revealed that the Chinese were paid at a rate of $1.50 per day while most EuroAmerican workers were paid from $2.50 to $3 per day, with men in higher positions and skilled workers getting as much as $6.[154] What is significant on this payroll sheet is that some EuroAmericans, such as M. A. Bianchi, were also paid at the $1.50 rate. Another interesting fact is that four individual Chinese miners and one Chinese "company," the Sing Kong Wah Company received a total of $788.63 compared to individual miner Ki Yack's $46.50. Both Sing Kong Wah and Ki Yack signed for their paychecks in English while China Ike, Ah Ung, and Ah Coon signed in Chinese. In addition, Ki Yack and the other individual Chinese miners purchased goods at the company store while Sing Kong Wah Company had no store bill, so it is likely that Sing Kong Wah provided the team of workers with all supplies necessary. Contrary to the labor union's assertions, the wage scale for Chinese also applied to EuroAmericans as Tenabo's payroll records indicated.

It was easier to unite a diverse audience using an anti-Chinese messages than almost any other issue. This was evident throughout the United States, as numerous scholars have demonstrated.[155] Politicians and newspapers that had supported big business and their use of Chinese labor often found it to their advantage to participate in the anti-Chinese movement to gain votes for their causes or to improve the circulation of their newspapers. Since Chinese immigrants could not be naturalized, they could not vote and therefore politicians and labor union leaders did not need to seek their support. The Chinese presence unfortunately corresponded to the rise of labor unions that found their unifying cause in the anti-Chinese movement.

Some mining communities did not have racial violence despite a sizeable minority population, while others began their violent anti-Chinese campaigns in the mid-1850s. Aurora and Bodie, two small mining towns in eastern

California, were examples where the Chinese and Mexicans were not targets of racial violence despite high crime rates that were typical of many western towns.[156] The Chinese may not have been targets of racial violence in Bodie because important businesses in town (the hotel, restaurants, and a casino) were owned by Chinese. More research into these mining camps would reveal the nature of the interethnic relations and reasons for the smaller number of incidents of hostility.

Violence was characteristic of most mining camps having a predominance of single men, numerous saloons, and few or weak government officials. In June 1856, EuroAmerican miners in Humboldt County, California, attacked a group of Chinese who had discovered gold. This, along with other events, led to the passage of many of California's anti-Chinese legislation.[157] The *Shasta Republican* (California), for example, reported in December 1856 that "hundreds of Chinese" had been "slaughtered in cold blood" during the last five years.[158] The troubles continued in many locations until the early twentieth century. When the Knights of Labor (founded in 1869) and other labor organizations began to grow, the anti-Chinese issue was popular as job competition became more intense due to economic depressions.[159] Labor organizers aggressively exploited the discontent and often violence resulted.

Chinese miners were aware of this problem and turned to membership in brotherhoods or *tang* for protection against EuroAmericans while they were mining. In 1877 the Chinese miners in Jackson County, Oregon, were attacked, robbed, and had their cabins burned to the ground.[160] In February 1885 the Chinese were expelled from Eureka, California; some returned once the hostility died down.[161] In 1903 the Chinese were briefly driven out of Tonopah, Nevada, a place incorrectly hailed as the "second Comstock Lode." These were just a few of the many anti-Chinese violent acts. Numerous western towns participated in attempts to drive the Chinese out of their towns with the use of force or with economic boycotts of Chinese businesses and EuroAmerican businesses that catered to the Chinese. By the early twentieth century, anti-Chinese violence declined as mining towns "busted" and people moved elsewhere.

In the 1870s the anti-Chinese sentiment moved into the larger realm of national politics and remained prominent until the passage of the 1924 Immigration Act that essentially closed the door to large-scale Chinese immigration. The Chinese "problem" led to the passage of the 1882 Chinese Exclusion Act prohibiting the immigration of Chinese laborers for ten years.[162] The federal government hoped to curtail the rapid increase of Chinese immigrants and passed additional laws extending and expanding these restrictions in response to the public's fears that the Chinese population and the competition for jobs would continue to grow. Agitators cited the inability of the Chinese to assimilate, their religious beliefs, and their general undesirability as justifications for restricting Chinese immigration. Dissatisfaction with the 1882 exclusion act eventually contributed to a wave of violence and robberies of Chinese miners and others, especially in areas with a growing or large Chinese minority population like Portland, Oregon, and Tacoma, Olympia, and Seattle, Washington, in the 1880s.[163]

Anti-Chinese sentiment contributed to a ten-year extension of the exclusion, with harsher regulations, with the passage of the Geary Act, as it was popularly called, in 1892. That year U.S. Senator William Morris Stewart (Nevada) commented to Congress, reflecting the general American attitude favoring more stringent laws, "The American people are now convinced that the Chinese can not be incorporated among our citizens, can not be amalgamated, can not be absorbed, but that they will remain a distinct element."[164] Although writers like Mary Roberts Coolidge and Reverend William Speer tried to defend Chinese immigration and immigrants, more sensational publications like P. Donner's *Last Days of the Republic* (1880) had a greater impact upon Americans, especially with illustrations showing the "imagined" Chinese takeover of Washington, D.C.[165]

Samuel Gompers, president of the American Federation of Laborers, in 1902 published his widely circulated pamphlet *Meat vs. Rice: American Manhood Against Asiatic Cooliesm, Which Shall Survive?* that emphasized the economic threat of "cheap" Chinese labor.[166] Numerous other publications, including the racist *Illustrated WASP*, highlighted the Chinese problem. These stereotypes were also reinforced in melodramas of the period as Bret Harte and others popularized the image of the Chinese as a trickster with many negative attributes.[167]

Loopholes in the exclusion laws and regulations allowed small numbers of Chinese to immigrate between 1882 and 1903 but the 1904 and 1924 immigration acts, along with more stringent BI regulations closed the door to large-scale Chinese immigration and helped to deter further anti-Chinese violence.[168]

With the decline of California's placer mining, the Chinese left mining and entered other occupational niches, especially cooking and laundry work, that were open to them in the 1870s and 1880s. The emergence of San Francisco and other cities with Chinatowns as manufacturing centers, the growth of

Chinese in agriculture, and the completion of the Central Pacific Railroad and other railroad lines, provided new opportunities. Those seeking the instant wealth from mining moved to neighboring states. In 1880, for example, of the 2,171 miners in eastern Oregon, 1,605 (73.9 percent) were Chinese.[169] Nevada, Montana, Wyoming, Washington, and British Columbia were among the new locations attracting Chinese miners.

The Chinese had come to the United States with great hopes of obtaining economic success. They had secured funds for the trans-Pacific trip and had joined Chinese American organizations for mutual aid and protection. They had brought traditional practices and values with them but had to make adjustments to their new-found environment. They encountered racism and prejudice that prevented many from realizing their hopes and dreams. The anti-Chinese movement, mob violence and mentality, derogatory publicity, and discriminatory laws at the local, regional, state, and federal levels drove many to return to China. However, as seen in examples in John Day, Tuscarora, and Island Mountain, some gained acceptance and ultimately preferred to remain in the United States.

2 Onward to Eastern Oregon

BY THE MID-1850S as the gold became harder to find in California, some Chinese miners remained in California or returned to China while others moved into unchartered territories in the nearby regions. There was an advantage in going to new areas because they might have the opportunity to mine unhindered by animosity and anti-Chinese mining regulations. The Chinese who traveled to new boomtowns either followed EuroAmerican miners or knew enough about finding gold to strike out on their own. Some, like those who went to Idaho, were guided to placer sites by friendly Native Americans; many more were killed by hostile Native American bands. Two neighboring territories, Oregon and Nevada, offered new beginnings. At first the Chinese migrated to southern Oregon but when hostility forced them to leave, some moved to the isolated area of the rugged Blue Mountains in Grant County in eastern Oregon. There Chinese miners and merchants dominated placer mining in the region and carved out unusual niches for themselves. An examination of the limited information that has been available provided insights into the dynamics of their experiences there.

From the outset the Chinese encountered difficulties in living and working in Oregon. As they tried to mine in Oregon the Chinese miners had to cope with EuroAmerican racism and Native American attacks. Oregon was organized as a territory in 1848 and achieved statehood on February 14, 1859. Beginning in 1851, Oregon saw the influx of miners of many nationalities. The announcement of the discovery of new placer sites in the Rich Gulch of the Rogue River valley in southern Oregon attracted miners to the area. By 1852 Jackson County and then Josephine County were established with a growing Chinese presence.[1] The main town in Jackson County was Jacksonville and its political leaders and miners dominated territorial and state politics until around the 1870s. In 1860 Jackson County's population was 84 percent to 95 percent EuroAmerican miners who wanted to keep foreigners, especially Chinese, out. Like California and Nevada, they wrote their own regulations to that effect. The EuroAmerican miners took a strong anti-Chinese stance and influenced legislation.[2]

Many of Oregon's political leaders brought their prejudice from California and Nevada. Anti-Chinese agitators from California influenced anti-Chinese activities locally and in politics. For example, Burnette A. Haskell from California continued his anti-Chinese campaigning in Oregon, stating that he preferred to be peaceful but encouraged violence if it was necessary.[3] By 1857 EuroAmerican miners adopted some of the same or similar discriminatory laws as California and Nevada regarding Chinese miners.

Hostile Native Americans and the new terrain delayed the establishment of towns until the mid-1850s and early 1860s for all miners. The Chinese encountered hostile Native Americans early in their migration to Oregon. In 1855 the *Oriental* (*Tung-ngai san-luk*), a bilingual weekly San Francisco newspaper, reported that the Rogue River Native Americans killed a large party of Chinese miners.[4] Word of the attack spread among Chinese miners so that many only traveled with a EuroAmerican guide or protector. Despite these challenges, some Chinese persevered in their quest for new mining opportunities. Upon arriving in the small town of Portland in 1861, Ah Ning wrote, "The country here is new found; it is wild, mostly still trees . . . the people have just come."[5] This could have described other parts of Oregon just as well.

Legal discrimination toward the Chinese was formalized early. In 1854 territorial legislators offered proposals against African Americans and Chinese, including one to prohibit them from entering or living in the state—but this bill died in committee.[6] The justification derived from eighteenth-century European pseudoscientific theories about racial differences, with peoples of color being inferior and subordinate, and the popularity of social Darwinism's "survival of the fittest."[7] The Chinese never accepted this notion of subordination and for centuries had given China the name of the "Middle" or "Central" Kingdom because of China's cultural, political, and economic influence over her Asian neighbors. As one of the oldest civilizations in the world with achievements in many fields, the designation of "inferior" was never a part of the Chinese mentality about themselves.

Landholding, suffrage, and taxation were the other areas of discrimination used against the Chinese. EuroAmerican miners in southern Oregon quickly influenced the drafting of the Oregon constitution, ratified in 1857, to deny land holding and suffrage to the Chinese. That same year Oregon followed California's lead in levying taxes on the Chinese to discourage them from settling in the state. The first was a mining tax of $2 per month per Chinese miner; a year later it was raised to $4 per month for both mining and conducting business. The justification, published in a letter to the *Oregonian*, was a fear of Chinese invasion and takeover as the Chinese bought out American miners and paid good prices for their claims.[8] Like California, Nevada, and other western states, in 1862 Oregon enacted a poll tax of $2, which had to be paid between January 1 and March 1 of every year, with monetary penalties accruing and forced labor required if payment was missed. This meant that until the tax was determined illegal by the courts, Chinese miners had to pay the state government $50 a year in taxes and fees just to be in Oregon. Later, other types of taxes were levied upon Chinese miners.[9] Nevertheless, these acts of discrimination and taxes did not discourage the Chinese miners.

The taxes on the Chinese funded county and state governments. By 1858 Josephine County in southern Oregon reported some 1,000 to 1,200 Chinese miners working in the area; all of the local government expenses were covered from the taxes paid by the Chinese.[10] This was similar to the $5 million (constituting 25 percent to 50 percent of the state's revenue) that was collected from the Chinese in California for the foreign miners license tax of 1850 and 1852, which continued until the federal Civil Rights Act in 1870 voided the laws.[11] In 1861, the state of Oregon netted $8,624 from the mining taxes collected in Jackson and Josephine counties—and this figure did not include the 20 percent of the total collected that the counties kept.[12] This tax represented a substantial contribution to the state treasury. Since the Chinese were prohibited from voting, politicians did not have to worry about catering to them. Levying taxes and fees was considered one method of driving them out of Oregon.

For Chinese miners the harshest restriction was in the state's constitution. The territorial legislators accepted statehood in 1859. Article XV, Section 8 of the Oregon constitution stated, "No Chinaman, not a resident of the state at the adoption of this constitution, shall ever hold any real estate or mining claim, or work any mining claim therein."[13] Lawmakers were pleased with this provision, but due to a legal technicality, in 1866 they were forced to change the wording slightly to prohibit only foreign-born Chinese from mining in the state.[14] The federal mining law that Congress passed in 1866 solved some of their problems in trying to discourage the Chinese through the precedent of local mining laws, especially special taxes, and the qualification of "intent to become a citizen" (see chapter 1). The tradition had been established in California, Nevada, Oregon, Idaho, and other locations that miners determined their own rules of governance for each district. In 1862 the "Laws and Regulations of John Day's Mining District" included the statement that "Chinese or Tartars are hereby prohibited from working these mines under any and all circumstances." Six other districts in Oregon included the same or a similar clause.[15]

Like other discriminatory legislation, these laws and mining regulations were ignored when convenient and enforced when hostility arose. According to Daniel Liestman, two important factors changed the minds of the EuroAmericans about enforcing these provisions: the need to sell depleted and unprofitable claims, and the development of industrial and capital-intensive mining that required wage laborers.[16] Like the railroad barons, many EuroAmerican mine owners found the Chinese dependable and "reasonable" workers, whereas others were undependable and expensive. They sought Chinese workers for their corporate mining operations. Ultimately, the frontier spirit and big business interests contributed to flexibility in the interpretations of the mining regulations and laws.

The Chinese mined in Oregon and purchased abandoned claims but they always faced the threat of having their gold or possessions taken away from them with no recourse. EuroAmericans who wanted to move to more profitable sites ignored the laws and regulations, selling unwanted claims to the Chinese. For example, as early as August 20, 1859, Ephraim Allen sold his mining claim of 150 yards at Wolf Creek in Jackson County, together with eight sluices, two picks, two shovels, two hatchets, one root ax, and one cabin, to a Chinese miner for $30.[17] More often than not in these early years of mining, the transfer of mining property was done informally and included equipment and cabins.

Another early harsh law that the Chinese had to contend with in Oregon targeted Chinese merchants. Unlike California and Nevada, Oregon's laws discouraged Chinese merchants from operating businesses within the state. In 1859 in an effort to enable EuroAmericans to dominate the business sector, Oregon required Chinese and Kanakas to pay a $50 per month tax if they were involved in trade or barter.[18] This gave a distinct advantage to EuroAmerican merchants and worked a hardship on the Chinese merchants. Chinese merchants were forced to make a bigger profit to survive. They usually did not charge a fee for their labor contracting or employment services but made their profits from the sale of goods.

When mining began to wane, the state legislators had to rethink their anti-Chinese position. In his master's thesis, Robert Wilson traced some of these efforts.[19] In 1864 one of the first actions was to repeal all former state laws relating to mining, leaving the regulations to local government. By 1866 Chinese were allowed to mine with a license issued from the county sheriff's office. In 1868, again following policies in nearby states, the Chinese were prohibited from working on public projects but, like other states, employers subcontracted with Chinese labor agents so that the public records showed only EuroAmerican companies on the payroll. These were similar to actions that had occurred in California, Nevada, and other neighboring states.

Jacksonville, the county seat of Jackson County, was founded in 1851 and settled in 1852. Chinese miners quickly moved into the town and the county. For thirty years Jacksonville was the most important and largest town in Oregon. There was a Chinatown on the Main Street between Oregon Street and First Street, and although this was a minor arterial, the EuroAmerican population was cognizant of the presence of "distinctive looking foreigners."[20] Like many other western towns, the citizens actively tried to force the Chinese to leave. They found some success in Jackson County as the Chinese population dropped from 634 in 1870 to 337 in 1880 and 223 in 1890.

A few prominent Chinese miners resisted the expulsion, most notably Gin Lin (variously spelled Chin Lin, Gen Len, Chinny Lin, and Gin Lan), a contract labor broker and miner, who purchased and leased placer claims along the lower Little Applegate River for over twenty years.[21] According to archaeologist Jeffrey LaLande, in 1864 Gin Lin purchased the Wilson Ranch at the mouth of Sterling Creek for $900, purchased or leased other properties, and reportedly took out $2 million in gold from his numerous mining claims.[22] Gin Lin also had an account in Jacksonville's famous Beekman Bank that totaled $1 million. Like EuroAmerican miners, he purchased hydraulic mining equipment from San Francisco to make his projects profitable. (Part of his equipment can still be seen on the historic "Gin Lin Mining Trail" that covers three-quarters of a mile and shows the complex water system and expensive equipment.) The 1,500-foot pipe reportedly cost $2,500 and fed a 400-pound nozzle to wash the dirt away. He had a crew of about fifteen Chinese residing in a boarding house that was next to the residences of some EuroAmericans. Unlike many of his contemporaries, Gin Lin discarded his queue (a hairstyle required of Chinese men to show subservience to their Manchu rulers) wore western dress, and probably spoke English. He was well liked by community leaders, including pioneer photographer Peter Britt, who took several photographs of him, and he loved to drive his buggy with a high-stepping horse around town. Popular lore alleged that he went to China three or four times, each time bringing a "wife" with him; she would then marry one of his workers.

The local press carried stories about Gin Lin's success in hydraulic mining in the 1880s. Once he exhausted his claims in Jackson County, he moved to nearby Josephine County around 1885. At that point he and his own wife no longer merited any media attention but it was widely believed that he, his wife, and Oregon-born children returned to China in 1897. Gin Lin was successful and wealthy and made friends with the EuroAmerican population despite the prevailing hostility. He has been remembered with the preservation of part of his mining operation. He and his workers were allowed to stay in Jackson County, but fellow countrymen, particularly Chinese merchants, did not fare as well elsewhere in southern Oregon.

In Jackson County Chinese miners had to purchase goods from EuroAmerican stores instead of Chinese ones. Some EuroAmerican merchants recognized the advantage of catering to Chinese miners and, like the Chinese merchants, ordered imported foodstuffs and other products to attract customers.[23] The Chinese preferred to patronize stores owned by fellow countrymen, especially those from the same county or district in southeastern China, but the high tax on Chinese businesses resulted in fewer Chinese merchants in southern Oregon. Some EuroAmerican merchants made lasting friendships with their Chinese customers. This was seen in the case of Kaspar Kubli of Applegate in Jackson County. Based on business records for 1864–65, some 106 Chinese miners patronized the Swiss immigrant Kubli's store. Kubli sold Chinese imported goods obtained from Tung Chong and Company in San Francisco, usually paying in cash but sometimes on credit.[24] The most popular items were Chinese food products and western work clothes.[25] Economic interdependence led to ethnic interaction and, in this case, it was positive since Kubli had many Chinese customers for several decades.

Following a western America anti-Chinese trend, beginning in the late 1870s and into the exclusionary period (1882–1943), mining and other companies, as well as labor union supporters, adopted a "white only" policy, often boycotting employers who hired Chinese workers and businesses catering to Chinese customers. The policy was largely ignored during times of prosperity while attempts were made to enforce it during periods of economic decline. This, in addition to the decreasing number of Chinese miners in Jackson County, contributed to the eventual closure of Kubli's store. During these periods of intense racism it was difficult for the Chinese to shop at non-Chinese stores;

at the same time the Chinese stores had difficulty getting merchandise from California since most were dependent upon EuroAmerican teamsters.

The media eventually tried to temper the anti-Chinese environment. Influential newspapers in Oregon took an ambivalent stance on the Chinese issue. Echoing negative appellations from California and the national media, in 1865 the *Morning Oregonian* (Portland) referred to the Chinese as "filthy and abominable" and in the next year added "long-tailed, moon-eyed nuisances" and "filthy rats."[26] But a change occurred when the *Oregonian* came under editorship of Harvey W. Scott from 1865 to 1910. Scott stood for law and order, denounced agitation against innocent Chinese, and tempered many of the articles that were sent from other newspapers.[27] In 1868 the *Morning Oregonian,* a supporter of business enterprises, predicted that the Chinese would help build the mining, manufacturing, and agricultural interests of Oregon.[28] Positive comments like that persuaded anti-Chinese organizations to boycott the newspaper periodically. Nevertheless, smaller newspapers followed the *Oregonian*'s new editorial policy of ambivalence or attempted to be objective rather than anti-Chinese like labor-supported publications.

According to Herman B. Chiu, who studied the small newspapers in four Oregon communities, most of the EuroAmerican population basically ignored the Chinese living in their midst.[29] However, when stories were written, many newspaper articles were either very negative or neutral about the Chinese. Often stories about China and the Chinese were reprinted from other newspapers describing the Chinese attacks on foreigners; for example, reports of the massacre of American missionaries during the Boxer Uprising of 1900 were serialized and projected a negative image. Sensational reports of local or regional crimes and criminals were highlighted and portrayed Chinese Americans in a bad light. Accounts of Chinese festivals, especially the celebration of Chinese New Year with noisy firecrackers, discordant music, and "foul-smelling" foods, reinforced the "foreign-ness" of the Chinese. That few news articles appeared in Oregon about the Chinese might have been due to the absence of access to the Chinese residents.

In comparison, in the late nineteenth century, the *Eureka Sentinel* in Eureka, Nevada—a mining town that thrived in the same period—carried numerous stories about their Chinese residents because Chinatown was located across the street from the newspaper office.[30] When things were dull, the reporter went across the street to find out what the Chinese were doing and reported it. Or the newspaper editor simply reprinted an old news article about the Chinese to fill space. In the first two decades of the twentieth century, the *Tonopah Bonanza* (Tonopah, Nevada) did not neglect their Chinese residents because, according to the editor's son, the editor ate lunch almost daily in the Chinese restaurant across the street from the newspaper office and printed noteworthy news that he learned during lunch.[31] Thus, the smaller number of negative stories about the Chinese in the local newspapers probably contributed to the less hostile and less violent interactions between Chinese and EuroAmericans living in eastern Oregon.

Despite these challenges, the Chinese moved to Oregon between 1862 and 1900 in large numbers. There were 3,330 Chinese in 1870; this figure increased to 9,510 in 1880 and rose again to 9,540 in 1890. Part of the increase between 1870 and 1880 was due to railroad construction and maintenance. The Chinese had done such an impressive job building the Central Pacific Railroad (completed in 1869) that other railroad companies hired them: Chinese worked on the Oregon and California Railroad from 1868 to 1870, the Oregon Pacific Railroad from 1875 to 1886, the Oregon Railway and Navigation Company along the Columbia River in 1879, and the Oregon Short Line in 1884, to name a few.[32] Among 25,000 railroad workers, approximately 15,000 were Chinese, which helped increase the Chinese presence in the state. This was a major contribution to the building of North America as the rail lines provided the means for settlement, shipment of goods, and industrialization. Once the construction work was completed, the workers often sought other opportunities in the state, such as mining. The railroads also brought the Chinese into areas that they had not explored before. (In the early years the Chinese population was concentrated in the Portland area but like Nevada, there were Chinese throughout the state, especially in mining towns.)

With the exception of Portland, most of the Chinese in Oregon were miners, that is to say independent prospectors, employees in a company-owned mine, owners or part owners in an operating mine, or shareholders in an operating mine. After 1860 the Chinese miners and merchants migrated to eastern Oregon where the rugged mountains and long, cold, snowy winters and dry, hot summers were a sharp contrast to coastal Oregon. In October 1861 gold was discovered near the south end of the Powder Valley; by the end of summer the multiethnic population grew to 4,000 in what became Baker County the following year. Miners, farmers, and ranchers flocked to the area.

For the Chinese, as well as others, traveling to and living in eastern Oregon was difficult.[33] The Chinese traveled on foot with their gear and provisions in wagons driven by EuroAmerican teamsters. The wealthier ones hired the teamsters to carry them as well.[34] Some may have had mules, horses, or wagons of their own. A few carried all that they owned on shoulder poles and walked. When visiting Jackson County, John Mullan of the U.S. Army wrote, "We observed in squads, the ubiquitous Chinaman, moving from mining locality to mining locality, fleeing from the kicks of one to the cuffs of the other, with no fixed abiding place to be called his permanent home."[35] This was applicable to eastern Oregon as well. Bears and other animals unfamiliar to the Chinese also posed a potential danger. The nature of the occupation required frequent moves as the miners, and the merchants and others who supported them, followed the gold.

Living in eastern Oregon had many dangers, one of which was trouble with Native Americans. The John Day River Valley was home to the Northern Paiutes, as well as the Cayuse and the Tenino tribes who also lived in southeastern Oregon and the Umatilla tribe in the northeast.[36] The Paiutes were fishermen and root diggers while the northern tribes were hunters, fishermen, and seed gatherers. All harassed travelers in eastern Oregon as well as fought among themselves. Thus the unsettled Native American situation led to a ban on EuroAmerican settlement from 1856 to 1858 and a military campaign to control the marauding Indians in the winter of 1866. By the end of 1868, an agreement was reached between the military and tribes that had the tribes settle in designated reservations. The peace allowed EuroAmericans and others to settle in eastern Oregon.

In 1866 there were at least three reports of massacres of anywhere from forty to two hundred Chinese traveling from California and Nevada to Oregon, Idaho, and Montana. One frequently told account was of the death of approximately forty to ninety Chinese at the hands of a Northern Paiute tribe near Baker City in Baker County, Oregon, just north of Grant County, on May 19, 1866.[37] Mutilated bodies were left scattered on the road. One survivor lived to tell the story. Six years later, on October 15, 1872, the *Territorial Enterprise* (Virginia City, Nevada), quoting the *Humboldt Reporter* (Winnemucca, Nevada), stated that two wagon loads of the bones of Chinese who had been scalped by Native Americans passed through Winnemucca en route to San Francisco and ultimately to China[38]—thus, approximately six years after burial, the bones were disinterred and scraped, cleaned, then sealed in a metal box and shipped via San Francisco to a final resting place in China.[39] Elmer Rusco, in an attempt to unravel the authenticity of these massacres, questioned, "If the Chinese were killed by Native Americans, we do not know why they were attacked with such extreme violence—a level of violence which has not been reported as directed against EuroAmericans in the area at this time." In general, Rusco concluded, the Chinese did not carry firearms, so they probably were more vulnerable to attacks. Thus, it seems likely that the massacres occurred.

Established in 1864 but not incorporated until 1874, Baker City was located with the Wallowa Mountains to the east and the Elkhorn Range, part of the Blue Mountains, to the west. The Powder River ran through the center of town and fed into the famous Snake River. By the late 1860s Baker City, Baker County, could be reached by overland stage five times a week and served as a major route between the Willamette Valley in the west and Idaho and Montana to the east. It was a major distribution and trade center. In 1884 it was a station along the Oregon Railway and Navigation Company line that connected the city to Portland and the Union Pacific line, giving it access to other parts of the nation. A second mining boom from 1890 through 1910 led to another growth in its population.

Chinese settled in Baker City. The 1870 census manuscript listed 275 Chinese miners, three hotel cooks, two cooks, ten merchants, ten involved in gaming, one physician, one tailor, and one butcher (all males).[40] After a decline noted in the 1880 census, the Chinese population rose again in 1900 with a total of 264 (4 percent of the city's total population of 6,663). By 1910 there were only thirty-seven Chinese out of the 6,742 residents of Baker City.

Little is known about the miners in eastern Oregon as individuals, but one exception was Ah Poo (b. 1831), who had entered the country through San Francisco in May 1864 and lived in Baker City in the 1890s. When mining declined he, like many other miners in Oregon, moved to Boise, Idaho, where he still lived and worked as a miner in 1903.[41] (Migration for the placer miners was generally regional and they did not go far from the previous site where they had worked.) Ah Poo told his brief story in his application for a duplicate Certificate of Residence, which the BI granted in 1903.

The Chinese established a Chinatown in Baker City that was bordered by Auburn Avenue on the south, Valley Avenue on the north, Resort Street on the west, and the Powder River on the east. The location of the river suggested that *fengshui* (geomancy) was used to select the location. This was similar to the geographical location of the Chinatown in Truckee, California. There were a half dozen stores, a gambling establishment, a "red-light district" located near the joss house, one cemetery with a stone funerary burner, and a substantial brick two-story joss house, which cost $10,000 to build in 1883.[42] As in many other locations, the Chinese had an extensive garden area and irrigated it from a well. Because Baker City had the largest Chinatown in the area, the Chinese in eastern Oregon and western Idaho often spent recreational time there. Eventually the Chinatown disappeared with only a few photographs to document its existence; the nearby Chinese cemetery was restored in 2002.

According to Howard Baker, who retired from the Oregon Department of Geology and Mineral Industries in 1991, the Chinese miners worked at Virtue Mine nearby "getting half of what the white guys did."[43] This statement reflected the old stereotypes about the Chinese. A few Chinese miners owned their own claims in the vicinity of Baker City. In addition to the purchase or lease of claims, the optional cost of registering the property with the county clerk's office, and the cost of constructing and maintaining ditches, the Chinese miners in Oregon and elsewhere in the American West purchased hydraulic equipment. They worked in large-scale hydraulic mining on McCully Fork west of Sumpter, at Rye Valley, and at Salmon Creek, and on placer and lode gold mines throughout Baker County. This equipment allowed them to mine low-grade sites profitably. In 1882, the Lum Sing Company of Oregon, with twenty employees and two hydraulic monitors, made nearly $15,000.[44] The initial investment was large but great profits potentially could be reaped.

The Baker City Chinese cemetery had forty-seven burials recorded between 1894 and 1948, with sixteen additional identified males and fifty others for whom no names or records are available.[45] Of the original forty-seven only one woman (who died between 1910 and 1919) and three men remain in the cemetery, one being Lee Chue (1882–1938), who was the youngest at age 56.[46] In accordance with Chinese tradition, the burials from this cemetery were disinterred, the bones cleaned, and each individual placed in custom- sized galvanized sheet metal boxes that were made by Cook and Emele Sheet Metal Works. The boxes were sealed and sent to China. Reburial occurred in the home village after the skeleton was carefully reassembled.[47] This was part of the arrangement that had usually been made in advance with one of the Chinese organizations connected with the CCBA or a district association. The body of a single or widowed woman was seldom exhumed and reburied in Chinese tradition. The three men probably remained in the cemetery because they died during Sino-Japanese War (1931–45) when the collection of bones and reburials were halted because of the war or because the deceased did not belong to an association, or possibly because they were criminals or fell into some other undesirable category.

As in other western states, the Chinese were active in constructing irrigation ditches that were used for mining and agriculture. EuroAmerican investors owned ditch companies that hired Chinese labor companies to construct the two major mining ditches. In 1863 construction of the El Dorado Ditch began; by 1878 it was the longest historic mining ditch in Oregon with water traversing over one hundred miles. It was five feet wide, seven feet deep, and had a grade of 4.8 feet per mile. Approximately one thousand Chinese probably worked on the construction. This was an engineering feat, and part of the ditch still remains. The second was the Sparta Ditch, built in 1871, that was about twenty-two miles long and located just twenty miles northeast of Baker City.[48] The Chinese maintained these ditches. One of the workers, Aw-wing, decided to settle in Sparta in a small wooden house. He became a good friend of the James Shaver family, posing for a rare photograph (with his Chinese three-stringed instrument) that is still in the possession of a Shaver descendant, Phyllis Badgley.[49] Aw-wing said that the music always reminded him of his home in China.

The 1870 census counted 2,476 miners in eastern Oregon; of them, 1,516 (61.2 percent) were Chinese.[50] As in other western states, some laws were simply ignored and some were voided through the terms of the 1868 Burlingame Treaty.[51] Consequently the Chinese were able to own mines that had been abandoned or were sold or leased to them. Some Chinese miners wanted their claims legally recognized and had their property recorded despite the expense involved. Archaeologist Lanban Richard Steeves studied county records in Baker, Grant, and Union counties in eastern Oregon for the period 1862 to 1900 and tallied four hundred sales of claims to Chinese miners by EuroAmericans.[52] The Chinese paid anywhere from $6,000 for three claims to $1 for seven claims.[53] Obviously Chinese mining companies purchased the expensive claims while individual miners bought the less expensive ones.

Gold was discovered in 1862 at Whiskey Flat, just south of Baker City, in the future Grant County. Grant was established as a county on October 14, 1864, along with Union County. Both had been part of Wasco County. Grant County, covering 4,533 square miles of eastern Oregon, was the largest county in the state at that time and was bordered in the north by the Blue Mountains, part of the larger rugged Columbia Plateau, located in the dry area of Oregon east of the Cascade Range (with the highest peak at 9,038 feet).[54] Two famous mining camps, John Day and Canyon City, were established by the John Day River at the base of the mountain range. The main supply center for John Day was Canyon City, a mining camp established in 1862 that quickly attracted several hundred men, many of whom had originally intended to prospect in Idaho but stopped en route as news reached them of discoveries in eastern Oregon combined with mining busts in Idaho. Within a year of the discovery, the mines in the area yielded $26 million worth of gold.

By 1870 when the gold had declined, Grant County's population dropped to 2,500 EuroAmericans and 940 Chinese (41.6 percent of the total county population, which included 162 Chinese miners).[55] The mining camps were Elk Creek, Granite, Marysville, Olive Creek, Union, Canyon City, and John Day. Near Granite the Chinese left their rock walls (measuring fifteen feet wide and twelve feet high, with some rocks six inches in diameter)—today called Ah Hee Diggings or the "Chinese Walls."[56] The miners moved these rocks by hand and carefully placed them with a sense of decoration and pattern. Similar stone walls could be found in Union Creek, about twenty miles southwest of Baker City near Phillips Reservoir, and in Island Mountain, Nevada, as well as at numerous other Chinese mining sites. The walls probably were used for sluicing.

According to Chia-lin Chen, the number of Chinese doubled between 1870 and 1880 in Elk and Olive Creek while the number of EuroAmericans, who left for richer areas, declined. In Union and Canyon City, the number of EuroAmericans, especially those in agriculture and ranching, increased and the Chinese decreased as they searched for mining opportunities elsewhere.[57] Based on the 1870 census manuscript of Grant County, the men of wealth were Jim Pang (age 30, a restaurant owner who boarded two miners and had a personal worth of $350), Hoy Hey and Chung Yoh (age 45 and 33, respectively, boarding house owners who were worth $150 each); and Sam Lee and Wong Woo (age 33 and 32 respectively, merchants or storekeepers each worth $600).[58] These men did not remain in Grant County for the next census, or if they did, the 1880 census taker assigned them different names. Grant County's Chinese population dropped to 905 (26.6 percent of the total county population) in 1880 and 326 in 1890.[59] Among the reasons for the population decline were passage of the Chinese Exclusion Act, lack of employment opportunities, and the depletion of placer gold.

However, the number of Chinese miners in John Day increased between 1870 and 1880. In 1870 John Day had 85 Chinese (81 of whom were miners) and 184 EuroAmericans (23 of whom were miners). By 1880 this figure had risen to 357 Chinese (including 298 miners), compared with the 201 EuroAmericans (only one of whom was a miner).[60] In 1870 the oldest Chinese miner was 70 years old, the youngest was a boy of 10, and the median age was 29.5 years with most in the 21- to 25-year-old range. By 1880 the age range was slightly older, 26 to 30 years old. By 1880 the EuroAmericans had left placer and hydraulic mining to the Chinese; at that time, 92 of the EuroAmericans were engaged in farming and ranching.

The 1880 census taker in Grant County, like the one in neighboring Idaho, was aware of the Chinese tendency to organize themselves in mining companies and noted this on the census manuscript. There were nineteen Chinese mining companies: Yung Gon Company (24 men); Gum Gow Company (21 men); Sip Goon Company (19 men); Ah Buck Company and Ah Hy Company (12 men each); Wan Goon Company, Ah Gin Company, An Goon Company, One Goon Company, Kin Goon Company, Suig Lee Company, Kam Wa Company, Ah Hog Company, and Tong Goose Company (11 men each); Po Lin Company and Mow Company (10 men each); Ye Ling Company (eight men); Sing Goon Company (11 men in two groups); and the Ding Company (4 men).[61] Of the 298 miners, 220 were working for Chinese bosses who probably had some previous knowledge or experience in mining when they staked the claims or worked the placer sites. The investment in hydraulic equipment required capital and only a few had sufficient funds, so working as a team or company was a necessity.

The EuroAmerican perception was that the Chinese miners were "wage-slaves" of the Chinese merchants and that belief justified EuroAmerican opposition to the presence of slavery and these Chinese mining companies.[62] The existence of the company miners indicated that the traditional Chinese practice of group mining was transplanted and that the profits were probably divided among the workers and supervisors as they had been in China. There is no evidence that these miners were wage-slaves.

Each crew had a headman and at least one man who served as a cook as well as miner. For example, Yean Hat of Middle, Grant County, a single man age 45 in 1880, had nine miners working in his company; Ah Buck, also age 45, a married man living without his wife, was in residence with his crew. With the additional exception of Kam Wa, none of the other John Day Chinese mining companies apparently had the company's owner on site.[63] Kam Wa probably was a shorthand reference to Kam Wa Chung (also known as Kam

Wah Chung), a 43-year-old merchant who lived with his business partner, Ah On, age 46 (both married men living separately from their wives) in John Day. If this was the case, it indicated the close tie between the merchants and miners with merchants operating mining companies.

There is no known record of how profitable these Chinese mining companies were—but the 1882 gold and silver production in the nearby Warren Mining District of Idaho might provide some indication.[64] In 1880, the Chinese population in Warren included 354 miners, five general merchants, five cooks, two laborers, twelve gamblers, four farmers, three gardeners, two barbers, and one each housekeeper, blacksmith, mule packer, laundryman, prostitute, woodchopper, wood sawyer, shoemaker, and doctor. Five Chinese mining companies employed about two hundred men in the creek bottom that extended for about one mile and reported the following production for 1882: Took Sing Company, $14,120; Lin Wo Company, $21,500; Hung Wo Company, $17,400; Wing Wo Company, $15,000; and Shun Lee Company, $11,260. Individual Chinese reported an average of about $1,000 per miner. The total production of the district was $126,450. This was an impressive amount for one year's work. Additionally, the figures probably represented an undervaluation because the Chinese always hesitated to show how successful they were because of the jealousy of other miners.

According to the 1880 census manuscript, John Day had ten merchants, the most notable being Kam Wa Chung and his partner Ah Ong; two brothers, We Lem (age 34) and We Gun (age 30), who lived together; and Ah Bongie (age 36) and Ah Hop (age 40). Get Lee (age 37) lived with his wife, Ah Loy (age 30), and a man who was undoubtedly a relative, Ah Quan (married, age 24). The youngest merchant was Kit Lee (single, age 19) who lived next to two miners. At his youthful age, he undoubtedly represented his kinsmen in this business and might have been sent overseas specifically to operate a general merchandising store in the gold fields. His closest neighbors were EuroAmerican farmers and several Chinese miners, suggesting that he managed a small store. The tenth merchant was Ah Bog (single, age 30) who lived with one of the town's two physicians, Dr. Chi Wah (single, age 34).

John Day's physicians were an interesting group. The other physician in town, Dr. Ah Look (age 36), lived with wife Suey Young (age 38). Both Dr. Chi Wah and Dr. Ah Look were probably hired by the Chinese mining companies or associations because the contract laborers, more often than not, demanded the services of a physician. It is likely that those hired by a com-

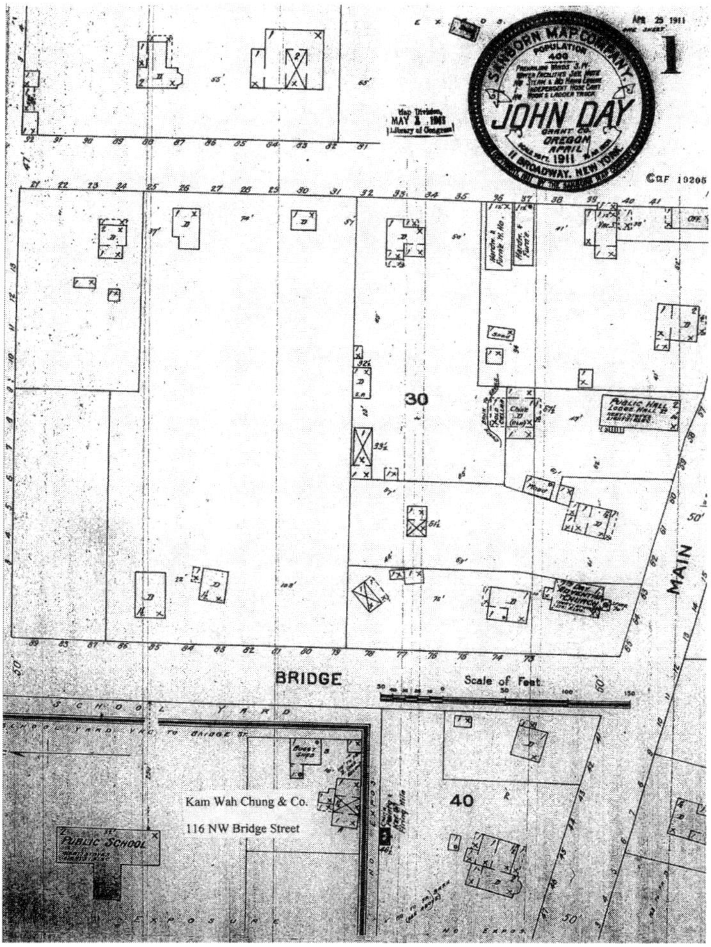

Sanborn map of John Day, Oregon, 1911. Kam Wah Chung and Company and Chinatown were located centrally in the vicinity of present-day Bridge Street. The building is now a museum.

pany or association had to treat their workers first. Some Chinese physicians treated non-Chinese patients as well. These men usually were fairly wealthy. Many EuroAmerican patients testified orally or in writing to the efficacy of traditional Chinese medical and herbal practices, which attracted other EuroAmerican patients.[65]

Grant County had three Chinese doctors in 1870 and five in 1880 who were all relatively prosperous and, in the tradition of Chinese physicians and herbalists, traveled to surrounding towns to care for patients. The doctors with some knowledge of English could treat the non-Chinese population; many of them became prosperous because their treatments were successful. Undoubtedly the majority of the EuroAmericans went to the three EuroAmerican physicians living in John Day in 1870 and 1880, but a small contingent, particularly women, became patients of Chinese physicians because of their reputation for efficacious treatments.

Chinese physicians could obtain their herbal remedies from Chinese druggists in Portland: for example, Dr. Wing Yuen Sai of the firm of Quong Shong Tong, on Second Street in Portland, was deemed by four prominent EuroAmericans as "an honorable man."[66] Although there is little or no documentation to substantiate this, the physicians probably could obtain some of the herbal remedies from Native Americans, who used the same or similar herbs of vegetable origins, or from locally grown plants and from animals in the vicinity, like bear paws.[67] But the majority of the pharmaceuticals were imported from China. Chinese pharmacopeias have a long tradition in China. If no Chinese doctor was in the vicinity, the Chinese had an herbal recipe book that covered cures for common illnesses; usually someone in the community had some rudimentary knowledge such remedies or cures.

Like miners, some Chinese physicians moved around a great deal. This was the case of Zhang Liang Rong Li (Rong Li was his mother's name), known as Dr. Wing Lee, of Portland and Salem, Oregon.[68] Wing Lee arrived in San Francisco around 1862 or 1864, stayed there for two years, then went to Albany, California; Boise, Idaho; and towns in Washington and Idaho before settling in Portland at 104½ First Street, and in Salem at 226 Front Street around 1883. His wife bore him several children, all raised in Oregon. By 1915 at the age of 77, his business, Wing Lee Tong Company, was worth an estimated $50,000.

In John Day EuroAmerican merchants outnumbered the Chinese merchants. There were eleven EuroAmerican merchants in 1870 and twelve in 1880. If the Chinese miners and other residents of John Day were like the Chinese in Pierce, Idaho and other locations, then the Chinese preferred to patronize Chinese-owned stores but also shopped at the EuroAmerican-owned stores that did not discriminate against them or discourage them from shopping there. Of course, the Chinese merchants had to be doing a good business to cover the taxes that Oregon levied on them.

Chinese merchants belonged to the privileged class of individuals who could travel to and from China. Not all merchants had sufficient funds to do this. The trip not only entailed the cost of travel but also the gifts that had to be distributed to relatives in China and the entertainment that was required to celebrate one's return. More often than not, it was simpler to send money home on a monthly or annual basis, usually ranging from $100 to $300. Some built homes for their family in China in the prestigious "overseas Chinese community" that often were of western-style designs and were protected by guard towers and sturdy walls enclosing the community.[69] For example, a merchant from nearby Baker City, Baker County, visited his native place in October 1890, leaving behind his stone store valued at $2,000 in real estate and $600 in personal property.[70] Like many other Chinese merchants, he had two partners to whom he entrusted the business while he was abroad. A few merchants were able to bring relatives (real or "paper" relatives) to handle their business while they were visiting in China.[71]

Unfortunately, family-owned, extended-family-owned, or partnership businesses often declined once the key person left or died.[72] Very few survived through two generations. Often these early Chinese merchants did not have wives and families living with them in the American West, so the business was passed to a son raised in China or a distant relative who had little or no background in the business.

In almost all of the Chinese communities in the American West, there were few Chinese women. This was not unlike the situation for EuroAmericans until the mining camps evolved into more settled towns with families.[73] In 1870 John Day had at least seven saloons in the EuroAmerican section of town. The rowdiness and hardships of living in such a remote and often lawless location discouraged the men from bringing their wives and daughters into the town. Traditional Chinese wives were not enthusiastic about living in such a place because they knew they would face the hardships of isolation, few women friends, persecution, and hostility. They also faced the possibility of being kidnapped because of the scarcity of women.[74]

In 1870 eastern Oregon had only forty-three Chinese women listed in the census manuscript and only ten women listed as "keeping house" in Grant County: Ah Quay (age 28) and Ah Yet (age 20) lived with the miner Ah Shu (age 42). Another two women, Yon Goo (age 22) and Gam Wee (age 18), worked in the laundry business in Canyon City and lived with the cook, Ah Yee (age 23). The physician Ah Tin (age 35) lived with Toy Lee (age 22) and Gam Sing (age 18). Ah Sally (age 34) took in washing and lived with Ah Law (age 40), a miner who probably was her husband. Ah Goods (age 18) kept house for Ah Ban (age 26), a laborer. Li Moa (age 24) kept house for He Ow, a gambler—in reality she probably was a prostitute (based on his occupation). The same situation was true for Ah Ho (age 20) who lived with the gambler Ah Yow (age 42). The latter two couples lived about five households apart and they were surrounded by large groups of Chinese miners. Husbands usually maintained the practice of keeping their wives

Mrs. Get Chor Chan nee Wong (d. 1906). Upper-class Chinese women, particularly wives of merchants, had bound feet or wore platform shoes so that it appeared as if they had bound feet. For this reason, these women seldom left their homes because of the difficulty of walking on the unpaved streets or wooden sidewalks of American mining towns. (Author's collection)

inside the home to protect them from the overwhelmingly large number of single males in the community.

In John Day and throughout the American West the merchants and physicians could afford to bring a first or second wife with them, but many preferred to leave their wives in China where they could care for the absent husband's parents and any children they might have. The 1880 census manuscript listed only one wife of a physician: Suey Young, age 38. Another woman named Ah Loy, obviously the wife of the merchant Get Lee, had no occupation listed. As historian Huping Ling has pointed out, Chinese women in the United States became more involved in their husband's business affairs, something that seldom occurred in south China.[75] Chew Fong Low (1869–1936) of Winemmuca, Nevada, and San Francisco, California, for example, worked in her husband's store, Jim Low and Company, from the 1880s to the early twentieth century. Because they had Paiute customers, she learned how to speak some elementary Paiute.[76] Other Chinese American women of the first and second generation in this early period performed similar tasks in small towns.

When they brought wives, Chinese men had to be concerned about the education and careers of their children. Although there is no example in eastern Oregon, a miner-merchant with Sing Kee and Company, Hangtown (present day Placerville), California, had five children, all born in Hangtown. Like many wealthier Chinese Americans of the time, he sent the oldest son and middle son to China for an education while assigning his youngest son to work for the Wing Hop and Company in San Francisco.[77] (Merchants who could afford it and the well-to-do sent their older male children to China for an education and to seek a wife.) His two daughters were married to men who were already in California. The shortage of Chinese women in the United States made it easy for fathers to negotiate marriages to Chinese men who were financially secure or had the promise of a prosperous future.

In keeping with tradition, Chinese women kept their maiden name or were known by a familiar name. The use of "Mrs." with the husband's last name was an adaptation that did not appear until the turn of the twentieth century. The tradition for married women was to remain cloistered in the home except during festivals or special occasions. With only two married women in John Day in 1880, it was a lonely existence.

Many of the men brought second wives, leaving the first wife and children to care for his parents. This was the case of Li Tom Shi, wife of merchant Lee Lung of Portland, Oregon, who applied to be admitted with their daughter. But admission was denied because she was the second wife, a status not recognized as legitimate in the United States.[78] In 1880 Mary Toy (age 25), whose occupation was "house servant," lived with four Chinese miners in Granite. She may have been a relative of one or more of the men and truly a servant or she may have been a prostitute or second wife.

No prostitutes as such were listed in the 1870 census but two appeared in the 1880 census. Married women usually did not socialize or have anything to do with prostitutes. However, nearby Baker County had fourteen prostitutes in 1870 and seventeen in 1880, so obviously the men spent some of their recreational time in Baker County. Prostitutes were known to travel to different mining camps at regular intervals, so the men did not necessarily have to go to Baker County. Only the upper echelon of Chinese prostitutes could restrict their customer list to Chinese men.[79] The majority of Chinese men (one-third to one-half of them married but living separately from their wives) had to make two major accommodations when living in the American West: to live without the comfort and protection of the nuclear and extended family, and to spend most of their adult lives separated from their wives. For those reasons, they created brotherhoods (such as secret societies), and employment families that filled the void but were not necessarily satisfactory.

In 1880 the other Chinese residents of John Day included several laundrymen, two blacksmiths, one shoemaker, one hog dealer, several laborers, several cooks, one gambler, one tailor, and one jeweler. The wide range of occupations indicated some degree of self-sufficiency in town. Pork was the preferred meat for the Chinese: one observer in Idaho noted that the Chinese there consumed a pound of pork per day, which was more than they would have consumed in China.[80] Pigs were easy to raise and often kept in willow fences near the cabin or house backed onto a hillside. The hog dealer was the only one in the vicinity but others were scattered elsewhere in other nearby towns such as Lovelock, Nevada.[81] Chickens, more difficult to raise, were regarded as a festive dish and usually purchased at the store. In addition to the rice and tea that was imported and purchased from the Chinese merchant, they also preferred to eat fresh vegetables and fruits. Common foods purchased at the stores included wheat flour, preserved fish, dried and preserved vegetables, spices, cooking oil, and some American products that resembled Chinese items, like maple syrup and Worchester sauce.

No gardeners or small farmers were listed in John Day. Presumably the produce came from Canyon City where there were three Chinese gardeners. In southeastern China farmers worked part-time as miners, so the occupations were close. This may have been the case as well in eastern Oregon. The other alternative was to purchase food, especially poultry, from EuroAmerican farmers in the John Day area—and this meant interaction with them. The purchasing of food by miners was a great incentive for these farmers, some of who became prosperous because of trading beyond their immediate area.[82] Pearl Becker, in the St. Helena (Montana) *Sentinel Mist,* April 29, 1963, recalled a memory that others shared in other places: "When my grandparents came to Oregon in 1877, there was a work camp of Chinese laborers near Rooster Rock. . . . They would buy poultry, eggs, butter, small pigs, and other farm products. They were very fond of white ducks, and would buy all my Grandmother could raise."[83] EuroAmerican teamsters brought goods in from other locations; all of the Chinese imports traveled into John Day by these freight handlers.

Chinese also worked as cooks and servants for EuroAmerican employers, giving them the opportunity to adapt to American life faster. Terry Abraham has demonstrated how some of the Chinese servants, such as Walter James of Olympia, Washington, began as a servant and rose to prominence in Minneapolis, Minnesota.[84] There were numerous examples of this upward mobility. Servants, ranch hands, and cooks for a family or hotel also might live with EuroAmericans. In Monumental, Grant County, for example, a Chinese laundryman lived with a EuroAmerican family. This was unusual. In the larger Chinese enclaves of Canyon City and John Day, the Chinese lived together but might live next door to a EuroAmerican person or family. Merchants usually lived on the premises of their stores, as was the case in Kam Wah Chung and Company.

Because Canyon City was so close to John Day, the Chinese knew each other and visited John Day during their recreational time. In 1880 Canyon City's Chinese population consisted of three merchants, two physicians, and two opium dealers (all of whom probably did business with the John Day miners) as well as the forty-seven Chinese miners who lived there. Additionally, there were five laundrymen, ten cooks, three gardeners, and four restaurant owners and workers. There also were three wood choppers—an occupation not found in any other Grant County mining town but one that was dominant in nearby northern Nevada. The wood choppers probably supplied the mills and townspeople with firewood as well as other wood products. Clearly, Canyon City's Chinese population was diverse in its occupations.

In a 1970 letter to Christopher H. Edson, author of *The Chinese in Eastern*

Oregon, 1860–1890, Mrs. Janice Justice, curator of the Grant County Museum, said that the Humboldt Mining Company, a prosperous hydraulic enterprise located near Canyon City, employed about sixteen to eighteen Chinese to carry away the large boulders created by the monitors that washed down huge quantities of the gold-bearing sediment from the mountainsides. But the census manuscript does not list any Chinese laborers there in 1870 or 1880, so the men must have been classified as "miners" despite the type of work they did.[85] (Nevada's census takers would have listed them as laborers and not miners.)

One Chinese miner described his experience in Canyon City in his application for a duplicate Certificate of Residence. Huang Gui (Wong Goey) revealed that he landed in Portland in 1868 and spent nine years as a miner in Canyon City but because he did not know English, he felt very isolated and stayed within the Chinese community.[86] He subsequently went to work for the Great Northern Railroad in Everett, Washington, where he was arrested in 1895 for not having in his possession the Certificate of Residence that had been accidentally destroyed a few days earlier. Because he had memorized his number (49,779) and it was traceable, he was issued a duplicate and could remain in the United States. The isolation Huang felt was not uncommon for those who knew little or no English.

The Chinese population in John Day grew even larger in 1887 when the Chinese living in Canyon City, where jointly owned Chinese and EuroAmerican mines were permitted by law, were forced to move. The Chinese had lived in a segregated section of Canyon City. When a fire in 1885 destroyed Chinatown, hundreds of Chinese moved two miles down the valley to John Day. John Day's estimated population increase was five hundred to six hundred people. The Chinese established their own social and business organizations as well as lineage, clan, and native-place associations based upon similar societies in southern China. However, the subsequent economic decline in mining and other occupations led to an exodus of many of the Chinese from this area by the turn of the century.

Although most of the Chinese miners in John Day worked in teams or for a Chinese company, according to the census manuscripts some individual miners either worked for themselves, in groups of two, or for EuroAmerican mine owners. The financial success and survivability of a lone miner was uncertain. Independent miners needed the protection of the local *tang* from other Chinese miners, hostile Native Americans, and jealous EuroAmerican miners. On the other hand, because of their independent nature these men were most likely to continue mining long after the EuroAmerican mining companies moved on.[87]

As the Chinese population grew, John Day's economic future looked promising despite the earlier declining gold resources. From the 1890s through early 1900s new mining discoveries and the use of hydraulic equipment revived the town's economy. In 1892 the Chinese produced $150,000 (14.4 percent) of the $1,297,409 gold and silver found in eastern Oregon.[88] On February 8, 1901, the *Blue Mountain Eagle* (a weekly newspaper in John Day) reported that the output of gold and silver in Grant County in 1898 totaled $176,231; in 1899 it rose to $303,681. But these figures did not accurately represent what the Chinese produced since they were reluctant to let the public know how successful or unsuccessful they were. The success attracted other Chinese to the area. For example, Ah Mow (aka Ng Moo) arrived in Portland in 1875 and by 1893 was living in John Day and working as a gold miner.[89] Once there, he joined the local Zhigongtang. In 1902, when he moved to Hanford, California, he, like many others, kept his Certificate of Residence and other important papers in the safe at the local lodge.

Because of the restrictive 1866 and 1872 mining laws, Chinese leased land and purchased it whenever they could. In Grant County from June 25, 1862, to October 1, 1888, county records showed sixty-two entries in which Chinese were one or both parties of record with the majority (forty-nine) being transfers of mining rights from EuroAmericans to Chinese. Additionally, two were sales between Chinese, two were purchases from Chinese to EuroAmericans, two were leases from EuroAmericans to Chinese, and seven were records of placer grounds and mining water rights originating with the Chinese.[90] According to the local newspaper, EuroAmericans owned the land that was rented to the Chinese miners in John Day.[91] Eventually some Chinese purchased the land: for example, the *Grant County Express* (June 2, 1887) reported that Z. A. Wallace of Long Creek had sold the claim he and his partner owned on Big Creek to the Ah Heng Company for $4,000.[92] Because of the high price the Ah Heng Company undoubtedly was a consortium of Chinese investors. It is likely that many more informal unrecorded transactions occurred. The Chinese took risks in purchasing and leasing land and property because the claims could be taken away from them.

By 1880 residential segregation in eastern Oregon began to break down. Most of the Chinese miners and men lived in boarding houses usually owned and operated by the Chinese company. Independent and small groups of miners also lived together. In 1880, Marysville, Grant County, had a population of sixty-four Chinese—sixty-three miners and one physician. A Chinese miner, Ah Hung (single, age 30), lived with two EuroAmerican miners and Ah Jim (single, age 31) lived next door to a EuroAmerican farmer and his wife. At the same time in John Day, some EuroAmerican residents were interspersed among the Chinese residential units and three Chinese laborers lived with a EuroAmerican laborer from California. The towns were often too small to segregate the population into separate ethnic groups although the larger ones like Canyon City and John Day had designated "Chinatowns."

The anti-Chinese sentiment in Canyon City not surprising. At the height of its gold rush between 1864, when Canyon City became the county seat of the newly created Grant County, and 1900, when an estimated $16 million in gold and silver had been recovered, the predominately EuroAmerian population did not want to share this prosperity with the foreign Chinese. Influenced by the anti-Chinese sentiment elsewhere, they supported the passage of the 1882 Chinese Exclusion Act. But EuroAmerican workers and their political supporters were not satisfied with the exclusion of Chinese laborers, feeling there were too many loopholes, so intensified agitation and violence led to the passage of the subsequent acts, most notably the renewal and extension of the 1882 act in 1892 along with the requirement for identification papers. When fire destroyed Chinatown, the residents of Canyon City refused to allow the Chinese to rebuild or settle in Canyon City, so the Chinese relocated to John Day.

One of the more infamous violent acts against the Chinese was the Snake River Massacre on May 25, 1887, involving the tragic and brutal murder of thirty-four Chinese miners who had been working in Hells Canyon on the Oregon side of the Snake River.[93] The miners had been working there since October 1886; in May they had accumulated about $4,000 to $5,000 in gold. Using traditional Chinese methods of boating against swift river currents, they used ropes and poles to pull boats carrying their equipment of rockers and sluices that were used on the gravel bars. Chea-po was the leader of the two crews of miners, all originally from the Punju area near Guangzhou. The leader of another crew working for the same company, Lee She, traveled to visit the men and accidentally discovered three bodies on the riverbank. Eventually ten bodies, some found as late as the fall of 1887. Some were scalped, hacked to death, and decapitated. Eight belonged to the Chea clan. An additional body was found later but the total estimated count was thirty-four dead.

At first Native Americans were blamed for the massacre because of an 1867 attack on seven Chinese miners working on the west bank of the Snake River about twenty miles above the Salmon River.[94] Nine Native Americans robbed the Chinese, killing two Chinese miners and wounding another. (At that time approximately 150 Chinese were working on the Snake River and the attack forced them to look in surrounding areas for other placer sites. Eventually Chinese miners returned to this lucrative area. On May 18, 1870, the EuroAmerican miners decided "to prevent Chinese emigration and colonization of the Snake River" and to forcibly drive them out.[95]But by the next year they allowed the Chinese to returned since the Chinese were "better adapted to this sort of mining and there is room here for 500 of them." "Let them come," one miner wrote.)[96] The EuroAmerican attackers in 1886 Snake River massacre allegedly dressed like Native Americans and scalped and beheaded their victims. The massacre made newspaper headlines throughout the nation.

The Chinese sought redress through the courts and the State Department in Washington, D.C. The subsequent legal entanglements were typical of the convoluted process that the Chinese faced when attempting to obtain some sort of justice for crimes committed against them. Lee She immediately reported the murders to the sheriff in Lewiston, Idaho, who said that since the crime was committed in Oregon, it was out of his jurisdiction. Meanwhile, the sheriff in Oregon claimed the murderers were in Idaho and he had no authority to pursue them especially since Idaho was still a territory. The Chinese Consul-General in San Francisco, working with the Sanyi (Three Counties) District Association to which the victims belonged, offered a $1,000 reward, and hired a special investigator, Joseph K. Vincent, to find the murderers. Vincent did very little and refused to assist government officials when the matters moved out of the realm of local authority. The Chinese minister in Washington, D.C., and federal officials became involved with the authorities in Oregon and Idaho as legal arguments continued. In August 1888, four of the seven men who had been arrested for the murder of ten of the Chinese miners were found not guilty in Joseph, Oregon—this despite the deathbed confession during the trial of 16-year-old Robert McMillan of Walla Walla, Washington, that all seven men were guilty.

Because some of the Chinese were scalped and beheaded, Native Americans had been blamed for the attack. But when McMillan made his confession, several newspapers throughout the nation carried the sensational story that the crime had been committed by EuroAmericans dressed as Native

Americans.[97] George S. Craig, who owned the cabin in Hells Canyon where the murderers planned their attack, commented to an interviewer after the trial, "I guess if they had killed thirty-one white men, something would have been done about it, but none of the jury knew the Chinamen or cared much about it, so they turned the men loose."[98] Shortly after the trial, all of the court documents mysteriously disappeared only to be found in 1995, which allowed journalist R. Gregory Nokes to examine the documents and give a more accurate historical account of the massacre.

In September 1888 Congress ratified the Baynard-Chang Treaty, which extended the immigration ban against Chinese laborers to allow only those Chinese with a minimum of $1,000 in assets to return to the United States and provided compensation to Chinese families for property losses and murders. But due to political maneuvers it was never signed by either the Chinese or American governments.[99] In the interim, the United States agreed to pay an indemnity of $276,620 for all of the losses and injuries suffered by the Chinese in the United States. But this did not include the Snake River deaths because the information was not yet available. Whereas China paid indemnities for the deaths of Americans in China, most notably during the 1900 Boxer uprising, this was one of the last payments that the United States made for deaths of Chinese in the United States. In recognition of what occurred there, in 2005 Hells Canyon in the Snake River was renamed Chinese Massacre Cove.

This event demonstrated how dangerous life could be for Chinese miners, how many deaths may never be discovered, how justice was not on the side of the Chinese, and why the Chinese mined in groups that shared the common bond of native place (in this case, Sanyi District)—because mutual trust and protection were vital in placer mining sites even though safety was uncertain.

With the influx of the Canyon City Chinese in 1887, John Day became a livelier place. Kam Wah Chung ("The Golden Flower of Prosperity") and Company was the center for daily social and recreational activities and the purchasing of supplies for its Chinese residents in John Day and the nearby areas.[100] According to Bob Wah, nephew of Ing Hay, Kam Wah Chung and Company was established in 1871 and advertisements for the business appeared in the *Grant County News* by 1883.

The 1880 census manuscript listed the name of the store's owner as Kam Wah Chung—which was actually the name of the store. (This was a common practice in the American West because Chinese names were difficult to pronounce.) Little is known about Kam Wah Chung except that he was 43

Kam Wah Chung and Company, built in 1866 and expanded, was the main structure in John Day's Chinatown and did not close its doors until the 1950s. Doc Ing Hay operated his Chinese medicine practice here; his partner, Lung On, ran the general merchandising store. (Author's photograph of present-day structure)

at the time and probably headed or owned one of the mining "companies" listed in the census. In 1887 the owner, at the age of 50, decided to retire or move elsewhere and sold the building to two newcomers, Lung On and Ing Hay, who had arrived in 1886. There were three other prominent Chinese merchants in John Day, See Ling and Quong Yuen Lung, who owned one store and Kit Lee, who operated another, smaller one. No information is available as to when these businesses opened or closed.

The new owners of the Kam Wah Chung store were interesting personalities.[101] Lung On (1863–1940, in pinyin, Liang Guangying) came from Xinhui, Guangdong, to San Francisco intent upon becoming a miner. He came from a wealthy merchant family and his father frequently wrote to him asking him to return to China to join in the family business there. Lung On left behind a wife and daughter, who, according to tradition, lived with his parents. He may have been related to Kam Wah Chung's partner, Ah On, and may have purchased the business through this connection. He spoke English, was a skilled businessman, and was the primary intermediary with the EuroAmerican community. Lung On took on the duties of providing assistance to those newly arrived from China and those wishing to immigrate. His letters schooled

Doc Ing Hay was well known for his medical and herbal treatments of patients in eastern Oregon as well as neighboring states. He and his business partner, Lung On, took over Kam Wah Chung and Company in 1887. Despite the declining Chinese population in John Day, the business prospered when their customer base became primarily EuroAmerican. Lung On later opened the first car dealership in eastern Oregon in the 1920s. (Courtesy of Oregon Historical Society, FSDM2)

prospective immigrants on how to answer the customs officials' questions when they arrived, suggesting that he might have been involved in illegal immigration and the "paper" relatives system. He undoubtedly was part of an international network that provided information about employment in the United States as well as loans for transportation costs to the United States.[102] These were functions of the Chinese associations like the Binggongtang—but there was no evidence in the store that Lung On was an officer of any Chinese association although it is likely that he was connected to one. He was a gambler, womanizer, and opium smoker. His outgoing personality was very different from that of his partner, Ing Hay.

"Doc" Ing Hay (1862–1952, in pinyin, Wu Younian) arrived in Walla Walla, Washington, in 1885 with his father. He had been trained as a Chinese herbal doctor and pulsologist in China. He came from Taishan, Guangdong, and had kinsmen in British Columbia, Washington, northeastern Nevada, and eastern Oregon. (Ing Hay's father returned to Guangdong and wrote to his son asking for money for Ing Hay's wife and son, whom Ing Hay left behind in China. Although Ing Hay wrote to his father and told him he intended to send for his son, he never did.) Ing Hay's knowledge of Chinese, both written and spoken, was excellent. He left behind many documents written in Chinese in the store, but he did not speak English well and depended on his partner for translations. Of the two men, he was known to be more eccentric and in his later years suffered from poor vision and deafness. Among the many artifacts in the Kam Wah Chung and Company Museum are his experiments with optical instruments. He continued the tradition of practicing Chinese medicine that had begun decades earlier in John Day.

Unlike the earlier Chinese entrepreneurs, Lung On and Ing Hay came relatively late to the United States. The 1882 Chinese Exclusion Act permitted merchants and physicians to immigrate, so the two men probably fell into this category. It was fortunate that Ing Hay arrived before 1892, when the extension of the 1882 act, known as the Geary Act, was passed. This legislation classified physicians and priests with laborers, thus prohibiting their immigration, and required all Chinese to carry Certificates of Residence for identification purposes.

In his statistical study of early Roseburg, Oregon, William G. Robbins showed that a direct relationship existed between wealth and length of residence in late nineteenth-century frontier towns.[103] This was true for Ah Lee Lake of Tuscarora and China Lem of Island Mountain, but Ing Hay and Lung On became wealthy because of the different services they offered to a changing population. They stayed in John Day until their deaths from natural causes.

The Kam Wah Chung store was located around the corner from Main Street and was conveniently located for John Day's residents. Chinatown was to the north of the store. The building, erected in 1866, was made of sandstone blocks quarried from the southern canyon. It may have served as an outpost for the U.S. Army when it handled minor troubles with Native Americans. An iron door protected the inhabitants from wild animals and any trouble that might arise. Ing Hay and Lung On added a wooden attic in the 1890s and a north wing around 1917. The wooden attic was probably divided into rooms to board workers; the price for sleeping in such an accommodation was about $1.50 per month.[104] As the most impressive building in John Day, it was not unusual for the store to take in boarders since EuroAmerican hotels seldom allowed Chinese to stay there. The north wing indicated a growing, rather than shrinking, business.

The first floor of the two-story building was divided into several rooms, including a consultation area and drug store for Ing Hay's patients, a bedroom for Ing Hay, a general merchandising area and bedroom for Lung On, bunk beds for visiting guests or workers, a kitchen, two altars with deities, and a post office. The probable boarding room area on the second floor later was used as a storehouse. The post office provided a link between the residents and the families that they left behind in China or other parts of the United States. Since Ing Hay and Lung On were literate, they not only read letters that the Chinese received but also could write letters for those unable to write. Some of these letters have been preserved in Kam Wah Chung Museum.

The religious aspect of the services offered at the Kam Wah Chung store exemplified the universalism of Chinese beliefs—a combination of Daoism, Buddhism, and Confucianism (especially with its reverence for the ancestors) was evident. Chinese American temples often had the "three religions" of China represented so that all the people could worship. The larger altar in the store was open to the public and visitors paid a small amount to pray there. The shrine was flanked by fortune-telling sticks, incense burners, candle-holders, and often, bowls of fruit and vases of flowers. (It is believed that the shrine came from the joss house, a separate building located in John Day but moved to Kam Wah Chung by 1900 when the Chinese population declined.) The small shrine in the building was typical of those found in homes; it honored family deities, ancestors, and protective deities, such as Hou Wang, also known as Mazu, the Empress who protected those who went abroad.[105] Chinese sayings flanked the altars.

Lung On and Ing Hay also were involved in burial arrangements since there was no obvious Chinese association in town to handle such matters. For example, in a telegram in the Kam Wah Chung files, a friend wrote, "I am shocked by the telephone call from Lung On that our friend Gonglin was shot and killed by an American. . . . Enclosed is $30 to help with the expenses for his funeral."[106] Like the Chinese cemetery in Baker City, the bones of many those buried in John Day's Chinese cemetery were later exhumed and shipped to their home villages in China for reburial.

Local residents often gathered in Kam Wah Chung's consultation area to play games, learn the latest news through newspapers and magazines, and relax. The place served as an employment center providing information about jobs in the area. Goods were imported and the Dollar Shipping Line, the largest Pacific coast shipping company (owned by Robert Dollar), regularly gave the store its shipping schedule and calendar for Chinese customers.

According to an advertisement in the local newspaper, the store carried Chinese and American products, and before 1894, Japanese products. Lung On and Ing Hay were aware of the 1894–95 Sino-Japanese War and probably knew about the anti-Japanese protests led by fellow Guangdong radical reformers Kang Youwei and Liang Qichao. Perhaps for this reason they stopped carrying Japanese-made goods. They kept in touch with events in China through newspapers and letters from their families in China. As a general merchandising store, Kam Wah Chung carried American food products as well as Chinese imported foodstuffs.

The store was decorated with Confucian sayings on the walls, probably penned by Ing Hay, but Lung On also regarded himself as a Confucian scholar. "Recompense injury with kindness," "Lack of forbearance in small matters upsets great plans," "The soft overcomes the hard," "Even the metal and stone can be melted by the warmth of sincere friendliness," "The sage meets worthy men," "Business starts in the spring," and "May the deities and men have good fortune for the entire year." [107] The writing showed a skilled hand in calligraphy, so it is not surprising that one or both men wrote letters on behalf of their clients to family members in China; one such draft from a man to his wife read, "Because I can get no gold, I am detained in this secluded corner of a strange land."[108] Unfortunately none of the large collection of correspondence at the present-day museum described their day-to-day living situation or the challenges they faced in John Day.

In 1901 the EuroAmericans in John Day formed a miner's union and the harassment that typified many other towns began. Mining was on the decline and the Chinese population was shrinking, so they became vulnerable. (By 1900 only one hundred Chinese were living in John Day; by 1910 the figure dropped to forty-seven in all of Grant County.) In 1905 a mob searched and ransacked Chinatown and ordered the Chinese out of town, a technique used in many mining towns throughout the American West. They broke into Kam Wah Chung and looted the store.

Lung On and two others were jailed for having opium in their possession; each had to pay a $100 fine because an 1887 Oregon law made the possession and smoking of opium illegal.[109] Three years later, in 1890, when Mon Luck, who was convicted of illegal possession of the drug, appealed to the Oregon Supreme Court on the basis of infringement of personal liberties for the use of a drug that was no more harmful than alcohol, the court responded that possession and smoking were demoralizing vices and injurious to the health and moral welfare of the community.[110] In 1905 the only EuroAmerican physician in John Day, Dr. J. H. Fell, charged Ing Hay with practicing medicine without a license, a common charge throughout the American West. But in the case of Ing Hay and others like him, supporters who had been helped or cured pointed out that no jury would convict these Chinese doctors and they were allowed to continue practicing. The relative tranquility of the 1880s was gone forever but despite the adversity, Kam Wah Chung and Company thrived because its two owners had become an integral part of the larger community. Some residents and descendants of residents recalled that the Chinese generally kept to themselves and remained isolated. One early account erroneously stated that they remained "apart from the main town [and did] not mingle with Americans."[111] Photographs and testimonials in the museum offer evidence to disprove this statement.

Lung On was the more entrepreneurial of the two men. In her biographical portrait of Lung On, Ruthanne Lum McCann said that he invested his profits in property and shares in dairies and gold mines, played in Chinese and American games, started the first automobile dealership east of the Cascades, dated EuroAmerican women, rode with white buckaroos, and provided temporary partnerships in the store for individuals seeking the status of "merchant" so they could travel to and from China (merchants belonged to the "exempt class" under the 1882 Chinese Exclusion Act and its extensions).[112]

One would have expected the two men to move to Portland, Seattle, or San Francisco when the Chinese population declined, but both were enterprising and creative and found John Day to their liking. Both men ignored pleas from their families to return to China. Ing Hay had a thriving practice treating Chinese and non-Chinese patients in person, as well as via mail from as close as California and as far away as Texas and by telephone. He had numerous testimonials, including one by Lillian Davis, who, in 1905, had been to see Dr. Fell and was told that she would always be a cripple because of her inflammatory rheumatism. But Ing Hay concocted an herbal remedy that cured her ailment.[113] Eastern Oregonians credited him for saving the locals from the flu pandemic of 1918, in sharp contrast to the high number of deaths from the flu reported in places like Portland. Thousands died in the United States but no one in eastern Oregon succumbed to the flu. Many testimonials to his skill have been preserved in the museum.

The herbal or drug store contained carefully labeled boxes of herbs as well as preserved bear paws, snakes, and dried seahorses. This probably is the largest extant collection of late nineteenth- to early twentieth-century Chinese remedies in the world. The fact that Ing Hay had eye testing equipment and lenses may have indicated that he also served as the local optometrist. His collection of medical books and scientific information indicated that he was well read and kept up to date in his field until he became blind and turned his business over to relatives.

These two married men, who experienced considerable financial success after mining ended, remained in John Day until their deaths and were buried there. In 1940 Lung On passed away; at that time his net worth was estimated at $45,000. Ing Hay tried to carry on the business; eventually his nephew, Bob Wah (1897–1966), came to assist him. Ing Hay died in 1952 and Bob Wah and his wife, Rose (1901–57) took over the business. They immigrated from Xiaping Village, Taishan, Guangdong, after the repeal of the Chinese Exclusion Act in 1943 under the qualification of "relatives." The couple were buried in the local cemetery. Before his death, Bob turned Kam Wah Chung over to the city, which in turned gave it to the state.

The building and its contents, a wealth of information and artifacts, are available for study. Everything was preserved intact until it was opened recently as a museum. Among the many items were $23,000 in uncashed checks, boxes of correspondence that now fill several large file drawers, a variety of books, herbal remedies, western drugs and food products, general store items like matches, Chinese deities, and personal belongings. These have been preserved in the Kam Wah Chung and Company Museum and Museum Office.

What is remarkable about the eastern Oregon community of John Day is that Ing Hay and Lung On remained there until they passed away (despite the small Chinese population in the twentieth century) because they had found an economic niche that provided the larger EuroAmerican population—their loyal customers—with much-needed services. The townspeople honored these two men by naming streets after them. Supporting the effort to restore the building and turn it into a museum were the Friends of Kam Wah Chung, Oregon State Parks, and Mary Oberst, the first lady of Oregon. John Day's Kam Wah Chung, which was refurbished and reopened in May 2008, is the earliest Chinese American National Historic Landmark site outside of California. It earned that designation in 2006.

Chinese miners and merchants migrated to eastern Oregon in the 1860s. Some were very successful despite cycles of violence and overt discrimination from an influential segment of the EuroAmerican population supported and encouraged by the passage of anti-Chinese legislation on the federal, state, and local levels. Like many frontier towns, some laws, such as the prohibition against owning abandoned mining claims, could be ignored, but the threat of enforcement was always present. Despite the high taxes that they had to pay, some Chinese were successful in mining and merchandising. As in Nevada and other western states, some came and stayed after the construction of the railroads to try their hand at mining. Although some of the media were hostile to the Chinese, some influential individuals, especially locally, took a more neutral stance and tried to encourage a more fair approach toward the Chinese who lived in their communities. The Chinese also faced challenges from hostile Native Americans. When Chinese miners were massacred at Snake River, the U.S. government would not award indemnities to the Chinese government despite its efforts in negotiating with the U.S. State Department. Chinese living abroad realized the weakness of the Manchus ruling China and eventually sought to overthrow the imperial government in favor of a republican form of government under Chinese leadership.

In the rugged terrain of eastern Oregon, the Chinese established communities where some of their leaders interacted with the local population who were also struggling to survive. Some of the miners and merchants were successful while others struggled, going from place to place searching for that elusive gold. Chinese merchants were involved in the formation of Chinese mining companies, and it appears that many were successful. Although there were no statistics from Grant County, nearby Warren, Idaho, reported significant mining successes for its Chinese mining companies. These companies required individual Chinese to work together and were based on traditional organization as in China. By banding together they could afford the equipment needed for hydraulic mining and extensive irrigation systems. Unfortunately, after 1907, mining again declined and much of Grant and Baker counties became agricultural lands.

Some wealthy Chinese miners like Gin Lin returned to China after spending over thirty years in Oregon. But economic success did not mean that one returned always to China, as was the case of Ing Hay and Lung On. They assisted the small Chinese population and larger EuroAmerican population by providing services and goods into the early twentieth century and were remembered by those who liked and accepted them as part of the community.

The Chinese left behind few physical reminders of their presence: the cemetery in Baker City, the Gin Lin Trail, the El Dorado Ditch, the Ah Hee Chinese Rock Wall, and the Kam Wah Chung and Company. Until recently the Chinese presence seldom has been mentioned in books and articles about Oregon and yet they helped build the state by constructing irrigation systems, railroad, trails, and mines; they patronized EuroAmerican businesses and farmers; and provided services needed in frontier communities, to name a few.

3 Eastward to Northeastern Nevada: Tuscarora

BY THE MID-1850S Chinese miners migrated to remote parts of Utah Territory, now called Nevada, from various parts of the West, especially California because of the new gold discoveries along the Carson River. Most of the Chinese lived in western Nevada in the Carson City and Comstock Lode areas where mining and lumbering were major industries. After the completion of the transcontinental railroad, they moved eastward. Between 1870 and 1890 the third-largest concentration of Chinese in the state was in northeastern Nevada, in Elko County, where new mining sites were discovered.[1] The Chinese miners and merchants in the new boomtown of Tuscarora had a different experience from those in Grant County, Oregon, primarily because Nevada allowed them to own property (including mining claims). They were successful even though the nature of mining had become more technical and the national anti-Chinese movement that led to the passage of the Chinese exclusion acts was intensifying. Some Chinese miners in Tuscarora found the riches that they were seeking and a few remained into the 1920s. Like Lung On in John Day, Chinese merchant Ah Lee Lake remained long after the mining boom was over in Tuscarora.

The early presence of the Chinese at the beginning of EuroAmerican settlement in Nevada (which achieved statehood in 1864) helped to shape their experiences. As in Oregon, EuroAmericans needed irrigation systems to cultivate the dry desert lands of Carson Valley for farming and mining. Gold had been discovered in the region in the spring of 1849 but EuroAmerican settlements were slow to be established because most of the gold seekers from the eastern United States were heading to California. Around 1855 the early Mormon settlers in present-day Genoa, near the eastern base of the Sierra Nevada, asked a Chinese labor contractor in San Francisco to send fifty Chinese to dig irrigation ditches in the Carson Valley. Some of them eventually settled in present-day Genoa. In 1856 Chinese workers constructed a ditch from two miles west of present-day Dayton, Lyon County, to Gold Canyon, located just south of present-day Virginia City.[2] Portions of this "China Ditch" still remain near Dayton. The Mormons, who were primarily agriculturalists, allowed the Chinese workers to remain.[3] (This tolerant attitude prevailed among many Mormons who themselves had experienced discrimination.) The number of Chinese increased to about two hundred, mostly placer miners. They built huts of stone, mud, and tule in "Chinatown" (later renamed Dayton), because they knew mining was usually ephermeral.[4] In 1857 the Johntown (so named for "John Chinaman") miners found gold in Six-Mile Canyon, five miles north of Gold Canyon; Chinese miners worked the claims there for several decades.[5] For unknown reasons, these early Chinese of Chinatown were not listed in the 1860 census manuscript.

A small EuroAmerican minority welcomed the Chinese. Reacting to this new migration, Genoa's *Territorial Enterprise,* April 21, 1859, stated, "We hope that the 'good time coming' [in mining] which has so long been in anticipation by the Celestials [Chinese] is near at hand." That materialized in 1859 when some fifty Chinese miners in Gold Canyon reportedly earned over $35,000 from their efforts. This unwanted publicity taught the Chinese to underreport or not reveal their discoveries whenever possible.

The biggest mining discovery was made public in 1859. The famous Comstock Lode, with its rich vein running through Virginia City and Gold Hill (originally Carson County and later Storey County), was the first major silver deposit in the United States. It quickly became internationally famous and many of the investors either came from or eventually settled in the San Francisco Bay Area, making the connection between the two locations inseparable for several decades. Although gold was also found there, silver was the main production. For this reason the Chinese called Nevada *Yinshan* (Cantonese, Gheum Shaan), or "Silver Mountain," while California was *Jinshan* (Cantonese, Gum Shaan), or "Gold Mountain."[6] Between 1859 and 1878, the Comstock Lode, named after one of the founders, Henry Comstock, produced approximately $400 million in silver and gold.

The fear of Chinese miners moving in prompted the Gold Hill miners in 1859 to pass the resolution that "no Chinaman shall hold a claim in this district."[7] Chinese were prohibited from working in the silver mines—but the capital investment required to do so was prohibitive for them anyway. Discouraged, the Chinese turned to various service industries. In Nevada's 1860 census manuscript the twenty-one Chinese listed included sixteen laundrymen, two cooks, two laborers, and one barkeeper.[8] There were no miners listed. Lee Kee (1824–1931), who had gone to Gold Canyon in the 1850s to mine, was typical of the disenchanted miners who moved further eastward for work. He ended up running a restaurant in Austin, Lander County, where he remained until his death at the age of 107 and was buried in the local cemetery there.[9] Although the general belief was that most Chinese did not find that pot of gold, a few did. Another Austin Chinese, who died in 1875 with $45,000 in the Bank of California, was among the few who were able to accumulate substantial wealth during these early years.[10] Most Chinese never let the community know the extent of their wealth and often preferred to deposit their money in Chinese banks—if they used a banking service at all. Those with families in China sent varying amounts of money to their families, often by way of the Bank of Canton, headquartered in San Francisco.[11] Others transferred funds through one of the Chinese organizations or stores to China.

One of the advantages the Chinese had in moving to Nevada was the right to buy, sell, and own property. Article I of the Nevada constitution, adopted in 1864, allowed "resident aliens" to buy, sell, and own property. Traditionally the Chinese immigrants valued land ownership, so having this right in Nevada was attractive to them. This, combined with the 1866 and 1872 mining laws allowed EuroAmerican miners to sell them property once an initial claim had been filed. (Usually this occurred after a site had been deemed no longer profitable.) A common practice was to obtain a claim through preemption, which involved filing necessary documents in the county recorder's office and putting up markers to show the boundaries but not purchasing the land.[12] Some Chinese leased their mining land from EuroAmericans or partnered with EuroAmericans for the purchase of mines, but the most popular method was to purchase abandoned or used claims from EuroAmericans. In most, if not all, cases, individual Chinese did not have sufficient funds to purchase or lease the more expensive claims, so they formed partnerships or companies or had their *tang* provide the funds. For example, in 1880 in Idaho, Alex Danskin leased his claims to the Hexingtang, an association that had forty-two men involved as partners for nine-nine years at the rental fee of $1 per year with a one-time payment of $12,500. Though nothing of this type was recorded in Nevada, this probably occurred there as well.[13]

When the construction of the Central Pacific Railroad (from 1863 to 1869) needed workers, some of the Chinese abandoned their jobs for this new opportunity.[14] Because their labor was so important to its completion, the Burlingame Treaty was negotiated and signed in 1868. In this treaty the United

States and China recognized “the inherent and inalienable right of man to change his home and allegiance,” allowed free emigration (something that the Qing government had refused to permit earlier), and guaranteed “the same privileges, immunities, and exemptions in respect to travel or residence, as may be enjoyed by the citizens or subjects of the most favored nation.”[15] The treaty allowed the Chinese to emigrate legally and prompted more to travel to the American West. The Central Pacific recruited 50 percent of its Chinese railroad workers from those who were already in the United States and, because of the treaty, the other 50 percent from China.

The Central Pacific Chinese construction crew of twelve thousand to fifteen thousand workers reached present-day Reno in 1868; thereafter, only about five thousand of them continued across Nevada because the construction work was much easier. The number of workers fluctuated until the crew that included Irish, Native Americans, and Mormons as well as the numerous Chinese, reached Promontory, Utah, in May 1869. Although often working in separate ethnic groups, some interaction occurred between the Chinese and others, which probably accounts for the development of friendships and acquaintances—as well as later hostility .

After the completion of the Central Pacific, some of the Chinese workers continued to work for the railroad doing maintenance, rebuilding track lines, and other jobs, while others worked on other railroad lines in Nevada or nearby states. The majority looked to mining, merchandising, laundry work, food service, gardening, the timber industry, roadwork, or other types of work to earn a livelihood. Working for the Central Pacific had trained some Chinese for lumbering and road construction. Their background in agriculture gave them experience in irrigation projects. The railroad lines also opened new areas of mining in many regions, including Deadwood, South Dakota, where, in 1880, there were 221 Chinese mining in the Black Hills.[16] It also paved the way for settlement of northeastern Nevada: Tuscarora in 1869 and Island Mountain in 1873.

Between 1870 and 1880 the Chinese population in Nevada increased dramatically. Virginia City and nearby Gold Hill, Storey County, attracted approximately 736 Chinese who worked in a wide variety of occupations (but none in mining).[17] Local residents estimated the Chinese population at over two thousand at its peak in the 1870s, rivaling San Francisco's Chinese population. Most Chinese worked in the service industry, particularly in restaurants, laundries, and hotels, as well as in the lumber industry. But on the Comstock there was a wide range of occupations such as doctors, dentists, gamblers, prostitutes, painters, masons, and barbers, to name a few. The Chinese provided services to the Chinese and non-Chinese population.[18]

There were few Chinese miners in the census manuscript. In 1880 Ah Jim (age 28) was the only Chinese miner in Storey County. He lived and worked in the vicinity of Six Mile Canyon.[19] Five other Chinese males lived in his household including a 10-year-old boy, Ah You. Early mining towns had a large population of single males who did not like to cook or wash their clothing and who sought recreation in saloons and gambling halls. The Chinese easily found jobs as cooks, laundrymen, and saloon workers.

Chinese servants were "fashionable," so many wealthy, prominent Comstock families had a Chinese servant or cook and some of these servants, especially in the households of political or business leaders, created a network with other Chinese. They shared information about new opportunities, new laws, and current events. For example, Nevada Senator William Sharon (Republican, 1875–81) was a major figure in the development of the Comstock prosperity. His Chinese servant kept in close touch with his cousin, Ah Kim (immigrated 1850), who had settled in Virginia City in 1860 and worked in Colonel John Van Buren's saloon.[20] Upon learning about the new opportunities in Eureka, Nevada, another mining town, both Ah Kim and Van Buren moved there and continued their close relationship until Ah Kim's death in 1881.

In the popular literature of the time, the Chinese were regarded as highly visible in the mining towns and new urban centers because of their distinctive appearance but they were only a small part of the mining population. In 1870, they numbered 3,123 (7.4 percent) with only 228 miners in a total state population of 42,491; in 1880, they numbered 5,416 (8.7 percent) with 343 miners in a total state population of 62,266; and in 1890, they numbered 2,833 (6.0 percent) in a total state population of 47,355.[21] (The number of Chinese miners is unknown because the 1890 census manuscript, stored in Washington, D.C., was destroyed in a fire.) One of the reasons that so few Chinese miners were counted as miners was because the Nevada census takers adopted a strict definition of miners (men working in mines to extract ore) that differed from laborers (those doing menial tasks connect with mining). The 1870 census listed the Chinese under the category of "miners," but by the 1880 census, the census takers refined the category and listed 102 Chinese placer miners, 164 miners, 2 as "in mining," and 73 unaccounted for in the occupational category but included in census summary as miners. There was little uniformity in the collection of data. Often the census takers could not get the information about age, birthplace and date, year of immigration, home ownership, and other data from individual Chinese and apparently preferred to simply omit some of these people if they could not complete the census form.

Table 2. Population of Chinese in United States and Nevada, 1860–2000, including Foreign-born and Citizens, 1900–1940, 1990–2000, and Clark and Washoe Counties, 1950–1990

Year	Total Chinese Population in U.S.	Total Population in Nevada	Chinese Population in Nevada	Percent of Chinese in Nevada	Chinese Males in Nevada	Chinese Females in Nevada	Ratio of Males to Females
1860	34,933	6,057	23	.4	—	—	
1870	63,199	42,491	3,123	7.4	2,817	306	9:1
1880	105,465	62,266	5,416	8.7	5,102	314	16:1
1890	107,488	47,355	2,833	6.0	2,749	84	33:1
1900	89,863	42,335	1,352	3.2	1,283	69	19:1
Foreign-born	80,853						
Citizen	9,010						
1910	71,531	81,875	927	1.1	876	51	17:1
Foreign-born	56,596						
Citizen	14,935						
1920	61,639	77,407	689	0.9	630	59	11:1
Foreign-born	43,107						
Citizen	18,532						
1930	74,954	91,058	483	0.5	410	73	6:1
Foreign-born	44,086						
Citizen	30,868						
1940	77,504	110,247	286	0.3	221	65	3:1
Foreign-born	37,242						
Citizen	40,262						
1950	117,629	160,083	281	0.2	205	76	3:1
Clark			56				
Washoe			82				
1960	237,292	285,278	572	0.2	388	184	2:1
Clark			225				
Washoe			249				
1970	433,469	488,738	951	0.2	567	384	1.5:1
Clark			457				
Washoe			411				
1980	812,178	800,495	2,979	0.4	1,490	1,489	1:1
Clark			1,725				
Washoe			1,089				
1990	1,645,472	1,201,833	6,618	0.5	3,180	3,438	1:1
Foreign	529,837						
Clark			4,185				
Washoe			2,121				
2000	2,432,585	1,998,257	14,113	0.7	N/A	N/A	
Foreign	988,857						

The Chinese settled in northeastern Nevada during and after the construction of the Central Pacific. In 1868 one group surveying the land for the Central Pacific discovered a rich underground spring and stayed there to farm, thus establishing the town later known as Carlin.[22] As a major transportation center with a roundhouse, Carlin attracted forty-nine Chinese, six of whom were women, to reside there by 1870.[23] Additionally, there were fourteen railroad workers, eight cooks, two merchants (Sing Car, age 30, and Loy Joy, age 40), seven laundrymen, eight laborers, and four miners. A decade later the number dropped to forty-six Chinese, including two railroad workers, thirty-six laborers, two clerks (who must be workers for the merchants in the 1870 census), two servants, two laundrymen, one boardinghouse operator, and one prostitute. Carlin remained vibrant, and in 1920 four Chinese merchants, Yee Hah (age 48), Lee Sing (age 54), Yee H. Wah (age 60), and his relative Yee N. Wah (age 49), operated stores there. Carlin was the transportation connection to the mines in Tuscarora, Island Mountain, and other northeastern Nevada mining towns.

In January 1869 the population of the railroad town of Elko, east of Carlin, was 230; one month later it grew to 1,500 because of the anticipated advent of the transcontinental railroad.[24] Elko was the next major train station and ranching center in northeastern Nevada and another important connection to the mines in Tuscarora and Island Mountain. In September 1870, sixteen months after the rail line was completed, Elko had 3,448 residents.[25] Among them were 108 Chinese living in the new town, many of them employed by the railroad as cooks, dishwashers, and laborers. Additionally, in Elko's Chinatown there were the usual restaurant cooks, laundrymen, and prostitutes. A decade later (1890) eighty Chinese, mostly laborers, lived in Elko. By 1900 Elko County boasted a population of 5,688 people with 849 living in Elko; by then, the Chinese population in the city had dropped to thirty-nine.[26] Two Chinese merchants, Yeben Tong (age 44) and Chung Yoon (age 49), remained in Elko because they continued to supply goods to Chinese in the region. Although no merchants were listed in the 1910 census, in 1920 Ny Gin (age 38), who was born and raised in California, owned the only Chinese store in Elko. He exemplified the second generation of Chinese Americans who were reaching their maturity. The census taker neglected to include the owners of the Hi Loy Store but immigration records showed that the store was still operating.

The Chinese merchants in Elko invested in mining and other properties. Some had their purchases officially recorded in the county recorder's office. For example, Hi Loy, a well-known Chinese American merchandising company in Elko whose owner was called Hi Loy (born in 1840 in China), was a partner with eight EuroAmericans in the Merrimac Mining District in Elko County, not far from Tuscarora. In 1887 the group sold the standard claim size of 1500 x 600 feet of mining property to S. G. Weston, who later incorporated all of his mines into the famous Lone Mountain Mining Company.[27] The area was noted for silver, copper, and zinc mining. This provided funds for the ten partners of the Hi Loy store to purchase a building to sell groceries, drugs, and general merchandise, and to rent rooms on the second floor of the store for $3 per month to boarders.[28] Hi (Hy) Loy, as a business firm, had opened in Virginia City in the late 1860s and was accustomed to buying and selling property and having that property officially recorded.[29] If the Elko store was a branch or part of the network, the owner was familiar with the importance of documentation according to American practices.

Most Chinese, however, used the informal, usually unrecorded method of transferring property in the late nineteenth century. The *Elko Independent* (April 18, 1870) noted that "a considerable portion of [the Cope Mining District's Russell and Grasshopper Gulches, which had been extensively worked by EuroAmerican miners] have been sold to Chinamen." But none of these transactions were officially recorded in the county records. Between 1866 and 1876, in the Boise (Idaho) Basin located near the Nevada-Idaho border, the Chinese bought numerous claims ranging from as little as $50 to as much as $10,000, depending on the size and quality of the claim and whether buildings, equipment, and water rights were included.[30] The practice of pooling financial resources occurred in other locations too, most notably Oregon, Idaho, and as far away as New Zealand and Australia.[31] In his doctoral dissertation on Pierce, Idaho, Darby Campbell Stapp discovered that the Chinese began to be very active in purchasing placer mines in the Pierce Mining District between 1866 and 1871, with the average price in 1866 at $744 and in 1867 at $816.[32] Elko County did not have such extensive records but because of its proximity to the Boise Basin, the prices were probably similar.

Like other western regions, water was a major concern and the Chinese worked on several irrigation projects. One of their notable projects provided water for the town of Elko. According to local historian Howard Hickson, the Chinese originally dug the "China Ditch" to water their fields at China Ranch (presently the Elko City Park), which was owned and operated by the merchant, Hi Loy (b. 1840) and his foreman Le Hi.[33] There was a wooden flume from Kittridge Canyon to a small reservoir; later, a nine-mile ditch from Osino to Elko was added to incorporate water from the Humboldt River.

On October 28, 1898, the Hexingtang (Hop Sing Tong), a secret society often using the term "company" on legal documents, sold a one-half interest in the Elko Water Company and Elko Water Works (the water ditch from Osino to the town of Elko and the pipeline from Kittridge to the pipes in Elko) for $1,000.[34] One might assume that Hi Loy (a company name but given to an individual in American documents) was an officer in the Hexingtang, which funded the initial and costly project. Numerous examples of similar irrigation projects were found in other parts of Nevada.

Therefore, it was not surprising that when nearby Tuscarora, a new mining town, needed water, the Chinese were hired and eventually stayed to mine. Located on the southwest side of Independence Valley at an elevation of approximately 6,200 feet, the Tuscarora mining camp was founded in the 1860s. Tuscarora was the highest-producing mining camp in northeastern Nevada prior to 1932.[35] (Placer mining declined by the early twentieth century.) The perennial water for mining, mills, and ranching came from the Tuscarora Mountains to the north, at approximately 8,100 feet high with Mt. Blitzen as the tallest peak, and the Independence Mountains to the south at approximately 10,000 feet high. Water from McCann Creek, part of the Owyhee River complex, was the site of much of the placer gold deposits. The town's proximity to Idaho and use of the Owyhee River led to investments in mining by residents of both states and undocumented migrations back and forth.[36] Mining often was regional as the important rivers and streams crossed state and county lines. Once the Central Pacific Railroad was completed, the main railroad town of Carlin, some twenty-two miles to the southwest, and Elko, fifty-two miles to the southeast, served as the gateways to Tuscarora.

Several accounts describe the founding of Tuscarora. The earliest account, in 1867, states that a group of miners from Austin, Lander County, Nevada, found placer deposits along McCann Creek, as it was later called. The miners met and decided to name the mining camp Tuscarora after a U.S. gunboat because one of the men had served on that gunboat. Another popular account gave credit to Stephen and John Beard for establishing the town in 1869. According Stephen Beard's reminiscences, he was part of a group of prospectors from Austin who arrived in Tuscarora in July 1867 as the result of a tip from a Shoshone named Captain Jim given to trader William Heath who organized the Austin miners.[37] In 1869 the Beard brothers hired two hundred Chinese workers to build a six-mile ditch from McCann Creek to increase the water supply for placer mining. The brothers remained involved with the Chinese and town affairs for many years.

The Chinese population grew rapidly because of the success in mining.

Many of the ditch diggers stayed to mine because the Beards leased them claims for 10 percent of the profits and furnished them with water "at a reasonable rate. . . . [They] flocked hither by hundreds, and in the course of a year extracted many hundreds of thousands of dollars worth of gold dust."[38] EuroAmerican owners of water rights in placer sites sometimes leased the site to the Chinese but charged them a substantial fee for the water, much higher than they charged EuroAmerican miners.[39] Tongue in cheek, the nearby newspaper, the *Daily Silver State* (Winnemucca, Nevada) called them the "Tuscarora Pioneers," whose industriousness led to the discovery of rich gold and silver quartz ledges, but added "Old Chinatown still remains in its primitive dilapidated ugliness and John [the Chinese] proudly claims that he is the 'phonee of Tustalola.'"[40]

On June 18, 1872, the *Los Angeles Times* reported that one-third of the Chinese labor force who built the Central Pacific Railroad went to Tuscarora. According to popular lore, in the 1870s Tuscarora had the second largest Chinatown in Nevada, with a population of 2,000 at its height, thus rivaling Virginia City's Chinatown. If only 5,000 Chinese were employed in railroad construction after the crews reached Reno in 1868–69, then this may well have been true. Roy Primeaux (1885–1969), who grew up in Tuscarora and whose father owned a general store, estimated that there were 2,500 Chinese in the town during the boom years.[41] In reality, the stable Chinese residential population probably numbered around 200. The census report in 1870 showed that Tuscarora had a population of 119, of whom 104 were Chinese and 15 were EuroAmericans.[42] The early large percentage of Chinese in relation to the EuroAmerican population helped shape the growth and development of the town.

According to the *Elko Independent* (April 13, 1870), the community welcomed the Chinese placer miner and ditch construction workers. Without their help, the EuroAmerican placer miners, farmers, and ranchers could not have prospered as quickly. This probably was similar to the initial reaction of EuroAmericans in other mining towns. The Chinese were allowed to work abandoned claims or to lease claims around McCann Creek and reportedly recovered from $2 to $15 per day per man, yielding approximately $700,000 to $7 million between 1869–70.[43] On April 23 and October 22, 1871, the newspaper claimed that the Chinese took out close to a half million dollars in gold that year, and estimated that Tuscarora's Chinese population was between eight hundred and one thousand people. That same newspaper on July 4, 1874, reported that each Chinese miner was making about $6 per day and still getting their water from the Beard brothers at $2.50 per day. For the

Chinese miners, making $3.50 per day was better than the average Chinese worker who was earning an average of $1 per day or $30 per month in other occupations like railroad construction work.

Like many biased writings of the time, local EuroAmerican historians described Chinatown as a place filled with "flimsy residences" and businesses "jammed together, and redolent with all the odors and smells characteristic of such enclaves" so that "when the wind was right, it could be smelled for miles when approaching Tuscarora from the east across Independence Valley."[44] Chinatown was noted for its games of chance, opium dens, and prostitutes, who served both Chinese and EuroAmerican customers. Like many small Chinatowns in rural America, there were rumors of subterranean chambers. But if San Francisco's Chinatown was a model for these, the "basement" rooms in reality were used for cold storage and to preserve fruits and vegetables. Descriptions of Tuscarora's Chinatown resembled writings about San Francisco's Chinatown; the link between the two was the popular literature that supplied the colorful language and perceptions, real or not.

Tuscarora continued to grow but its Chinese population declined in relation to its EuroAmerican population in the 1870s. This change in ratio also resulted in a change in attitude: once the Chinese became a minority, they were treated with disdain. In 1871 another settlement began two miles away: New Tuscarora boomed because of the discovery of a silver lode and as the home of EuroAmerican miners. Like the Comstock, the Chinese were prohibited from working in silver mines; whenever a mine owner attempted to employ them at the mines or mills, a mob emerged to demand their dismissal.[45] The Chinese were allowed to work the placer sites, especially the abandoned ones, but not the profitable silver mines.

The discovery of new mines and the construction of new stamp mills contributed to the mining boom of the early 1870s. The 1875 state census for Tuscarora listed thirty-seven Chinese miners, four merchants (Ah Gow, age 30; Ah Sing, age 25; Ma Song, age 35; and Hung Sing, age 50), fifteen Chinese in unspecified occupations, four laborers (including one woman), two laundry workers who were women, and five men working in the Chinese general stores.[46] The listing may not have been complete. Among these sixty-seven individuals, merchant Ah Gow was the most interesting.

In 1872 Ah Gow's personal property was valued at $400; two years later it had risen to $600.[47] Ah Gow speculated in property by purchasing a lot in nearby Cornucopia with Mong Chung.[48] In 1878 he owned four houses and lots on Front Street in Tuscarora, worth $780, and had personal property valued at $470.[49] By 1882 he had a small house on the east side of Front Street, worth $250; sixty acres of land on McCann Creek, valued at $100; two small businesses on the east side of Front Street adjoining the south side of the Silver Bush Mine, valued at $100; and a house on the west side of Front Street adjoining the gambling house on the south, worth $100. He also owned horses and wagons for a total personal property value of $1,075.[50] He may have been related to another younger man also named Ah Gow (b. 1854), who, in 1880, was a miner in Island Mountain. Ah Gow's story was contrary to the stereotypical image of the Chinese sojourner who did not own property, houses, wagons, and horses. From these statistics, Ah Gow obviously was a prosperous businessman for his time.

By the summer of 1877 the total population of Tuscarora rose to nearly three thousand, making it almost as large as Elko. That year Tuscarora had at least twelve saloons, several boarding houses and hotels, specialty shops, several general merchandising stores, and numerous services, including nine law offices. The saloons were an integral component of the lives of most miners. A band, drama group, social organizations, and church groups provided recreation and social activities for the EuroAmerican residents who anticipated the development of a settled community as families were established. Several stage lines also served the town. Two newspapers began publication in 1877 and then merged into one a year later. The *Tuscarora Times and Mining Review* was not openly hostile to the Chinese and carried stories about crimes committed by and against the Chinese; stories about Chinese associations, women, and festivals; and laudatory articles about some of the Chinese residents, especially merchant Ah Lee Lake. As in many frontier settlements with a Chinatown, the newspaper regularly noted Chinese New Year's celebrations and repeated stories criticizing tales of opium dens and the crimes associated with smoking opium. The newspaper also reported anti-Chinese boycotts and activities in other parts of the state in the 1880s and commented upon the departure of the Chinese in 1886–87 because of the town's economic decline. The few Chinese who remained were well known by the townspeople and a more positive attitude toward them evolved.

The mining boom was in full swing between 1876 and 1886; during this period racial hostility was not evident. The bullion produced in Tuscarora represented a substantial percentage of the county's mineral production, and in 1878 the state mineralogist reported the total shipment valued at $1,212,337.[51]

Mining crews of different ethnicities could be seen working together. A photograph of a multiethnic mining crew showed Chinese, Mexicans, and perhaps EuroAmericans working together, which was not surprising in this location (but would have been in the anti-Chinese communities in California).[52] The local press in 1878 noted what may seem to be an unusual occurrence: Tuscarora had "a Chinaman who talks Spanish like an old Castilian."[53] This may indicate links between the overseas Chinese in countries outside of North America, most likely immigration through Mexico or Latin America. But Chinese speaking other languages could be found in other Nevada towns as well.[54] Undoubtedly this individual assisted the multiethnic work crews and was an example of one of several Chinese who knew Spanish. Additionally, it was not unusual to find in local records for this area Chinese with the first name of Pedro or Felipe, indicating some links to Spanish societies.

Chinese success in mining continued until the turn of the twentieth century. On July 11, 1882, the *Tuscarora Times and Mining Review* carried a story

Multiethnic mining crews in Tuscarora were not uncommon in the late nineteenth century. The mining bosses and prominent members of the community influenced public opinion about Chinese coworkers so the hostility toward them was minimal. (Courtesy of Northeastern Nevada Museum, Elko)

about the Chinese engaged in placer and quartz mining, pointing out that wealthy Chinese in San Francisco assisted their fellow countrymen in developing any enterprise that seemed promising. This may explain the miners' ability to purchase expensive mining equipment. Their gold discoveries often were not reported in the official records since Chinese miners had their own assayers and deposited their gold at the Bank of Canton in San Francisco, Chinese businesses, Wells Fargo, or other institutions at other locations. However, the *Tuscarora Times-Review* (March 26, 1881) noted that even in 1881 it was an unusually favorable season for the Chinese miners, "some of whom have made big white men's wages since the flow of the water [from the Beard brothers] commenced," and estimated that some one hundred Chinese were "busily sluicing" with no EuroAmericans in sight. In 1881 the Chinese also worked a quartz claim in this district; the local press erroneously claimed it was the first occurrence in the state.[55] The Chinese continued to build ditches in the area. During the off-season they hauled sagebrush to the silver mines, caught salmon in the river, and did road work, such as building the road between Carlin and Tuscarora.

The Chinese bought and sold claims, often to other Chinese. One example of such a sale was Hong Sing and Tai Kee of Tuscarora, who transferred mining claims to Quong Hi (company name) of Tuscarora—forty acres of the Black Hawk Mining Claims, also known as the Eureka Gulch Placer Claims, for $120 on March 13, 1886.[56] The sale price included equipment and all mineral rights. Although nothing is known about Hong Sing and Tai Kee, the Quong Hi and Company was very active in Tuscarora in mining and in legal disputes. The owner of the company was known as Quong Hi (since EuroAmericans often did not separate the name of the owner from the name of the business), but his Chinese family name was Tan (Cantonese, Tom). According to the Chinese business partnership records, in 1887 Quong Hi and Company was owned by six members of the Tan family. It was among the largest Chinese stores in Elko County with a valuation of $1,000 in both 1888 and 1890; by 1893 it had dropped to $500.[57] Quong Hi was not hesitant to take matters to court: for example, in 1889 Quong Hi sued Sam Fook Lo for the sum of $123.75 and costs, which was satisfied when the constable of Tuscarora, John Merteer, seized Lo's house, lot #43 on block J, in Tuscarora.[58] In December 1892 the company sued Piedmont Gold and Silver Mining Company and was awarded $144.80 in damages and $22.15 in costs.[59]

In 1894 Quong Hi and Company sold all of its personal property in their brick store to Hom Tong of Tuscarora and had the transfer recorded in the recorder's office.[60] Usually these kinds of transactions were done informally but Hom Tong requested the official filing. In 1899 Quong Hi and Company officially had closed. Based on this evidence, the owners of Quong Hi and Company were active in mining enterprises, knew American laws, and were not hesitant about going to court against EuroAmericans—but also against Chinese, instead of using the Chinese informal tribunal system. This was an important transition as Chinese merchants moved in the direction of following American business practices. The reasons for the failure of the business is not known but may have been due to competition from other Chinese-owned stores in a declining economy. But it also could have been due to the loss of leadership at the top, which was so crucial in a family or extended family business.

The lives of the Chinese in Tuscarora centered around two secret societies that existed there: the Hexingtang in Old Tuscarora and the Zhigongtang ("Active Justice Society") in New Tuscarora. In Old Tuscarora's Chinatown, the Hexingtang headquarters was the main structure and center for social activities. The Hexingtang had possible links to China's Tiandihui (Heaven and Earth Society) and Sanhehui (Triads), secret societies rumored to be connected with illicit activities like opium, gambling, and prostitution in south China and with branches in the American West.[61] The wealth of the Hexingtang in Elko, the closest lodge, was impressive: $8,255 in 1882.[62] Many of the "tong wars" in San Francisco and other locations were fought between the Hexingtang and Zhigongtang historically and into recent times. However, certain individuals could belong to both organizations, especially when the elders strove to achieve harmony in the Chinatown communities and stop the wars. In rural communities, membership probably was limited to one or the other organization.

When New Tuscarora was established in 1871, some of the Chinese moved there and established a Chinatown with a Zhigongtang headquarters. In larger Chinese communities, family and regional associations (*huiguan*) as well as guild organizations played leading roles, but in these small western towns, birthplace, name, and occupation had to yield to other types of bonds, especially those of secret fraternal organizations.[63] The Zhigongtang was originally organized in China in 1674 as an anti-Manchu political secret society and was considered to be related to the Hongmen secret society (although many believed it was an offshoot of the Tiandihui). In the Three Kingdoms period (third century AD), Liu Bei, Guan Yu, and Chang Fei became sworn brothers

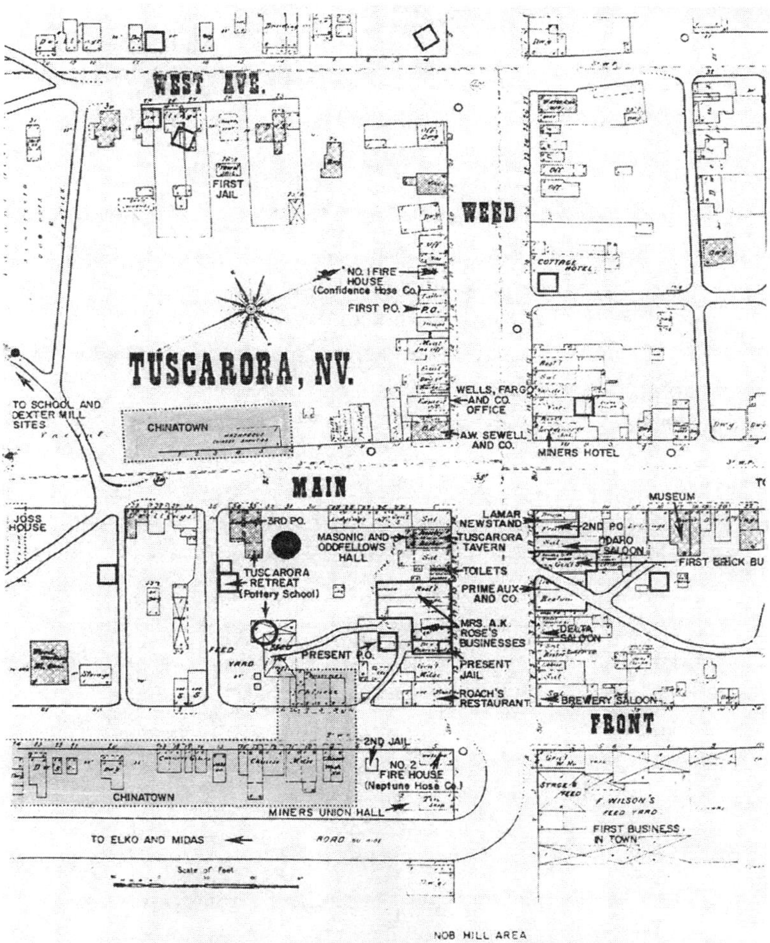

Sanborn map of Tuscarora, 1880, showing old and new Chinatown. Old Chinatown had the Hexingtang lodge on Main Street while New Chinatown had the Zhigongtang lodge on Front Street, as seen in this 1880 Sanborn Fire and Insurance Map.

in the Peach Garden. The idea of blood brothers became popular for dissident or socially marginalized groups throughout the Chinese diaspora.

Taiping rebel Luo Yi has been credited with starting a new American-based organization Zhigongtang in the 1860s with its American headquarter in San Francisco. Like the Hexingtang, other branches were established in many overseas Chinese communities, particularly in mining communities like Marysville, California, and commercial centers like Portland, Oregon. Unlike the colonial governments in Southeast Asia and Hong Kong, the American government decided that the Zhigongtang was not a threat to the United States and allowed it to flourish. By 1900 there were over thirty lodges in the United States. As a Hongmen society, the Zhigongtang was related to the Guangdetang (Cantonese, Kwong Duck Tong), a Siyi organization; the Xiyitang (Hip Yee Tong), a Sanyi organization; and the Danshantang (Tanshan Tong), whose members originated from Zhongshan. It also had connections with the Binggongtang and the Yixingtang (Yee Sing Tang).[64] The primary goal of the Zhigongtang was political: to rid China of the alien Manchu rulers and reestablish Chinese rule in China.

For this reason Chinese revolutionary leader Sun Yatsen sought the political and financial support of the organization and assisted in its reorganization in 1904 to become an integral part of the Chinese revolutionary, anti-Manchu movement. Sun was an active member of secret organizations in China and the brotherhood linked him with these overseas organizations. When Sun appealed to overseas Chinese to establish a republican form of government based on the three principles of democracy, nationalism, and socialism ("people's livelihood," or state capitalism), he found enthusiastic support among Chinese Americans and their secret societies, especially the Zhigongtang. In 1911, Sun raised $20,000 at one gathering from San Francisco's Chinatown; $3,000 from the Chinese in the railroad town of Winnemucca, Nevada; and $200,000 from New York's Chinatown.[65] The donations were substantial considering that the average Chinese was earning only $1 per day. When Sun overthrew the Manchus, he established branches of the Nationalist Party (Guomindang) in overseas Chinese communities that often replaced the earlier fraternal organizations and the power of the secret societies declined. By the 1920s the power of the merchant elite filled the void.

Membership in the Zhigongtang was restricted. In the United States, the organization also was a mutual aid society open to anyone nominated by a member regardless of surname or place of birth. The *Nevada State Journal* (Reno) claimed in 1911 that 90 percent of all Chinese in the United States belonged to the Zhigongtang—but this figure probably was an exaggeration.[66] Nevertheless, it had support from many Chinese Americans and with the dues collected from its membership, the organization could build impressive lodges in various Chinatowns and sponsor elaborate funerals for its local leaders that often were regarded as newsworthy by the local newspapers. Like many of the other organizations, the Zhigongtang also preserved certain Chinese traditions, especially the celebration of Chinese New Year, which occurred on the first day of the lunar calendar (early January to mid-February on the Gregorian calendar). Firecrackers and traditional music marked the celebration that included a festive banquet for members and their friends. Almost every newspaper in towns having a substantial Chinese population in the American West took note of the activities. Unlike the New Year celebration in China where the wives, children, parents, and relatives were an integral part of the festivities, the celebration was modified to accommodate the predominately bachelorlike society.

The Binggongtang, which called itself the "Second Independent Order of Chinese Free Masons," separated from the Zhigongtang in 1874 because, in addition to mutual aid services, its goals included control of local gambling and prostitution along with importation and sale of opium. It was one of the several organizations that allegedly assisted in illegal immigration and the phenomenon of "paper sons, daughters, and wives" that began after the 1882 and 1892 Chinese exclusion acts.[67] The Zhigongtang did not favor these illegal activities but eventually, in the twentieth century, may have participated in some to survive financially. The two organizations were often confused with one another but in reality were very different during these early decades. The Binggongtang flourished in Seattle where it had enough financial support to build an impressive building with stained glass windows on the second floor. The national lodges of both organizations still exist in San Francisco's Chinatown.

Certain clans supported the Zhigongtang and played leadership roles. Based on the nineteenth-century account books of the society found in Barkerville, North Cariboo, British Columbia, the Wu (Ng in Cantonese) clan from Taishan, Guangdong, were active members of the Zhigongtang—and many of the Wu Chinese in Barkerville, British Columbia, were related to one another.[68] It is possible that merchant Lem Hong Ng of Island Mountain also was a member of the Zhigongtang like many of his fellow kinsmen.

With the advent of Tuscarora's EuroAmerican Masonic Lodge in 1878, the Zhigongtang was viewed as the "Chinese Masonic" order because of the similarities in rituals and insignia. The connection had been made in other locations and many Zhigongtang and Binggongtang lodges proudly displayed the English sign "Chinese Free Masons" on their buildings. This may have contributed to the warmer personal relationships between the Chinese and EuroAmerican Masonic leaders and members.

The Zhigongtang's power and prestige rose in the period from the 1880s to 1900s and later declined in the 1920s and 1930s, but still exists today. A

Zhigongtang building in Elko was larger in size and had a bigger membership than the one in Tuscarora.[69] The Elko lodge lasted longer, though; when the Chinese left Tuscarora, the altars were moved from Tuscarora to Elko and eventually was moved to Las Vegas, Nevada. Officers of the Elko lodge undoubtedly visited the Tuscarora lodge and provided an informal networking (*guanxi*) system that was characteristic of traditional Chinese secret societies.

One of the Zhigongtang's rivals for power was the Chinese Consolidated Benevolent Association (CCBA, or Chinese Six Companies), which did not usually establish branches in small rural towns. Although there was a CCBA branch in Virginia City, this probably was due to the large Chinese population there and its proximity to San Francisco, that fostered close financial and organizational ties between the two cities. The transitory nature of mining communities, in general, did not warrant the construction of CCBA branches.

The Zhigongtang built an impressive two-story wooden headquarters on the main street of New Tuscarora with a floor plan and appearance that was similar to other Zhigongtang lodges in other towns in the American West, such as in Monterey and Santa Cruz, California.[70] An earlier building (built

The two-story Zhigongtang lodge in the foreground (right) was the most impressive building in New Tuscarora's New Chinatown. Several Chinese merchandising stores were on Front Street; the Primeaux's store was around the corner on Weed Street. (Courtesy of Northeastern Nevada Museum, Elko)

in 1880 at a cost of $1,800) burned in 1901. Ah Lee Lake, probably with the assistance of the headquarters in San Francisco, volunteered to supply the $3,000 needed for the reconstruction.[71] The editor of *Tuscarora Times-Review* (November 23, 1901) felt that since there was no insurance and Ah Lee Lake was not responsible for the fire, the citizens of the town should help defray the expense through a subscription. This was an unusual act of generosity on the part of the EuroAmerican community. The new building, completed in 1902, was thirty-six feet long and sixteen feet wide.[72] There was no mention of how the new building was financed.

According to general plans for similar organizational buildings, the first floor was a social and recreational center with a kitchen in the rear and lodging available for visiting members. Gambling, story-telling, reading newspapers and magazines, playing musical instruments, and smoking opium were common activities.[73] The second floor was the meeting place of the secret brotherhood with lanterns, altars, and deities. The building and interior were organized in accordance with the principles of *fengshui.* Since carpenters and wood yards were located in San Francisco's Chinatown, some of the ritual items probably were built there. But the deities and some of the more elaborate decorations usually originated from south China and were shipped to San Francisco and then to Tuscarora by rail.

One altar usually featured a statue or a portrait of Guan Yu, who was noted for his loyal and righteous life. Other deities, folklore heroes, supernatural beings, and Chinese ancestors probably were present in statue or pictorial form. The altar was flanked on both sides by traditional fighting weapons, silk lanterns, silk tapestries, colorful triangular silk flags, and silk brocades with a myriad of silver mirrors worked into them, all typical of Zhigongtang lodges. On top of the altar table were items such as flower vases, dishes with fresh fruits such as oranges and apples when in season, divination devices such as *Yijing* (Classic of Changes) sticks, incense, and incense burners for burning "joss sticks." Some of the altar pieces were made of silver and there was a report of "a silver dragon with jeweled teeth and a spring-loaded tail, which moved whenever anyone propelled it across the temple floor."[74] EuroAmericans often called the building a "joss house," which comes from the Portuguese word *deos* ("deity") because of the worship of deities that took place. Musical instruments also were stored on the second floor for ceremonial and recreational use and the local "Chinese band" played the instruments to welcome the returning victorious Tuscarora school teams. Auspicious sayings written on silk or special paper probably decorated the walls.

One wall displayed the thirty-six oaths and twenty-one regulations of the

In the 1950s Tuscarora's Zhigongtang Altar was moved to Las Vegas. It is pictured here at the tourist attraction called Frontier Village. An image of Guan Yu, the God of War and Literature, is above the intricately carved and gold-leafed altar decoration showing segments of the story of the Three Kingdoms. A pair of embroidered silk fans flank the altar and a bowl of *yijing* or fortune telling sticks, is in the foreground. Parts of the altar were donated to the Nevada State Museum, Las Vegas. (Courtesy of Nevada State Museum, Las Vegas)

Zhigongtang that were recited by the members. The opening resolution read, "We vow to re-establish our Han [Chinese] nation . . . at this ancestral tablet. . . . We shall remember the 128 martyrs of the Shaolin Temple [whom the Manchu imperial army massacred when they took over China]."[75] Twenty-four rules concerned fiscal policies and revenues, duties of members, and the settlement of disputes.[76] The seventh oath and third regulation forbade members from revealing the organization's secrets to outsiders on the penalty of death. Social rules forbade coveting another's wife. The second set of nine rules concerned mining, including the size of a mine allotted to each person and the punishments for violations of rules. Additional regulations were spelled out on a variety of topics. These were faithfully recited during official meetings.

Nationally, both the Hexingtang and Zhigongtang grew in power, influence, and membership in the 1890s and 1900s partially because of the anticipated success of the 1911 republican revolution in China, the pressure placed on joining one of the organizations for mutual aid, and the lack of protection afforded the Chinese by the local community's law enforcement agencies. The two leaders of the Tuscarora Chinese community and respective heads of the Hexingtang and Zhigongtang were Hop Lee and Ah Lee Lake.

Hop Lee (b. 1842), a married man living apart from his wife, was twenty-three years older than Ah Lee Lake. In the 1870s Hop Lee owned the Hop Sing (Hexing) general merchandising store that provided supplies to the local population, as well as a house and lot opposite the store on Front Street, valued at $400. In 1878, his personal property was valued at $500.[77] This showed an increase from 1877 when tax records indicated his worth at $300 for real estate and $250 for personal property.[78] Hop Lee's personal property rose from $1,050 in 1880 to $1,800 in 1881 as Tuscarora's mining boomed.[79] Part of his increasing prosperity may have been related to the financial resources available to him from the Elko branch of the Hexingtang. In 1880 Hop Lee lived with his clerk, Lee Ling (age 19) and a young gambler, Hin Bin (age 17), who were both single. During this era it was common for store employees to live with their boss and thus an "employment family" was created since there were no wives and children living with them. By the mid-1880s Hop Lee went bankrupt, could not tap any pooled resources, and eventually moved to Winnemucca, Nevada, where he owned a store and additional property. (One of the effects of the 1882 Chinese Exclusion Act was the declining number of Chinese customers with whom merchants could do business and members in fraternal organizations.)[80] In contrast, Ah Lee Lake, who found living in Tuscarora to his liking and was able to earn money, continued to remain in town until after 1910.

Ah Lee Lake was born in 1855 in China and immigrated in 1869, suggesting that he had worked on the construction of the Central Pacific and was among the thousands released from railroad construction in April or May 1869. He probably followed relatives or friends into mining and to Tuscarora.

Dressed in a traditional silk robe around 1880, Ah Lee Lake was Tuscarora Chinatown's community leader, merchant, labor contractor, and long-time resident. (Courtesy of Northeastern Nevada Museum, Elko)

He was married, but the census manuscript does not list a wife living with him, so undoubtedly she remained in China as many Chinese wives of this generation did (because of Chinese tradition and the Page Act of 1875 that discouraged Chinese women from immigrating.)[81] Or, because his visits to San Francisco were occasionally noted in the local press, she may have lived in San Francisco's Chinatown where life for a Chinese woman was safer and more comfortable.

In the early 1880s he established a store called the Ah Lake Company and had personal property valued at $100 according to the county assessor.[82] In comparison, in 1883 merchant Lem Hong Ng of Island Mountain had a valuation of $200; Quong Hi and Company of Tuscarora, $800; and Sam Wah Company of Tuscarora, $1,490 (including three houses, several lots, merchandise, six horses, and three wagons).[83] The wealth and prosperity of the merchants varied according to mining situation, but it is notable that Ah Lee Lake was at this time a relatively young man at age 25.

In 1888 Ah Lee Lake was a partner in the general merchandising firm of Quong Hing Lung and Company, a labor recruiter and contractor, and intermediary between the Chinese and EuroAmerican community.[84] The store carried teas, groceries, liquors, and "fancy goods" for Chinese and EuroAmerican customers in the town and in the general area. At first Quong Hing Lung and Company was not as prosperous as Quong Hi and Company. According to county tax records, Quong Hing Lung had a personal property valued at $700 and $1,400 in 1888 and 1890 respectively, but by 1893 the company had become the most important Chinese general store in town with a valuation of $1,000 compared to Quong Hi's $500.[85] By 1899 Quong Hi had closed and Quong Hing Lung's assessed value had dropped to $500, bringing it closer to Lem Hong Ng's store in Island Mountain (valued at $300), but rose again to $1,000 in 1900.[86] These fluctuations were related to Tuscarora's economy.

According to the Chinese business records kept by the U.S. Department of Treasury and now part of the INS records, in 1895 Ah Lee Lake operated a general store with his partners Guing Lee, Fook Chin, and Wing Yuen Chin (also known as Wing Goon Ching).[87] When the Department of Treasury's Bureau of Immigration needed support letters about the reputation of the business, S. Davis of Wells Fargo; Logan Ervin, a merchant; Robert Johnson, a hardware merchant; Fred Wilson, Stage Line president; C. Watkins, deputy sheriff; and J. Meteer, sheriff, all sent in letters of support.[88] Typically, Chinese merchants who dealt with the larger community realized that it was to their advantage to know prominent EuroAmericans (especially the sheriff) who could intercede on their behalf in legal matters because the American government officials placed a higher value on testimony from EuroAmerican community leaders than from anyone in the Chinese community.[89]

According to the 1900 census manuscript, Ah Lee Lake lived in a house with his five partners: Fun Louie (b. 1851) who had been married for forty-one years and immigrated in 1885; Wing Goon Ching (b. 1862) who had been married for 28 years and immigrated in 1882; Lung Lee (b. 1864) who had been married for thirty-five years and immigrated in 1882; Fook Chin (b. 1861) who had been married for thirty-nine years and immigrated in 1881; and Hoy Lee (b. 1864), who had been married for thirty-six years and immigrated in 1882.[90] All of the men lived separately from their wives, who probably remained in China. They also immigrated around the same time, suggesting chain migration. Each of these merchants could read, write, and speak English, therefore they could interact with the EuroAmerican community. That they were in their thirties and early forties meant that they were all in the same generation, and the Lees were probably related to Ah Lee Lake while the Chins may have been in-laws or from the same village in China. The expansion of the partnership from the three in 1895 to six members in 1900 allowed the company to survive the economic downturn in Tuscarora at this time by pooling their funds.

Ah Lee Lake had community responsibilities. According to county tax records he was one of the wealthiest Chinese in Elko County and therefore ranked close to Lem Hong Ng of Island Mountain. Like many Chinese merchants throughout the state, he paid the annual $4 per person poll tax for himself and others.[91] Undoubtedly he was an important intermediary between the Chinese and EuroAmericans. Numerous documents in the Elko County Recorder's Office, including the Death Books, contain his signature, which was very good in both English and Chinese.[92] His Chinese calligraphy indicated that he probably had a good basic traditional Chinese education. In some of these government records, Ah Lee Lake's name has been misinterpreted as Lee Gee instead of the correct version of Li Li (pinyin, based on his Chinese signature).[93] There is neither a record of his permanent return to China nor of his death in the United States, so his fate remains unknown. But he was one of the "old-time" residents and leaders of Tuscarora and still lived there in 1910.

Ah Lee Lake was also one of the rare Chinese individuals who merited the attention of the local newspaper. One day in 1886 he was robbed of $600 in gold coin, $600 worth of jewelry, and other items.[94] (This was an indication of his economic success.) Another news story told about the "Bomb Day" celebration in February 1890. The Chinese celebrated the birthday of Bok

Kai (also spelled Bok Eye, "Water Deity") on the second day of the second month of the Chinese lunar year. Members of the Zhigongtang brought this tradition from China and newspaper stories carried reports of the activities in Evanston, Wyoming; Marysville, California; and numerous other western towns. It was called "Bomb Day" because twenty rockets, some filled with candy, fruit cakes, nuts, coconut candy, little prizes, and other "gifts" were fired.[95] One bomb had a good fortune ring with the number four—the person who got that ring became the ceremonial leader of the community. The newspaper reported that Ah Lee Lake won over the manager of Quong Hi.

When he claimed his position Ah Lee Lake was dressed in a robe of midnight silk embroidered in red, blue, and green, decorated with silver dragons, exotic birds, and delicate flowers. He has also been photographed in an ermine-lined silk robe that undoubtedly kept him warm during the cold winter months.[96] Although he had traditional, expensive Chinese outfits, he also wore western clothing, one indication of adapting to the American lifestyle. The local newspaper reported that he visited China twice, once in 1891 and again in 1897, the latter lasting ten months.[97] The purpose of his visits was not given, but undoubtedly he visited his family and made arrangements for the purchase and shipping of goods. While he was in China, his partners managed the store. Ah Lee Lake visited San Francisco's Chinatown frequently, probably to buy goods and keep up his networking system. (He even traveled by train to New York.) In 1903 the newspaper reported that while in San Francisco, he entertained a group of "American Tuscarora friends at a theatre party."[98] He was known for bringing gifts to community leaders when he returned from his travels, including a very expensive gift for the postmaster.

Fragmentary information gave more insight about him. He was a good friend of the Antoine Primeaux family (French-Canadians who owned one of Tuscarora's three main EuroAmerican general merchandising stores). They lived across the street from each other.[99] The *Tuscarora Times Review* (September 30, 1897) commented, "Lake has many friends among our residents, gained by scrupulous honesty and liberality rare among the people of his race." On March 21, 1903, the newspaper stated "[He is] a rare specimen of a 'white' celestial, and . . . numbers his white friends, of both sexes." This was an interesting commentary on the leader of a minority group.

As was true elsewhere in Nevada, the Chinese did not just own mining claims. The Chinese placed a high value on land ownership. Elko County records showed that the Chinese bought and sold property, some of which was located elsewhere in the state. In 1869 Mon Chung paid county taxes on his house and lot in Carlin, valued at $60, but lived and worked in Tuscarora while Sing Saw had a house opposite Billings Stables in Elko, valued at $100.[100] For comparison, Suig (or Sung) Lee's house and lot and Ahe's house in Mountain City in 1872 each were valued at $100 for tax purposes—the same as Ah Gow's house in Tuscaroa.[101] Quong Yuen and Company owned two houses and one lot in Tuscarora at the rear of Pat Leonaides's saloon and one house in Cornucopia, valued at $300 for the real estate and $450 for personal assets in 1877.[102] Sing Hung (on the tax rolls as Hing Hong) owned a house and lot on Weed Street, not far from the Tuscarora Kethridge Livery Stable, valued at $200 and personal property at $200. These individuals and business owners probably constituted the Chinese American middle class in Tuscarora and Elko County because they had sufficient funds to invest in property.

Based upon photographs and remains of the Chinatown houses, residences there were small; made of adobe bricks, wood, or metal siding; and had metal roofs. The lumber might have been shipped from the wood yards in San Francisco's Chinatown.[103] Lumber was scarce in this part of Nevada, so they used whatever was available and inexpensive. The structures were similar to others found in transient mining communities and Chinatowns throughout the American West. None of these other property owners, however, made it into any of the census manuscripts so little is known about them. In all likelihood, the census taker assigned them names that were different from those in the Elko County Recorder's Office.

By 1880 the Chinese had become a minority in Tuscarora, but some had moved to nearby mining towns. The 1880 census recorded 224 Chinese living in Tuscarora (total population was 1,634). Elko County that year had 639 Chinese, so Tuscarora represented roughly one-third of the county's Chinese population. In addition to Hop Lee and Ah Lee Lake, there were a few other prominent Chinese merchants in the town: Suig Hung (age 33) owned a general store and his clerk, Go Sing (single, age 40) lived with two married men, Ah Gee (age 38), a cook, and Ock Tip (age 32), a gambler.[104] Two men, Ah Tee (age 33) and Leung Yeung (age 40), owned grocery stores. These men were, in general, in their thirties and probably could have continued doing business in Tuscarora for another decade or two. Otherwise not much is known about them.

The 1880 census enumerated others in Tuscarora. There were five miners: Lem Tung (single, age 30), Ah Fow (single, age 23), Chow Ah (single, age 30), Hing (married, age 22), and Mann Ah (single, age 30). Most of the Chinese were cooks (45), wood choppers (25), laundrymen (20), gamblers (14), and servants (11) but fifty, including three young women in their early twenties, were listed without any occupation.[105] Hi Loy (single, age 60) was in the latter category and may have been the entrepreneur from Elko. The large number of wood choppers was due to the fact that Tuscarora, like Cornucopia, used sagebrush to fuel the steam-powered hoisting-and-pumping systems at the mines. Although only twenty-five men were listed in the census in this occupation, the popular belief expressed in the local literature was that five hundred Chinese were collecting sagebrush for this purpose.

Two Tuscarora Chinese assayers, who had learned their trade from EuroAmericans, kept the Chinese mining successes confidential. EuroAmericans frequently complained that they did not know how much gold the Chinese found. Chinese miners traditionally sent their gold and other wealth to San Francisco through the Bank of Canton or Wells Fargo.

Medical care also was very important. In the 1880s Tuscarora still had two Chinese doctors. Doctor Frea (b. 1832, and single) lived with the miner Hing. The other was Long Yut or "Dr. Jet" (b. 1817) who, according to the 1880 census manuscript, could not read and write English. Dr. Jet was quite popular and was known as "the pioneer Chinese medicine man of Mountain City, Cornucopia, and Tuscarora."[106] To practice medicine in Nevada, one had to have a medical diploma, so Hong Lee (China Lem), from Island Mountain, signed a translation of the medical diploma for Leong or Long Yut of Tuscarora for the Elko County Recorder's Office in 1876. The translation read:

> This certifies that Long Yut has attended a medical school in the city of Canton in the Empire of China for a period of ten years, that on account of his learning and ability in the profession of medicine and surgery, taught to said Lung Yut at said medical school, the degree of Doctor of Medicine has been conferred upon him by the faculty of said institute of learning. Dated 12th day of July A.D. 1876 by Chas. Ak Chow, teacher in said school of medicine and surgery.
> Signed: Hong Lee[107]

This document demonstrated the link between China Lem and Dr. Jet and served as a connection between the two communities of Tuscarora and Island Mountain.

These physicians were important to the well-being of the Chinese residents and, like the other Chinese doctors in Nevada and elsewhere, they treated EuroAmerican patients. Between 1860 and 1900 approximately 57 Chinese doctors were practicing in Nevada compared to 633 EuroAmerican civilian doctors.[108] The efficacy of Chinese medicine was praised and received

EuroAmerican testimonials in numerous Nevada newspapers. For example, the *Gold Hill News* (Gold Hill, Nevada) on January 31, 1866, reported how a Virginia City Chinese doctor had been summoned after "the best medical talent" had failed to treat a EuroAmerican miner suffering from a paralytic stroke and had successfully treated the patient so that he regained his sight and partial use of his arm and leg. Chinese doctors believed their practices were rooted in several thousand years of practical experience, beginning with the *Yellow Emperor's Classic of Medicine* (*Huangdi Neijing,* third millennium BC) as well as the numerous compilations on medicine and pharmacopeias written in the Qing dynasty. For this reason they also believed that their methods were more effective than western medicine, which was in its infancy and relied on practices like the use of leeches for bloodletting. By the time Doc Ing Hay was practicing in John Day, Oregon, Chinese medicine had established a good reputation, especially among people who had little access to western medicine or who believed that Chinese medicine was more effective.

Medical care was essential since western hospitals and doctors usually refused to treat Chinese patients. When the Central Pacific's Chinese construction and maintenance crews were in Elko, they discovered that they could not be admitted to the Elko County Hospital (built in 1869) on the basis that they were not citizens, so the Chinese raised funds to build a two-ward Chinese hospital in 1873 and hired Dr. Ken Fung, a graduate of the School of Medicine and Surgery in Guangzhou, to serve as the first resident doctor of the hospital.[109] Elko's Chinese hospital admitted EuroAmerican patients. When the discrimination policy at the county hospital stopped, the Chinese hospital closed its doors and the Chinese and lower-class EuroAmericans went to the public hospital.

Many Chinese left China with knowledge of basic folk remedies for illnesses or purchased basic self-help books like the *Golden Mirror of Medicine* (cost: $2.25), but the Chinese doctor provided more sophisticated care.[110] In addition to importing Chinese medicines, the Chinese doctors also relied upon harvesting plants originally from China that were grown in the American West, such as *hyoscyamus niger,* or "stinking nightshade," used as an antispasmodic remedy and cure for toothaches, earaches, and rheumatism. (The odor of the fresh plant allegedly drove off rats too.)[111] Another plant from China was the *ailanthus atissima,* or "Tree of Heaven," which was planted in many mining communities and had many health benefits. Its roots relieved indigestion and constipation and its wood was suitable for fuel and light carpentry work. Its leaves were used as adjuvants, or modifiers, for other drugs.[112] Occasionally Chinese doctors also shared information with Native

Americans who used the same or similar herbs and plants to cure illnesses. Like many Chinese physicians or herbal doctors, Native Americans treated the non-Chinese population as well. With the departure of the two physicians, the Chinese community in and around Tuscarora and Island Mountain were left without a Chinese doctor. The possibility of getting a replacement was very difficult since the 1892 Geary Act re-classified Chinese doctors as laborers and thus prohibited them from immigrating to the United States. Although a EuroAmerican physician practiced briefly in Tuscarora, the closest doctors often were in Elko, Salt Lake City, or Boise.

According to the local press, Dr. Jet left Tuscarora in 1885 to return to China partly because of his opium addiction. (Dr. Jet's addiction probably began because of his need for a pain suppressant.)[113] Opium had long been a staple medicinal product in the East and West before 1840. In 1729 the emperor of China tried to ban the importation of opium for smoking because of its addictive nature. The Opium War (1839–42), which took place in Guangdong, was fought over the issue of whether the British and other foreigners could continue to import and sell opium in China.[114] The Chinese lost the war against Britain and as a result, the sale and distribution of opium became widespread in China, particularly Guangdong. Chewing opium, a much older practice dating back to the ninth century, had no addictive properties but smoking it led to addiction. A small amount could be used to lessen the pain from the hard physical labor of miners and railroad workers. In Dr. Jet's case, it gave him relief from arthritis and other ailments related to aging. This was its primary use.

Historians and archaeologists often believed that the smoking of opium was widespread among the Chinese in the American West. Several studies demonstrated that this was not true. The number of Chinese who were arrested and incarcerated in the Nevada state prison between 1865 and 1904 showed that of the 1,727 (1 percent of the prison's eighty-nine-year population) Chinese in prison, only seventeen were there for violations of the opium law.[115] In Storey County, which included the Comstock's famous Virginia City Chinatown and its opium dens, only fourteen Chinese (17 percent of all arrested) were charged with violations of the opium law between 1877 and 1890, but only eleven Chinese were found guilty and had to serve jail time and/or pay a fine.[116] The number should have been higher if so many were addicts. Archaeological digs of railroad and mining camps in Nevada and elsewhere produced many fragments of opium bowls and pipes. At one railroad site near Carson City, the Chinese camp showed an obvious physical separation between those who smoked opium and those who did not.[117] Twelve of the thirteen Chinese skeletons found buried in Carlin, Nevada in 1996, showed bone fractures, some of a serious nature—their pain undoubtedly was alleviated by opium or some type of opiate.[118] Only one was a heavy smoker; six were light smokers or probable smokers based on denture examinations. These men could have been tobacco or opium smokers. The Chinese knew that usage had to be judicious and that there was the possibility of addiction.

Recreational smoking became popular among the Chinese and EuroAmericans. When the smoking of opium spread to EuroAmerican youths who visited the opium dens of the various Chinatowns, the EuroAmerican anti-opium campaign began. In the mid-nineteenth century the outcry against opium smoking and alcohol became more virulent. By 1876 there were attacks in the newspapers against opium smoking and its "contamination of white people" because "John Chinaman" had brought his vices with him.[119] In 1874 and 1875 San Francisco passed local bans on the smoking of opium and on the operation of opium dens. Other cities and towns followed San Francisco's lead. States also passed laws against opium. In 1877 the Nevada Legislature restricted opium to medical use by prescription from a legally practicing physician distributed through druggists and apothecaries and made it illegal to smoke or possess an opium pipe.[120] Imprisonment and fines for the sale and use of opium were added in 1879 and the police moved in quickly to close the Chinese opium dens.[121] Oregon passed similar legislation in November 1885; during the next two years at least four Chinese served time in the state penitentiary for "frequenting an opium den" or "unlawful selling and giving away of opium."[122]

The anti-opium laws were directed primarily against the Chinese. Law enforcement agents in Nevada liked to trick Chinese into selling small medicinal amounts of opium to Native Americans so that the Chinese seller could be arrested.[123] The Native Americans were rewarded with bottles of liquor. In 1883 a federal tariff was placed on the importation of smoking (not medicinal) opium and in 1887 there was a federal prohibition on the Chinese importation of smoking opium. In 1890 the government passed a tax on opium. In 1909 the federal ban on the importation of all opium for nonmedical purposes became law. In 1914 the Harrison Narcotics Tax Act (Ch. 1, 38 Stat. 785), the first major narcotics law, was passed to control the importation and distribution of opiates and eventually led to the arrests of Chinese opium dealers. In 1924 the U.S. Treasury Department Narcotics Division (the first federal drug agency) banned all legal narcotics sales. The result was the beginning of the widespread practice of the illicit drug trade. But by the time opium distribution and smoking were illegal, many of the Chinese miners had passed from the scene. In the early twentieth century addicts were the primary clients who got their supplies from the secret societies or merchants who hid the illegal opium in goods imported from China.

The Chinatowns were large enough to attract Chinese from surrounding areas to visit during their holidays and recreation days. Chinatowns had gambling, opium dens, and prostitutes who entertained the Chinese and non-Chinese alike. As a general rule, those involved in these activities moved around and often set up temporarily in local boarding houses or other structures having sufficient space. One anonymous informant said that his grandfather told him the railroad company had train cars devoted to these types of entertainment that were available on pay days.

During the height of the regional and national trend of anti-Chinese movements, the racism that occurred in Tuscarora could be considered relatively moderate. Hostility over job opportunities took place in 1878 when the EuroAmerican sagebrush gatherers attacked the Chinese with weapons, thus setting a precedent for later mob action.[124] Nevertheless, the Chinese remained in this occupation: the 1880 census manuscript listed twenty-five Chinese woodchoppers, whose work was critical providing the fuel for the stamp mills. There were alleged conflicts between Native American and Chinese woodchoppers, but these incidents did not merit attention in the local press. In July 1883 a EuroAmerican mob in Tuscarora forced the dismissal of Chinese workers in the silver mines.[125] In keeping with the complaints from the growing labor unions, the issues were a shortage of jobs for EuroAmericans and the low wages paid to the Chinese. Generally, the Chinese were relegated to more menial tasks that EuroAmericans did not want to do.

By the late 1880s, as anti-Chinese societies and labor unions grew in the region and articles in the local newspapers reported such activities as the boycotting Chinese businesses, tensions between the Chinese and EuroAmericans increased. Numerous minor incidents occurred. For example, in 1886 in an effort to drive out the Chinese laundry, EuroAmericans attempted to boycott the laundry and replace it with one under EuroAmerican ownership.[126] As in other locations, loyal patrons thwarted the attempt. In many neighboring towns signs appeared in restaurants saying "No John's fixings here," or "No Chinaman working here." EuroAmericans were encouraged to patronize businesses that had no connections with the Chinese.

The anti-Chinese movement even penetrated the local drama club. In 1886 the members of the club, which performed in nearby towns as well, presented "Nevada," a play about a typical mining camp. Win Kye, a "Chinaman," was one of the characters and was depicted as a person who could not be trusted and had to be carefully watched. Eventually Jube, a "darky miner," drove Win Kye out of the camp. Nevada did not have a large African American population at this time so the few who lived in Nevada often sided with EuroAmericans against the Chinese.[127]

(Although the Tuscarora drama club performed in Island Mountain, there was no mention in the local newspapers that this particular play was ever performed there.)

By publicizing anti-Chinese activities elsewhere, the local press played a role in intensifying hostility toward the Chinese and, by 1877, persuaded the majority of the population to join the movement. The atmosphere was not as friendly as that in Island Mountain, Nevada, or Hite Cove, California, where the primary EuroAmerican mine owners hired Chinese workers and established a friendlier attitude toward the Chinese, as will be demonstrated in chapter 4.

There were a number of Chinese women in Tuscarora compared with the only single woman recorded in Island Mountain in 1880. Like elsewhere in American Chinatowns, EuroAmericans regarded most of the women as prostitutes. As Michelle Lettieri demonstrated in her study, EuroAmerican missionaries contributed to the stereotype of single Chinese women as prostitutes and census takers regarded all but the first wife as prostitutes.[128] The Chinese tradition of several wives and concubines offended EuroAmerican Christians. Between 1850 and 1910 the number of Chinese men greatly exceeded that of Chinese women in the United States. The Page Act of 1875 and other exclusionary laws made it difficult for Chinese women to immigrate.[129] Moreover, Chinese tradition required women to care for their in-laws, especially when their husbands were overseas.

Of the thirty-nine Chinese women living in Elko County in 1880, twenty resided in Tuscarora; eight were married and living with their husbands; two were married and heads of the household: Ah Homo had a 5-year old son—the only Chinese child in the 1880 census manuscript—and lived with her single 23-year-old sister, while Gun Ho had two Chinese single female boarders living with her.[130] Ten women were single and seventeen women, some of whom may have been prostitutes, did not state an occupation. Elko County in 1880 had six Chinese prostitutes; one, Ah Hee (age 25), lived in Island Mountain. This differs from the 1870 statewide census when census takers often labeled Chinese women as prostitutes, harlots, or whores, thus lending credence to the need to pass the Page law banning prostitutes from immigrating to the United States. Because of the proximity to Island Mountain, it would not be surprising if the prostitutes of Tuscarora visited Island Mountain on a regular basis or the Chinese men of Island Mountain visited Tuscarora whenever they could. Several of the single women lived in small groups of two or three. The ages of the women ranged from sixteen to forty-eight.

Information about Chinese women was limited. Census takers had a difficult time finding and counting Chinese women because of the Chinese tradition that females remain cloistered in the home. Chinese women also did not like the difficulties of living in American mining towns where they had little or no support or contact with other Chinese women. Most Chinese women could not speak or understand much English and were further isolated if they did not speak or understand the Chinese dialect of their husbands. The local newspaper reported several stories about Chinese prostitutes, but none of the women mentioned matched the names of the women, single or married, in the data from different census years.

Usually stories in the local press about Chinese prostitutes involved disagreements over the ownership of a prostitute, their opium addiction, or death. For example, the *Tuscarora Times and Mining Review* (April 16 and June 3, 1884) related the story of "China Pete," a prostitute who worked in Hong Gee's brothel. The story also revealed part of the inner workings of the community. Hong Gee sold China Pete to a man in Sacramento for $950. But her lover, China Jim, discovered the transaction, killed Hong Gee, and was wounded in the process. During the investigation, it was revealed that in 1877 Hong Gee used China Pete as collateral to Hop Lee, the Hexingtang leader and merchant, who subsequently went bankrupt. In 1882 China Jim advanced Hop Lee the money for China Pete and therefore claimed to be her owner. (The newspaper used the story as a commentary directed to U.S. senators advocating Chinese immigration in order to show them that Chinese women were a "degraded specimen of female humanity.")

Before the matter could be brought before the district court, the Chinese "tribunal," headed by Chinese community leaders, heard the case and decided that China Pete had to go to Sacramento to her new owner; that China Jim had to relinquish her but would not be prosecuted for the death of Hong Gee; and that Ah Wee, who had beaten China Pete for refusing to go to Sacramento, was cleared of all charges. The Chinese felt that since they came from the same region in China and had the same values, the redress of grievances and the restoration of harmony (the latter being an important Confucian concept) were internal community decisions.[131] Western lawmakers often accepted the decisions of Chinese "tribunals" that functioned like the informal court system in China so that problems involving only the Chinese could be solved within their own community. This also meant that the local sheriff did not have to become involved in matters concerning the Chinese.

Unlike the Virginia City newspapers, Chinese marriages in Tuscarora did not make the news. According to county records, the earliest official marriage that took place in Tuscarora was between Sam Chung and Annie Youck on December 12, 1879. When Pong Sing married Ti Toy on February 10, 1880, the Episcopal minister J. W. Pendleton performed the ceremony before Charles Abbot and E. R. Baynton. A small group of close friends attended the wedding. What is significant about the latter marriage is that these two individuals had adopted Christianity and had a western religious ceremony. When Justice of the Peace W. S. Hillman married Chuck Hop to Ah Cook on March 8, 1888; J. Young to Ah Lin on March 10, 1888; Lee Sung to Ty You on March 12, 1888; Loock Ten to Hong You on September 8, 1888; and Lee You Hover to Loye Howe on November 10, 1891, all of the couples had EuroAmerican witnesses but their marriages did not merit mention in the local newspapers.[132] The individuals were not listed in the census manuscripts so there is no additional information about them. This suggests that there were more women in Tuscarora and Elko County than the census taker enumerated.

The birth of Chinese children also was not reported in the newspaper. In the mining town of Tonopah, Nevada, in the same time period, the newspapers often noted the birth of Chinese Americans. The County's *Book of Records* listed two female children, Mildred Chin (b. July 18, 1913) and Mabel Chin (b. January 11, 1915), born to On Chin, a cook who was born in California in 1879, and his wife How or Tom Shee.[133] The couple had three more children after Mabel was born. The parents were concerned about the education of their children and were probably pleased to learn that the state school superintendent felt that Chinese children had the same right to attend public school as everyone else.[134] The family, however, eventually relocated outside of Nevada by 1920.

As elsewhere in the state mining became more technologically advanced in the 1880s. By 1884 there was a 1,000-foot wooden flume for a hydraulic monitor in Tuscarora's Eagle Ravine and sluices were used in the other gulches for placer mining.[135] The equipment was purchased from San Francisco. Hydraulic mining extended the mining season by at least one month or more so that the *Tuscarora Times and Mining Review* (July 23, 1884) reported that the Chinese had "done unusually well." The Chinese usually used a Little Giant, the most advanced nozzle of the day that allowed mining of low-grade sites. Hydraulic mining had been halted in California in 1884 because the destructive force of the water broke down gravel banks and leveled mountains.[136] (This kind of environmental concern did not spread to Nevada and other neighboring states until years later.) Hydraulic mining was dangerous: for example, the *San Francisco Bulletin* (July 27, 1881) reported the deaths of Chinese miners due to the mishandling of hydraulic equipment.

Mining successes contributed to merchant success, so several Chinese stores in Tuscarora's Chinatown also prospered. The earliest "old-time" merchant (about whom little is known) was Ti Kee who, in 1884 after the decline in placer mining, decided to leave for New York City where he planned to open a tea store.[137] But some companies persisted: Yuen Chong Lung (owned by four members of the Louis clan and Fong Din Look) and Quong Sing and Company (owned by four members of the Lee clan) were among them.[138] The Sam Wah Company, flourishing in the 1880s, owned buildings, houses, horses (varying in number from four to eight), and wagons.[139] The decline of mining resulted in a transition into other occupations and lifestyles.

By 1885 the Chinese built a ditch that began west of Beard Hill on McCann Creek to south of Battle Mountain before reaching Old Tuscarora and passing four Chinese placer camps.[140] The local newspaper reported that by the end of the 1885 season the Chinese had taken out over $30,000 worth of gold.[141] At its zenith, Tuscarora had more than five thousand people of many ethnicities and sent to San Francisco an average of $500,000 per month in gold and silver for a considerable period.[142] Beginning in 1884, the price of silver was less than the production costs so by 1891 Tuscarora's population dropped to between twenty-five hundred and three thousand as the gold was depleted and the profits became smaller. Chinese mining companies gave way to more independent miners. The ever-present dangers of mining were becoming more apparent. For example, in 1892 Ah Way, an independent miner, was sluicing in the Eureka Gulch just west of town when a cave-in occurred; he was killed instantly.[143] Many members of the community searched for him that evening but his body was not recovered until the next morning.

At the turn of the twentieth century, Tuscarora began to decline. Unfortunately the destruction by fire and water of the 1890 census manuscript left a great gap in tracing individuals. The *Compendium of the Eleventh Census: 1890* reported a total of 1,080 residents in Tuscarora and a Chinese population of 311.[144] By 1897 only one thousand people lived in Tuscarora. Many of the residents had moved to Idaho. Around 1900 the two pioneer ditches that the Chinese constructed, the McCann Creek Ditch and Three Mile Creek with its extension to the Six Mile Creek Ditch, were abandoned and local ranchers acquired the water rights.[145] Placer mining yielded meager results but since the Chinese had taken about $1 million in gold between 1870 to 1900 from the area serviced by the two ditches, miners assumed there was little remaining in this location.

In 1900 there were only 192 Chinese in Elko County, and the entire population of Tuscarora was 669. During the next few years, many left after the closing of famous mines such as the Grand Prize Mine and Dexter Mine and Mill. By 1907 Tuscarora ceased to be a major mining town and many of the residents moved to nearby towns, especially Elko.

The 1900 census manuscript listed no Chinese women in Tuscarora or Island Mountain and only three, whose occupations were not given, in all of Elko County. Therefore, like many communities in the American West, single males in a variety of menial jobs with few or no Chinese women around characterized the Chinese population.

The 1900 census manuscript for Tuscarora included Ah Lee Lake and his five partners who operated Quong Hing Lung, and seven miners. These miners differed from the earlier miners—they were older: Yin Hai Anan (age 50), Yem Fong (age 59), Tong Ham (age 50), Wa Ham (age 60), Luck Hong (age 52), Yen Ton Mah (age 74), and Tem Yee (age 49). With the exception of Mah who had EuroAmerican neighbors, they all lived in Chinatown in the same neighborhood as Ah Lee Lake and his partners, but they all owned their homes and lived without any roommates.[146] There also were nineteen laborers (who may have been miners or mined in their spare time). Finally, there were six gardeners aged 40 to 60 and who had lived in the United States for several decades; seven laundrymen; twelve cooks; and one barber. The trend for this aging male population was to move into occupations that did not require the hard physical labor they had performed in the 1870s and 1880s.

The 1910 census listed fifteen Chinese among the 336 people living in Tuscarora. Their occupations were cook (4), farmer (2), laundrymen (3), and miner (6). Seven of the men were married and living apart from their wives, so another trend was the growing number of married men who probably were more stable (since they had to provide for their families in China) than the eight single men. Two of the miners in Tuscarora in 1910 exemplified the changes in the miners' profile: Fueng Sue (single, age 61) did not speak English but could read, and Moi Lung (married, age 70) spoke English and immigrated in 1869.[147] They lived separately and not close to each other, indicating that they had integrated into the community.

In 1920 the population of Tuscarora dropped to 164 with only five Chinese: a laundryman, a ranch hand, a restaurant owner, and two miners. There were no merchants. Two men were married and three were single. The two miners were Yeu Tou Mah (age 74), who had immigrated in 1864; and Lee Wing (age 66), who had immigrated in 1870. Both men were single and lived separately, but Mah still lived in a EuroAmerican neighborhood while Wing lived next door to Sam Sing, a ranch hand, and Charlie Wah, a laundryman.

Although the county recorder's office has birth records of two Chinese girls to a Chinese couple, none of them were listed in the 1910 or 1920 census manuscript. The last Chinese resident of Tuscarora, Yan Tin, died in 1927. By that time, the town's population was very small. Seven years later, a group of students visited Yan Tin's garden and one found a can of gold dust and nuggets valued at $1,200 buried among the plants.[148] In 1972 Mrs. Nora Trembath (b, 1891), one of the town's dozen residents, remarked that the last of the Chinese residents (implying Yan Tin) in accordance to Chinese tradition of allowing the "spirit" to return to one's birthplace, had his bones exhumed and reburied in China "a while back," thus ending the Chinese presence in Tuscarora.[149]

The Primeaux family exemplified the bonds between the EuroAmericans and Chinese in Tuscarora. Whenever Mrs. Primeaux could not fix dinner for her children, she sent them to a Chinese neighbor with some meat and the Chinese man cooked their meal, adding his own vegetables and rice. Her two sons, Antoine and Roy, were in the Chinese band that greeted the Tuscarora sports teams when they returned from games played nearby and that was featured in many public events such as the Fourth of July parade.[150] Antoine served as Elko's postmaster and Roy operated a general store in northeastern Nevada before he became a judge. In 1953 Roy and Antoine (1911–2004) donated over one hundred items including Chinese musical instruments, many from their Chinese friends, to the Nevada State Museum in Carson City, thus commemorating the Chinese presence in Nevada.[151] Antoine Primeaux also added numerous Chinese artifacts to the existing collection of Northeastern Nevada Museum in Elko, thus creating an impressive permanent exhibit commemorating the Chinese role in the history of northeastern Nevada.

Tuscarora currently is privately owned and no extensive archaeological site excavations have taken place (with the exception of those done by the Bureau of Land Management's archaeologist, Eric Dillingham), so government and privately held documents, newspaper reports, oral histories, and memoirs provide the basis for information about the community. Tuscarora essentially became a ghost town sometime during the 1920s or 1930s. Today the current population is estimated at anywhere from a dozen to sixty inhabitants and boasts of a famous pottery school.[152]

The discovery of gold in the Carson Valley brought Chinese miners into Nevada and their ability to buy and sell land made their experiences in Nevada much different from that in Oregon. However local mining regulations and anti-Chinese movements, coupled with the decline of mining resources in western Nevada led them to look eastward along the Central Pacific route. Just as the Chinese finished working on the construction of the first transcontinental railroad, the mining camp of Tuscarora was established. Chinese built the needed irrigation system for placer mining and became the largest segment of the population. With later discoveries and the growth of the EuroAmerican population, they experienced a reversal in their status. This was in keeping with the majority of Chinese mining camps in the American West. During the years of prosperity, they bought and sold property. They established two secret societies that were closely connected to the two community leaders who were merchants. A few were able to marry and have families. Once the economic decline began, the EuroAmerican population joined the ranks of the anti-Chinese movements and discrimination and racism became commonplace until the perceived threat of the Chinese diminished as they moved away. For Tuscarora, this change took place around the turn of the twentieth century. The Chinese had made an impact upon the community by building the town and irrigation system and in sharing their culture with those who befriended them. Ah Lee Lake played an important role in Tuscarora; both the Chinese and EuroAmericans recognized his contributions and positive activities. Chinese Americans were remembered long after the last Chinese resident passed away. But unlike John Day, Oregon, there was little physical evidence remaining to recall their presence with the exception of artifacts donated to museums by friends such as the Primeaux family.

Tuscarora's story is important to understanding the Chinese role in the developments that took place in establishing a mining town. The two secret societies provided services for their membership and extended their influence to neighboring Chinatowns. Chinese from smaller communities moved to or visited Tuscarora and vice versa. Unlike many other mining towns, especially those in California, different ethnic groups worked together for the Chinese and EuroAmerican mining companies or as individual independent miners. The atmosphere of hostility among different ethnicities was not as obvious if and when it existed at all. The frontier spirit of cooperation was more important as the community struggled to survive when the mining boom ended. As industrialization and technological improvements occurred, more and more of the miners had to work in groups not unlike those in China. A few of the older generation of independent miners continued on as long as they could make a living.

Merchants like Ah Lee Lake found that profits could be made from the miners and he became accustomed to life in Tuscarora. He obviously enjoyed himself so much that, like Ing Hay and Lung On of John Day, Oregon, he did not want to return to China when the economic decline occurred. All three men were married and living separately from their wives, so the emphasis on family that characterized Chinese life in China was not as meaningful to them. Ah Lee Lake's fate after 1910 was unknown as no documents could be found indicating that he died or returned to China.

4 Farther East: Island Mountain and Gold Creek

THE COMPLETION OF THE Central Pacific Railroad in 1869 opened numerous other potentially rich placer gold sites in northeastern Nevada. Island Mountain, and the later town of Gold Creek that encompassed it, was first settled in 1873 and abandoned between 1918 and 1930. It exemplified the boom-and-bust mining towns of a shorter duration than did eastern Oregon towns and nearby Tuscarora. Island Mountain, located twenty-five miles south of the Nevada-Idaho border on the main stage coach route, was a major stop between the Central Pacific train stations of Carlin and Elko, Nevada, to the south, and the transportation centers at Franklin and Boise, Idaho, to the north. Because of its small size and relatively isolated location, Island Mountain demonstrated an economic and social interaction that was not as apparent in John Day and Tuscarora but may have existed elsewhere. It offered a sharp contrast to the predominately anti-Chinese sentiment that prevailed elsewhere in mining towns.

Emanuel "Manny" Penrod (1826–1913), the town's founder, hired Chinese for the irrigation projects needed for mining in Island Mountain.[1] He helped create a positive atmosphere for those Chinese who stayed. The Chinese constituted the majority of the town's population for most of its existence—interaction with the other residents, primarily EuroAmericans and Native Americans, was unavoidable. In 1880 Chinese miners were a part of a multiracial community that was 76 percent Chinese. The Chinese population grew in the 1890s when two hundred Chinese worked on the construction of the Sunflower Reservoir to provide additional water for mining and farming. Some of these workers remained in Island Mountain but, beginning in 1900, most had moved on as the economy faltered. In general because of the small size of the community and the economic interdependence of its residents, a more harmonious multiethnic relationship resulted than could be found elsewhere. The dynamics of this situation included invitations to Chinese and EuroAmerican dinners and recreational activities, social practices that were unusual for this time period.

Around 1896 the EuroAmericans established a new town called Gold Creek some three miles away. Since most of the EuroAmericans moved to the new community, the town of Island Mountain became known as Gold Creek's Chinatown.[2] Gold Creek's advantage was its location on level ground while Island Mountain was a hillside community.

By 1900 the character of the region had changed and the Chinese only represented 5 percent of the population in Island Mountain Mining District that included Gold Creek. A series of excellent historic photographs taken by Mrs. Hilda Matthey in August 1903 showed Island Mountain's Chinatown was still thriving with residents and teamsters, but apparently only a few made the town their permanent home.[3] By 1907 only thirty people lived in nearby Gold Creek and agriculture was the main occupation.[4] Chinese continued to live in and around Island Mountain at least through 1917 when the world war and the 1918 pandemic became the focus of the community's attention so that the passing or departure of the last Chinese resident went unnoticed in the local newspapers. Island Mountain became an isolated ghost town because of the construction of a new highway some ten to twenty miles away at the edge of the new Wild Horse Reservoir. The town of Gold Creek also failed: a fire destroyed most of the town in September 1921, with the exception of the Hardman Hotel and a few other buildings. In January 1929 Henry Moffatt bought the Hardman Hotel and the other remaining buildings—he eventually moved all of them to another location because of the shortage of wood—so only the concrete sidewalks of the town remained. Between 1929 and 1930 the owners officially abandoned the town. Only a partially paved sidewalk leading into the "town" remained.[5]

In August or September 1873, Emanuel Penrod arrived in an area that had experienced gold strikes in nearby Mountain City, Placerville, Bruneau (also spelled Bruno) City, and Tuscarora. Upon the advice of a teamster-mining partner named Crate Rousselle, Penrod panned the gravel of a creek (now known as Penrod Creek) and found a rich placer gold deposit. The partners reportedly found several $50 gold nuggets.[6] They knew they had struck it rich!

The Island Mountain Mining District was organized on October 11, 1873, and named after the approximately 8,000-foot-high isolated, loaf-shaped mountain that was snow-capped in winter and surrounded by mist in spring (which made it look like an island in the clouds).[7] The district was at the southeastern flank of Tennessee Mountain, an area that showed ancient volcanic turbulence. According to a geological analysis, the district was underlain

Emanuel "Manny" Penrod was the founder of Island Mountain and brought Chinese workers to Island Mountain beginning in 1874–75. (Courtesy of Nevada Historical Society, Reno)

mainly by slate, shale, and limestone with fluvial gravels being prominent.[8] Quartz veins contained gold, silver, and arsenopyrite. The fairly coarse placer gold in the gravels was worked to a depth of seven feet.

The potential riches of the area were developed with the use of new equipment and technology. The Penrod-Rousselle partnership became more successful by the next summer. Lacking capital and sophisticated equipment, they used picks, shovels, and sluice-boxes, and recovered gold worth $19.45 per ounce.[9] In November 1873 Penrod joined forces with a Mr. Mayon of San Francisco, who supplied better mining equipment. Their company, Penrod, Mayon, and Company, which employed twenty miners (mostly Chinese), produced $3,000 worth of gold during the first six weeks of operation.[10] Mayon bonded several claims in the region and shipped hydraulic mining equipment to Island Mountain.[11]

By the 1850s hydraulic mining using high-pressure water jets through a large canvas hose via a nozzle (called a monitor) from a tank dislodged large volumes of auriferous gravel deposited in ancient river channels.[12] A "Little Giant" invented in the 1870s improved the system, but sources of water were critical and about twenty men were required to work the giants. Unfortunately, this system caused environmental problems such as washing away hillsides and dumping huge amounts of tailings into creeks. The Lum Sing Company in Mormon Basin, Oregon, with a crew of twenty, used hydraulic equipment in the 1870s and 1880s. Miners in Nevada also favored using the system because of its efficiency in recovering gold. In the 1870s through the early 1900s Chinese and EuroAmerican miners invested a substantial amount of money in hydraulic equipment from San Francisco and elsewhere. Lone miners could not afford to buy the equipment, so companies were formed to raise sufficient funds.

Mayon's equipment arrived by midsummer 1874. Water ditches, iron piping, a hydraulic "giant," and a flume to carry off the tailings were set into place. Other smaller companies were organized and some great profits were made: for example, Stanhope and Company sold their Comet mine in Hope Gulch for $10,000 in the 1870s.[13] Mayon's estimated investment was about $4,000; he sold half of his interest to a Minnesota company for $60,000—a handsome profit—shortly thereafter. These kind of profits attracted other investors from the East into the area.

Penrod and others undoubtedly used Chinese workers to help build eight canals and ditches between 1873 and 1878 that made successful mining and agricultural production possible.[14] In June 1874 the Owyhee Water and Gravel Company began hydraulic operations after the completion of a large reservoir and five miles of canal.[15] The *Elko Independent* (August 15, 1874) reported that the Owyhee company hired forty Chinese for this construction project. The only extant ditch, the Owyhee Canal, had a complicated gravity system with sturdy iron flood gates made by Joshua Hendy of San Francisco to control the movement of the water.[16] Parts of the ditch were over six feet deep and covered many miles.[17] Thompson and West's *History of Nevada* described the ten—mile-long canal (with three miles of branches) that was built at a cost of $10,000 and was under the ownership and control of Penrod.[18] Chinese miners had to depend on Penrod for the use of water much like the Chinese in Tuscarora depended on the Beard brothers. The Owyhee Canal enabled more extensive placer mining and a faster recovery of gold.

How many men were employed in irrigation construction was unknown, but the government estimated that on average one person was needed for every ten miles of ditch construction—and more if there were hills and other obstacles.[19] In Oregon the Ah Fat Company used one thousand Chinese workers to dig the two hundred–kilometer El Dorado ditch, the longest ditch on the West Coast as of 1870.[20] According to a retrospective article in the *Gold Creek News* (February 11, 1897), Penrod had trouble working the property at first, but "Chinamen in his employ were known to have returned home loaded with gold." It was estimated that they could earn $9,000 in only a few weeks during the mining season.

Typically there were numerous fluctuations in mining in the early years. The conditions at Island Mountain were far from ideal. According to the *Elko Independent* (July 4, 1874), the winter of 1873–74 was an extremely wet one—and the abundance of water contributed to the discovery and early success of placer mining in the Island Mountain District. The winters often were so harsh that few people lived in the district during the entire year. The same issue of the newspaper described the method used by the Chinese to extract placer gold. They used sluices, but, as the newspaper article described, they ran "the dirt through only about six or seven boxes, with one riffle (wooden slate) in each." Different types and sizes of metal grizzlies [metal plates with holes], fragments of which were found a century later, separated large rocks from the gold-bearing sands prior to the sand being run through a sluice or rocker. As done in China, gold and sand were often separated by the use of quicksilver (mercury) to extract the gold.

Emanuel Penrod did not subscribe to the anti-Chinese prejudice found in western Nevada. Penrod moved his family from Genoa to Island Mountain. His early mining success contributed to his decision to run for assemblyman from Elko County in 1874.[21] He won the election and moved to Carson City, leaving his mining business to his three sons (Alexander, William Allen, and James) and sons-in-law. As a member of the Nevada Legislature beginning in 1875, Emanuel Penrod was acutely aware of the growing northern Nevada anti-Chinese sentiment based primarily on economic competition. But he was a practical man who realized the need for Chinese laborers in Island

Mountain, so he did not support anti-Chinese legislation.[22] He worked on economic issues and helped establish a state university.[23] He prided himself on his familiarity with minorities and proudly stated in his letters that he knew the Native Americans and all his children had been raised with Native American servants.[24] After he returned to Island Mountain from Carson City a year later, he sold mining rights and property to the Chinese, something the anti-Chinese agitators wanted to stop. His leadership abilities shaped much of the development of Island Mountain and the acceptance of the Chinese there.

Penrod's mining success drew the interest of people from other states. California, New York, Colorado, Minnesota, and Iowa investors took note of the developments in Island Mountain. Major newspapers in the state, like the *Territorial Enterprise* and *Carson City Appeal*, gave accounts of the mining successes in Island Mountain and around the state. At Island Mountain Chinese and EuroAmerican miners reportedly recovered gold worth as much as $2.50 per pan and $30 per person per day for those using rockers.[25] According to archaeologist David W. Valentine, these were excellent recoveries for that period.[26] Also among the investors were Dr. and Mrs. Heinrich Matthey of Iowa. On a 1903 trip Hilda Matthey, a professional photographer, took photographs of Island Mountain and some of its Chinese inhabitants, thus providing pictorial documentation of their lifestyle .

Penrod continued his mining successes. In one season in 1897 he took out $11,000 from his Anti-Comstock Mine.[27] He had staked out eighty acres of placer ground and probably used Chinese workers to build the early water ditch from Martin Creek near Bruneau City to the head of the east fork (Fuzzi Gulch) of Gold Creek.[28] On this site he employed some twenty miners to work the land.[29] At one point Penrod sold out his mining claims, but bought his property back for about $15,000. These kinds of transfers were not uncommon. He and his sons became even more active in mining.[30] Penrod's early success reportedly netted him $250,000 from his operations in Island Mountain and Bruneau City.[31]

Penrod was a community leader in Island Mountain. He held the prestigious post of postmaster from 1884 to 1887, when the mining "bust" led to a drastic decline in the local population, thus rendering his service unnecessary.[32] In 1891 Penrod and his son Alexander discovered the Oro Grande, the most productive lode mine in Alder, located about eight and a half miles from Gold Creek, and built a three-stamp mill there. James Penrod continued to develop the claims there through the early 1900s.[33]

During the first twenty years of its existence, Island Mountain mining sites yielded tremendous returns. According to one estimate about $800,000 in gold was extracted from Gold Creek (Fuzzi Gulch), Hammond Canyon (Patterson Gulch), Penrod Creek, Big Bend Creek, Mill Creek, Martin Creek, Poorman Creek, and Coleman Canyon (Hope Gulch).[34] Another source reported that between 1873 and 1901 the Island Mountain Mining District recovered an estimated forty thousand ounces of gold. This made it one of the most productive placer areas in Nevada during this period and the Chinese were an important part of the mining successes.[35]

Gradually, Penrod became less active in mining. In 1892 he sold his claims to W. B. Duvall, who then changed the name of the company from Island Mountain Mining, Milling, Land, and Investment Company to Gold Creek, Nevada, Mining Company with Henry Mayham as president.[36] Penrod remained in the area for the next three years. One of his projects was the construction of the four-hundred-foot Golden Dream tunnel along the ledges of the mountains. The Chinese who worked with him reportedly took home a substantial amount of gold that they could send back to their families in China.

By the turn of the twentieth century Penrod had more or less retired. His last big bonanza was working the Constitution Mine with his son-in-law Walter Stofiel.[37] In May 1897 Penrod constructed another three-stamp mill; in its first nine days of operation, the mill produced a $1,000 bar of gold. After moving to California, Penrod and his wife frequently returned to Island Mountain and Gold Creek, but after his wife's death in 1901, he spent more time in Watsonville and Vallejo, California, with his daughter's family than he did in Nevada. Nevertheless in his correspondence, he pointed out that he always remained a "citizen of Nevada." Emanuel Penrod died in Vallejo, California, in 1913.[38]

Members of the Penrod family continued to live in Island Mountain despite the mining decline in Gold Creek after 1899. In 1900 James Penrod (b. 1863) lived there as a miner and rancher with his wife Cora and their four children.[39] Penrod's mill in Tennessee Gulch still operated, processing ore from Penrod's Oro Grande as well as Burkhart and Stauts's Gold Bug mine. In 1910 James was still living in Gold Creek; the local press reported that he did not leave until around 1921.[40] The Elko County Recorder's Office showed William Allen Penrod and Alexander Penrod were active in mining around the turn of the twentieth century. Eventually most of the Penrod family moved to California.

The *Gold Creek News* (March 4, 1897) provided a description of the Island Mountain Mining District as the reporter traveled on the Van Drielen stage: On the road from Elko the snow-capped peak of Island Mountain was seen.

At the northern base was the new town of Gold Creek and to the north of it the mines nestled in semicircles in the mountains. The stage stopped at Stofiel's Store and Station, seven miles from Gold Creek. After passing several creeks, bridges, and East Owyhee, the reporter reached Gold Creek and then headed past the old Penrod residence and Hugh Martin's 250-acre ranch near the Little Sunflower Reservoir to Island Mountain's Chinatown at the junction of the Hope and Patterson gulches. The reporter's description ended with a visit to China Lem's store, which had become a favorite community gathering place and a major stage stop as well as a shopping center for general supplies and foodstuffs. The highlight of the trip was the rice whiskey provided by Lem Hong Ng, or China Lem, who had been there since the 1870s.

Gold Creek, a planned community, was just three miles east of Island Mountain but only a few blocks had structures on them.[41] In January 1897 John Hardman (b. 1855) announced that by the following spring he intended to relocate his Carlin hotel-boarding house, the Hardman House, and a liquor store to Gold Creek because "everyone he meets is talking about Gold Creek."[42] The *Gold Creek News* (March 4 and 11, 1897) reported that the three-story Hardman House accommodated 170 people and was the center piece of the town.[43] The post office was established that year in the hotel-store and Mary Hardman became postmistress after Hugh Martin left the position. Next to the hotel was the one-story office of the Gold Creek Company, with its assay office at the rear, and behind that was a well that went down some eighty-seven feet but still did not have water.[44] There were a few residential homes but otherwise the growth of the town never reached the anticipated and hoped-for population. The Chinese, however, preferred to remain in Island Mountain and did not settle in the town—with the exception of the hotel's cook.

A second mining boom began in late 1896 through January 1897. By 1897 the Gold Creek Company employed twenty men in the mines. Gold Creek's population grew to five hundred, with three hundred on the mine payrolls alone.[45] The Gold Creek Townsite Company was capitalized in Denver at $2 million and the Gold Creek Improvement Company at $100,000.[46] A newspaper, *Gold Creek News* (which began publication on December 14, 1896), and its successor, *Mountain City News*, promoted the mining community and provided insights about the region's development and the Chinese living in the area. The Gold Creek Nevada Mining Company, with its leader and general manager Major John L. Robertson, acquired ten thousand acres of placer ground and fifty lode claims with funds from New York, and in the process revitalized the community.[47]

The community thrived from 1897 until 1900. The *Gold Creek News* (January 14, 1897) described the conditions in Gold Creek: EuroAmerican miners earned $3 a day for ten hours of work, while teamsters earned $6 to $8 a day for four-horse teams, and reservoir laborers, many of whom were Chinese, earned $2 a day. There was sufficient water from the winter snows and the Sunflower Reservoir and wood was obtained from Mountain City and Elko. Board was listed at $5.25 to $7.00 per week.

Travel to nearby towns became easier with more frequent stagecoaches and connecting trains. Roads were constructed to link the new boomtowns to the main railroad stations. Stage and freight lines sprang up and passed through Island Mountain to and from Mountain City, Nevada, and Boise, Idaho.[48] J. D. Franklin initiated his tri-weekly North Fork–Gold Creek stage line in June 1900 that connected with the Tuscarora-Elko Stage at Dinner Station, thus making the availability of lumber (primarily cut for Tuscarora) and ranch products more accessible.[49] From Island Mountain the stage traveled to Elko to the south and Carlin and Winnemucca to the southwest. Travelers also could reach the Oregon Short Line by stagecoach to Mountain Home, Idaho, one hundred miles to the north.[50] Transportation was vital to the development of this relatively isolated region.

The miners wanted a larger reservoir to assure a steady supply of water. The lack of water, especially during drought years, hindered the growth of placer mining, so more effective irrigation was very important. About two miles from the end of the Owyhee Canal was the approximately two-acre "Little Sunflower" reservoir. Miners wanted it expanded to impound water to extend hydraulic mining into the summer season.[51]

The Corey Brothers Company from Ogden, Utah, was hired to construct the reservoir. It would be fed by a long ditch running across the hillsides.[52] Construction of the enlarged Sunflower Reservoir began in January 1897. The Corey Brothers hired 289 workers (about two hundred or more were Chinese) for $2 per day.[53] Chinese and non-Chinese workers were paid the same for the same type of work; supervising personnel were paid more. The reservoir, designed to hold 821 million gallons of water and cover an area of 137 acres, was a tribute to its designer and the Chinese work crew.[54] In its first season, it attained a maximum depth of 19 feet 8 inches, holding 310 million gallons of water.[55] The reservoir's dam measured 600 feet by 40 feet, was 44 feet high, and was an impressive sight. The core of the reservoir was solid masonry. Fed by the Martin, Mill and Big Bend creeks, the 4-foot wide inlet ditch carried 3,000 miners' inches (75 cubic feet per second) of water over a 3.5 percent grade for eight miles to fill the massive reservoir. Later a bypass ditch that was 2,700 feet long was constructed twenty-five feet higher than the top of the water to direct the excess water around the reservoir to Slate Creek.[56] On May 13, 1897, a small boat named the *Kazoo* sailed from the intake ditch down to the reservoir carrying Robertson and his friend Captain Nicholas Barlow.[57] They probably used the boat to help clear the ditch of accumulated snow drifts as well as for regular repairs. The reservoir continues to be a major feature in the area.

With the completion of the Sunflower Reservoir, hydraulic mining proved to be successful. By June 10 a pipeline some 2,185 feet long was laid along the full length of the gulch; the ground had a vertical descent of 235 feet. In July 1897 using massive water cannons the miners blasted away at the Crevice Gulch hillside where the loosened gravel ran through 6-inch-wide sluice boxes to sort the gold from the tailings.[58] The exposed bedrock also was mined with pick and shovel to obtain the gold. A track 200 to 300 feet long, much like the logging flumes, was probably built by the Chinese to haul gravel from the cracks between the bedrock to the sluice boxes.[59] A hydraulic giant washed the dirt and gold into large sluices in Coleman Canyon.

The success of the Crevice Gulch operation was astounding, but the Gold Creek Mining Company had amassed huge financial debts. Among their many financial difficulties was the Corey Brothers' lawsuit seeking $24,000 to cover some of their construction expenses. As a result of this lawsuit, the land holdings of the Gold Creek Mining Company were transferred to the Corey Brothers, who sold much of the land to recover their losses.[60] Public auctions were held. By the early twentieth century mining there had declined because of the issue of water rights and the depletion of placer gold.

In the wake of the bust, the population of Gold Creek declined quickly. By 1902 the Hardman Hotel was the only business left. But miners still returned to Island Mountain: in 1910, out of the seventy-eight residents, thirty-one were still involved in mining as prospectors, miners, and mining engineers, but no Chinese miners were listed. However, the Chinese rancher named Joe Nep was also a miner according to a newspaper report about his death. Of Gold Creek's 1880 EuroAmerican residents, only a few stayed through the turn of the century. In 1888 John French (b. 1830 in Ohio), the mining engineer, married Ella (b. 1854 in Indiana) and by 1900 had two daughters and a female boarder, the local school teacher, living with them. Another man, James Tippett, who boarded with the Martin family in 1900, remained until 1910. James Penrod first stayed with his family; in 1920 he was listed in the census alone.

But some activity continued to occur: between 1918 and 1935, miners extracted 230 ounces of gold, and between 1936 and 1940, 299 ounces.[61]

The Island Mountain District was subsumed into the Bruneau District, which was centered around Bruneau (Bruno) City (founded in 1869), which also disappeared. The mining towns of Island Mountain, Gold Creek, and Bruno City faded into the rural landscape, living on only in people's memories. The area's economic profile changed from mining to agriculture and the Chinese population moved elsewhere.

The Chinese were among the first settlers in Island Mountain. In 1875 the Nevada state census manuscript listed one Chinese cook and twenty-five Chinese miners, as well as twenty-seven EuroAmericans, two of whom were children, living in Island Mountain.[62] Considering only the adult population, this meant that Island Mountain consisted of 50 percent Chinese and 50 percent EuroAmericans. No individual names or ages were given but most of the Chinese lived in a boarding house operated by Mr. and Mrs. P. Fairchild and

In 1903 Hilda Matthey photographed Pekin Avenue in Island Mountain's Chinatown with horses in front of or near Lem's store. Hangchow Street was behind Pekin Avenue. (Author's collection)

their two children. Fairchild, from Iowa, was a miner and had two other EuroAmerican miners living in the boarding house. Interracial boarding houses in small mining communities in Nevada were not unusual. In all probability, Fairchild was the superintendent of the mining crew. Hugh Martin and his family established another household of EuroAmerican miners, laborers, and a teamster. The Martins, who became ranchers, remained in the area for many decades; their descendants now live in Elko. While the newspapers in neighboring communities printed stories about the anti-Chinese movements and eventual passage of the 1882 Chinese Exclusion Act, the residents of Island Mountain were largely unaffected—they worked together and continued to live interdependent lives.[63]

Island Mountain reflected the influence of its Chinese residents. The town was located on a gentle hillside at the junction of the Hope and Patterson gulches, about three miles by dirt road away from Gold Creek (which was on the other side of a hill on level ground at the northern base of the main mountain).[64] The town's main street was called Pekin Avenue after China's capital city and the secondary street was Hangchow Street, named for a resort area in China. All of the streets were actually leveled dirt roads. Foundations of at least fourteen structures can still be detected on the main street. Other buildings were located in the vicinity. Henly, one of the Chinese miners who spoke English and served as the guide for the visiting Matthey family in 1903, had his home off of the main street and away from the main town. The Penrod home was in the opposite direction about a mile and a half away on the way to Gold Creek, but only the remnants of their vault remains.

Familiar elements of *fengshui* and the feeling of stability probably accounted for the Chinese remaining in Island Mountain instead of moving to the new town of Gold Creek.[65] The main creek ran parallel to the first part of the Chinatown and willow trees grew nearby. Willow trees, not found in nearby areas, grew along the border of the creek, their interlacing roots protecting the banks from erosion. The Chinese knew that the growth of willow trees meant water was available and that the wood from the willow trees could be used to make charcoal, furniture, window frames, brooms, fences to pen in animals, roof beams, poles, and other household items. In numerous locations throughout the American West, the Chinese used willow branches just as they did in south China. Additionally, due to its salicylic acid content, the bark and leaves of the tree had the medicinal attribute of being a remedy for aches and fever. On a more practical note, the Chinese in Island Mountain did not feel the need to uproot themselves and move three miles away to Gold Creek since buildings were already established and provided a modicum of comfort.

Some of the Chinese moved to Island Mountain from neighboring transient mining towns. Mountain City, one of the closest mining towns, was a typical mining community that rose and fell quickly. Originally named Cope after Jesse Cope in April 1869, the camp grew to three hundred residents and was renamed Mountain City. By the end of the year there were seven hundred people, twenty saloons, a dozen hotels, six restaurants, and two breweries serving the primarily single male population. The first shipment of ore to San Francisco assayed at $420 per ton; once that news was out, miners flocked to Cope. By the end of 1870 the population reached one thousand, and the Chinese population numbered forty-six: twenty miners, seven cooks, seven laundrymen, four laborers, and eight in unknown occupations.[66] The town had more than two hundred buildings. By 1875 (just six years later) as placer mining declined, the population shrank to sixty-seven people. This pattern of fast boom and bust was not unusual in this era and in this area.

During Mountain City's brief prosperity, the Chinese created a suburb called Placerville, where fifty homes were built—forty of them belonging to the Chinese.[67] Although none of the names of the Placerville Chinese match the names in the census manuscript of the 1880 Island Mountain and Tuscarora Chinese residents, in all probability some moved from Mountain City to Island Mountain and neighboring mining towns when the bust came. Since Mountain City was Nevada's gateway to southern Idaho, some undoubtedly tried their luck in the Idaho Basin and other Idaho mining towns as well.[68] By 1880 there were only three Chinese remaining—two miners (Ah Check and Ah Sam) and one cook (Ah Hong)—who were part of the thirty-four residents in Mountain City and that now included Placerville.[69] Like Island Mountain, mining eventually yielded to ranching, although the 1890s saw a minor resurgence in mining activities. Productive mining there fluctuated during the twentieth century. Only recently has Mountain City's population grown to about 150 residents, most of whom are ranchers and Native Americans.

One of the Chinese miners, Ah Ching (b. 1848) moved from Placerville to Island Mountain between 1870 and 1880.[70] According to the deed records in the Elko County Recorder's Office, he, along with Lung Wah (b. 1840) and Wo Sing (not in the census), purchased twenty acres of land, known as Hope Gulch, from J. C. Baker, W. L. Morley, and J. Talbott in Island Mountain for $1,600 in gold coin.[71] (The original claim was filed by William Kidd in May 1874 and sold by Kidd to J.C. Baker and W. L. Morley in December 1875.)[72] Chain migration, not only of Chinese but also EuroAmericans, was common at this time. According to the census records, the Chinese miners in Island

Mountain had been living in the United States for several years before Island Mountain was established and generally were men in their thirties and forties.

Other Chinese miners moved to Island Mountain from other areas. After the completion of the transcontinental railroad, ephemeral mining towns located in the vicinity experienced cycles of boom and bust. American Canyon, Columbia, Cornucopia, Winnemucca, and Mardis in Nevada as well as towns in Oregon and Idaho were located close enough to send miners to the new sites. One group of Chinese miners moved to Island Mountain from Tuscarora.[73] Tuscarora was the closest town with a large Chinatown and probably attracted the Island Mountain residents with its recreational activities. One of the owners of a local general store moved from Tuscarora to Island Mountain when his brother died (or returned to China); both brothers were called "China Lem." Often friends and relatives from the same place in China spread the word about new mining discoveries.

Although no records substantiate this, most of the Chinese in Island Mountain probably were born in Taishan or one of the other Siyi districts.[74] Men born in Taishan traditionally migrated overseas during periods of overpopulation, rebellion, banditry, economic dislocation, and political or social disorders—all of which characterized that area in China in the late 1860s.[75] The fact that a Chinese cemetery was in nearby Carlin, Elko County, Nevada, for men from Taishan suggests that Siyi men were more populous than men from Sanyi or other South China areas.[76] When the Chinese labor "bosses" in Elko County needed to hire workers, they undoubtedly preferred to recruit from the labor pool of men from Siyi. Because these men had common regional and district unity, they shared a similar culture, customs, food tastes, and spoken language which meant that they could work together and adapt more easily to their new environment.

Occasionally Chinese from a more unusual area could be found. Two brothers, surnamed Nep (pinyin, Ni), came from the district Sihui located in western Guangdong.[77] The Neps were part of a small Chinese clan in a district not known for emigration. But they probably left for the purpose of survival and closely identified with their countrymen from southeastern Guangdong—this association would not have occurred had they remained in China. The Nep brothers remained until their accidental deaths, Suey in 1898 and Joe in 1915.[78]

According to the 1880 census, Island Mountain had seventy-one inhabitants: fifty-four (76 percent) Chinese, of whom forty-five (83 percent) were miners; the remainder included four cooks, two woodchoppers, two merchants, one laundryman, one "loafer," and one prostitute. The other residents were six Native Americans: two women, one young son, two hunters, and one medicine man. Also listed were eleven EuroAmericans: two wives, one male farmer, two male teamsters, and six male miners.[79] In this census, the only Penrods listed were Allen Penrod (age 30) who was born in Illinois, and his wife, Rebecca (age 19) who was born in Iowa. Emanuel, his wife, and other children were away or living elsewhere. With the exception of the man who was born in Prussia, the other EuroAmericans were second-generation with the following birthplaces: New York (2), Ohio (3), Utah (1), Pennsylvania (1), and Virginia (1). They did not seem to have the anti-Chinese prejudice that characterized the American West at this time.

In most mining communities and rural areas, Chinese settlements grew because of the necessity for people to band together for social and economic benefits and for mutual protection against the hostile attitudes of EuroAmerican miners, residents, and officials as well as the American practice of segregating the population by race or ethnicity. In Island Mountain, where non-Chinese lived next to Chinese in a multiracial, multiethnic setting, this was not the case.

Of the fourteen households in Island Mountain in 1880, seven were Chinese: Household 3 (2 woodchoppers); Household 5 (7 miners, 1 cook); Household 8 (13 miners, 1 grocer); Household 9 (1 prostitute, 1 gambler, 1 loafer, 1 miner); Household 12 (5 miners); Household 13 (10 miners, 1 cook); Household 14 (6 miners, 1 cook, 1 laundryman, 1 merchant). In addition, there was the Chinese cook, Ah Chung, who lived with Mr. and Mrs. Sharp (Household 4).

The details of each household were revealed in the 1880 census manuscript. Household 1 consisted of Allen and Rebecca Penrod. Household 2 was the home of a farmer, Joseph Everett (age 54), a widower from New York. These two households were farther away from the main streets of Island Mountain. Household 3 consisted of two young Chinese woodchoppers, Ah Lue (age 18) and Ah Fat (age 24); both men later moved to Franktown, a major lumbering town near the state's capital, Carson City, to cut wood with a larger contingent of Chinese woodchoppers.[80] Wood was an essential material that provided fuel for stamp mills, for stoves and heaters, and for furniture, sidewalks, and buildings. Household 4 consisted of the home of mining boss G. J. Sharp (age 26) from New York, his wife Artie (age 23) from Utah, and their Chinese cook, Ah Chung (age 33). Since Artie was born in Utah, it is probable that the Sharps were Mormons like the Penrods. Sharp was a young mining boss who apparently earned enough to afford his own cook. In the 1870s and 1880s throughout Nevada and the American West it was very fashionable to have Chinese cooks and servants in the household.[81]

Table 3. 1880 United States Census Manuscript for Island Mountain

Chinese names are given with nomenclature "Ah" first as it appears in the census manuscript.
The census taker was not able to distinguish Chinese last names and first names.

Household	Name	Age	Sex	Race	Occupation	Birth place	Single/Married	Other census
Hshd 1								
1.	Penrod, Allen	30	M	White	Miner	IL	M	
2.	Penrod, Rebecca	19	F	White	Keeping House	IA	M	
Hshd 2								
3.	Everett, Jos[eph]	54	M	White	Farmer	NY	Wd	
Hshd 3								
4.	Ah Lue	18	M	Chinese	Wood chopper	China	S	
5.	Ah Fat	24	M	Chinese	Wood chopper	China	S	
Hshd 4								
6.	Sharp, G. J. (?)	26	M	White	Mining Boss	NY	M	
7.	Sharp, Artie	23	F	White	Keeping House	UT	M	
8.	Ah Chung	33	M	Chinese	Cook	China	S	
Hshd 5								
9.	Ah Choo	32	M	Chinese	Miner	China	S	
10.	Ah Loy Le Jr.	38	M	Chinese	Miner	China	S	
11.	Ah Jim	30	M	Chinese	Miner	China	S	
12.	Ah Oldman	60	M	Chinese	Cook	China	S	
13.	Ah Pony	41	M	Chinese	Miner	China	S	
14.	Ah Ben	30	M	Chinese	Miner	China	S	
15.	Loy Gum	35	M	Chinese	Miner	China	S	
16.	Ah Charley	46	M	Chinese	Miner	China	S	
Hshd 6								
17.	Indian Jim	40	M	Indian	Hunter	NV	M	
18.	Indian Tom	65	M	Indian	Medicine Man	NV	Wd	
19.	Aleck	42	M	Indian	Hunter	NV	M	
20.	Maggie	30	F	Indian	Wife	NV	M	
21.	Gertie	25	F	Indian	Wife	NV	M	
22.	Willie (son of Maggie)	2	M	Indian	Son	NV	S	

Table 3. (cont.)

Household	Name	Age	Sex	Race	Occupation	Birth place	Single/Married	Other census
Hshd 7								
23.	Gilruth, Austin	42	M	White	Teamster	OH	S	
24.	Arundel, Jabez	24	M	White	Teamster	PA	S	
25.	Ginn, R. W.	25	M	White	Miner	VA	?	
Hshd 8								
26.	Lem Hung Lee	40	M	Chinese	Grocer	China	S	
27.	Ah Won	31	M	Chinese	Miner	China	S	
28.	Ah Muck	43	M	Chinese	Miner	China	S	
29.	Ah Ong	42	M	Chinese	Miner	China	S	
30.	Ah Bing	33	M	Chinese	Miner	China	S	
31.	Ah Sam	33	M	Chinese	Miner	China	S	
32.	Au Yoy	38	M	Chinese	Miner	China	S	
33.	Ah Gee	36	M	Chinese	Miner	China	S	
34.	Ah Hung	31	M	Chinese	Miner	China	S	
35.	Ah Yem	31	M	Chinese	Miner	China	S	
36.	Ah Charley	20	M	Chinese	Miner	China	S	
37.	Ah Sing	30	M	Chinese	Miner	China	S	
38.	Ah Loye Sr. (?)	67	M	Chinese	Miner	China	Wd	
39.	Ah Chung	35	M	Chinese	Miner	China	S	1870 Cope
Hshd 9								
40.	Ah Hee	25	F	Chinese	Whore	China	S	
41.	Ah Tony	35	M	Chinese	Gambler	China	S	
42.	Fung Lo	31	M	Chinese	Loafer	China	S	
43.	Ah Sup	28	M	Chinese	Miner	China	S	
Hshd 10								
44.	Tippett, James	34	M	White	Boss Miner	OH	S	1900 Gold Cr
Hshd 11								
45.	French, J. L.	46	M	White	Miner	OH	S	
46.	Groehn, J. A.	46	M	White	Miner	Prussia	S	

Table 3. (cont.)

Household	Name	Age	Sex	Race	Occupation	Birth place	Single/Married	Other census
Hshd 12								
47.	Ah Fred	60	M	Chinese	Miner	China	S	
48.	Ah Long	18	M	Chinese	Miner	China	S	
49.	Ah Chew	19	M	Chinese	Miner	China	S	
50.	An Gow	26	M	Chinese	Miner	China	S	
51.	Ling Hoy	52	M	Chinese	Miner Boss	China	S	
Hshd 13								
52.	Wah Sung or Lung	40	M	Chinese	Boss Miner	China	S	
53.	Ah Shep	40	M	Chinese	Miner	China	S	
54.	Ah Lee	31	M	Chinese	Miner	China	S	
55.	Ah Gee	30	M	Chinese	Miner	China	S	
56.	Wah Lee	28	M	Chinese	Miner	China	S	
57.	Suig Lee	41	M	Chinese	Miner	China	S	
58.	Ong Gee	33	M	Chinese	Miner	China	S	
59.	Long Wa	38	M	Chinese	Miner	China	S	
60.	Ah Chuck	43	M	Chinese	Miner	China	S	
61.	Ah Foy	31	M	Chinese	Miner	China	S	
62.	China Sam	30	M	Chinese	Miner	China	S	
Hshd 14								
63.	Ling Wo	43	M	Chinese	Boss Miner	China	S	
64.	Sam Wo	34	M	Chinese	Miner	China	S	
65.	Ling Gee	36	M	Chinese	Miner	China	S	
66.	Hop Wo	39	M	Chinese	Miner	China	S	
67.	Hoy Lip	30	M	Chinese	Miner	China	S	
68.	Charley Sing	34	M	Chinese	Miner	China	S	
69.	Sam Lee Wah	39	M	Chinese	Wash Man	China	S	
70.	Lem Hung	41	M	Chinese	Store Keeper	China	S	
71.	Hong Gee	32	M	Chinese	Miner	China	S	

Based on the United States Census Manuscript for 1880 Nevada, Island Mountain District.

Household 5 was a small dormitory of seven Chinese miners and a cook. All of the men were single, the oldest at age 60 served as cook; the miners ranged in age from 30 to 46. By looking at the Chinese names, one miner probably was the adult son of a man living in Household 8 because of the term "Junior" attached to his last name. The cook probably raised vegetables in a small garden that existed just off the creek.

Next to them lived six Native Americans. Two of the men were hunters, one was a medicine man, two were wives, and one was the 2-year-old son of Maggie, one of the wives. There was an abundance of wild game in the area, so the hunters probably provided the meat for the miners. Their relationship with the Chinese miners might have paved the way for positive Chinese-Shoshone interactions and the marriages that took place. In the ensuing years, a popular belief was that some of the Chinese men of Island Mountain married the Shoshone women "Indian style" with the chief's permission and that the women praised the good treatment that they received from their Chinese husbands.

Unlike marriages and cohabitation between EuroAmericans and Chinese, which was forbidden by an 1861 Nevada law, marriages and cohabitation between Chinese and Native Americans was not prohibited by law.[82] Idaho and Oregon followed suit and also forbade EuroAmerican and Chinese marriages. Ruth Bilheimer, who studied these marriages in the Paiute community of Schurz, Nevada, reported that the women found their Chinese husbands more reliable and caring but eventually returned to Schurz to raise their children.[83] Some of the children kept close contact with their Chinese fathers and grandfathers, as seen in the example of the family of Sam Leon of Bodie, California, and Reno, Nevada.[84] Although Sam's married daughter lived in Schurz, she and her children visited Sam on a fairly regular basis and all of his children and grandchildren attended his funeral when he died. According to his granddaughter Juanita Pontoon, the family maintained the practice of eating rice and some of his grandchildren still speak Cantonese.[85] The local newspapers in western Nevada took delight in noting these Chinese–Native American relationships and their children. In an 1884 article, for example, a reporter commented that there was a "half-breed girl, whose father is Chinese cook and her mother a Piute [sic] squaw. She is about 13 years old, quite smart, and her features, with the exception of her eyes which are Mongolian, show her Indian origin."[86] For the Chinese men, this was a way to have a family in the American West.

The close proximity of the homes in Island Mountain and the different occupations of the men suggested that there was interaction and interdependence in the early settlement. Household 7 had three EuroAmerican men: two teamsters and one miner. Austin Gilruth (age 42, from Ohio) worked with Jabez Arundel (age 24, from Pennsylvania). R. W. Ginn, a 25-year-old miner from Virginia, was probably a friend of Arundel. In this relatively isolated community, the teamsters performed an essential role because they transported goods and gold.

Next to this EuroAmerican house was Household 8, which had the largest group of Chinese miners. It was conveniently located next door to the "recreational center." Lem Hong See (Lem Hung Lee, age 40 or 41), was the grocer in this household with thirteen miners. The teamsters probably brought in food and other products that he sold to the community. Ah Chung (age 35), who lived in nearby Cope Mining District in 1870, was among the miners living in this household.[87] This may indicate that this was one of the early residential structures in the town as well as a newly formed Chinese mining "company," or group. The Chinese miners ranged in age from 20 to 67, the latter being a widower whose son, Ah Loye Jr., lived in Household 5. All the men were reported to be single.

Household 9 was the recreational house with the only female resident, a prostitute, Ah Hee (age 25), a gambler, Ah Tony (age 35), a loafer, Fung Lo (age 31), and a relatively young miner, Ah Sup (age 28). As the only prostitute in town in 1880, Ah Hee probably had a variety of clients, both Chinese and non-Chinese.[88] Since Tuscarora, Carlin, Elko, and Boise were linked to Island Mountain by a regular stagecoach route, other Chinese prostitutes may have visited Island Mountain on a regular basis and used Ah Hee's abode as their base for their Chinese and non-Chinese clients.[89] Some female artifacts were found in the archaeological excavations that suggested where Household 9 was located.

For those Chinese, EuroAmerican, and Native Americans who preferred gambling to female company, Ah Tony provided games of chance. The most well-liked games were *fan tan* (a counting game), *pai kow* (a type of Chinese dominoes; both were later popularized in the 1970s to customers in Nevada casinos), *pak kop piu* (Chinese lottery, later adopted in Nevada as keno), and *mah jong* (similar to a card game but played with tiles). Chinese chess and the game of *Go* also were played. Pieces from these games, coins, and tiles have been found in almost all Chinese archaeological mining community sites. Island Mountain was no exception. Although Fung Lo was listed as a loafer, he probably performed a variety of duties for Ah Hee and Ah Tony or may have offered other types of service. Traditionally Chinese gaming establishments offered refreshments so Fung Lo may have had additional duties as a cook. Ah Sup was their link to the predominantly single Chinese miners and may have been the "money man" for the household or may have worked under the direction of their neighbor, James Tippett. As soon as the wealth of the Chinese community began to diminish, this entire household probably moved quickly to another location. Nearby Tuscarora had larger Chinese gaming houses and houses of prostitution; in all likelihood, the professionals traveled and visited smaller Chinese communities like Island Mountain on a regular basis when such establishments were no longer around. Several Shoshones from Mountain City reported that their fathers visited Chinatown's gambling house in the early twentieth century but the location among the fourteen structures could not be determined.

Household 10 was James Tippett's residence and since he appeared in the 1900 census manuscript for Gold Creek, it is probable that he remained in the district throughout this period. As a single, 34-year-old male born in Ohio, he worked as the "boss miner." He lived next door (Household 11) to two single miners, J. L. French (age 46, also from Ohio), and J. A. Groehn (age 46, from Prussia). These two older men probably were Tippett's assistants. The Ohio connection may have been how French came to Island Mountain.

Household 12 was a small boarding house headed by Hoy Ling (age 52), a boss miner, who lived with Ah Fred (age 60) and three younger men: Ah Long (age 18), Ah Chew (age 19), and An Gow (age 26). This was next to a larger boarding house (Household 13) that was headed by the boss miner Sung or Lung Wah (age 40), and housed ten other men who ranged in age from 28 to 43. One can assume that these men were more experienced miners than Household 12's young miners.

Household 14 was the last structure on Pekin Avenue and in subsequent census years may have been the first household counted. Ling Wo (age 43), was the boss miner, living with eight men including the store keeper Lem Hung (age 41). These two men were the oldest in this household of men in their thirties. Lem Hung may be the name for "China Lem," who remained in Island Mountain until at least 1917. The household included the only laundryman in Island Mountain, Sam Lee Wah (age 39). Mining was a dirty occupation, so a laundryman was important in the community.

Often an experienced miner teamed up with novices in the occupation and the more experienced man served as a "boss." In the 1880 census manuscript Lung Wah (age 40, possibly the same as Sung Wah?) and Ling Wo (age 43, possibly the same as Wo Sing?) were two of the three boss miners. They headed Household 13 consisting of eleven men and Household 14 consisting of nine men respectively. Hoy Ling (age 52), the third boss miner, headed a smaller group of five men in Household 12. The elevation in occupational status to boss miner was not uncommon. In such situations, the boss miners supervised the Chinese workers for the EuroAmerican mine foremen, guaranteed the number of men present at the site, determined the work and pay of each individual so that higher skilled jobs, such as wood chopping, received more money. The boss also handled food and health concerns.[90] Sometimes the boss miners also headed a Chinese mining company like the ones found in China and Oregon. This suggests that the Chinese organized themselves into mining groups or companies rather than working as individual miners and that Island Mountain's Chinatown had at least three distinctive Chinese mining "companies" or groups under the supervision of "bosses."

The phenomenon of Chinese mining "companies" was observed as early as 1854 when a writer named James Mason Hutchings (1820–1902) witnessed two factions of Chinese fighting over the rights to a mining site in California; this was also seen in eastern Oregon.[91] The companies and boss miners were usually divided by place of birth in China or grouped by clan or family ties or related by marriage. American mine owners preferred to have Chinese headmen control the workers hired through Chinese labor contractors but generally had EuroAmerican supervisors and office workers overseeing the work. The same organizational system was evident in railroad construction throughout the American West. By the 1900 census, when some census takers were able to ascertain more accurate renditions of Chinese names, none of the three Chinese boss miners or any names resembling these individuals appeared with correlating birth dates.[92] In all probability, these men had settled in another location in the United States or returned to China.

However, not all boss miners returned to China. There is no information about anyone in Elko County, but in nearby California the case of Won Woo was an example of a mining boss who remained in the United States.[93] According to his 1904 application for a duplicate certificate of residence, Woo, like many first-generation American immigrants, opted to remain in California. All of his fellow co-workers in the Calaveras County, California, Firstborn mine returned to China to live in retirement or semi-retirement because the mine had been very profitable. However, Woo had adapted to American life during his thirty years of living in the area, first as a railroad worker and then as a mine foreman, and probably felt that contemporary Chinese lifestyle was too restrictive and "old fashioned." At age 56, he now had sufficient funds to comfortably support himself. Like many other Chinese at the time, he had to pay an attorney to assist him in getting another certificate of residence from the Bureau of Immigration. Some of the Chinese miners in Island Mountain might have earned enough to return to China.[94] On the other hand, men like Woo, Ing Hay, Lung On, Ah Lee Lake, and China Lem remained after the mines were no longer prosperous.

The residential pattern of the fourteen households in 1880 suggests that there was no spatial segregation. Class lines also apparently were blurred. A single EuroAmerican miner from Ohio who could afford a single dwelling lived next to two EuroAmerican miners on one side and a household that was made up of a Chinese prostitute, a Chinese gambler, a Chinese loafer, and a Chinese miner on the other. The hostility and residential segregation that characterized so many of the 1870s and 1880s mining communities in many parts of the American West was not evident in Island Mountain, thus making it unusual. When the dwellings of the non-Chinese residents were abandoned, the Chinese probably took them over. Often the transfer of property was informal, so it is not known whether they purchased the dwellings, leased them, or simply moved in.

Unlike many other Chinese communities in Nevada, such as Virginia City, where approximately one-third of the Chinese men were married but living apart from their wives, in 1880 the Chinese miners in Island Mountain were all single men with an average age of 35.[95] Two miners were 60 and 67, making them the seniors in the group. The 19-year-old was the youngest Chinese miner. The census taker could have been mistaken or did not bother to check the "married" column since it was unusual to have only single men listed.

The miners living in boarding houses regarded their abode as temporary and primarily for sleeping. They often worked in shifts and rested according to their work schedules. As Daniel Liestman pointed out, "Homes in China were highly adapted to the local environment . . . [and often used the traditional method] of creating walls of tamped earth in wooden frames."[96] Typically whatever was available locally was used in the construction of the dwellings.

Like many Chinese immigrants with an agricultural background, the men raised their own vegetables in a garden that was a drainage bottom opposite the row of buildings.[97] A creek fed by the twenty-foot-wide reservoir near Pekin Avenue was used for irrigating the garden.[98] The produce was grown for their consumption, sold to Chinese cooks, and sometimes sold to the larger community. Carrots, onions, potatoes, lettuce, and other produce were preserved in barrels filled with river sand for use in the winter. Chinese cabbage, which took only three months to grow, was a main crop that could be preserved well in the sand for the winter months. Archaeological evidence in front of several of the dwellings included fragments of wooden barrels with river sand.[99] The location of the garden itself is unknown.[100] Mining water was diverted for planting; pumps were often built to move the water. With the passage of time and the silt deposits, the Island Mountain gardens disappeared. However, Chinese terraced gardens are still found outside of Winnemucca, Nevada.[101] Gardening was usually an auxiliary occupation for the miners.

Although there was no printed record of appreciation for the fresh vegetables in Island Mountain, in the same time period other mining communities in Nevada, particularly Virginia City, expressed their great praise for the Chinese gardeners. In nearby Elko, Wah Sing, a potato grower, provided the locals with potatoes, carrots, and turnips as his major crops and made enough money by 1886 to return to China.[102] In Hawthorne, Nevada, the merchant and vegetable peddler Chung Kee taught the Paiutes from Schurz how to irrigate the dry desert landscape for farming.[103] The availability of fresh produce enhanced a miner's diet and health. EuroAmerican miners usually were not interested in agricultural work, so the Chinese "gardener" or farmer filled this void.

Although there are no known records of Chinese miners from Elko County who became farmers, there was the history of Wong Ah Lung, also known as Wong Shee Chew.[104] He was born in How Boy village, Kaiping District, Guangdong, around 1849 and immigrated to San Francisco in 1868. He worked for three years as a miner in Virginia City and made enough money to establish a merchandising store that operated for ten years in nearby Auburn, Placer County, California. Later, he became a farmer in Penryn, Placer County, for the next ten years. He made enough money to make one trip to China between 1874 and 1878. He subsequently married but like most Chinese men, left his wife and children (if there were any) in China. His story indicated that although he had been a miner and a merchant, he was most comfortable being a farmer as his ancestors had been.

There was ample wild game (such as sage hens) and fish (including wild salmon from the Owyhee River) for the community. The Chinese probably purchased pigs, chickens, and ducks from the EuroAmerican farmers if they did not raise them in town. The fact that Suey, one of the Nep brothers, had gone to Gold Creek to purchase two chickens for Chinese New Year indicated that this occurred.[105] Evidence of a wide variety of animal and fish consumption was seen in the fragments of bones uncovered during the archaeological excavation. The Chinese merchant usually imported canned fish, preserved and pickled vegetables, canned meats, rice, and tea from China through a California wholesaler or middleman.

Local newspapers reported only one serious crime involving the Chinese in Island Mountain. George W. Mardis, a rancher and miner born in Pennsylvania in 1834, also owned freighting horses and hauled ore to and from Island Mountain and Mardis Mining Districts to the railroad station at Deeth. Five Chinese miners lived and worked in Mardis, not far from Island Mountain. In September 1880, New York Charlie, a Chinese resident of Island Mountain, allegedly robbed and murdered Mardis for the gold he was hauling.[106] The case achieved some notoriety because New York Charlie had six toes and left his footprint near Mardis's body. According to one of numerous accounts, the local vigilante committee promptly lynched New York Charlie after a "trial" at Stofiel's store despite Charlie's protestations of innocence.[107] Another account stated that the posse found New York Charlie in the future Gold Creek area and the Chinese community leaders asked the posse if they could take over the case because Mardis had been carrying $250 to buy supplies for the Chinese in Elko.[108] The posse agreed. The Chinese "tribunal" found Charlie guilty of a crime punishable by death.[109] Both accounts are believable, the final result was the same, but the money was never recovered. New York Charlie's and Mardis's funerals occurred on the same day: both were buried in the present-day Gold Creek Cemetery. Like other grave markers, New York Charlie's headstone was removed by vandals in the mid-twentieth century, so there is no evidence of where his grave was located.

Census manuscripts and other government documents did not shed any light on the community's development between 1880 and 1900. The critical 1890 census manuscript was destroyed by fire. Another set of documents, the 1892–93 Chinese Certificate of Residence interviews, required by the stricter 1892 Chinese Exclusion Act, could not be located for Island Mountain or Tuscarora. However, these depositions must have been taken by a Bureau of Immigration agent from either Salt Lake City, San Francisco, or Sacramento. By 1900 almost all of the Chinese listed in 1880 for Island Mountain apparently had left the town.

The 1900, 1910, and 1920 census manuscripts for Elko County did not contain matching names and ages of any of the aforementioned 1880 Chinese individuals with the exception of three men, Lee Suig or Suig Lee, Ah Chee, and China Lem (who is discussed below separately). In 1880 Lee Suig or Suig Lee (b. 1838, immigrated 1861) was a placer miner working for Lung Wah in Island Mountain. Based upon the spelling of his name and a match of his birth date, by 1900 Suig Lee had moved to Tuscarora.[110] He was listed as a laborer who was in partnership with the gardener, Siu Lee (b. 1856). At 61, he had given up mining as his main occupation unless the category of "laborer" included some aspect of mining. Since Ah Lee Lake was the most prominent Chinese in Tuscarora, if both men had the family name of Lee, there was probably a kinship relationship and indicative of chain migration.

Among the fifty-one Chinese living in Tuscarora in 1900, only six were miners, and they all made enough money to own their own homes. Their profile differed from the Island Mountain Chinese miners of the 1880s. In Tuscarora only one (age 60) was single while the other five were married. However their average age was 53 and all had immigrated between 1872 and 1882, indicating that they were about the same age as the 1880 Island Mountain Chinese miners. Taking into consideration the Bryan, Elko County, Chinese placer miners, who numbered two (one, age 61 and married for forty-three years, and the other, age 60 and single), the data suggests that Chinese placer miners in this region were decreasing in number and becoming elderly.[111] That many were married but living separately from their wives suggested they had been married before they left China—or made enough money to go back to China, marry, and returned to the American West without their wives. Most who had mined earlier had changed their occupation because of the decline in placer mining and probably moved into the service or agricultural occupations.

Table 4. Chinese Population by Nevada Counties, 1870–1920*

County	Date established	1870	1880	1890	1900	1910	1920
Churchill	1864	16	32	30	7	9	17
Douglas	1864	23	159	56	19	14	17
Elko	1869	439	613	311	191	151	93
Esmeralda	1864	56	242	277	115	64	8
Eureka	1873	—	633	284	101	30	14
Humboldt	1861	220	529	377	225	162	78
Lander	1862	218	387	87	71	24	13
Lincoln	1866	23	100	34	72	32	18
Lyon	1861	116	390	86	39	24	15
Nye	1864	6	66	23	7	59	44
Ormsby	1861	769	988	760	152	118	73
Storey	1850	749	639	245	76	44	13
Washoe	1861	221	526	217	246	155	155
White Pine	1869	292	107	46	31	25	32

*Roop (1859), Mineral (1911), and Clark (1909) counties are not included.

Bureau of the Census, *Compendium of the Eleventh Census: 1890,* Table 14, Chinese Population by Counties, 1870, 1880, 1890, p. 520, and *Fourteenth Census: 1920,* Vol. 3, Population by states.

The second "long time" resident of Elko, Elko County, was Ah Choo. There is the possibility that Ah Choo's name became spelled Ah Chee in the 1900 Elko City census. His age, 52 in 1900, his date of immigration of 1871, his single martial status, and his home ownership despite his occupation as a day laborer, suggested that he had accumulated some wealth earlier elsewhere. He was not listed in the 1880 census manuscript for Elko County. In Elko, he headed a household that consisted of two young relatives, probably cousins. One cousin, Ah Chee Ang (b. 1855; Ang is another rendition of Ng), had married in 1874 and had immigrated in 1882. The other cousin, F. Yew Ong (Ong is yet another spelling for Ng), was born in California in 1871 and married in 1897 but living separately from his wife. The establishment of related households was typical among the Chinese in this exclusionary era (1882–1943). As members of the Wu (pinyin)/Ng/Ong/Ang/Eng clan, these men were probably linked as kinsmen to Lem Hong Ng of Island Mountain.

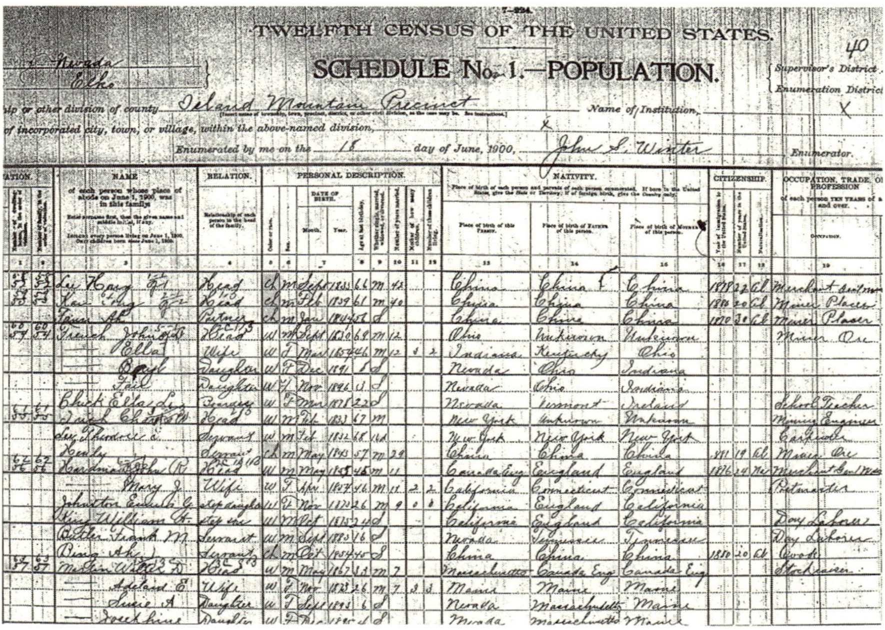
TWELFTH CENSUS OF THE UNITED STATES.
SCHEDULE No. 1.—POPULATION.

Census manuscript (also called population schedules) for Island Mountain precinct, 1900. The first three entries are China Lem and two Chinese miners. Information gives head of household, date of birth, age, married (with length of time) or single, place of birth, immigration date, occupation.

By 1900 the character of Island Mountain/Gold Creek changed as more EuroAmericans and EuroAmerican families settled there. Of the ninety-one residents, only five were Chinese: Hong Lim or Lem (b. 1833, married), merchant and popularly known as China Lem; Kan Fong, (b. 1839, married in 1860, immigrated 1880), a placer miner; Ah Fann (b. 1844, immigrated 1870, single), a partner in mining with Kan Fong; Henly (b. 1843, married in 1871, immigrated 1881), a miner; and Ah Bing (b. 1854, immigrated 1865, single), a cook for John Hardman (b. 1858 in Canada, naturalized) and his wife, Mary (b. 1856 in California). Hardman owned a general merchandising store, large hotel, and salon in Gold Creek. The only other Chinese miner in a nearby town was Sing Quin Gee (b. 1864, married in 1888, immigrated 1890), who lived in Mountain City. The Chinese varied in age but each had been in the United States for ten to twenty years. Kan Fong had spent half of his married life in the United States without his wife by his side.

The 1910 census manuscript listed three Chinese men in Island Mountain: China Lem, listed in the census as Lim or Lem Hong (b. 1833, married in 1858, immigrated 1878), a store keeper; Joe Carney 1841–1915, immigrated in 1865), who owned a ranch and because of his age, could also have been the person commonly known as China Joe, the miner; and Bing Ah or Ah Bing, the Hardman's cook at the Hardman Hotel.[112] Most of the long-time residents of Gold Creek remembered China Lem, China Joe, and Ah Bing. By 1920 Ah Bing had left and was replaced by Charlie King (b. 1874, married), who cooked for the Hardmans and was the only Chinese remaining in the district. The usual method of obtaining a Chinese cook was by having the previous cook recommend a friend or relative, so Ah Bing and Charlie King might have been related since relatives often turned over their jobs to another relative. In almost all mining communities in the American West, Chinese cooks had a reputation for providing good food—essential in keeping single men in the location—so many mine and hotel owners actively sought Chinese cooks.

Despite the friendliness and reliance upon each other, there were still elements of racism. Daniel Liestman pointed out that trade was the mainstay of the relations between Native Americans and Chinese since the Chinese served as the "middleman minority" between the Native Americans and EuroAmericans.[113] David McKinney, a Shoshone, often visited Island Mountain with his father. His father liked to gamble with the Chinese and probably communicated in pidgin English since members of both ethnic groups knew only limited English. This was not uncommon in certain parts of the American West.[114] McKinney recalled that when he was a child the Native American children teased the obese Chinese cook (probably Ah Bing or Charlie King).[115]

They pointed out that his pants wiggled when he walked and often fell down. McKinney also recalled throwing rocks at certain Chinese individuals. However, these pranks never developed into the violent anti-Chinese actions. By contrast in Tonopah, Nevada, in 1903 a mob spurred on by union leaders drove the Chinese out of town, killing one old laundryman; and in Reno, in 1908, citizens burned Chinatown in the winter, leaving one hundred fifty Chinese without a place to live.[116] In general, the Chinese stayed in Island Mountain because the community was usually accepting and friendly toward them despite the antagonism elsewhere in the county, state, and nation.

There were several stories about the local Chinese. Peter Bastida, who was born and raised in Gold Creek, recalled that Charlie King was fond of chukar and sage hen and often went hunting.[117] One day, while the Bastida family was having a picnic in their backyard with friends, Charlie accidentally killed the family's pet badger, Bob, who was eating scraps from the picnic. Charlie had mistaken Bob for a wild badger and thought he was doing the family a favor. The children were so heartbroken that Charlie, hoping to soothe their grief, gave them each a dollar—no small sum of money in those days. In 1930 Charlie was listed in the census as a 68-year-old widower cooking in a camp in South Fork, Elko County.[118]

Merchant China Lem was the Chinese community leader of Island Mountain and there is only fragmentary information about him. His background has not been clearly documented in the census records. In 1870 there was a miner named Hong Lee (b. 1845), who was able to read, living in Mountain City, but this individual may or may not have been China Lem of Island Mountain.[119] The identity of China Lem, the familiar merchant-grocer of the turn of the twentieth century, could have been one of two men in the 1880 census manuscript (and a close examination of the 1900 and 1910 census manuscripts only contributed to the confusion). In Household 14, the storekeeper, Lem Hung (b. 1839, age 41, single) lived with a laundryman, Sam Lee Wah; a boss miner, Ling Wo; and six other miners. In Household 8, the grocer, Lem Hung See (or Lee?) (b. 1840, age 40, single) had a similar name. China Lem's advertisement in the *Gold Creek News* gave the names Hung Li and Hong Lee. The EuroAmerican residents recalled that when one brother died or returned to China, the other moved from Tuscarora to take his place around the turn of the twentieth century. It is possible that Household 14 became Household 1 in the 1900 federal census with the address 1 Pekin Avenue, so that Lem Hung was the first China Lem.

In the 1900 census manuscript China Lem is listed as Hong Lee (b. 1834, age 66), merchant, who had been married since 1898. This suggests that he went to China in the late 1890s, married, and then returned to the United States—but a search of records of the Bureau of Immigration had no one with immigration papers by that name or the name Hong Lee/Lem Ng or any combination therein. The year of his immigration was listed as 1878 and it was noted that he was literate. The census taker in 1900 was probably more accurate than the one in 1880, nevertheless it is difficult to determine which man was China Lem who lived in Island Mountain from the 1890s through 1916. The census taker in 1910 listed Hong Lim (or Lem) (b. 1834, age 76), a storekeeper who had been married since 1854 (more realistic than the earlier account with the date 1898), who could read and was head of his household. (One of his neighbors was James E. Penrod, a miner and one of the sons of Emanuel Penrod.) This Chinese individual had immigrated in the late 1860s. Both the 1900 and 1910 census takers indicated that he lived not far from John R. Hardman. Census information in these small communities was not always accurate.

The Chinese family name of "China Lem" was revealed in a letter from the mayor of San Francisco noting Elko's Chinese donors to the 1906 San Francisco Earthquake and Fire Chinatown Rebuilding Project: $2 from Lem Hong Ng (in Chinese, Ng Lem Hong with the family name first, and in pinyin, Wu Linhong).[120] Based on this information, it is obvious that he was a kinsman to the Eng/Ung/Ng/Ing (Wu in pinyin) clan who were prominent merchants in Elko; to Doc Ing Hay in John Day, Oregon; and the large Ng/Eng/Ung (and similar spellings) clan who settled in Seattle and Port Townsend, Washington.[121] For decades Seattle's International District hosted Ng clan gatherings for kinsmen in the American West.[122] Members of this same clan, originating in Taishan, Guangdong, were prominent in North Cariboo District, British Columbia, in the 1880s and were members of the Zhigongtang in Barkerville, British Columbia.[123] The Ng clan also played a prominent role in the Zhigongtang in Port Townsend.[124] This suggests that China Lem might have been connected with Ah Lee Lake, the head of the Zhigongtang in Tuscarora, if he was a member of the organization.

Hung Li and Hong Lee,[125] two brothers who were both called China Lem, sold groceries and dry goods between 1878 and 1918 or later.[126] In 1881 the Elko County Recorder's Office listed Hong Lee's personal wealth as $200, making him one of the more prosperous Chinese in the county.[127] Chinese merchants who had EuroAmerican customers understood the importance of advertising in the local newspaper and supporting the efforts of small-town newsmen. A fairly regular advertisement for the Hong Lee store appeared in the *Gold Creek News* in 1896 and 1897.

China Lem was an "institution"—in a lengthy description of Gold Creek, published in the *Gold Creek News* (March 4, 1897), the story concluded, "If one has made the round trip [from Gold Creek to Island Mountain] he is now ready to stop at Chinatown . . . and receive Lem's friendly greeting. A moderate indulgence in that Chinese rice beverage will make the distance down to the [Gold Creek Mining] Company house not seem so long."

An undated photograph of the store itself from the C. A. Laing Collection at the Northeastern Nevada Museum showed that the foundation of Lem's store was partially constructed of rock with a porch covered by an awning.[128] China Lem stood in the foreground in a Chinese outfit, along with a hat that many Chinese in the American West liked to wear, and smoking a Chinese-style tobacco pipe. The store had barrels, boxes, and other objects in front. The front wall extended down to the ground. On the far side of the store were approximately six horizontally aligned short boards that tied the building to the structure next door. The front door was probably no taller than Lem. There

J. W. DEANE,
Formerly of Equitable Bld'g., Denver, Col.
ELKO, NEV.
Mines and Mining Investment.

HENDERSON BANKING CO.,
(Incorporated)
Transacts a General Banking Business.
Elko, - - - - Nevada.

Gold Creek Hotel,
JOHN B. ABEL, Proprietor.
NEWLY AND HANDSOMELY FURNISHED THROUGH-OUT.
Best Appointed House in Eastern Nevada.
RATES $2.00 TO $4.00 PER DAY.

Hardman's Saloon and Lodging House,
J. R. HARDMAN, PROPRIETOR.
Fine Foreign and Domestic
Wines, Liquors and Cigars.

R. R. BOWLES, Gen. Mgr., ... Elko ....
CHAS. W. WALDRON, Res. Mgr., ... Gold Creek ....
The Elko-Gold Creek Lumber Co.
MANUFACTURERS AND DEALERS IN
LUMBER,
Sash, Doors, Moulding, Shingles, Lath and all Kinds of Building Materials and Builders' Hardware.
★ Furniture and Undertaking. ★
GOLD CREEK AND ELKO, - - - NEVADA.

HONG LEE,
General Merchandise
Fine Display Rich Silks
Just Received, a Large Stock of Chinese Rice Whisky.
CALL AND BE CONVINCED.
Everybody knows me as "Lem," and I have been in business h[ere] 18 years.
NO. 1. PEKIN AVENUE (CHINATOWN) GOLD CREEK, NEVADA.

Hong Lee believed in promotion and regularly submitted the advertisement in the lower-right corner to the *Gold Creek News*, the local newspaper so that his customer base included non-Chinese.

was a six-paned airtight window near the front door. The top of the window was approximately the same height as the doorway. The panes of glass in the windows were framed with willow branches that had been split perfectly to tightly accommodate each piece of glass. The back of the store abutted the hillside, a common construction technique in Nevada and other parts of the rural American West. The roof was partially sod over timbers and partially boards covered with canvas. The front porch floor was constructed of milled lumber and the awning was held up by a frame with two round log posts. (After 1897 much of the milled lumber came from nearby North Fork where a sawmill had been built.)[129] Roofing material was not placed over the milled lumber rafters of the porch so that sunlight could shine through. Flashing between the front of the building and the roof was present.

Della Baker Johns (born in Elko, raised in Gold Creek, and the daughter of Lem's teamster Franklin Baker) occasionally went with her parents to Lem's store and talked about her experiences.[130] She described the interior of the store: the walls were lined with horizontally "stacked" willows, about one inch in diameter, tightly lashed together. The ceiling also was lined with willows of uniform size. The store's main room had a table made of a wooden barrel with boards across the top and simple willow chairs that patrons sat in probably to visit and catch up with the local gossip. Heat came from a small carved-out area of the floor and wall where a large pot of some kind made out of pottery or metal held hot coals and had a metal screen over it. The room also contained the typical straw carrying bags that the Chinese commonly used for shipping or transporting goods.

Della did not visit the other room or rooms in the store. She knew that Lem and his roommate, "Old Joe," lived in a separate dwelling but never visited that place.[131] According to Della, Old Joe never cut his queue, which poked out of the top of his skull cap and was quite long—long enough to be pulled around to lie on his chest. If the weather was cold and a warmer hat required, Old Joe and the other Chinese men having a queue simply put a warmer cap over the skull cap. Della recalled that the Chinese miners wore American-made baggy canvas overalls, thick-soled Chinese boots, and black quilted jackets. The combination of American-made and traditional Chinese clothing was typical of Chinese living in Nevada. In other locations, as seen, for example, in a photograph of a Dayton Chinese, the Chinese quickly adopted American-made boots, which were sturdier than the Chinese boots.

According to Della, some of the other buildings in Chinatown had roofs partially made of wild rye grass thatch and some huts had tents as the roofing.[132] Peter Bastida, who was born and raised in Gold Creek, said that the

Chinatown "huts" looked very much like frontier sod houses—depressions dug out of the hillside with rock or log foundations and timbers or poles set close together to make a base for the layers of dirt (similar to the mud bricks of South China) piled on top.[133] Based upon the Laing photograph, the building next to Lem's had a pitched roof covered with thatching. A log lay at the top of the left wall extending to the front of the structure perhaps about thirty centimeters. It supported a rafter that extended to the roof peak.

Lem was dressed in traditional Chinese clothing in the two photographs. The loose-fitting cotton Chinese garments were comfortable for work and easy to sew, unlike the more complicated American wear. However, many Chinese miners wore Western clothing, especially Levi's-type pants, because Chinese clothing was not suitable for the rough outdoor work of placer, hydraulic, and quartz mining. According to Liping Zhu, at one placer mining site in the Boise Basin, 86 percent of the recovered artifacts were of U.S. manufacture and only 14 percent were of probable Chinese origin.[134] Many Chinese had adopted western footwear because traditional Chinese footwear of cloth or silk was too delicate for the rough work of miners.

Archaeological finds in Island Mountain's Chinatown during the summers of 1999 through 2001 included Chinese tableware and ceramics, Chinese liquor jars, Chinese medicine bottles, and cans or ceramic food containers. Approximately 94 percent of the ceramic artifacts, most of which were broken, were of Chinese origin or Chinese-style ceramics of American or European manufacture. The porcelain table wares were primarily bowls and cups of three main decorative designs: winter-melon green (often mistakenly called celadon, and the most expensive), bamboo, and Four Seasons. However, the Double Happiness and Four Flowers designs, also commonly found in Chinese sites of the period, were not found. The most commonly found wares were Chinese brown-glazed stoneware that originally contained foodstuffs and liquor imported from China; some had "maker marks" imprinted on them. Preserved fruits or vegetables, soy sauce, and condiments were often packaged in green or brown-glazed stoneware. That he carried American ceramic goods suggested that Lem was practical and used or sold what was readily available, thus making accommodations to American life.

Despite its relative isolation, the Chinese community was able to import Chinese foodstuffs, such as pickled vegetables (transported in tins or brown or green glazed pottery ware), dried vegetables, preserved fruits (seeds found), fish (packed in tins; bones found), medicines bottles, tins for opium, and numerous types of liquor bottles. Lem's store sold soy sauce, canned fish and oysters, dried oysters, dried tomatoes and mushrooms of various types, canned water chestnuts and bamboo shoots, dried bean curd, pickled vegetables, canned meat, and other staples like rice, flour, and sugar.[135] American canned foods, including condensed milk, coffee, and butter, were also sold. A maple syrup tin (Log Cabin brand) was among the items found in one of the dwellings. This was used for a Cantonese dessert as well as a sweetener for other dishes. Lea and Perrins Worcestershire Sauce also was a popular EuroAmerican product among the Chinese and was found in Island Mountain and other Chinese sites in the American West.[136]

Canned goods and other products from China were shipped in barrels to San Francisco or Sacramento and then redistributed in smaller containers to Chinese stores throughout the country. His Chinese products undoubtedly came to his store via the Central Pacific Railroad from San Francisco or Sacramento and from Carlin or Elko by a teamster such as the Baker brothers. He probably purchased the products from stores owned by clansmen in California. Based on court records, Lem's American groceries came from Salt Lake City, Utah.[137] One of the Mormon residents probably introduced him to the Salt Lake City firm.

Alcoholic beverages were a popular item in his store. The bottles of rice wine and brandy were consumed for pleasure, used for medicinal purposes in soups or rubbed on the body as an analgesic. Alcohol also was offered to the deities in tiny porcelain tea cups, especially at New Year and on festival days.[138] According to Hugh Martin Jr., rice wine and Chinese brandy (*Ng Gai Pei*) were favorites for all in the town.[139] Discovered at the site of Lem's store during the Forest Service archaeological dig was a high-quality Chinese wine bottle—with a lustrous blue glaze—substantiating news reports about his rice wine, and indicating that he served and sold good-quality rice wine. Archaeological evidence also showed other types of Chinese wine vessels and a variety of American beverage bottles including champagne, whiskey, gin, beer, soft drinks, and lemonade.[140]

The dig also produced several American products including a ceramic doorknob; a 1892 lock; coyote traps; axes, shovels, and pickaxes; a variety of ammunition, black powder, lead balls, and shotgun shells; a wide array of textiles and clothing, including wool pants and shirts; various clothing fasteners, including Levi's metal buttons; suspenders, and boots (four complete boots and fragments of ten others).[141] The store sold a selection of western and Chinese clothing, especially for daily wear. There also was a part of a traditional Chinese lock. The discovery of a lady's silver filigree buckle and clasp and a stone from a piece of jewelry indicates that females also shopped at or visited the store. American cans of food products, kerosene cans, English-produced china fragments, a commercial-sized coffee grinder, farming equipment, tools, raincoats, rubber boots, leather shoes, barrel hoops, axe heads, portions of shovels, nails, and milled lumber were also present.[142] Lem's store undoubtedly was a smaller version of the northern California Kwong Tai Wo (probably situated in Marysville), whose 1871–96 record books have been preserved in the Ethnic Studies Library at the University of California–Berkeley and detailed the sale of food products, tools, hardware, household goods, clothing, personal accessories, books, drugs, and ceremonial items.[143]

Like all Chinese merchants, Lem used an abacus for accounting; this was found intact in the site of his store in 2001. The quality of the wooden frame was excellent. The design was typical of late nineteenth-century Chinese abacus. Most Chinese merchants treasured their abacus, so this might have indicated that a serious illness and sudden departure caused him to leave it behind.

During the excavation, aspects of daily life were revealed. A part of a wok uncovered showed that the Chinese favored cooking in the traditional style. Some cooking was done outside, using a big pot or barrel with a screen over it as the stove.[144] Since the Chinese did a lot of stir-fry cooking, the food was cooked quickly and the houses had no cooking odors. A wooden barrel outside of the store contained pure river sand that was used to preserve food throughout the winter. Interior cooking probably included making soup, rice porridge, and other slow-cooked dishes. Since imported Chinese goods probably were expensive, the Chinese had to supplement their resources with locally grown herbs, vegetables, and fruits as well as American foodstuffs. Rice and tea were mainstays of their diet and were imported from China. Pork, beef, and chicken were the primary meats, supplemented by wild game, including deer, ducks, quail, sage hen, and chukar from the region. The site contained bone fragments of these; the indications were that a Chinese cleaver was used to cut up the meat. Duck and quail eggs could be easily obtained and preserved and shell fragments were present on the site. Fish was very popular with southern Chinese and could be caught easily in the Owyhee River and its tributaries. The site had many types of fish bones, indicating that some of the fish were imported from China and some were local species.[145] Canned fish, such as Dace, was popular, as seen in bone fragments. In comparison with the diet of the time in southeastern China, the Chinese in Island Mountain probably ate a healthier and more varied diet with a better selection of food. They had incorporated some American food products into their diet while trying to maintain traditional Chinese foods.

These archaeological finds and documentary evidence indicate that as traditional as Lem seemed to the outside world in his clothing and habits, he had made adjustments to his situation in the American West. He was not a sojourner because he could have left when many of his fellow countrymen and relatives departed after the mining bust. He had made EuroAmerican friends in Island Mountain and from all indications, did not plan to leave even after the death of his good friends, the Nep brothers.

By 1915 the store had been improved with wood panels and was much more in line with western architectural style, demonstrating increased prosperity. A photograph from the Baker family collection showed men, including the Baker brothers (who were teamsters), gathered in front of the store before a hunting excursion. The size and value of the store may have been similar to ones in nearby Chinatowns. In 1882 Chung Fung sold George Dick a newly erected brick building in Tuscarora for $40 "on the north side of Front Street and the south side of Weed Street, 25 feet south from the brick and adobe building erected by the Hop See Company, southerly along the northerly line of Front, 12½ feet at right angle easterly 100 feet and at right angle northerly at 12½ feet."[146] In 1887 Yee Sing Nan sold Hong Yet Tong Company a building that was on the west side of Front Street, Tuscarora, for $185.[147] The deed's description was "the third house, northerly from Hogle Corral, 13 feet wide on Front Street, back 65' in a westerly direction, two stories with a cellar." All contents in the structure were included, so a general store was worth more. In

China Lem "modernized" his storefront after 1900. Many of his EuroAmerican friends, including the Baker brothers, stopped there before and after going hunting. (Author's collection)

1877 in nearby Cornucopia, the Sing Chong Company, also known as the An Gow Company, was sold to Quong Yuen for $1,000.[148] In a larger community like Elko, the price was even higher. In 1910, Hop Sing sold Ung Fung the Hi Loy Company, Block J, in Elko for $2,000, which included all goods and merchandise.[149] Lem's store probably was worth something in between $40 and $2,000, but probably closer to $1,000. In the 1880s, the Elko County tax assessor listed Lem's personal property worth for tax purposes as $300, which was much less than the $800 that Chinese merchant Hop Lee of Tuscarora was valued at.[150]

Lem's store was the neighborhood store, so he had to interact with the EuroAmerican and Native American population. Knowledge of English, however limited, was important for the Chinese merchant to transact business. The close connection between Chinese miners and merchants was evident. Miners needed Chinese and American supplies and foodstuffs and felt more comfortable purchasing goods from a Chinese merchant like Lem.

Hugh Martin Jr., whose family came from Nova Scotia and whose father served after Emanuel Penrod as postmaster of Island Mountain, recalled his memories of Lem:

> [He] was a nice old Chinaman. Everyone liked him. He always had a little gift for every person who came to his store—a cigar, maybe, or a drink of Chinese brandy—, or if the customer was a lady, he might give her a little Chinese silk handkerchief. After Lem died, the store was taken over by his brother, Hong Li, [also eventually known as China Lem] from Tuscarora. Hong was just as nice as Lem had been; and one or the other of the Li brothers was in business here for close to forty years.[151]

Martin also commented about celebrating Chinese New Year in Island Mountain.[152] In China, families met for dinner on New Year's Eve and during the week, the Chinese entertained good friends. The Chinese immigrants always celebrated this favorite festival, often inviting EuroAmerican friends to meals, and continued the practice of celebrating and gift-giving, especially to children, thus introducing the larger community to this Chinese tradition. Chinese men, longing for the family life that was so familiar in China, often treated children of any race and ethnicity with special kindness, especially during Chinese New Year. This was the case in Island Mountain.

Martin recalled, "Our Chinese couldn't afford lot of fancy fireworks like they had at Chinese doings in Elko, but there were plenty of loud firecrackers and lots of queer cookies and candies."[153] He also said that Lem gave him all the cookies and candies he could eat and sacks filled with more to carry home.[154] Other children, including a Shoshone, David McKinney, recalled the same.[155] Lem always had sweets for the children but Della Baker Johns did not like the bitter mint, or horehound candy that he usually gave her. She recalled that Lem often gave her father sardines and crackers and her mother received silk handkerchiefs. The practice of gift-giving to close friends and acquaintances at this time of year was a tradition in China that Lem continued in Island Mountain.

It was not uncommon for the local Chinese merchant to sell opium, which could be done legally until the passage of local and federal anti-opium laws much later.[156] In 1909 a federal law prohibited the importation of smoking opium, and the Harrison Narcotics Tax Act of 1914 made the simple possession of opiates illegal. As in most late nineteenth-century Chinese sites, fragments of opium tins and pipes, the base of a spirit lamp to light opium, and small metal opium stirrers were found during the excavation.[157] The opium bowls were of the cheapest grade of opium pipe bowls available. Lem was personally opposed to smoking opium but he may have carried the opium tins and pipes due to customer demand. Della recalled how her mother had planted poppies one spring day and when Lem saw them, he insisted she dig up the plants "because they were bad." Mrs. Baker grudgingly consented because he was so adamant. The absence of numerous opium paraphernalia, as seen in other excavated Chinese American store sites, suggest that Della was correct in asserting that Lem was against opium smoking and did not smoke himself.

For those who did not smoke opium Lem's store was a place to play traditional Chinese games and listen to the latest news or reminisce about home.[158] Chinese gaming pieces were found in several locations in town; many were in the vicinity and inside of Lem's store. The most interesting artifact found during the 2001 archaeological dig at China Lem's store was a small fragment of a book in Chinese. The paper was of better quality than newspapers and the printing indicated that book was published in China. The two partial pages described the new republican government established in China after 1912 thus indicating that China Lem, like many Chinese merchants in the American West, could read Chinese and retained an interest in events in China. He probably also kept the local Chinese abreast of news about China. Many of the Chinese who were able to read and had books or newspapers from San Francisco's Chinatown or China set aside time on a regular basis to keep others in the community informed. This helped them to feel connected to the larger world even though they were geographically isolated.

Interactions with the EuroAmerican and Native American children were not limited to holidays. Martin and his friends also caught horned toads and traded them for candy at Lem's in the late 1870s and early 1880s. The toads (actually lizards) were packed in black pottery jars (which had formerly contained brandy), then covered with alcohol and sent to China for medicinal purposes.[159] Pine nuts were another popular item from Nevada, often the result of trading with Native Americans, which the Chinese merchants also sent to China where they were valued for their vitamin and high-protein properties.[160] Therefore, Lem's business activities included both importing goods from China and sending specialty items to China.

Although Chinese physicians could be found in every major Chinese community prior to 1892, the Chinese in Island Mountain had to travel to Tuscarora, where two doctors were listed in the 1880 census manuscript, but none by 1900.[161] Whether the Chinese ever consulted the Native American medicine man who lived in the hamlet is unknown but it was certainly a possibility since there were some similarities between Chinese and Native American herbal medicines. In 1900 the nearest Chinese doctor was Ow Quang (age 36, immigrated in 1872), who lived in Tecoma, Nevada, near the border of Utah.[162] Gold Greek did not have a EuroAmerican physician until 1897 when the Corey Brothers Construction Company contracted with a doctor.[163] Medical care in frontier America was difficult to obtain.

However, most Chinese knew traditional folk remedies and undoubtedly practiced preventive medicine by preparing various soups and teas to ward off common illnesses. The presence of gingko nuts, a favorite health food of the Chinese, in the Carlin Chinese cemetery from the turn of the twentieth century indicated that this health food was used.[164] Gingko nuts cooked in a rice gruel for better health was a common southern Chinese dish. Scattered throughout the Island Mountain residential area were empty, full, and partially full bottles of *bozhu yin,* Chinese pills for diarrhea and stomach pains, indicating that this was a commonly used remedy. Archaeological evidence showed that Vaseline, bitters, and aspirin also were in the store. Several Chinese American mining sites had various bottles of EuroAmerican bitters, suggesting that it was a popular medication that the Chinese adopted.

Throughout Nevada were many stories, passed down orally, about the kindness and generosity of the Chinese in times of need.[165] Della Baker Johns recounted one such story. One winter her mother, Margaret Tennille Baker (b. 1889), heard that her oldest sister, Daisy Davis (b. 1878), had been left without provisions by her husband.[166] Both women were married to teamsters. Mrs. Davis, who lived near Allegheny Creek, unsuccessfully tried to provide food for herself and her four children by shooting game and trapping rabbits. When Mrs. Baker heard that they were starving, she skied to Lem's store and explained the situation. Despite Lem's grumblings about the possible dangers in the bad weather, he gave Mrs. Baker on credit sacks full of canned goods, rice, flour, and other staples, and even included a small bottle of wine gratis. Lem then helped Mrs. Baker balance the weight on her back so that she could bring these provisions on her skis to her sister's—a task she would have been unable to do without Lem's help. Mr. Davis eventually was found in Elko where he was having a good time in the local taverns. The Baker and Davis families praised Lem for his generosity and kindness and, according to Della, they never forgot his help during this emergency.

The Bakers in turn helped Lem when the need arose. One example of this reciprocal assistance was when Lem was swindled. Two traveling confidence men persuaded Lem to purchase $110 worth of goods, primarily groceries, from them instead of his usual source in Salt Lake City. Lem gave them the money, but later heard that the men were arrested for swindling customers in nearby Mountain City. In March 1911 they were tried for fraud before Judge Klatte.[167] Lem could not testify in court because it had become common legal practice to prohibit the Chinese from testifying against "whites" in criminal cases. One of the justifications for this was that most Chinese were not Christians.[168] Additionally, in the famous case of *People v. Hall* (1854), the California Supreme Court held that Chinese could not testify against whites because allowing them to do so would "admit them to all the equal rights of citizenship . . . a race of people whom nature has marked as inferior."[169] The practice was not uniformly applied throughout the American West because some mining communities such as Bodie, California, occasionally allowed the Chinese to testify to convict non-Chinese criminals, especially in particularly violent and rough-and-tumble towns like Bodie.[170] Lem could and did testify about the circumstances surrounding China Joe's accidental death and other civil matters involving only Chinese, but not in criminal cases against EuroAmericans. Franklin Baker was so upset that he went to court on Lem's behalf. Because of Baker's testimony, the court ordered the swindlers to pay back Lem's money as well as pay back some of other men who had placed smaller orders with them.

Della also recalled that Lem and his friends were invited to share meals at her parents' home as well as at the Martins's home. Mrs. Baker served whatever she would normally cook, but because the Chinese men were there, rice was also a part of the menu.

No one recalls what happened to the second Lem, also known as Hong Li. In his eighties, he probably died or went to a neighboring state. Della mentioned that when he was sick, her parents or the Martins would take him to a nearby physician. The closest hospital was in Elko: ten beds in the home of Dr. Shaw from 1919 to 1923, and Elko General Hospital, completed in 1921. A search of obituary records and other materials yielded no information about Lem but the last recorded taxes he paid was in 1916.[171] The store was listed in Wang Kin's *International Chinese Business Directory* (1913) as one of five or six general merchandising companies in Carlin, the closest major transportation center.[172] At the time, newspapers were filled with stories about the 1918 flu pandemic and the war instead of stories about Chinese residents. No one recalls what happened to Lem after about 1918.

Three miners also became well known in the Island Mountain community, but they also had other occupations. Henly lived in a house around the bend from Peking Street and also worked as a servant for Charles Irish (b. 1833 in New York, married but living separately from his wife), a mining engineer who lived next to the French family. Henly probably got his name from the Elko County Commissioner T. Henley, or Elko County Recorder S. Henley, or Joshua Hendy, the San Francisco maker of mining equipment used in Island Mountain.

When Hilda Matthey visited Island Mountain with her husband and children in late August 1903, she took a photograph of Henly, who was her guide, and his home (or workshop). The photograph showed single dwelling with a door and windows, very much like middle-class American dwellings of the time. The fact that both Henly and Lem had glass windows in their homes was in contrast to the windowless designs of the New Zealand Chinese miners' homes that archaeologist Neville A. Ritchie studied.[173] Henly's house had sheets of metal, similar to those on the houses in Tuscarora, covering part of the roof for protection against the heavy winter snows. A black-and-white spaniel-type dog was on the porch. Nearby was a wall constructed of rock tailings set carefully in decorative patterns and sorted into piles of different sizes, a characteristic of a Chinese mining site. Non-Chinese miners tradition-

In 1903 Hilda Matthey photographed Henly's house/workshop as she toured Chinatown. A black-and-white spaniel and other goods are on the porch. A substantial structure, the house/workshop was around the bend from Chinatown. (Author's collection)

ally threw the tailings in random piles, but the Chinese usually constructed a wall that, according to Australian archaeologist Barry McGowan, was used as "puddlers" to break down the wash dirt or other mining tasks and was noted for its neatness.[174] Scattered housing behind the building may have been temporary residences of other miners. Little else is known about Henly.

The Chinese were very practical about the construction of their buildings. Since mining was an ephemeral occupation and one never knew how long one would reside in a particular location, most of the houses in Island Mountain's Chinatown were not built to last. But Henly's house resembled homes in South China and was more substantial. The residences on Pekin Street abutted the hillside, which formed the back part of the structure. This was a common architectural technique and provided cool relief from the summer heat and warmth in the cold winters. Unlike the Idaho Basin, wood was not in abundance, so the buildings were constructed of wood frames, tamped earth, and miscellaneous materials. They were small by western standards, usually consisting of two rooms.[175] The bedroom was in the rear and the living room, which also served as a kitchen, was in the front, closest to the street. The stove, which also served as a heater in the winter, was in the back part of the first room or by the front door. This was a relatively standard layout of homes in Guangdong. Since ancient times in China small shopkeepers had their store in the front and lived in the back room or rooms. If there was a business, the shop was the first of three rooms and usually was a gathering place for friends since homes were small.

In addition to China Lem and Henly, two miners were community notables. China Joe and Suey, brothers who worked as miners during the mining season, died and were buried in Island Mountain. In November, 1897, Emmanuel Penrod sold a placer claim in Tennessee gulch for $150 to two Chinese who were residents of Mountain City: Suey (also spelled Sui; in pinyin, Nie Shui; d. 1898) and his brother, China Joe or Shee (in pinyin Nie Shu) Nep (aka Joe Carney). Suey did not profit much from the investment but apparently China Joe did. Suey's death was reported in the Gold Creek newspaper and forest ranger August Rohwer, in his article about Gold Creek, also noted his passing.[176] Suey had been drinking at Gold Creek's saloon and walked home with a couple of chickens thrown over his shoulders for the forthcoming Chinese New Year celebration. (The saloon obviously did not have a segregation policy.) It was a cold winter and a storm developed suddenly. Suey was found frozen to death under a tree near the Hugh Martin house on January 2, 1898.[177] According to Hugh Martin's oral interview, Suey lived about ten miles from Gold Creek, which placed his home farther away than Island Mountain but closer than Mountain City. Martin said that Suey raised horses as well as worked for EuroAmerican mine owners. Other residents of the region had died under similar circumstances, so Suey's death was not unusual but he was the only Chinese known to die in this manner.

China Joe was a more interesting personality. He played cards and hunted with the EuroAmerican and Native American men. He died at the age of 74 on August 21, 1915, after having lived in the Island Mountain for thirty years.[178] His name, as such, did not appear on the census manuscript of 1900, but he may have been the rancher "Joe Carney" in the census manuscript for 1910. At the coroner's inquest, aspects of China Joe's life were revealed. He had

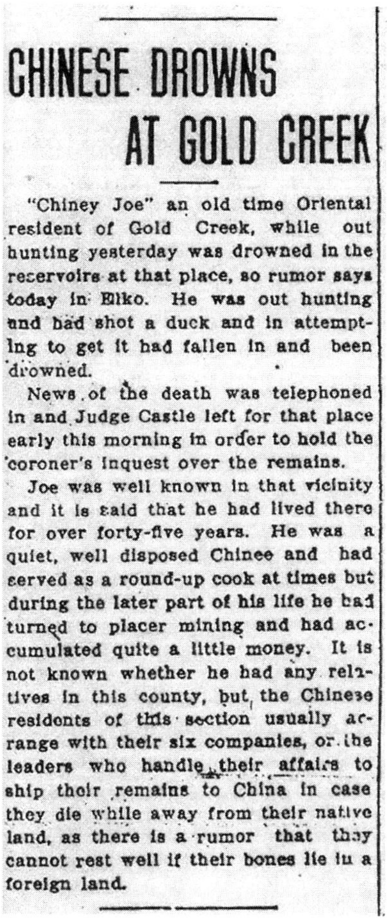

CHINESE DROWNS AT GOLD CREEK

"Chiney Joe" an old time Oriental resident of Gold Creek, while out hunting yesterday was drowned in the reservoirs at that place, so rumor says today in Elko. He was out hunting and had shot a duck and in attempting to get it had fallen in and been drowned.

News of the death was telephoned in and Judge Castle left for that place early this morning in order to hold the coroner's inquest over the remains.

Joe was well known in that vicinity and it is said that he had lived there for over forty-five years. He was a quiet, well disposed Chinee and had served as a round-up cook at times but during the later part of his life he had turned to placer mining and had accumulated quite a little money. It is not known whether he had any relatives in this county, but the Chinese residents of this section usually arrange with their six companies, or the leaders who handle their affairs to ship their remains to China in case they die while away from their native land, as there is a rumor that they cannot rest well if their bones lie in a foreign land.

China Joe's death made the newspaper in a story that reflects the sentiments of the times. (Source: Elko Free Press, August 23, 1915)

lived in Elko County for over forty-five years. He continued to own and work the mine that he had purchased from Emmanuel Penrod, and perhaps other mines as well. At the inquest in 1915, China Lem said that China Joe regularly sent $1,000 back to his family in China. This was more than the usual amount of around $300 that most Chinese of the time sent to their families. On the morning of August 21, China Joe went duck hunting with Bob McKenzie and accidentally drowned in the Sunflower Reservoir. McKenzie, Walter D. Martin (b. 1867, a stock rancher), and several other people tried without success to rescue him; they could not reach his body until the next day. When they found him he still had a duck clutched in his hand. China Joe's death and the attempted rescue were reported in detail in the local newspaper.[179] The newspaper devoted a significant amount of space to his obituary, indicating that he was a well-known and probably a well-liked figure in the community.

Although the newspaper reported that he probably was going to be reburied in China by the Chinese Benevolent Association (Chinese Six Companies), he was buried on August 23, 1915, in Island Mountain.[180] Like his brother's, China Joe's headstone was written in both English and Chinese.[181] Lem regularly remembered the brothers on Qingming Jie (Clear Brightness Festival), which occurred in the spring, usually around early April, and on the Feast of the Hungry Ghost, which occurred in the fall, usually sometime in September.[182] The former festival involved cleaning the grave site and offering prayers and food for the spirits of departed relatives and close friends, while the latter was observed to pacify the ghosts of strangers and the uncared-for dead.

Hugh Martin recalled that Lem was upset because the alcoholic beverages that Lem had placed on China Joe's grave disappeared but the food did not. It was obvious to Hugh that the local cowboys or Native Americans had drunk the liquor but would not touch the food.[183] Throughout the American West the Chinese performed funerary rituals dating back to 300 BC or earlier, and in rural towns, more often than not the funerary food and liquor offerings "disappeared." Nevertheless, the EuroAmerican and Native American residents took note of Lem's honoring of his friends.

Because Suey and Joe were born in the northwestern part of Guangdong province, an area not noted for the emigration of its residents, and because they belonged to a small clan (Nie, or in Cantonese, Nep), they would have been "outsiders" among the Chinese from the Siyi and Sanyi districts of southeastern Guangdong. However, in this small community, regional and local identity and clan identity yielded to "national" identity and the fact that they were all Chinese was more important to the Chinese men of Island Mountain. Thus, as many of the residents noted, Lem felt badly about the loss of his two friends. It is highly unlikely that their district association exhumed their graves and sent their bones back to China because there was not a viable district association or burial society in the immediate area. The brothers remain buried in Island Mountain to this day but the location is unknown since the grave markers were removed (around the 1950s).

These men were long-time residents of the area and were not sojourners. They lived between two worlds—that of China where their wives and families (parents, relatives, and possibly children) were, and that of the American West where they earned a good living and, from a comparative perspective, led a good life. They did not limit their circle of friends to Chinese immigrants but were friendly with EuroAmericans and Native Americans.

Another Island Mountain resident who later moved to Tuscarora was the laundryman Charlie Wah.[184] In the 1880 census manuscript for Island Mountain there was a laundryman named Sam Lee Wah (b. 1841), who may have been related to or was another name for Charlie Wah. In predominantly male mining towns, Chinese laundrymen could make a good living. Almost every mining town in the late nineteenth century in the American West had at least one Chinese laundry. The investment in the business was minimal: an estimated $5 would cover the washtubs, benches, irons, kettles, drying racks, and stove (which could be split in half and carried elsewhere on a shoulder pole) as long as there was a stream nearby.[185] At the standard rate of 25 cents per garment, a laundryman could earn $10 per day by washing forty pieces, thus earning more than the salaried Chinese worker at $2 to $3 per day. These men usually knew how to wash, iron, and care for material, having been in the cottage industry of textile production that had been replaced by western imported material. Clothes were dampened for a better finish, and some heated the irons in groups on the side of the stove and rotated their use for a faster result. Although there is no concrete information about the laundrymen in Elko County, in nearby Eureka County, Sam Kee amassed a considerable fortune. When he died in 1878, he had a savings account of $18,000.[186] Although Wah is not a Chinese last name, several laundries or laundrymen in the area had Wah as part of their names: in Tuscarora in 1880 (Hop Wah, b. 1850), in Elko in 1900 (Gun Wah, b. 1829, immigrated 1875), and in Carlin in 1910 (Yee Wah, b. 1858, immigrated 1881).

Among the Cantonese, it was a common practice to try to monopolize a specific trade in an area and to pass on a profitable business to a fellow clansman. The laundryman Charlie Wah advertised in the *Gold Creek News* in late 1896 stating that he did first-class work at his laundry at 9 Pekin Avenue; during the next year he expanded his appeal to note that he delivered anywhere in Gold Creek. Charlie Wah left Island Mountain in June 1897. Although his name did not appear in the 1900 census for Island Mountain, by 1910 a Charlie Wah, age 65, lived Tuscarora and had a laundry business. He was prosperous enough to own his own home and business, but like many "long-time" resident Chinese, he was getting on in years. His name did not appear in the 1920 census. When Charlie left, a new laundryman took over in Island Mountain.[187] The Hop Lee

Company, a laundry at No. 9 Pekin Avenue, Chinatown, advertised in the *Gold Creek News*, "First class laundry work. Spring Water. Mend clothes. Washed clean. Clothing called for and delivered." His advertisement, he hoped, was more appealing and informative than his predecessor's.

Most of the stories revealed a friendship that had developed between Lem, China Joe, and other Chinese and members of the larger community. The Chinese were no longer strangers in the community and did not represent an economic threat. If their personalities lent themselves to positive interactions with other members of the community, then the hostility from the "Yellow Peril" era of the 1870s and 1880s was forgotten. Because of the Chinese exclusion laws in 1882, 1892, and 1902, and the declining Chinese population, the Chinese had to interact with the larger community and could do so only by learning English and adopting some American customs. At the same time, the EuroAmericans became more tolerant of Chinese practices. Both came to rely on each other economically in this small community. The interdependence and lack of economic threat opened the door to positive social interactions such as sharing meals together and going hunting and fishing.

By the 1920s Island Mountain's Chinatown had become a ghost town. As the decades passed the original nineteen buildings were reduced to dugout depressions and only fourteen foundations arranged in a single row 260 meters long and 25 meters wide remained. Often the wood from the abandoned buildings was removed for firewood or for the construction of another structure.

Nearby Gold Creek also became a ghost town. A fire in September 1921 destroyed most of its buildings. Elko County records showed that Island Mountain's population was higher than the census records: 111 residents in 1900; 78 in 1910; 91 in 1920; and 48 in 1930.[188] Gold Creek and Island Mountain had been abandoned.

In 1930 the Elko County census manuscript showed that thirty-five Chinese (a merchant and his family, a laundry owner and his family, cooks, and other laundrymen) lived in nearby Elko; two in Carlin (railroad employees); and three lived in Montello, South Fork, and Tobara Elestion—a total of forty—a substantial decrease from the ninety-three living in Elko County in 1920. Island Mountain and Tuscarora had disappeared from the census rolls. The decline in the Chinese population of Nevada continued until new immigration laws enacted after 1965 spurred new growth. Gradually, some Chinese moved back to Elko County.

Island Mountain and Gold Creek were small communities. Because Island Mountain's founder, Emanuel Penrod, recognized the need for Chinese workers and adopted a policy of working with them, he provided a harmonious atmosphere. Other residents followed his lead. This allowed the Chinese merchant China Lem, and his friends and associates who were miners, to live in Island Mountain for many decades without the racism and anti-Chinese prejudice present in other mining towns. China Lem and Joe and Suey Nep could have returned to China, but like Ing Hay, Lung On, and Ah Lee Lake, they chose to stay. They were not sojourners but rather accepted members of the community who shared their culture and customs with both EuroAmericans and Native Americans. Their contributions and goodwill were remembered by friends long after the town disappeared.

Conclusion

CHINESE MINERS AND MERCHANTS in the three relatively small, isolated communities of John Day, Oregon, and Tuscarora and Island Mountain, Nevada, faced situations similar to those in other mining towns elsewhere in the American West, and in mining communities elsewhere in the Chinese diaspora, most notably British Columbia and New South Wales, Australia. In sharp contrast, the Chinese in South Africa were "coolie laborers" and suffered harsh treatment during their short tenure there. This experience resembled some of the attempts to use Chinese workers to replace African American slave labor in agriculture in the southern United States.

Because many of these Chinese-dominated nineteenth-century mining towns in the American West disappeared, there were few written records. But some artifacts found in archaeological excavations provided some information about their lives. Although Chinese participation in mining in the American West declined in the twentieth century, some individuals persisted in mining (and a few were relatively successful). However in general most of the Chinese found other employment.

Studies of Chinese miners and merchants in Idaho provide yet another perspective on their experiences, and one that may have been more typical of many mining towns in the American West. Liping Zhu examined the Chinese experience in the Boise Basin.[1] The Chinese first moved into Idaho in 1856 but kept their successes secret. Gold strikes in nearby locations became newsworthy in the early 1860s and Idaho became a territory in 1863. That same year numerous Chinese migrated to the Boise Basin along with many EuroAmericans. Two years later they moved into Idaho City when EuroAmerican owners of abandoned mining claim were anxious to sell to them. The situation was similar to that in Oregon in its early mining history but in the end, the dynamics were different. Hostility developed between EuroAmerican laborers on one side and the Chinese and those who encouraged the Chinese to move to Idaho City on the other side.

According to Zhu, the number of Chinese miners in Boise County grew to 1,621 in 1870, and then declined to 969 in 1880, 202 in 1900, and 62 in 1910, while the EuroAmerican population increased throughout this period, quickly regaining the status as the majority of the population.[2] The discriminatory foreign miners tax was levied against the Chinese but they avoided paying it. According to the deputy sheriff of Shoshone County, only 20 percent of the Chinese miners there complied with the $4-per-head tax required by the territorial legislature.[3] The great distances and small number of collectors contributed to this nonpayment.

Yet, despite anti-Chinese legislation and actions, a few Chinese thrived. One of the most successful miner-merchants was Loke Kee, who arrived and started mining in the Boise Basin in 1863, then owned a general store in Idaho City, and in 1906 returned to China with his large and extended family after accumulating some $60,000 to $90,000 in personal wealth.[4] Shortly after his arrival in Hong Kong, Loke Kee died and the fortunes that he left to his extended family diminished thereafter. It was a sad, but was not an atypical, commentary on a rise from rags to riches only to have the next two generations lose the hard-earned money that had been accumulated.

The experiences of the Chinese in Pierce, Idaho, had many of the same characteristics seen in John Day, Tuscarora, and Island Mountain—except that there was overt violence and racial hostility. Darby Stapp and others have written about Pierce: founded by the Chinese, then taken over by EuroAmericans who, in the end, abandoned it in favor of the Chinese.[5] With the adoption of a mining district law in 1861 that was similar to the mining regulations found in Oregon and Nevada, the Chinese were excluded from mining in Pierce, the oldest placer mining camp in Idaho.[6] Economic necessity, especially the need to sell worked-out mines, led to the adoption of an amendment in 1864 (first in Oro Fino, then in Pierce and other mining towns) that allowed the Chinese to own claims as long as they paid the monthly taxes of $4 (later raised to $5) to the county government. Like the poll taxes in California and Nevada, this tax was eventually repealed.[7] For those earning an average wage of $2 or less per day, the monthly tax was a great hardship and discouraged many Chinese from staying in Idaho.

Once the Chinese could own mining claims in Pierce, their numbers increased and they became the majority population between 1870 and 1895. According to Stapp, they bought mining property, including gulches, that ranged in price from $10 to $9,200, with most of the larger purchases made between 1866 and 1890. Groups of Chinese, probably using the traditional rotating credit system for the capital investment, bought the larger claims.[8] As early as 1865 the Yanghe Association, whose members came from Zhongshan, sent forty miners from Nevada to Pierce to work in a mine that members of the association probably funded.[9] This gave them an early presence in Pierce and was different from the Siyi-dominated mining towns of Tuscarora and Island Mountain in Nevada because of their more urban instead of rural background.

In 1870 the population of Pierce grew to 14,999 residents, including 455 Chinese men and eight Chinese women with an average age of 32 years. Like John Day, most of the men (411) were miners. The Pierce census manuscript listed gamblers (14, who provided recreation for the workers), hotel cooks (3, who catered to the bachelorlike society), blacksmiths (3), gardeners (3, who provided produce for the people), laundrymen (2), and one each of the following occupations: trader, hotel keeper, merchant, hotel waiter, barber, doctor (who treated primarily Chinese patients in and around the area), brothel keeper (for whom the eight women worked), and Chinese employment agent (who was responsible for groups of workers and who kept in contact with the EuroAmericans about job openings). This profile of occupations showed a greater number of gamblers, blacksmiths, and gardeners than John Day, Tuscarora, and Island Mountain.

The eight women ranged in age from 20 to 40 and were listed as prostitutes in the 1870 census perhaps to add support for the passage of the 1875 Page Act.[10] Although Stapp believed that the women probably worked for a *tang* or other Chinese organization, the fact that four established their own households by themselves (numbers 196, 200, 201, and 220) suggests individual entrepreneurship was possible. They also may have had a different occupation—but the bias of most census takers was to list Chinese women as prostitutes. By 1880 there were no Chinese women in Pierce, an indication of the community's economic decline and increased racial tensions.

In reaction to the growing Chinese presence, EuroAmerican miners influenced legislation. For example, in 1867 the Owyhee Miners' League in Owyhee County was the first labor union in the state to write a platform for the anti-Chinese movement. The virulent anti-Chinese attitude was evident in northern Idaho, especially in Coeur d'Alene, located in present-day Shoshone County, so the spread of anti-Chinese sentiment throughout the central and northern part of the state was not surprising as the EuroAmerican miners and others moved around the state.[11] In Idaho it was not unusual to hear about a Chinese person being ridiculed, robbed, beaten, or driven out of town.

In 1870 there were 4,274 Chinese in Idaho; of the 6,579 miners in the state, 3,853 (58.6 percent) were Chinese.[12] This figure was larger than the number of Chinese in Oregon in the same period. According to Rossiter W. Raymond, the Chinese were working two-thirds of all the claims in Idaho.[13] Part of the reason may have been that Idaho did not achieve statehood until 1890, so fewer restrictions were placed upon the Chinese in mining. Chinese were very visible and, some believed, very successful, but they faced different kinds of challenges that made Idaho less desirable as a place to work.

Trouble with Native Americans, economic downturns, and additional discriminatory policies contributed to the Chinese departure from Idaho. The Nez Perce war of 1877 discouraged all non–Native American men from making the area a permanent home. Although there were stories of Native Americans showing Chinese miners where to find gold, tension existed between some of the tribes and the Chinese, including rumors of Native American massacres of Chinese. Living in larger towns offered better protection from hostile Native Americans, so, as in other western states and territories, the Chinese gravitated toward populated areas, particularly in the Boise Basin where Chinatowns offered some protection. Eventually, many of the placer deposits were played out and miners of all races gradually began to leave.

By 1880 the state's Chinese population dropped to 3,379 as they moved to other neighboring states.[14] In 1882 Pierce became the county seat; but as mining declined, the town (whose population had declined by the turn of the twentieth century) became part of Clearwater County in 1911. Some believed that the Chinese could sense a forthcoming mining "bust," and were among the first to leave the future ghost town.

Although Pierce had some residents who had good relations with the Chinese, criminal activities intensified anti-Chinese animosity. In 1885 Pierce experienced its most famous anti-Chinese event with the brutal murder of one of the town's foremost citizens, D. M. Fraser.[15] Five Chinese were charged with his death; eventually a vigilante group hung the men. If the Chinese were guilty, then this could be regarded as justifiable in a frontier society but there was no concrete evidence or trial. In 1886 the unwarranted murder of thirty Chinese miners outside Lewiston continued the trend of rising anti-Chinese violence and racism. The number of Chinese in Pierce and other parts of Idaho dropped even more rapidly when, in 1889, Judge Willis Sweet decided that they could not hold mining claims. In 1890 the Idaho legislature barred Chinese from holding mining lands.[16] In 1892 there was a report in Pierce City of EuroAmericans attacking the Chinese and taking their gold.

By 1900 the Chinese population in the town numbered only 64 gold miners, while the EuroAmerican population grew to 135 gold and quartz miners. The ratio of Chinese to EuroAmericans miners reversed and that trend continued. The last Chinese merchant, Ah Duck, left Pierce in 1908, but some Chinese miners remained, with 19 recorded in 1910. By 1920 there were fewer than 10 Chinese; in October 1932, Ah Fong, the last and one of the best-loved Chinese in the area, was shot and killed.[17] The complete absence of Chinese in Pierce was in contrast to the eventual situation in John Day, where the Chinese stayed until the post–World War II era.

The Chinese initially had constituted one-third of the population of Idaho but the number dropped to less than 1 percent in a matter of decades. Their departure has been studied from several perspectives. In his dissertation, Samuel L. Couch cited the reasons he believed accounted for the population decline: "(1) depletion of the mining resources, (2) the Chinese Exclusion Act of 1882 and its subsequent extensions, and (3) the peculiar migrant status of the Chinese 'sojourners.'"[18] The validity of the sojourner status must be questioned since some Chinese (for example, Ing Hay and Lung On, Ah Lee Lake, Joe and Suey Nep, and Pierce's Ah Fong) felt no desire to return to China. Added to this must be the development of new technology in gold mining that made it impossible for the Chinese to compete with the new, larger gold mining companies and the rising tide of anti-Chinese sentiment in Idaho. Archaeologist Ronald L. James investigated why the Chinese were no longer found in Twin Falls, Idaho, and concluded that after large-scale industrial lode-mining emerged, the Chinese were driven out so that by 1910 there were only 859 Chinese in this predominately metal mining state.[19] (Liping Zhu, on the other hand, asserted that Idaho provided the opportunity for some Chinese gold miners and merchants to realize their dreams despite economic competition, racial prejudice, and frontier living, and that most Chinese Americans in Idaho were better off than their counterparts in China.)[20] Without women, there were no children and no families, the essential elements in a traditional Chinese community, so the Chinese were not as motivated to remain. Moreover the Chinese could not find economic niches that allowed them to continue living in Idaho. Looking at northern Idaho, archaeologist Priscilla Wegars discovered that hostility against the Chinese kept the number of Chinese miners there very small.[21] A hostile environment with a declining economy offered little reason to stay.

Although the Chinese in general experienced anti-Chinese mining regulations, discriminatory taxes and state laws, and federal exclusion legislation, they persisted in areas where they could make a living. Once placer mining declined, most Chinese left. These patterns occurred in mining towns in Oregon, Nevada, and Idaho, but within each community, different dynamics converged to make the place hospitable or not to Chinese merchants and miners. When new opportunities arose elsewhere, miners went there.

One of the most attractive new areas was British Columbia in western Canada. Some of the Chinese experiences there were similar to those found in the western United States. Archaeologist Ying-ying Chen told the story of early Chinese residents in the North Cariboo District of British Columbia.[22] The Chinese first arrived in the late 1850s from the American West; by the early 1860s most left Taishan and the other Siyi districts and traveled directly to British Columbia in search of gold. They dominated the mining community of Barkerville and other mining towns in North Cariboo. Like the Chinese in Tuscarora, they established organizations for protection and created mining companies. One of the most powerful and prominent was the Zhigongtang, established in Mau-si (historic location unknown) in 1876 and Barkerville in 1882. The Zhigongtang acknowledged the leadership of the San Francisco lodge and created some rules that were different from lodges elsewhere, such as the requirement to obtain a mining license from the Zhigongtang.[23] Instead of merchandising links through San Francisco and Sacramento, they had goods shipped through Seattle and ports in British Columbia. By the 1870s the Chinese imported hydraulic mining equipment and were very successful until the gold resources in North Cariboo began declining between 1877 and 1931.[24] They had a longer gold mining experience than did the Chinese in the United States but had to endure unfamiliar weather conditions and an isolation that allowed them to make their own gradual adjustments to Canadian life.

Another similar experience occurred in New South Wales, Australia. Gold was first discovered in Sydney, New South Wales, in 1851; several rich mines quickly developed throughout the country, attracting Chinese miners. Archaeologist Barry McGowan and others have studied the Chinese mining experience there.[25] Chinese farm workers and servants, who began to move to Australia from Fujian province in 1848, gave up these occupations in the wake of the discovery of gold in New South Wales. Their traditions, language, values, and system of organization differed from the Chinese from neighboring Guangdong province to the south. Beginning in 1853 the Guangdonese began arriving in Australia. Whether organizations clashes and other problems at the mining sites occurred is unknown. The 1861 census counted 24,724 Chinese in Victoria; the population dropped thereafter as a result of the depletion of gold as well as anti-Chinese legislation, taxation, and other discriminatory actions.[26] The pattern was similar to that in the American West.

In 1901 new goldfields opened elsewhere in Australia and some 29,153 Chinese immigrant males and 474 females relocated to the new sites.[27] They represented 70 percent of Australia's total population, but gradually became a minority. Because they were closer to China, they could maintain more Chinese traditions than those who moved to the American West. By 1911 the Australian census indicated that only 21,856 Chinese males and 897 females (51 percent of the total population) lived there; only about 7 percent were in mining and most, about 40 percent, were in agriculture. Some, of course, may have mined part-time or seasonally but spent most of their time farming, as they had done in China.

The experience of the Chinese in South Africa was not one of settlement and independence for miners like most other locations in the Chinese diaspora. From 1903–4 until 1908, using Chinese labor contractors in Tianjin, Shanghai, and other locations, the Chamber of Mines Labour Importation Agency of South Africa brought 63,296 Chinese mine workers to South Africa as a solution to the shortage of labor faced by the mining companies.[28] In 1906 the Chinese constituted just over 35 percent of the total unskilled labor force in South Africa. Many died as a result of the dangerous work and the health hazards of living in Africa as well as the harsh treatment and beatings that the mine owners and supervisors meted out. By 1910 all of the imported Chinese mine workers who had not deserted or died, returned to China.[29] This was Chinese contract labor at its worst and was found in other locations such as Cuba, where nineteenth-century Chinese worked on the island's sugar plantations.[30] Many Chinese going overseas to work did not know the kind of conditions they would have to endure. The experiences in South Africa were at the opposite end of the spectrum for Chinese gold miners from those in the American West.

There are only a few examples of successful Chinese miners in the early twentieth century in the American West. Some Chinese miners remained in California but eventually transferred their claims to others who came after them. One example was Ah Kai, who remained in Dutch Flat, California, in partnership with George Wright and Associates.[31] Between 1910 and 1915 he was a part of a hydraulic mining operation called You Bet Mining Company; during eight months in 1910 the company took out an estimated $150,000 to $300,000 in gold. The rich find was noteworthy enough to be publicized in the *Los Angeles Times.* The partnership with a EuroAmerican allowed Ah Kai to become familiar with local mining regulations and members of the EuroAmerican community. By 1915 Ah Kai, as head of the Chinese mining company, sold his interest and made a substantial profit. Nothing else is known about him, but there were others in similar situations.

Lone Chinese miners were few and far between during the early twentieth century. Two Nevada miners, Sam Yet and James Chang On, and one Idaho miner, Doc Lee, are examples.

Sam Yet of Searchlight, Nevada (born in San Francisco in 1868 to Wong Yet and Susie Yet, an English woman), was noted for developing some of the richest mines in the dry desert area. He worked his five claims from 1905 until 1927 as a lone miner. He had married a EuroAmerican woman who died in the early 1900s. He became depressed until Searchlight's sheriff encouraged him to continue to work. In 1912 Sam Yet's estimated worth was $500,000 to $750,000.[32] In 1928 he sold five of his claims to B. D. Young, A. P. Coroman, J. R. Denny, and J. Winberger for $45,000.[33] When he died, he left his fortune to the local sheriff.

James Chang On (b. 1876 in San Francisco; family name Chen), had, like many Chinese, a typical career that covered several occupations. He worked as a cook in a restaurant in Winnemucca, Nevada, in 1900.[34] He joined a revolutionary movement in Latin America and later fought for the 1911 Revolution in China after meeting Sun Yatsen in Winnemucca. Unfortunately On was captured by the Qing imperial army and imprisoned. When the Qing government discovered that he was an American citizen, they released him. Before returning home, he stopped in his ancestral village in the Sanyi area where he met and married Chow See. In 1913 On returned to Lovelock, Nevada, and opened the Northern Cafe on Broadway and Ninth, serving American and Chinese cuisine to the general public (including train passengers) as well as to the inmates in the local prison next door.

By 1920 On was investing in mining property with EuroAmerican partners and bought and sold real estate in the area. Around 1924 he moved his wife and four children to the mining camp of Rochester, where he operated a boarding house for miners and also did some mining. When the mine closed, On and his family returned to Lovelock where they were the only Sanyi family in town. There he opened the Wing Lee Company, which sold Chinese goods (tea, wine, and herbal medicines), American general merchandise, and secondhand items. The backyard of his store became a gathering place for other Chinese workers in Lovelock. On read the newspapers and the Chinese discussed politics and other events under the shade of a large tree. It was fortunate that On could speak several dialects of Chinese because the other Chinese in town came primarily from Taishan. After On's death, his son Frank continued the family's interest in a mine at Star Mountain (near Lovelock) while earning a living as one of the town's mechanics. He mined for gold as a recreational hobby until his death in the 1990s. Frank Chang (real family name Chen) is remembered in a small museum established in the family's honor in Lovelock.[35]

Finally there was Doc Lee of Boise Basin, Idaho, who immigrated at age 21, eventually settling in Idaho in 1864.[36] He was still panning for gold in 1930 at the age of 91. He died in his cabin holding his pan and leaving a net worth of $127 in silver, $15 in greenbacks, and $5 in gold dust—which was more representative of the average Chinese miner of the time. The search for gold, some believe, is in the "blood" and certainly continued for a long time in these three twentieth-century cases.

Chinese miners and merchants came to the American West with great hopes and dreams of wealth. They encountered prejudice and hostility while trying to earn a living. Fortunately, some of the mining regulations that prohibited EuroAmerican miners from selling or leasing mining property to the Chinese were ignored shortly after the EuroAmericans abandoned their sites; in addition, the Chinese were resourceful enough to search out new areas to mine that were not heavily populated or were primarily agricultural towns. Their efforts were hampered by federal mining laws passed in 1866 and 1872 that severely restricted the ability of the Chinese to participate fully in placer mining. As well, a decision by the Montana Supreme Court denying Chinese the right to own mining claims was a common obstacle to success. Nevertheless, most Chinese miners and merchants obeyed the federal and local laws and contributed to the development of the region through their payment of taxes and fees. For example, in its early years, the government of Jackson County, Oregon, relied upon the taxes collected from the Chinese; likewise, the California state government collected one-fourth of its budget from the

Foreign Miners Tax (passed in 1850). Contrary to popular belief, Chinese bought and sold property and mining sites and went into partnerships with EuroAmericans to stake claims and invest in and own mines. They also purchased houses and other property.

When mining declined in California, the Chinese moved to neighboring states. The miners brought with them knowledge about mining techniques, irrigation systems, cultural values, and organizational structure from China and adapted them to the American environment. Little is known about the mining techniques they employed but the fact that they ordered some of their equipment from China, such as the rocker, and modified other equipment, such as the long tom, indicated that previous experience helped them to efficiently extract the gold.

Miners and merchants worked together. Many Chinese merchants also were involved in mining or had an interest in a mining company. The traditions of teamwork under a single leader or boss man, loyalty to one's fellow workers, the need for mutual protection, a strong work ethic, patronage of Chinese businesses, and networking with kinsmen or men in their fraternal organizations gave them advantages over the more individually minded and independent early EuroAmerican miners. Some did not have to endure the hostility and violence that characterized much of the Chinese experiences in California, Colorado, and Idaho. Although the discriminatory mining regulations and laws followed them from California, when they worked in isolated, difficult-to-reach areas in places like John Day, Tuscarora, and Island Mountain, the Chinese mined in relative peace unhampered by the prevailing racism. They were much less limited by anti-Chinese movements and laws than were others elsewhere.

Many of the merchants and miners adopted some American values and customs. Miners strove to become merchants because of Americans' esteem for businessmen. Moy Jin Mun (1848–1936) was one individual who exemplified the Chinese miner-to-merchant success story and his life was not unlike others. Born in the small rural village of Hoy Young On Fun, Taishan, Guangdong, to a schoolteacher and his wife, Moy watched his uncle return to the village as a rich man because of his success in the goldfields in the American West.[37] In 1860 he and his uncle spent six and a half months crossing the Pacific, arriving in San Francisco in February 1861. Moy attended a mission school in Chinatown and learned English. At the age of 15, he worked as a garden "boy" for the family of Leland Stanford in Sacramento, who also employed his older brother.

The lure of the goldfields led Moy to Moss Platt, California, to work over abandoned claims. There he made enough money to fund a trip back home for a year. During that time, he married and a year later, as was typical, left his wife behind in China. By 1874 he was in Truckee, California, where he was caught up in an anti-Chinese riot, but found shelter and protection in the home of an Irish police officer who had befriended him. Moy continued to mine for gold and became a labor contractor for railroad companies. His status had risen. By 1881 he made enough money to return to China to bring his wife to San Francisco, where he opened an import-export store on Grant Avenue (then called Dupont Street). Moy had achieved the coveted status of merchant in the United States and was more privileged than the hundreds of Chinese miners who could not bring their wives to America.

In 1884, because of his skills in English, Moy became the first official Chinese interpreter for the U.S. District Court in California. But after suffering losses in the 1906 San Francisco earthquake and fire he began mining again. Upon his subsequent return to San Francisco, he became an interpreter for the immigration service at Angel Island, hoping to accumulate wealth to open another import/export store (which he did). He then became a community leader and activist. He worked to end the "tong wars" in California's Chinatowns and helped achieve peace among the *tang*s in 1924. After the stock market crash of 1929, he retired to a modest lifestyle but continued to be active in community affairs until his death in 1936.

Merchants served the Chinese mining community in many ways and often became wealthy as a result. They were the leaders of mutual aid organizations that assisted the miners in adjusting to American life by helping them pay taxes, informing them about the laws, and trying to protect them from anti-Chinese movements and violence. In rural American West, the Zhigongtang was the most powerful and influential secret society. Others, like the Hexingtang, also existed. The secret brotherhoods were the major providers of services to miners. Because of the 1882 Chinese Exclusion Act and the other Chinese exclusion acts that followed until 1924, the Chinese recognized the need to achieve the status of merchant so that they could afford to travel to China and to have some degree of respectability and acceptance in the American society. Although contrary to Confucian ethics, the Chinese in Guangdong also were reaching the conclusion that business was a good occupation. Chinese Americans found the American tradition of valuing entrepreneurship so miners became merchants if they were rich enough, had some intelligence, and had some educational background.

Chinese merchants assisted the miners in many other ways. The merchants often were labor contractors or "headmen" in small mining companies, provided the goods necessary for the miners to survive, and created organizations offering them protection, recreation, services, and maintenance of important traditional festivals. The majority of Chinese merchants could read and write Chinese and were conversant in English. They were skilled in using the abacus, which permitted them to add, subtract, multiply, and divide quickly. They wrote letters on behalf of the illiterate and read letters from home to them. The penmanship of Lung On and Ah Lee Lake indicated that they were well-educated in both English and Chinese. Their signatures on government documents indicated that American officials felt comfortable in turning to them for advice on a variety of matters. Merchants also served as important liaisons between the Chinese and EuroAmerican communities, and introduced the EuroAmerican community to Chinese traditions such as Chinese New Year and Qingming, the Festival in Remembrance of the Dead.

The Chinese merchants also interacted with EuroAmericans and some Native Americans. As suppliers of goods, an economic interdependence arose and sometimes this, in combination with some elementary knowledge of English, opened the door for social interaction and cultural exchange, creating a more harmonious society (one of the main goals of traditional Confucianism). The Chinese of John Day, Tuscarora, and Island Mountain had an advantage over many other mining communities because they did not experience the high degree of racism and discrimination that prevailed elsewhere.

Cultural values, work ethic, knowledge, and organizational systems gave the Chinese miners an advantage over EuroAmerican miners in working abandoned claims. Some miners and most merchants had to interact with the other settlers, speaking in English or broken English, and as a result, learned to work and live together in relative harmony with non-Chinese peoples. They transplanted some of their festivals and traditions and shared them with others. In turn they learned about American culture and values. Despite widespread racial prejudice and discriminatory laws, some Chinese miners achieved a modicum of wealth and returned to China while others remained in the United States. The Chinese merchants made their fortune by selling goods to the miners, so when mining declined, they also had to look elsewhere for their livelihood.

The 1924 Immigration Act that established a quota of one hundred Chinese to be admitted annually essentially ended the threat of the Chinese overpopulating the United States, allowing a more congenial atmosphere to develop. "Cheap Chinese labor" became a thing of the past. At the same time, the second generation of Chinese Americans had matured and began to take leadership roles in their communities, graduating from high schools and colleges, and becoming active politically. Racism and anti-Chinese movements still existed but not to the degree of the late nineteenth century. Two major events in China—the Japanese invasion and colonization of Manchuria in 1931 and the Sino-Japanese War (1937–45)—further helped to change American attitudes about China and the Chinese in the United States to a more positive image. Americans found the Japanese to be the aggressors and supported the "underdog" Chinese, who became America's partner during World War II. By 1940 in the United States, the Chinese were in the service industry (30.4 percent of those employed), managers (20.6 percent), operators (22.6 percent), sales workers (11.4 percent), and clerical workers (11.4 percent).[38] They were no longer miners and general laborers, but increasingly were becoming businessmen.

During the latter half of the nineteenth century, the Chinese contributed to the building of many American cities and towns, especially in the rural locations that were relatively isolated and mountainous with inhospitable weather but rich in gold. They were noted for their irrigation systems, especially canals and reservoirs, but also for building roads and participating in logging. They constructed railroad lines that helped transport goods and people across the United States, and also built narrow gauge lines that connected mines with main rail lines so that the gold and silver could be easily transported. They cut wood for fuel for stamp mills, trains, and stoves, and to build homes. They provided fresh produce from their gardens. Chinese doctors provided medical care.

Many of the Chinese miners in this study lived in the American West for several decades. Those who knew English, either because they were talented in languages or had studied English in south China or at a missionary school in an urban Chinatown, adjusted to the rural communities more easily and felt comfortable enough to continue mining despite its decline, as was evident in the towns presented. What is surprising is that merchants who were married—and some who had children—were not interested in returning to China even when the economy of the towns declined. Doc Ing Hay, Lung On, Ah Lee Lake, and China Lem were not sojourners but first-generation Chinese Americans who spent the rest of their lives in America away from their families.

The Chinese miners and merchants left an imprint on the landscape of the three mining towns of John Day, Oregon, and Tuscarora and Island Mountain, Nevada. Our examination of these men and their western American communities offered different perspectives about the experiences of Chinese gold miners and merchants who have been generally ignored or forgotten in history books. The construction of irrigation systems lasted long after the Chinese left. They made friends with EuroAmericans, some of whom felt that it was important for others to know about the Chinese despite the national and regional trends of anti-Chinese sentiment. In John Day, the Kam Wah Chung and Company Museum stands as a tribute to Chinese contributions. Some of the possessions the Chinese left behind in Tuscarora are now in the Nevada State Museum in Carson City and the Northeastern Museum in Elko. With the emphasis on the anti-Chinese movement, the positive contributions and friendly relationships between the Chinese and others are often neglected in recounting the history of the Chinese in the United States. Yet the lives of the Chinese miners and merchants presented in this study and the many instances of positive interactions between the ethnically diverse members of the small mining communities in which they lived has helped to shed new light on the history of the Chinese in the American West.

Notes

The following abbreviations are used in the notes:

Census	United States Bureau of Census, *Characteristics of the Population,* title varies with date of publication.
Census manuscript:	National Archives and Records Administration, dates vary from 1860–1930, on microfilm.
DSS	*Daily Silver State* (Winnemucca, NV)
EDS	*Eureka Daily Sentinel* (Eureka, NV)
EFP	*Elko Free Press* (Elko, NV)
GCN	*Gold Creek News* (Gold Creek, NV)
INS	Immigration and Naturalization Service
IS	*Idaho Statesman* (Boise)
NARA	National Archives and Records Administration
NSJ	*Nevada State Journal* (Reno)
SHPO	State Historic Preservation Office (Nevada), "Find People."
TE	*Territorial Enterprise* (Virginia City, NV)
TTMR	*Tuscarora Times and Mining Review* (Tuscarora, NV)
TTR	*Tuscarora Times-Review* (Tuscarora, NV)

Introduction

1. Hom, *Songs of Gold Mountain,* 184. See Zhu, "No Need to Rush," 42–57; Zhu, *A Chinaman's Chance;* Zhu and Fosha, *Ethnic Oasis*; Rohe, "After the Gold Rush," 2–19; Rohe, "Chinese River Mining," 14–29; and Rohe, "The Chinese and Hydraulic Mining," 73–91.

2. Williams, "The Chinese in the California Mines, 1848–1860"; Kanazawa, "Immigration, Exclusion, and Taxation," 779–805; Barth, *Bitter Strength;* Sucheng Chan, "Chinese Livelihood," 273–307; and Ping Chiu, *Chinese Labor.*

3. Wyman, "Mining Law in Idaho," 14–22.

4. Rusco, "The Chinese Massacres of 1866," 3–30, estimated 50 to 150 Chinese prospectors traveling from California through Nevada to Idaho were killed in the spring of 1866.

5. Emmons and Becker, *Statistics and Technology of the Precious Metals,* 237.

6. Sucheng Chan, "Chinese Livelihood," 280, n. 14.

7. Census, 1870; Ping Chiu, *Chinese Labor,* 27; and Sucheng Chan, "Chinese

Livelihood," 286, n. 32. On John R. Hite's millionaire mine, see Mendershausen, *Treasures of the South Fork,* and Giacomazzi, *Trails and Tales of Yosemite and the Central Sierra,* 106–8.

8. Hite discovered gold in 1861 and employed Chinese workers to bring the equipment to his 10 stamp mill in 1864 and his 20 stamp mill in 1874, to pave roads through the mountains, and to work on his mines.

9. Population figures are based upon the Census, 1870, 1880, 1900. The population schedules of each census were reproduced by the National Archives and Records Administration (NARA) Service on microfilm and are referred to as census manuscripts. The 1940 census manuscript is the latest release. The census manuscript for 1890 accidentally was destroyed.

10. Ping Chiu, *Chinese Labor,* 38.

11. Census figures 1870–1900. See Table 2 in chapter 3 of this book. See also Greg Lee Carter, "Social Demography," 73–89.

12. Sucheng Chan, "Chinese Livelihood," 286, n. 32.

13. Todd M. Stevens, "Brokers Between Worlds," 117.

14. *NSJ,* July 20, 1872.

15. Rohe, "After the Gold Rush," 18.

16. See Sucheng Chan, "Introduction," 1–61.

17. Ibid. See also Sucheng Chan, "The Changing Contours of Asian-American Historiography," 125–47; and Gary Okihiro, *Columbia Guide.* See also Rose Hum Lee, *Growth and Decline,* and Yu, *Thinking Orientals.*

18. Siu, *Chinese Laundryman,* and his article, "The Sojourner," 34–44; and Yang's defense of the use of the term in "The 'Sojourner Hypothesis' Revisited," 235–58.

19. See Barth, *Bitter Strength,* for a background.

20. Daniels, *Coming to America,* 102.

21. Tsai, *China and the Overseas Chinese*; Daniels, *Asian America*; and Sucheng Chan, *Asian Americans,* laid the foundation for the new studies of Chinese Americans. See also Hune, "Rethinking Race," 79–85.

22. Marcus Lee Hansen, *Immigrant in American History*; Higham, *Strangers in the Land*; and Handlin, *The Uprooted.*

23. Wunder, "What's Old," 50–58.

24. See note 11 above and Sucheng Chan, "Introduction."

25. See Lai, *Becoming Chinese American*; Ling, *Surviving on Gold Mountain*; Marie Rose Wong, *Sweet Cakes*; Shehong Chen, *Being Chinese.*

26. Geertz, *Interpretation of Cultures.* Stapp, "Historic Ethnography," evaluates the literature with a focus upon the Chinese and mining in chapter 1.

27. See Hune, "Rethinking Race," 79–85.

28. Hunt-Jones, "Heart of a Community."

29. Dillingham, "Tuscarora Greenstrip."

30. Sucheng Chan, "Chinese Livelihood," 281. Ah Louie and Company claimed 240 feet at Buckeye Bar along the Yuba River and Sham Kee claimed 4,200 feet eight miles outside of Marysville also along the Yuba River, both in Yuba County. Chinese also purchased claims in Yuba County beginning in 1856.

31. Frederick, *Rugged Justice*, chapter 3.

32. Knapp and Pigott, "Archaeology and Anthropology," 300–304.

33. Sandmeyer, *Anti-Chinese Movement*; Saxton, *Indispensable Enemy*; Daniels, *Anti-Chinese Violence*; and Pfaelzer, *Driven Out*.

34. Ying-ying Chen, "In the Colonies," provides an excellent background.

35. Harrison to Temple Letter, 1877, cited in ibid, 216.

36. McGowan, "Archaeology," and Ritchie, "Archaeology and History," are two of the several examples of work in this field.

Transliteration of Names

1. Louie, *Chinese American Names*.

2. On a discussion of "Americanized Chinese" and the Joseph and Mary Tape case, see Ngai, "History as Law and Life," 62–90.

3. Non Chong Yee and his wife (Mrs. Sam Gibson) were listed in the Ormsby County Tax Records in the 1870s–early 1880s (Nevada State Library and Archives, Carson City, Nevada, provided by State Archivist Guy Rocha). Four of the five family members returned to China in 1886 and the fifth, the oldest daughter Ah Cum (1876–1929), married merchant and vegetable peddler Chung Kee (1847–1909) of Hawthorne.

4. For more information, see Christman, "Women Zhonghua Huiguan," who looks at the CCBA in China, Vietnam, and San Francisco.

Chapter 1. The Coming and Early Challenges

1. Spence, *Search for Modern China*; Mei, "Socioeconomic Origins of Emigration," 219–47; Zo, "Chinese Emigration into the United States," chap. 3; Faire, "Plight of the Farmers," 3–37; and Woon, "International Links," 139–72.

2. Tsai, *China and the Overseas Chinese*, 12. See also Tsai, *Chinese Experience*.

3. Wen, "Breaking Racial Barriers," 13–19. Wen is the family name.

4. Taiping rebel Yet Low was just one of many who escaped to the United States. See Chung, "Between Two Worlds"; Cassel, "To Inscribe the Self Daily"; and Murray K. Lee, "Ah Quin."

5. For a general background, see Spence, *Search for Modern China*.

6. Irick, *Ch'ing Policy*; and Kwong and Miscevic, *Chinese America*, 24–25, 55–56, 58, 101.

7. Pan, *Encyclopedia of the Chinese Overseas*, 65.

8. Based on the *xianzhi* ("county gazetteers") that he examined, Yong Chen placed less emphasis on the political, social, and economic dislocations, which were not unusual in his opinion, and more on the potential for enrichment that the Chinese in Guangdong envisioned ("Internal Origins," 521–46).

9. Siu-lun Wong, "Chinese Family Firm," 59; P. Steven Sangren, "Traditional Chinese Corporations," 391–415.

10. See Guanhua Wang, *In Search of Justice*, 29–30, for the 1880 statement of petition by merchants to the Qing government.

11. Kung-Ping Wang, "Mineral Resources of China," 633; En-Han Lee, "China's Response," 55–76.

12. Dorian, *Minerals, Energy*.

13. Zhu, "No Need to Rush," 45–46.

14. My translation; poem in Mao, *Tang Song ci*, 27.

15. SHPO, Nevada census database, "Find People," 1900.

16. Song Yingxing (Sung Ying-hsiang) of the Ming dynasty (1368–1644), quoted in Golas, *Science and Civilisation*, 30. Golas's work is the most authoritative account in English on the subject.

17. Chung, "Between Two Worlds," 179–84.

18. Golas, *Science and Civilisation*, 239–55; see Steeves, "Chinese Gold Miners," on some of the unique technological aspects of mining of Chinese American miners; and Valentine, "Chinese Placer Mining," 37–53.

19. Golas, *Science and Civilisation*, 246–47.

20. Jung, "Capitalism," 31–34.

21. Golas, *Science and Civilisation*, 146. A Chinese miner died of mercury poisoning and was buried in Carlin, Elko County, Nevada. See Chung, Frampton, and Murphy, "Venerate These Bones," 107–46.

22. Jung, "Capitalism," 31.

23. In 1867, $9,031,504 (21.7 percent of total) in gold was exported to China from San Francisco, which was more than exported to any foreign country and second only to that sent to New York, $23,355,903 (56.0 percent). Figures are from a chart in Steeves, "Chinese Gold Miners," 151, table 7, based on data from Browne, *Mineral Resources*, and Browne and James "Reports upon the Mineral Resources." The figure for the silver and gold shipment is from Raymond, Statistics of Mines, 528.

24. McGowan, "Archaeology," 11.

25. Valentine, "Chinese Placer Mining," 37–53, and McGowan, "Ringbarkers," 31–46. On rare occasions, EuroAmerican mining sites had neatly stacked tailings—but the Chinese could have preceded the EuroAmerican miners.

26. Sun, "Mining Labor," 59–60, details this. See also Bulmer, "Sociological Models," 61–92.

27. Golas, *Science and Civilisation*, 400.

28. Ibid, 393–94.

29. James C. Jackson, *Chinese in West Borneo*.

30. Li, *Wan Qing*, covering the period 1884 to 1911 and Sun, "Mining Labor," 45–67.

31. Hardesty, *Archaeology of Mining and Miners*; Hardesty et al., *Riepetown*; Craddock, *Early Metal Mining*; Fredlund et al., "Archaeological Investigations"; Hardesty and Hattori, "Archaeological Studies"; James and Lytle, "Ruins of a World"; LaLande, "Sojourners," 29–52; Lingenfelter, *Hardrock Miners*; Rohe, "After the Gold Rush," 2–19; Rohe, "The Chinese and Hydraulic Mining," 73–91; Rohe, "Chinese River Mining," 14–29; Striker and Sprague, "Excavations"; Valentine, "Historical and

Archaeological Investigation"; Meade, "Production of Gold," 1–26; Vanderburg, "Placer Mining"; and Williams, "Chinese in California Mines."

32. Hittel, *Resources*, 258–62; Hittel, Marshall, and Waite, *Discovery of Gold*; and Umbeck, "A Theory," 421–37.

33. Portable Chinese stoves are in several Nevada museum collections.

34. Liestman, "Nineteenth-Century Chinese," 20.

35. Based on my observation at Chinese archaeological sites.

36. Borthwick, *Three Years;* Borthwick, *Gold Hunters*, 255; and Steeves, "Chinese Gold Miners," 32–33.

37. Umbeck, "A Theory," 421–37, describes the system.

38. Iris Chang relates this story in *Chinese in America,* without any references to the source, but the tale is very probable.

39. The original Chinese text is in Liu, *Meiguo huajiao shi*, 37.

40. Ping Chiu, *Chinese Labor,* 11.

41. See McKeown, "Conceptualizing," 306–37.

42. Barth, *Bitter Strength,* 191–93, is a basic work on this period and discusses labor contractors. See also "The Chinese Companies and Their Dealings with Their Countrymen," *San Francisco Bulletin,* November 24, 1865.

43. On Gift, see Cohen, "George W. Gift," 157–78.

44. Couch, "Topophilia," 113. The crossing and experiences on board ship and the Bureau of Immigration interrogation upon arrival have been detailed in Barde, *Immigration.*

45. See Pan, *Encyclopedia,* 76, 91, and Zhou, *Huaqiao Huaren baike quanshu.*

46. Records at NARA, INS RG 85, Entry 137, indicated that many of the applicants for duplicate certificates of residence had been funded by relatives and family members. This was also the case when they went to New South Wales in the 1860s, as noted in George Preshaw's diary of June 4, 1860, cited in Lindsay M. Smith, "Identifying Chinese Ethnicity," 19.

47. Zo, "Chinese Emigration," 215–29.

48. From "Biography of Lee Chew," 164–75.

49. This will be elucidated in my forthcoming article on the 1905 Chinese census.

50. See Yen, "Chinese Workers."

51. Hsu, *Dreaming of Gold,* and Jue, "Chin Gee-hee," 31–38, discuss Chin's career. Moy Jin Mun's (1848–1936) career is described in Chinn, *Bridging the Pacific*, 71–75. See also Todd M. Stevens, "Brokers," chapters 1 and 3; Chin, *Golden Tassels*, 85–90, on industries and labor contracting; and McConnell, "Historical Geography," 225, on the decreasing importance of labor contractors.

52. Stevens, "Brokers," 115.

53. For a detailed discussion of the 1882 Chinese Exclusion Act and the role of Chinese merchants, see Stevens, "Brokers." Stevens looked at 2,500 unpublished case files involving Chinese Americans in Seattle and Portland for this study.

54. NARA, San Bruno, INS RG 85, Admission of Gee Ton, aka Gee Hoy Quon, in 1919, Casefile 18055/4–28, testimony of his father, Gee Kue Quong. In pinyin the family name is Zhu.

55. Lai, "Chinese Regional Solidarity," 19–60.

56. On the Ng (Ung) clan in Carlin, see Chung, Frampton, and Murphy, "Venerate," 107–46.

57. Zhu, *A Chinaman's Chance,* 110, 124, 193–94. Kee is not a Chinese family name.

58. On the Low family, see Chinn, *Bridging,* 102–4. Low sold goods in northern Nevada, southern Idaho, and eastern Oregon. After his death, his wife returned to China briefly but had changed so much that she realized she could not live there. She eventually settled in San Francisco, where she built the first modern apartment house on the outskirts of Chinatown and helped fund her son's establishment of the nightclub, the Forbidden City.

59. Valentine, "Historical," discusses Wong Kee in detail. See also his articles, "American Canyon," 107–30, and "Chinese Placer Mining," 37–53. A photograph of Wong Kee and Death Valley Scotty can be found at the Nevada Historical Society, Reno, Chinese file.

60. This is detailed in Couch, "Topophilia." Appendix A is a sampling of Chinese departing for China, most of whom were miners.

61. Liestman, "Nineteenth-Century Chinese," 19.

62. See Armentrout-Ma, "Urban Chinese," 107–35; Liu, "Chinese Merchant Guilds," 1–23; and Burgess, "Guilds," 72–80.

63. Walter N. Fong, "Chinese Labor Unions," 23–27. Fong is talking about guilds.

64. Hoy, *Chinese Six Companies.* Hoy neglected to include the En Kai Association in his list. See Chinn, *Bridging,* 5. The functions of the district associations and Six Companies were outlined by the Secretary of the Chinese Consulate General in New York. Tow, *Real Chinese.* See also Sinn, "Xin Xi Guxiang," 375–97; Qin, "Six Companies," gives an excellent account of the organization and demonstrates that the Six Companies was not the main Chinese labor broker but primarily the defender of the Chinese during anti-Chinese movements, demanding indemnity payments, litigating on behalf of the Chinese, and lobbying for immigration legislation. See also Lawrence Douglas Hansen, "Chinese Six Companies," 37–61; and Di Wang, "Huaren shequ de chongtu," 93–101, who felt that the district associations, family associations, secret societies, and guilds expanded their powers in the United States because of the dependence of the Chinese immigrants upon them, which prevented the immigrants from assimilating into the American society.

65. On Sanyi, see Lai, *Becoming Chinese American,* 77–142.

66. Todd M. Stevens, "Brokers," chapter 3; for rotating credit, see Wu, "To Kill Three Birds," 565–84.

67. United States Consulate General, Control Unit, *Index of Clan Names by Villages for Hoiping [Kaiping] District, Chungshan [Zhongshan] District, and Toishan [Taishan] District.* Hong Kong, 1965, NARA, San Bruno, California.

68. Chinn, *Bridging,* 4–5.

69. Hom, "'Fallen Leaves,'" 36–50.

70. Yip, "Association," 109–17.

71. Carl T. Smith, *Chinese Christians,* chapter 2.

72. Freedman, "Immigrants," 25–48.

73. Chung "Zhigongtang," 231–49; Ownby and Heidhues, *"Secret Societies"*; and Mak Lau Fong, *Sociology*.

74. "Horrible Slaughter of Tong War as Narrowly Averted in Portland, Suey Woon, Whose Master is Lee Kee, Runs Off with Don Gow Doi," *Oregonian* (Portland), March 20, 1910.

75. Ying-ying Chen, "In the Colonies"; Lister and Lister, *The Chinese;* and Lyman, Willmott, and Ho, "Rules," 530–39.

76. *IS*, March 22, 1896.

77. There have been several news articles on this, see, for example, "Caught a Rare Bird," *IS*, November 15, 1902, on Johnnie Doane, a EuroAmerican member of the Zhigongtang, and "Freemasonry of the Chinese," *IS*, July 12, 1905, on four EuroAmerican members in Spokane, Washington.

78. McClain, *In Search of Equality*, 205–7; and Lydon, *Chinese Gold*, 200–202.

79. The Bureau of Immigration reported their enforcement efforts to Congress in Cong. Rec., 59 Cong., 1 sess. (1906), Doc. 847 "Facts Concerning the Enforcement of the Chinese Exclusion Laws," 162 pp., online in the U.S. Congressional Serial Set, v. 4990 Session v. 50.

80. For more information on this complex topic, see Tong, *Chinese Americans*, 70–72.

81. Nicolini, Yescas, and McDow, "Chinese Camp," 49–50. The commemorative plaque at Chinese Camp, California, incorrectly stated that the first tong war occurred in Chinese Camp. See also Minke, *Mother Lode*.

82. Ping Chiu, *Chinese Labor*, 31.

83. Liestman, "Nineteenth-Century Chinese," 20. Figures from Wikoff, "Idaho County," 41–42.

84. Stapp, "Historic Ethnography," 59, table 2, gives the number, cost, and average for Chinese purchases between 1864 and 1871. By 1880 the Chinese constituted 80 percent of the population of Pierce, Idaho.

85. There are several books and articles on Hakkas/Kejias, see, for example, Leong, *Migration*.

86. NARA, Washington, DC, INS, RG 85, Applications for Duplicate Certificates of Residence, Entry 137, Box 3, case file 133763 for Chung Kee Sing, dated 1901.

87. Pan, *Encyclopedia*, 76, and Zo, "Chinese Emigration." This system also was used in establishing businesses and purchasing property.

88. For more on Chung Kee, see Chung, "Ah Cum Kee," 179–95.

89. See Sucheng Chan, "Chinese Livelihood," 273–307; Sucheng Chan, *This Bittersweet Soil*; and Tsu, "'Unskilled Chinaman,'" 474–95. See also Conlin, *Bacon*.

90. Sucheng Chan, *Asian Americans*, 28, gives 85 percent for 1860; see also her article, "Chinese Livelihood," 280, and her book, *This Bittersweet Soil*. The occupational figures are from the 1870 and 1880 census of the population.

91. Boswell, "Split Labor Market Analysis," 360.

92. This theory on sojourners was introduced through the Robert E. Park School of Sociology at the University of Chicago in the 1920s and expanded by several scholars, most notably Siu, "The Sojourner," 34–44; Siu, *The Chinese Laundryman*; and

more recently detailed by Couch, "Topophilia"; and Yang, "'Sojourner Hypothesis,'" 235–58. See also Yu, *Thinking Orientals*; Anthony Chan, "Myth"; Woon, "Voluntary Sojourner," 673–90; and Glick, *Sojourners*. The sojourner is defined as a stranger who spends many years of his life in a foreign country without being assimilated by it and has deep emotional ties to the land of his birth. This is very controversial.

93. Aarim-Herlot, *Chinese Immigrants,* 89.

94. NARA, Washington, DC, INS, RG 85, Applications for Duplicate Certificates of Residence, Entry 137, Box 11, File 143114.

95. Aarim-Heriot, *Chinese Immigrants,* provides an excellent coverage of this situation.

96. Pitt, "Beginnings," 23–38.

97. Ping Chiu, *Chinese Labor,* 12.

98. McKanna, "Enclaves of Violence," 401–4.

99. "History of the Sierra County Sheriff's Gallows." Online.

100. Chinese Merchants of San Francisco, Message to Governor Bigler dated January 30, 1855.

101. *San Francisco Bulletin*, September 20, 1858.

102. Simmel, *Conflict.*

103. Paul, "The Origin," 185–89.

104. United States Department of Agriculture, Census Office, *Statistical View of the United States: Compendium* (Washington, DC, 1854), 394. Figures are approximate. See also Rohe, "After the Gold Rush," 3–26.

105. Choy, Dong, and Hom, *Coming Man.*

106. Ibid., 19.

107. Alfred T. Jackson, *Diary* 222–23.

108. McKanna, "Enclaves of Violence," 391–423.

109. Mann, *After the Gold Rush.* See also Blackburn and Ricards, "Unequal Opportunity," 19–38.

110. Information from Hagaman and Meals, "Chinese Quarter."

111. Mann, *After the Gold Rush,* 254, table 33. In 1870 Mann breaks the figures down into men and boys, women and girls, but I have added them together.

112. Miller, *Unwelcomed Immigrant.*

113. Mann, "The Decade," 484–504, and *After the Gold Rush.*

114. Peffer, *If They Don't Bring Their Women,* details the situation for women.

115. Choy, Dong, and Hom, *Coming Man.*

116. Paul, "The Origin," 185–89.

117. Ping Chiu, *Chinese Labor,* 16.

118. Ibid., 12, and Kwong and Miscevic, *Chinese America,* 45.

119. *People v. Naglee,* 1 Cal. 232; 52 Am Dec. 312 (1850); Mears, *Resident Orientals,* 213.

120. McClain, "The Chinese Struggle," 545.

121. *Trinity Times* (Weaverville, California), January 20, 1855.

122. Paul, "After the Gold Rush," 2.

123. Mann, *After the Gold Rush,* 116.

124. Carranco, "Chinese Expulsion," 328.

125. Mann, *After the Gold Rush,* 183–94.

126. *People v. Hall,* 4 Cal. Rep. 399, 405–6; see the Supreme Court opinion delivered by Chief Justice Murray with the concurrence of Justice Heydenfeldt at http://www.cetel.org/1854_hall.html; Doo, "Dispute Settlement," 630–31 and McClain, "The Chinese Struggle . . . The First Phase," 548–50.

127. Stahler, "William Speer," 113–29.

128. Torok, "Reconstruction."

129. Chung and Rusco, "Anti-Chinese Movement."

130. In 1878 the Federal Circuit Court in San Francisco ruled that the Chinese were ineligible for naturalization (*Ah Yup,* 1 F. Cas. 223 [C.C.D. Cal 1878]) based on the wording of 1 Stat. 103 (1790) that restricted the right of naturalization to "any alien, being a free white person." This was upheld in the Chinese Exclusion Act (22 Stat. 58, 1882) forbidding the granting of citizenship to any Chinese person. An excellent coverage of cases that made it to the Supreme Court is Hyung-chan Kim, *Asian Americans.*

131. *Baldwin v. Franks,* 120 U.S. 678 (1887); McClain, "The Chinese Struggle," 349–73.

132. Mining Law of 1866, 14 Stat. 251, 242–43; Placer Act of 1870, 16 Stats. at Large, 217; and General Mining Law of 1872, 17 Stat. 91 (later codified with others as 2318–46 U.S. Rev. Stat.).

133. A substantial body of literature was written on the 1866 and 1872 mining laws. See, for example, Libecap, "Government Support," 354–85; Davis, "Fifty Years," 897–908; Ary et al., *Mining Law of 1872*; and Mayer, "1872 Mining Law," 624–45. See also http://bulk.resource.org/courts.gov/c/F1/0104/001/00000192.txt on court cases involving the Chinese and the determination of the ownership of mining property.

134. "Crusade in Siskiyou County Against the Chinese Miners," *San Francisco Bulletin,* March 24, 1860.

135. Stapp, "The Historic Ethnography," 57.

136. Rich and Farnham, *Lawyers Reports Annotated,* 813–87, online at http://bulk.resource.org/courts.gov/c/F1/0104/001/00000192.txt. summarized case; the cases of *Tibbitts v. Ah Tong,* 2 Pac. 759, and *Chapman v. Toy Long,* 4 Savvy, 28 Fed. Cas. No. 2,610, on the inability of the Chinese to locate and possess mining claims because they are aliens ineligible for naturalization.

137. 30 U.S. Code 22; see discussion in Valentine, "American Canyon," 125. On the Chinese exclusion from being naturalized citizens, see Sayler, *Laws Harsh as Tigers,* 207, 210.

138. Leshy, *Mining Law.*

139. Mayer, "1872 Mining Law," 645.

140. "The Territory of Montana, Plaintiff and Respondent, v. 3000 Feet of Mining Ground, and Fouk Lee, Defendant and Appellant," 487–99.

141. Ibid., 495.

142. Wyman, "Mining Law," 14–22 ;and Zhu, "No Need to Rush," 54.

143. Allison French, "Pierce City Mines," *Spokesman-Review* (Spokane Falls, WA), August 6, 1891.

144. On the entrance fee tax which was in force in 1869, see *IS*, July 1, 1869.

145. Borthwick, *Gold Hunters,* 144.

146. Rohe, "Chinese River Mining," 19.

147. Sucheng Chan, "Chinese Livelihood," 280.

148. Information from exhibit at Dutch Flat Historical Society and Museum, 1999.

149. Bowles, *Across the Continent*, Letter 23 on the Chinese dated August 18, San Francisco.

150. Chang, *Chinese in America,* 40.

151. Raymond, Statistics of Mines, 3.

152. Zhu, *A Chinaman's Chance,* 103, details his argument.

153. Fong and Markham, "Anti-Chinese Politics," 183–210. See also Miller, *Unwelcomed Immigrant*; Saxton, *Indispensable Enemy*; and Sandmeyer, *Anti-Chinese Movement.*

154. The payroll record can be found at the Nevada State Library and Archives, Carson City, Nevada, Box SECSTATE-0321, File #51.

155. Three significant works on the anti-Chinese movement are Sandmeyer, *Anti-Chinese Movement,* Daniels, *Anti-Chinese Violence,* and Saxton, *Indispensable Enemy.*

156. McGrath, "The Heritage," 247–60.

157. Carranco, "Chinese in Humboldt County," 139–62.

158. Story reprinted in the *San Francisco Bulletin,* December 18, 1856.

159. Schwantes, "Protest" 373–90.

160. Currier, "Chinese Web," 46.

161. Carranco, "Chinese in Humboldt County." See also Karlin, "Anti-Chinese Outbreak," 271–83; Wortman, "Denver's Anti-Chinese Riot," 275–91; and Elmer Rusco, "Chinese Massacres," 3–30.

162. For additional information on exclusion laws related to the Chinese, see for example, Erika Lee, *At America's Gates*; Gyory, *Closing the Gate*; Hing, *Making and Remaking Asian America*; Hune, "Politics of Chinese Exclusion," 5–28; Calavita, "Paradoxes," 1–40; Calavita, "Chinese Exclusion," 203–26; Calavita, "Collisions," 249–82; Fritz, "Nineteenth Century," 347–72; and Hutchinson, *Legislative History.*

163. There are many works on this subject, some of which have been summarized in Tood M. Stevens, "Brokers," chapter 5.

164. *Cong. Rec.*, 52 Cong., 1 sess. (April 23, 1892), 3559.

165. Coolidge, *Chinese Immigration*; Speer, *Oldest and Newest Empire*; and Donner, *Last Days.*

166. This pamphlet is in the Bancroft Library, University of California–Berkeley collection.

167. Romeo, "Irony Lost," 108–36.

168. *Cong. Rec.*, 59 Cong., 1 sess. (1906), House of Representatives, "Facts Concerning the Enforcement of the Chinese Exclusion Laws," Doc. 847, and *Cong. Rec.*,

81 Cong., 2 sess. (1950), Senate, "Report of the Committee on the Judiciary Pursuant to S. Resolution 137, Report 1515 "Immigration and Naturalization Systems of the United States," 53, give the historical background and figures. See also Erika Lee, *At America's Gates,* Part II.

169. See Edson, *Chinese in Eastern Oregon.*

Chapter 2. Onward to Eastern Oregon

1. Chia-lin Chen, "A Gold Dream," 33.
2. Farnham, "Development," 29–45.
3. Chia-lin Chen, "A Gold Dream," 41.
4. *San Joaquin Republican* (Stockton, CA), November 24, 1855, reprinted the article that reported seventy Chinese miners killed in a "wholesale slaughter."
5. *Oregonian* (Portland), March 25, 1861, quoted in Liestman, "Nineteenth-Century Chinese," 17.
6. See Todd M. Stevens, "Brokers," 160–67.
7. See Anderson, *Vancouver's Chinatown.*
8. *Oregonian,* October 31, 1857; see Currier, "Chinese Web," 24.
9. Oregon Legislative Assembly, 1st session, 1860, *Laws and Journals,* 49–52.
10. Wilson, "A History," 20–21.
11. Takaki, *Strangers,* 81.
12. Todd M. Stevens, "Brokers," 170, n. 41.
13. Oregon Constitution, Article XV, Section 8.
14. Oregon Legislative Assembly, "An Act to Tax and Protect Chinamen Mining in Oregon," 4th sess., 1866, *Laws, 1866–1872,* October 24, 1866, 41–46, quoted in Edson, *Chinese in Eastern Oregon,* 46.
15. Oregon Constitution, Article XIV. See Edson, *Chinese in Eastern Oregon,* 49; and Steeves, "Chinese Gold Miners," 45.
16. Liestman, "Nineteenth-Century Chinese," 19.
17. Blue, *Mining Laws,* 140.
18. Wilson, "A History," 20.
19. Ibid., 21–22.
20. On Jacksonville, see Ross, "Jacksonville," 19–25.
21. LaLande, "'Celestials,'" and "Sojourners," give a detailed description of Jacksonville, Kubli's store accounts, the miner Gin Lin, and the archaeological findings in that area. LaLande noted that popular items in Kubli's store were Chinese imported foodstuff and American work clothes and boots ("'Celestials,'" 39–41).
22. LaLande, "Sojourners." See also Kingsleynews.com, "Unlike Most Chinese."
23. Although business records of EuroAmerican-owned stores in John Day have not been uncovered, a few business records of merchandising stores serving the Chinese have been preserved in the Ethnic Studies Library, University of California–Berkeley and discussed in LaLande, "'Celestials,'" and Stapp, "Historic Ethnography."
24. Kubli's business records, University of Oregon, Special Collections Library, Eugene, Box 12.

25. LaLande, "'Celestials,'" points out the adaptations that the Chinese made.

26. Quoted by Herman B. Chiu, "Power," 65.

27. Chia-lin Chen, "A Gold Dream," 37.

28. *Oregonian,* August 24, 1868.

29. Herman B. Chiu, "Power," 59–78.

30. Based on a visit to the newspaper office in the 1990s.

31. Oral interview with editor's son in Tonopah, Nevada, 2001.

32. For an overview of Oregon history, see the Oregon Historical Society website, http://www.ohs.org/education/focus. For information on Oregon's railroad construction, see Currier, "Chinese Web," 31–33. See also Farnham, "Development," 39.

33. *Weekly Oregonian,* April 1, 1853, July 15, 1854, and August 3, 1861, cited in Edson, *Chinese in Eastern Oregon,* 11.

34. Elmer Rusco, "Chinese Massacres," 8, based on stories in the *Territorial Enterprise* (Virginia City, NV) in April and May, 1866, and *Owyhee Avalanche* (Boise, Idaho), June 23, 1866.

35. John Mullan, U.S. Army, "From Walla Walla to San Francisco" in *Washington Statesman* (Walla Walla, WA), December 6, 1862, quoted in Wilson, "A History," 11.

36. See Toepel, Willingham, and Minor, *Cultural Resource.*

37. *An Illustrated History,* 520; and Bancroft, *History of Oregon,* 31: 521.

38. Elmer Rusco, "Chinese Massacres," 12. The six-year interval was the minimum time for the process of exhuming the bones. See Crowder, "Chinese Mortuary Tradition," 195–240.

39. Burial practices are described in Chung and Wegars, *Chinese American Death Rituals.*

40. Census manuscript, 1870, Baker City, Baker County, OR.

41. Ah Poo's story is told in NARA, Washington, DC, INS RG 85, Applications for Duplicate Certificates of Residence, Entry 137, Box 1 (an unnumbered file box).

42. This information is from Perry N. Stokes, Library Director of the Baker County Library District, and the website http://www.oregongenealogy.com/baker/baker/chinese.htm. The population figures are from Edson, *The Chinese,* 34 and 36.

43. Lisa Britton, "In the Footsteps of Chinese Miners," *Baker City Herald* (August 7, 2008).

44. Liestman, "Nineteenth-Century Chinese," 20.

45. "Chinese Cemetery, Baker City," online.

46. He may be Chue Gem Lee, who arrived in San Francisco in 1889, NARA, San Bruno, INS, RG 85, Casefile 226834, Box 11.

47. "Chinese Heritage" online; recollection of Herman C. Webb, who worked for Cook and Emele Sheet Metal Works; and Hom, "'Fallen Leaves,'" 36–50.

48. "The Chinese in Baker County," online; and "Chinese Heritage, Baker County," online.

49. "Sparta, Baker County," online, has the photograph of Aw-wing.

50. Edson, *Chinese in Eastern Oregon,* 32.

51. On the Burlingame Treaty see Kim, "Burlingame," 337–54; and Golove, "Treaty-Making," 1075–319.

52. Steeves, "Chinese Gold Miners," 45.

53. Ibid., 45–47.

54. For background information on Grant County, see "Grant County History, Oregon State Archives," online, and "Grant County in the Beginning," online.

55. Herman B. Chiu, "Power," 60; and NARA, Census manuscript, 1870, Microfilm reel 2, for more information on the Chinese in Grant County. The 1870 Oregon census also can be found online at http://www.rootsweb.ancestry.com/~cenfiles/or, but when compared with the census manuscript, some of the Chinese names were omitted.

56. Wegars, "Ah Hee Diggings," 119–20.

57. Chia-lin Chen, "A Gold Dream," 52.

58. NARA, Census manuscript, 1870, Grant County, OR. Some of the information is available online at http://ftp.rootsweb.ancestry.com/pub/usgenweb/or.grant/census/1870. My interpretations of the handwriting differ somewhat from the online version.

59. Census, *Eleventh Census,* 36, 521.

60. Chia-lin Chen, "A Gold Dream," 55–56, did these calculations. His figures differ from Edson, *Chinese in Eastern Oregon,* 32–35.

61. Edson, *Chinese in Eastern Oregon,* 25, did not count all of the companies and Chia-lin Chen, "A Gold Dream" was unaware of the significance of the designations; based upon the NARA, Census manuscript, 1880, Oregon, Grant County.

62. Edson, *Chinese in Eastern Oregon,* 25.

63. NARA, Census manuscript, 1880, Oregon, Grant County.

64. The information on Warren, Idaho, is from Fee, "Idaho's Chinese Mountain Gardens," 75.

65. For more information on Chinese medicine in this period, see Haiming Liu, "Resilience," 173–91; and Haiming Liu, *Transnational History;* Barlow and Richardson, *China Doctor;* Sohn, *Healers;* Loomis, "Medical Arts," 496; Hallmark, "Chinese Health Hazards," 60–79; Barnes, "Alternative Pursuits"; Amanda M. Smith, "Choosing Chinese Medicine," 24–31.

66. NARA, Portland, INS File M1638.2, Casefile 453, on Dr. Wing Yuen Sai, Portland, OR. See also Thornton, "Exceptions," 50–59.

67. The sixteenth-century Chinese pharmacopeia of 1,892 substances with 8,160 plant herbs was familiar to Chinese physicians and the information was summarized for common ailments in pamphlets readily available to Chinese travelers.

68. NARA, Washington, D.C., RG 85, Entry 137, Box 27, Casefile 54007/22, on Dr. Wing Lee provides this information from his application for a duplicate certificate of residence.

69. Pan, *Encyclopedia,* provides an overview.

70. NARA, Portland, Oregon, INS RG 85, M1638, 2, Casefile 373, on Leong Sun, cited in Thorton, "Exceptions," 53.

71. On paper relatives and the system to work around the Chinese exclusion laws, see Lau, *Paper Families.*

72. Siu-lun Wong, "Chinese Family Firm," 58–72.

73. The census manuscript for John Day in 1870 listed seventy-six EuroAmerican women, most of them children in farming families, in a total population of 280. Census manuscript, 1870, Oregon, Grant County, John Day.

74. Lyman, "Marriage," 321–30. See also Peffer, *If They Don't Bring Their Women Here.*

75. Ling, "Family and Marriage," 43–63.

76. Chinn, *Bridging,* 102–5.

77. NARA, San Bruno, California, RG 85, INS, Casefile 9870/7, on admission of native-born Ah Wy in 1902. Sometimes the entire family went back to China and some of the sons returned: Casefile 923/69 on Yuck Lum, arriving 1902, born in Dutch Flat, California, in 1889 to merchant Poon Duck Tie and his wife Yee Mon.

78. NARA, Washington, DC, INS RG 85, Entry 137, Boxes 14 and 16, Casefile 1355, petition of Lee Lung, merchant, for writ of habeas corpus for Li Tom Shi (wife) and Li A Tsoi (daughter), dated August 18, 1900. Lee Lung was a prominent merchant and agent for the North Pacific Steamship Company that solicited Chinese passengers to and from the United States. He was a partner in businesses in Portland and Astoria, Oregon; Baltimore, Maryland; New York City, and Hong Kong.

79. For a background on Chinese prostitutes, see Hershatter, *Dangerous Pleasures,* and Yung, *Unbound Feet.* Even in the United States there were different categories or rankings of Chinese prostitutes.

80. Liestman, "Nineteenth-Century Chinese," 18.

81. Mary K. Rusco, "Counting the Lovelock Chinese," 319–28; and Mary K. Rusco, "Chinese in Lovelock," 141–51.

82. Farnham, "Development," 29–45.

83. Quoted in Chia-lin Chen, "A Gold Dream," 82.

84. Terry Abraham, "Stepping Stones," and Walter James, "Walter James," 75–86.

85. Edson, *Chinese in Eastern Oregon,* 16.

86. NARA, Washington, DC, RG 85, Entry 137, Box 33, "Miscellaneous," No casefile number, Wong Goey. Testimonies from EuroAmericans carried weight with the government so the fact that he did not know any went against him in his original arrest.

87. Farnham, "Development," 39.

88. Jones, *Oregonian's Handbook,* 70 and 292, quoted in Steeves, "Chinese Miners, 146.

89. NARA, Washington, DC, INS RG 85, Casefile 53569/120.

90. Steeves, "Chinese Gold Miners," 46.

91. Ibid., 52, from the *Grant County Express* newspaper file in the Grant County Museum archives.

92. Steeves, "Chinese Gold Miners," 52.

93. The event was so sensational that much has been written about it. Stratton, "Snake River Massacre," 215–130, which has been updated by Nokes, "'A Most Daring

Outrage,'" 326–53 and his book, *Massacred for Gold*. See also Liestman, "Horizontal Inter-Ethnic Relations," 327–49.

94. *Idaho Statesman* (Lewiston), April 18, 1867.

95. Ibid., May 19, 1870.

96. James and Lytle, "Ruins of a World," 6 and 12.

97. The massacre made national news, see, for example, "An Old Snake River Tragedy. A Chinese Massacre in 1887 Brought to Light Again," *The State* (Columbia, SC), October 1, 1891, *Bismarck Tribute* (Bismarck, ND), October 2, 1891, and *Macon Telegraph* (Macon, GA), October 16, 1891.

98. Highberger, "Snake River Massacre," 4.

99. See *Fok Young Yo v. U.S.*, 183 U.S. 296 (1902), 185 U.S. 296; *Li Sing v. United States*, 180 U.486, 490, 45L.Ed 634, 21 Sup. Ct. Rep. 449; *United States v. Gee Lee*, 50 Fed. 271, 1 C.C.A 516, 7 U.S. App. 183.

100. "Kam Wah Chung & Co. Museum," online; Barlow, *China Doctor;* Chia-Lin Chen, "A Gold Dream"; Sarvis, "Gifted Healer," 62–69; and Steeves, "Chinese Gold Miners." Both Doc Hay and Lung On left a large collection of writings that are on file at the museum in several file cabinets and on CDs.

101. Additional information about these men can be found at the Kam Wah Chung and Company Museum, John Day, OR.

102. For more on the migrant networks, see McKeown, *Chinese Migrant Networks* 69–86.

103. Robbins, "Opportunity," 279–96.

104. This was the price for sleeping in one of the four upstairs rooms at the Wah Yuen Lung Kee and Company store in Reno, Nevada. NARA, San Bruno, California, INS, RG 85, Chinese Partnerships, Casefile 13561/231, for Wah Yuen Lung Kee and Company.

105. For a more detailed discussion, see Grimwade, "Gold, Gardens," 50–57. On Mazu, see Ruitenbeek, "Mazu," 281–329.

106. Oregon Historical Society, Kam Wah Chung Collection, Microfilm 74, Reel 3.

107. Some of the translations were done by Chia-lin Chen, "A Gold Dream," 113; and others by me for the Oregon Park Service.

108. Chia-lin Chen, "A Gold Dream," 92.

109. Ibid., 111–112. Idaho also passed an anti-opium possession and smoking law in 1887. Zhu, "How the Other Half Lived," 27.

110. *Ex Parte Mon Luck, Mon Luck v. Sears*, 29 Ore 421, 427–428 (1896), see also *State v. Ah Sam*, 14 Ore 347 (1887) and Wunder, "Chinese and the Courts," 206–7.

111. *An Illustrated History*, 443.

112. McCunn, *Chinese American Portraits*, 57–61 on Ing Hay and Lung On.

113. Ibid., 57.

Chapter 3. Eastward to Northeastern Nevada: Tuscarora

1. Kraus, *High Road;* Myrick, *Railroads;* Yen, "Chinese Workers,"; Lake, "Construction"; Bain, *Empire Express;* "Central Pacific Railroad," online.

2. See Ronald M. James, *Roar and Silence.* Portions of the Chinese Ditch and the building that house a Chinese store remain intact in Dayton today.

3. Chung, "Destination," 111–39.

4. Hazlett, "Historical Sketches," 21–22; and Chung, "Destination," 111–139.

5. The Chinese miners in Six Mile Canyon were listed in the 1870 and 1880 census manuscripts for Nevada but not in the 1860 census.

6. *Yinshan* was engraved on the altar pieces from one of the Zhigongtang headquarters in Carson City, Nevada, and presently is in the collection of the Nevada State Museum, Carson City.

7. Wright, *The Big Bonanza,* 40.

8. SHPO, "Find People," 1860 census.

9. Shawn Hall provided the information about Lee Kee.

10. *NSJ,* September 10, 1875.

11. See Barde, *Immigration,* 150–62, 169. Also called the Canton Bank.

12. Sucheng Chan, "Chinese Livelihood," 281.

13. Zhu, *A Chinaman's Chance,* 101.

14. See "Central Pacific Railroad," online.

15. The Burlingame Treaty, 16 Stat. 739 (July 28, 1868), Article V, can be found in Hing, *Making and Remaking,* 201–2.

16. Zhu and Fosha, *Ethnic Oasis,* covers the history and archaeological dig of the Chinese in the Black Hills.

17. Carter, "Social Demography," 73–89, gives a breakdown of all the Chinese in all Nevada counties. See also Lingenfelter, *Hardrock Miners,* 51–65, and his papers at the University of California–San Diego library.

18. Blackburn and Ricards, "Chinese of Virginia City," 51–72; and Blackburn and Ricards, "Prostitutes and Gamblers," 239–58.

19. SHPO, "Find People," 1880, Storey County.

20. *EDS,* November 19, 1881, details Ah Kim's life and death.

21. Census, 1870–1900, Table 2. See also Carter, "Social Demography," 73–89.

22. On the Chinese in Carlin, see Chung, Frampton, and Murphy, "Venerate," 107–46.

23. SHPO, "Find People," Elko County, Carlin, 1870 and 1880 statistics.

24. *TE,* January 19, 1869; February 21, 1869; and September 28, 1870.

25. Census manuscripts 1870–1900 Nevada, Elko County.

26. SHPO, "Find People," 1880–1920, Elko County, Elko.

27. Elko County Recorder's Office, Miscellaneous, Book 3: 549, dated November 14, 1887. In 1887 Weston and his partners, Edward Reily and George Bliss, discovered the King Mine; in 1888 Weston became the district recorder. Hall, *Old Heart,* 46–47.

28. NARA, San Bruno, INS, RG 85, Casefile 13561/281, and Elko County Recorder's Office, Bill of Sales, 267, Casefile 3466, dated 1898. The partners were all Ung (Ng or Wu in pinyin). By 1910 six of the partners were in China and only four ran the store.

29. See, for example, Storey County Recorder's Office, Book of Deeds, Book 30:

81, sale of property from Samuel Cohen to Hy Loy for $100, dated April 6, 1870. Numerous examples appear in Storey County's deed books.

30. Zhu, *A Chinaman's Chance,* 98.

31. See Ritchie, "Archaeology."

32. Stapp, "Historic Ethnography," 59, based upon the Pierce Mining District Records, 1861–90; and Stapp, "Documentary Record," 3–32.

33. "China Ditch," online.

34. Elko County Recorder's Office, Deeds, Book 25: 359–60.

35. Hall, *Connecting the West;* Hall, *Old Heart.* See also Patterson, Ulph, and Goodwin, *Nevada's Northeast Frontier,* 541–73, 654–63.

36. Ryan, Annual Report, 18.

37. Patterson, Ulph, and Goodwin, *Nevada's Northeast Frontier,* 655.

38. *DSS,* May 31, 1878, reporting a story from the *TTR.* See Vanderburg, "Placer Mining." Antoine Primeaux provided me with this and many other newspaper clippings that he had typed in his research on the Chinese in Tuscarora.

39. Emmons and Becker, *Statistics and Technology,* 238.

40. *DSS,* May 31, 1878.

41. Vanderburg, "Placer Mining," 77.

42. Census manuscript, 1870, Nevada, Elko County, Tuscarora.

43. Maureen Johnson, *Placer Gold Deposits,* 19–20. The figures most likely are an exaggeration. See also Nevada State Legislature, "Biennial Report of the State Mineralogist," 17, 18, 193.

44. Patterson, Ulph, and Goodwin, *Nevada's Northeast Frontier,* 660.

45. *TTMR,* July 25 and 26, 1883.

46. Nevada State Legislature, *Appendix,* 1875 Elko County census.

47. Elko Country Recorder's Office, Tax Assessment Rolls, 1872 and 1874.

48. Elko County Recorder's Office, Tax Assessment Rolls, 1878.

49. Ibid.

50. Elko County Recorder's Office, Tax Assessment Rolls, 1881. There is no Gow Ah or Ah Gow listed in the census manuscripts for Tuscarora, 1860–1900.

51. Nevada State Legislature, "Biennial Report of the State Mineralogist," 17–18.

52. Nevada Historical Society, Reno, Chinese file.

53. *Elko Post,* November 16, 1878.

54. Chung and Rusco, oral interview with Frank Chang of Lovelock in the 1980s.

55. *TTR,* July 23, 1881.

56. Elko County Recorder's Office, Deeds, Book 16: 577. There are more records.

57. Elko County Recorder's Office, Tax Assessment Rolls, 1888, 1890, and 1893.

58. Elko County Recorder's Office, Writs of Attachments, 1869–1899, filed and dated May 31, 1889.

59. Elko County Recorder's Office, Index to Miscellaneous Records 1869–1941, action dated November 23, 1892 (organized by date).

60. Hom Tong's name does not appear on the census manuscripts for 1880 and 1900. Elko County Recorder's Office, Index to Bills of Sale, 1890–1937, Book 1, 39.

61. For more information on the Hexingtang, see Reynolds, "Chinese Tongs," 612–23; and Culin, "Chinese Secret Societies," 42–43. Both contain misleading and inaccurate information. See also Blythe, *Impact;* Ownby, *Brotherhoods;* Stanton, *Triad Society;* Cai, "On the Origin," 481–508; and Murray, *Origins.*

62. Elko County Recorder's Office, Tax Assessment Rolls, 1882.

63. Chung, "Zhigongtang," 231–49. Two archaeological digs uncovered artifacts and documents from the organization: Ying-ying Chen, "In the Colonies," for British Columbia; and Lister and Lister, *The Chinese,* for Tucson. Zhigongtang artifacts from Tuscarora are housed in the Nevada State Museums in Carson City and Las Vegas.

64. Ying-ying Chen, "In the Colonies," 115, 289.

65. "Yankee Chinese to Hail Republic. Dr. Sun Yat Sen Issues Call to Countrymen in America to Aid Cause," *Oregonian,* October 14, 1911.

66. *NSJ* (Reno, Nevada), October 14, 1911.

67. For a detailed discussion of the system of illegal immigration, see Lau, *Paper Families.*

68. Ying-ying Chen, "In the Colonies," 51–54.

69. As an example of the relative values, the "China Mason House," as the tax assessor labeled it, was larger in Elko and valued at $900 while the one in Tuscarora was valued at $400. Elko County Recorder's Office, Tax Assessment Rolls, 1893.

70. This can be seen by comparing photographs of the two buildings. The photograph in Monterey, California, is displayed in the Cannery Mall. Lydon, *Chinese Gold,* 267, has a photograph of the Zhigongtang in Santa Cruz in the 1940s, which resembles the Tuscarora and Monterey lodges.

71. *TTR,* November 19, 1901.

72. *Weekly Elko Independent,* January 19, 1900.

73. State and local laws made opium importation and smoking illegal beginning in the 1870s. The Harrison Narcotics Tax Act (Chap. 1, 38 Stat. 785), passed in 1914, was the federal law attempting to stop the opium trade and practice. See Lowe, "Pipe Dreams," 178–93; Mark, "Opium in America," 61–74; and Ahmed, *Opium Debate.*

74. Patterson, Ulph, and Goodwin, *Nevada's Northeast Frontier,* 660.

75. Translated from the banner originally in the Zhigongtang lodge in Carson City, Nevada, now housed in the Nevada State Museum, Carson City.

76. The rules and regulations have been translated in Lister and Lister, *The Chinese,* Appendix.

77. Elko County Recorder's Office, Tax Assessment Rolls. 1878.

78. Elko County Recorder's Office, Tax Assessment Rolls. 1877. Hop Lee was born in 1832.

79. Elko County Recorder's Office, Tax Assessment Rolls, 1880 and 1881.

80. Liu, "Old Linkages," 582–609.

81. Lau, *Paper Families;* Peffer, *If They Don't Bring Their Women Here;* and Erika Lee, *At America's Gates.*

82. Elko County Recorder's Office, Tax Assessment Rolls, 1883.

83. Ibid. The details on the assessment were not uniform.

84. NARA, San Bruno, INS, RG 85, Files 13561/140 on Quong Hi and Company.

85. Elko County Recorder's Office, Tax Assessment Rolls, 1888, 1890, and 1893.

86. Elko County Recorder's Office, Tax Assessment Rolls, 1899 and 1900. Hong Lee's is listed as being in Gold Creek.

87. Fook Chin (b. 1861, immigrated 1881) and Wing Yuen Chin (b. 1862, immigrated 1882).

88. NARA, San Bruno, INS, RG 86, Casefile 1356/139 on Quong Hing Lung, investigation dated December 1895, with photographs.

89. This was true when "return certificates" were issued. See Dickman, "Living with Exclusion."

90. Census manuscript, 1900 Nevada, Elko County, Tuscarora.

91. Elko County Recorder's Office, Tax Assessment Rolls, 1870. Ah Lee paid $40, meaning he paid for nine other individuals as well. These taxes were levied upon all residents but usually only the Chinese paid for people other than themselves and their immediate family members. Some original receipts can be found in the Nevada State Library and Archives in Carson City. The records of the poll taxes collected were not always listed in the tax assessment rolls. In Nevada the poll taxes were collected until 1910 and finally repealed in 1966. The rate varied from $2 to $4 per person.

92. See, for example, on the death of Mun Quong (age 38) on May 15, 1890, Elko County Recorder's Office, Death Book 1 (1890), 288.

93. This correlation is based upon the dates of his visits to China, which were publicized in the local newspaper. NARA, San Bruno, INS, RG 86, Casefile 1356/139 on Quong Hing Lung, dated December 1895, with photographs and signatures. On his return in 1913, see NARA, Washington, DC, INS, RG 85, Box 368, Case ID 236101, Casefile 10362/00013.

94. *TTMR,* April 9, 1886.

95. The celebration has been interpreted incorrectly and can be found in McElrath, *Aged in Sage,* and retold by Howard Hickson in "Howard Hickson's Histories," online. See also Chace, "Returning Thanks"; and *Dancing with the Dragon.*

96. Photographs of Ah Lee Lake are available at NARA, San Bruno, INS RG 85 "Chinese Partnership Records," Casefile 1356/139 on Quong Hing Lung, and at the Northeastern Nevada Museum, Elko.

97. *TTMR,* November 12, 1891. See also *TTR,* March 21 and April 7, 1903, for his trips to San Francisco.

98. *TTR,* April 7, 1903.

99. Chung interviews with Antoine Primeaux, son of the Tuscarora merchant, in Elko, 1999. The fact that they lived close to each other was confirmed in the 1900 census manuscript.

100. Elko County Recorder's Office, Tax Assessment Rolls, 1869–1870, on microfilm. He does not appear in any of the Nevada census manuscripts, 1860–1930.

101. Elko County Recorder's Office, Tax Assessment Rolls. 1872.

102. Elko County Recorder's Office, Tax Assessment Rolls, 1877.

103. Valentine, "Historical," details this.

104. Census manuscript, 1880, Nevada, Elko County, Tuscarora, for household 28.

105. LuAnn Caressi compiled the data. See also Census manuscript, 1880, Nevada, Elko County, Tuscarora.

106. *TTMR,* October 15, 1886.

107. Elko County Recorder's Office, Index to Miscellaneous Records, 1869–1941, Book 2: 344, dated July 22, 1876.

108. Sohn, *The Healers,* 29. See also Duane A. Smith, "Comstock Miseries," 1–12; and So, "Ethnic Doctors," 75–82.

109. Sohn, *The Healers,* 29, on the Chinese hospital, and Mills, *Sagebrush Saga,* 89, on the Elko County Hospital.

110. Culin, "Practice of Medicine," 1–3.

111. Couch, "Topophilia," 136.

112. Ibid.

113. Chinese men in mining and railroad towns often suffered from serious injuries due to work and/or discrimination. See Schmidt, "Forgotten."

114. There are many studies of opium use in China and the United States. For a background, see Spence, *Search for Modern China,* chapter 7; Ahmed, *Opium Debate;* and Auerhahn, "Split Labor Market," 411–40.

115. Nevada State Legislature, "Biennial Report of the Warden."

116. Storey County Courthouse, Arrest Records, 1864–90.

117. There are several studies on this topic. See, for example, Wrobleski, "Archaeology of Chinese Work Camps."

118. Schmidt, "Forgotten," details the skeletons. One was mummified and fell into a different category of examination.

119. See numerous articles in the *Sacramento Daily Record-Union* and *San Francisco Post* in 1876. See also Auerhahn, "Split Labor Market," 422.

120. Statues of the State of Nevada, 8th Session of 1877 and Nevada Revised Statutes, vol. 27, Sec. 453, 056.

121. *TE,* March 29, 1879.

122. Ahmed, *Opium Debate,* 64. This work should be used with caution.

123. See, for example, NARA, San Bruno, U.S. District Courts, RG 21, District of Nevada, Casefiles 5501 (Charlie Hong), 5502 (Ah Fai, aka Ah Tai), 5503 (Tom Lung), 5504 (Gee Toy, aka Gee Sue Tom), and 5505 (Ah Boo) on Narcotic Inspector Harry Haley and his assistant and mentee, Special Indian Agent G. W. O'Neil, on their entrapment (present-day terminology) of Chinese selling *yen shee* (Cantonese) to Native Americans.

124. Mills, *Sagebrush Saga,* 66.

125. *TTMR,* July 25 and 26, 1883.

126. *TTR,* February 16 and 20, 1886. This tactic was common.

127. For more information on African American and Chinese relations, see Aarim-Heriot, *Chinese Immigrants.*

128. Lettieri, "Maximize Our Missions," discusses this.

129. The ratio of Chinese men to Chinese women was 19:1 (1860), 13:1 (1870), 21:1 (1880), 27:1 (1890), 19:1 (1900), and 14:1 (1910). See Daniels, *Asian America,* 69.

130. These statistics are from SHPO "Find People."

131. The system of dispute settlement and mediation is discussed in detail in Doo, "Dispute Settlement," 627–63.

132. Elko County Recorder's Office, Index to Marriages, 1869–1949, by date. Nothing else is known about these couples.

133. "Shee" indicates in Chinese that the woman is married and How or Tom (most likely Tom) was her maiden name.

134. *TTR,* June 22, 1883.

135. On the hydraulic mining endeavors, see *TTMR,* March 22, April 17, and May 28, 1884.

136. See Greenland, *Hydraulic Mining;* and Crouch, "Hydraulic Mining," online.

137. *TTMR,* February 26, 1884. He might be Ahe Tee (age 33), a grocer in Tuscarora in the 1880 census manuscript, see SHPO, "Find People."

138. NARA, San Bruno, INS, RG 85, Casefiles 13561/140 on Quong Hi and Company, 271 on Yuen Chong Lung, and 295 on Quong Sing Company. In numerous records, the name of the company, such as Quong Hi, mistakenly was listed as the individual's name.

139. The company was not recorded by the U.S. Treasury Department's Bureau of Immigration but was listed in the Elko County Recorder's Office, Tax Assessment Rolls, for example, in 1883 through 1886.

140. Government Land Office Plat Map, 1885, T. 39 N., 51 E.

141. *TTMR,* May 19, 1885.

142. *GCN,* January 14, 1897, provides this detailed description of Tuscarora.

143. *TTR,* May 9, 1892.

144. U.S. Congress, Miscellaneous Documents of the House of Representatives, 1st Sess., 52nd Congr., 1891–92, U.S. Bureau of the Census, *Compendium of the Eleventh Census: Part 1,* vol. 50, part 3, 401, 520.

145. Vanderburg, "Placer Mining," 77.

146. SHPO, "Find People."

147. SHPO, "Find People," 1910 and 1920, Elko County.

148. Accounts differ on where the gold was found. This is archaeologist Mary Rusco's version.

149. Hillinger, "Saga of Tuscarora."

150. *TTR,* February 11, 1886; July 31, 1890; July 8, 1897; and July 4, 1898, gave examples. Antoine and Ellen Primeaux's 1993 oral history is on file at the Northeastern Nevada Museum in tape and transcribed form. The author interviewed Antoine several times in the 1990s.

151. *Humboldt Star* (Winnemucca), September 3, 1953. Many musical instruments and unusual items such as a Chinese cigar maker's knife and gold dust cleaners were among the more than one hundred items.

152. Dillingham, "Tuscarora Greenstrip." There have been less than two dozen residents living in Tuscarora since the 1930s but it is still considered a ghost town.

Chapter 4. Farther East: Island Mountain and Gold Creek

1. Most of the information regarding Penrod's life comes from the *GCN*, February 11, 1897, his letters at the Nevada Historical Society (Manuscript #1416), and his obituaries in the *NSJ*, Apri114, 1913 and *Tonopah Bonanza* (Tonopah), Apri115, 1913.

2. Hall, *Old Heart*, 98–103, 129, 131, 133.

3. The photographs, taken by Mrs. Hilda Matthey of Davenport, Iowa, and donated by Louis and Roz Van Houten of Keystone, Colorado, are in the Northeastern Nevada Museum, Elko, File 1291, numbers 1–26 (Gold Creek and vicinity), in the Forest Service (Humboldt-Toiyabe National Forest–Elko), and in my collection.

4. *Polk's Nevada Gazetteer and Business Directory*, 1907–8, "Gold Creek."

5. Elko County Recorder's Office, Deeds, Number 34.

6. Granger et al., "Geology"; Lincoln, *Mining Districts;* Patterson, Ulph, and Goodwin, *Nevada's Northeast Frontier*, 615.

7. Hall, *Old Heart*, 98. See also Frampton et al., "Class III."

8. *GNC*, March 4, 1897.

9. Nevada State Legislature, *Appendix*, Special 1875 Census for Elko County, 28. The names are listed without designation as to location but by using the 1880 census manuscript with the names of those who remained in the town, the separations can be made.

10. *TE*, June 8, 1875. The Mayon in question is probably T. H. Mayon who became famous in Amador County, California.

11. Stretch, *Biennial Report*, 28. On hydraulic mining, see Kelley, "Forgotten Giant," 343–56; and Greenland, *Hyraulic Mining*.

12. Supernowicz, "Contextual History."

13. Hall, *Old Heart*, 100.

14. Between 1873 and 1878, eight canals and ditches were built with Chinese workers and recorded in the Elko County Recorder's Office, Miscellaneous Records, Books 1 and 2.

15. Hall, *Old Heart*, 99.

16. *GCN*, March 4, 1897. A few of these gates still exist.

17. I walked in several miles of the ditch system; this figure is an estimate.

18. Angel, *History of Nevada*, 394.

19. Emmons and Becker, *Statistics and Technology*, 237.

20. Liestman, "Nineteenth-Century Chinese," 20.

21. *Carson City Appeal*, September 26 and October 9, 1873.

22. This is revealed in the Nevada State Legislature, *Appendix to Journals of the Assembly and Senate*, Seventh Session.

23. Nevada State Legislature, *Journal of the Assembly*, Seventh Session (1875): 10, 19, 24, 32, 89, 103–4, 115, 118, 125, 133, 155.

24. Penrod, "Letters and Writings. ."

25. Granger et al., "Geology," 75, and Patterson, Ulph, and Goodwin, *Nevada's Northeast Frontier*, 615.

26. Personal communication, May, 2007.

27. *GCN,* August 6, 1897.

28. Hall, *Old Heart,* 90.

29. Rohwer, "Gold Creek Area."

30. Elko County Recorder's Office, Deeds, Book 11, 192.

31. Hall, *Old Heart,* 101.

32. Carlson, *Nevada Place Names,* 143.

33. Hall, *Old Heart,* 87–88.

34. Ibid., 88.

35. In the seven-year period between 1934 and 1941, the site yielded 529 ounces of gold; 552 ounces of silver; 1,900 pounds of lead; and 300 pounds of copper—valued in all at $19,039.

36. *Elko Weekly Independent,* April 23, 1893; and *GCN,* February 11, 1897.

37. In 1877 Walter Stofiel (b. 1855 in Pennsylvania, d. 1905) married Lydia Penrod (d. 1897), one of Emanuel Penrod's two daughters. Stofiel's store was in competition with China Lem's; he later relocated to Stofield (later called Wildhorse), some twenty miles away. See Hall, *Connecting,* 37.

38. *NSJ,* April 14, 1913; and *Tonopah Bonanza,* April 15, 1913.

39. Census manuscript, 1900, Nevada, Elko County, Island Mountain.

40. Census manuscript, 1910, Nevada, Elko County, Island Mountain.

41. Elko County Recorder's Office, Deeds, Book 24: 464–93, with map of townsite on 492–93.

42. *GCN,* January 28, 1897.

43. Hall, *Old Heart,* 101, 103.

44. *GCN,* March 4 and 11, 1897.

45. Hall, *Old Heart,* 101.

46. Murbarger, "Sidewalk," 1, 21.

47. *GCN,* December 24, 1896.

48. *GCN,* June 17, 1897, described the stagecoach rivalry.

49. Hall, *Connecting,* 30–31.

50. *GCN,* December 24, 1896.

51. Although there was no additional information about this reservoir and canal system, Jacqueline Beggs' detailed study of the 1874–92 construction of the Lake Chabot Dam in San Leandro, California, provides some comparative insight. Chabot hired five hundred Chinese and one hundred EuroAmericans to build the dam and reservoir; the Chinese workers modified his engineers' plans and made the system more efficient. Beggs, *Chinese Laborers,* 7–24. For details on the Sunflower Reservoir, see *GCN,* April 8 and 29, 1897.

52. *GCN,* April 8, 1897.

53. *GCN,* January 28, 1897; and Murbarger, "Sidewalk to Nowhere," 19.

54. *GCN,* February 4, 1897.

55. *GCN,* April 8, 1897; June 24, 1897.

56. *GCN,* April 8, 1897.

57. *GCN,* May 27, 1897.

58. *GCN,* April 11, June 17 and 24, and July 16, 1897.

59. *GCN,* July 16 and 30, 1897.

60. Information on the Corey Brothers and E. O. Wattis of Utah Construction Company, builders of Hoover Dam, is at the Stewart Library, Weber State University, Ogden, Utah.

61. LaPointe, Tingley, and Jones, *Mineral Resources,* 125.

62. Nevada State Legislature, *Appendix to Journals of the Assembly and Senate,* Eighth Session (1877); Elko County Census, 227–28.

63. See Sayler, *Laws;* Daniels, *Asian America;* Gyory, *Closing the Gate;* Erika Lee, *At America's Gate;* and Sucheng Chan, *Asian Americans,* on exclusion.

64. *GCN,* March 4, 1897 has a long description of Gold Creek and Island Mountain.

65. On *fengshui* and Chinese mining communities, see Couch, "Topophilia."

66. Statistics on Mountain City from SHPO, "Find People," 1870 to 1920.

67. In 1992 the Forest Service under the direction of Fred Frampton excavated two of the Chinese homes.

68. See Zhu, *A Chinaman's Chance,* and Wegars, "History and Archaeology," for a background.

69. Census manuscript, 1880, Nevada, Elko County, Mountain City.

70. Census manuscript, 1870, Nevada, Elko County, Cope Mining District.

71. Elko County Recorder's Office, Deeds, Book 11: 700.

72. Elko County Recorder's Office, Deeds, Book 7: 192–94.

73. Hall, *Old Heart,* 65–79.

74. In the late nineteenth century, 90 percent of the Chinese in the United States were born in the Siyi district, especially Taishan, Guangdong. The other three counties are: Kaiping/Hoiping, Xinhui/Sunwu, and Enping/Yanping.

75. Hsu, "Migration," 310.

76. Chung, Frampton, and Murphy, "Venerate," 107–46.

77. This was noted on their headstones in Island Mountain's Chinese cemetery, which disappeared sometime in the 1950s—but a photograph of the headstones still remains.

78. This information is based the photograph of their headstones. Suey died in 1898 but the headstone incorrectly reads "1897."

79. Census manuscript, 1880, Nevada, Elko County, Island Mountain.

80. This was determined through a lawsuit filed in June 1883 in which M. Hogen owed Ah Lue $378. Washoe County Recorder's Office, *Ah Lue v. M. Hogen,* Box 138, Case 2110 dated June 6, 1883, on microfilm.

81. Abraham, "Class, Gender, and Race."

82. Nevada Territory Laws ch. 32, sec. 1, 3, 1861. Nevada was the first in the nation to pass a law specifically barring marriages between whites and Chinese. The Nevada territorial law stated, "If any white man or woman intermarry with any black person, mulatto, Indian, or Chinese, the parties of such marriage shall be deemed guilty of a misdemeanor," with a prison term added. Sohoni, "Unsuitable Suitors," 587–618; Karthikeyan and Chin, "Preserving Racial Identity," 1–39; and

Pascoe, "Miscegenation Law," 44–69. Bilheimer, "Pawns," investigated Chinese-Paiute marriages.

83. Idaho Territory General Laws at 604, 1864; Oregon Laws at 10, secs. 1–2, 1866; Bilheimer, "Pawns." See also Liestman, "Horizontal," 327–50.

84. Oral interview with Juanita Pontoon of Schurz in 1991.

85. Ibid.

86. *Daily Free Press* (Elko, NV), September 12, 1884.

87. Ah Ching from Placerville would have been 32 years old in 1880; Ah Chung's name appears in the 1870 census manuscript for Cope and probably was the same person living in Island Mountain.

88. On prostitutes, see Hirata, "Free, Indentured, Enslaved," 3–29; Ling, *Surviving;* and Yung, *Unbound Feet.*

89. Student work on Chinese prostitutes in Nevada can be found in the University of Nevada, Las Vegas, Lied Library, Special Collections.

90. See *Mining and Scientific Press,* January 18, 1879; and Goss, *Life,* 65.

91. Hutchings quoted in Williams, "Chinese in California Mines," 85.

92. In 1910 there was a retail merchant named Wah Lung (b. 1846, immigrated 1876, married) in Elko but he was younger than the Wah Lung of 1880 Island Mountain.

93. NARA, Washington, DC, RG 85, Entry 137, Box 11, Casefile 143114.

94. Lists of Chinese departing from San Francisco between 1880 and 1900 might include some of these names but none could be located.

95. Chung, "Their Changing World," 203–28.

96. Liestman, "Nineteenth-Century Chinese," 17.

97. Zhu, *A Chinaman's Chance,* 112–16, discusses the merits of Chinese gardeners and their methodology. One can assume that a similar situation existed in Island Mountain/Gold Creek.

98. Many of the measurements cited in this work were made under the direction of the archaeologists, particularly Fred P. Frampton.

99. Hunt-Jones, "The Heart of a Community," listed the artifacts uncovered.

100. Sucheng Chan, *This Bittersweet Soil.*

101. I visited the site in the 1990s.

102. *EFP,* March 6, 1886.

103. The information on Hawthorne comes from the local Chinese vegetable gardener's grand-daughter, Shirlaine Kee Baldwin, who has writings from her uncle and papers from her relatives.

104. NARA, Washington, DC, INS, RG 85, Entry 137, Box 13, Casefile 52089/63. Wong is the family name.

105. *GCN,* January 28, 1898.

106. There are several versions to this story. See, for example, Ashbaugh, *Nevada's Turbulent Yesterday,* 290. The Mardis story was part of the Gold Creek tour; see *GCN,* March 4, 1897.

107. Patterson, Ulph, and Goodwin, *Nevada's Northeast Frontier,* 605.

108. Hall, *Old Heart,* 92.

109. An account of a Chinese tribunal session observed by Deadwood policeman Charley LaBresche in 1884 is recounted by Zhu, "Ethnic Oasis," 22–23.

110. Census manuscript, 1900, Nevada, Elko County, Tuscarora.

111. Census manuscript, 1900, Nevada, Elko County, Bryan.

112. Census manuscript, 1900 and 1910, Nevada, Elko County, Island Mountain.

113. Liestman, "Horizontal," 327–49.

114. Ibid., 346–47.

115. Fred P. Frampton interviewed McKinney and walked around Island Mountain with him.

116. Chung and Rusco, "Anti-Chinese Movement," 35–45.

117. Ispisua, "Island Mountain," 15–16.

118. Statistics from Census manuscript, 1930, Nevada, Elko County, South Fork.

119. SHPO "Find People," for 1870 Mountain City.

120. This letter (dated April 26, 1906) is in the Northeastern Nevada Museum, Elko, collection. Ng donated $2, as did several other Yee and Ng kinsmen. The local Zhigongtang donated $5 and several of the large merchandising companies donated $10.

121. On the Eng clan in Port Townsend, see Liestman, "'The Various Celestials,'" 93–100.

122. The Ng clan gatherings in Seattle was related to me by an Ng whose Americanized family name is Tuai.

123. Ying-ying Chen, "In the Colonies," 71–72. Thirty-six members of this clan were there.

124. Liestman, "'The Various Celestials,'" 94.

125. According to immigration records, Hong Lee was the name of a merchandising company in Carlin, Nevada, but actually was located in Island Mountain. The Ng merchants in Carlin gave the Department of Treasury officer the information and he mistakenly placed the firm in Carlin. See NARA, San Bruno, INS, RG 85, Hong Lee Company, Carlin, Casfile 13561/284.

126. For more information, see Hunt-Jones, "Heart of a Community."

127. Elko County Recorder's Office, Tax Asssessment Roll, 1881, listed both at $200.

128. Ispisua, "Island Mountain," 12–15.

129. C.A. Laing lived in Gold Creek and, in 1935, had settled in North Fork, Nevada. Elko County Recorder's Office, Bill of Sales, Book 3, File 64078 dated July 20, 1936.

130. Hall, *Connecting*, 30–31.

131. Ispisua, "Island Mountain," 12–15.

132. Ibid.

133. Ibid., 15–16.

134. Zhu, *A Chinaman's Chance*, 72.

135. Spier, "Food Habits," 80, lists some of the imports recorded at the U.S. Customs House at San Francisco in 1852; oral interview with Chinese food importer in San Francisco, Anna Kwock, who took over her family's importing business, 1970.

136. Striker and Sprague, "Excavations," 22.

137. *State v. B.C Hall and H.E. Tichenor,* March 13, 1911, Elko County Justice Court Records, Index to Criminal Docket, Book 1, Elko County Recorder's Office.

138. Maxine Chan of the Wing Luke Museum, Seattle, lectured on this. See also, Ying-shih Yu, "Han [Dynasty]," 58–60.

139. Murbarger, "Sidewalk to Nowhere,"; and interview with Hugh Martin.

140. Merchant's letter communicated to Reverend William Speer of San Francisco quoted in Gust, "Animal Bones," 190.

141. Hunt-Jones, "Heart of a Community," details the finds, 108–80.

142. Ibid. See also Striker and Sprague, "Excavations," 7.

143. Sando and Felton, "Inventory Records," 151–76.

144. Ispisua, "Island Mountain," 15.

145. The collection of bones found was not too dissimilar from those discussed by Longenecker and Stapp, "Study of Faunal Remains," 97–124; and Gust, "Animal Bones," 177–214.

146. Elko County Recorder's Office, Deeds, Book 14: 691, dated July 10, 1882.

147. Elko County Recorder's Office, Deeds, Book 17: 239, dated January 11, 1887.

148. Elko County Recorder's Office, Deeds, Book 8: 646–47.

149. Elko County Recorder's Office, Bill of Sale, Book 1: 267.

150. Elko County Recorder's Office, Tax Assessment Rolls, 1880–1884. The two figures come from the 1880 roll.

151. Murbarger, *Sovereigns,* 179.

152. Stepanchuk and Wong, *Mooncakes,* 1–40; and Hoy, "Native Festivals," 240–50.

153. Murbarger, "Sidewalk to Nowhere," 5.

154. Murbarger, *Sovereigns,* 179.

155. Chung, interview with Fred P. Frampton, 1993.

156. Lowe, "Pipe Dreams," 178–93; Ahmed, *Opium Debate;* and Mark, "Opium in America," 61–74.

157. On the typical archaeological finds involved with opium, see Wylie and Fike, "Chinese Opium Smoking," 255–306.

158. This kind of physical separation of those who smoked and those who did not has been observed in many archaeological digs of Chinese railroad camps throughout Nevada and elsewhere.

159. Murbarger, *Sovereigns,* 179.

160. Archaeologist Penny Rucks has done some preliminary research into the pine-nut trade between the American west and China.

161. Census manuscript, 1880 and 1900, Nevada, Elko County, Tuscarora.

162. Census manuscript, 1900, Nevada, Elko County, Tecoma.

163. Actually there were two doctors; the first became dissatisfied with the financial arrangements. *GCN,* February 4 and June 17, 1897.

164. Chung, Frampton, and Murphy, "Venerate," 107–46.

165. Oral interviews with Chung, various dates and locations throughout Nevada.

166. Statistics from Census manuscript, 1910, Nevada, Elko County, Island Mountain; story from oral interview with Ispisua, "Island Mountain," 12–15.

167. *State v. B.C Hall and H.E. Tichenor,* March 13, 1911, awarded China Lem (Hong Lee) $110, money he had paid to the swindlers. Franklin Baker testified on Lem's behalf as an eyewitness when the money changed hands. Other claims were much smaller. Elko County Justice Court Records, Index to Criminal Docket, Book 1. See also *EFP,* March 17, 1911, which stated the swindlers were Hall and Vincent.

168. Lammers, "Accommodation," 457, points out that the court made allowances for Chinese testimony through taking an oath upon the blood of a freshly decapitated rooster. But even then the testimony did not have to be accepted as truthful. See Wunder, "Chinese in Trouble," 25–41; Janisch, "Chinese, Courts, and the Constitution"; Cole and Chin, "Emerging," 325–64; and McClain, *In Search of Equality,* detail the background and problem.

169. *People v. Hall,* 4 Cal. Rep. 399, 405–406 (1854). Naturalization was denied to the Chinese in 1870. For a summary important of legislation and cases involving Asian Americans, see Hing, *Making and Remaking,* Appendices A to C.

170. McGrath, "Heritage," 247–60.

171. Elko County Recorder's Office, tax records on microfilm, 1900–1920. The records showed, for example, that the store paid $300 in taxes in 1900.

172. *International Chinese Business Directory,* 1913, Elko County; photocopy in possession of author from Maxine Chan. The other stores were Quang Sing, Quong Wah, Quong Wing, Wuong Wing Woo, and Sing Lee. Two laundries also were listed: Sing Lee and Wah Lee.

173. Ritchie, "Form," 337–38.

174. Barry McGowan feels that the carefully placed rocks in the tailings are characteristic of a Chinese site, but Jeffrey LaLande disagrees. See McGowan, "Typology and Techniques," 34–45; McGowan, "Archaeology," 11–17; LaLande, "Sojourners," 332; and Ritchie, "Archaeology."

175. See Zhu, *A Chinaman's Chance,* 66–69, for a discussion on the homes in the Idaho Basin and South China and the size of a New York urban worker's living quarters in 1893.

176. Rohwer, "Paper," and Murbarger, *Sovereigns.*

177. *GCN,* January 28, 1898. See also Elko County Recorder's Office, Death Record, 1898.

178. Elko County Recorder's Office, Death Record, 1915; Coroner's Inquest, held August 24, 1915.

179. *EFP,* August 23, 1915.

180. Elko County Recorder's Office, Death Record, 1915; Coroner's Inquest, held August 24, 1915. See Nelson, "Final Journey," 70–76.

181. Photograph in the Northeastern Nevada Museum, Elko.

182. The celebrations occur in accordance to the lunar, not Gregorian, calendar.

183. Murburger, *Sovereigns,* 179; Frampton, interview with McKinney; festivals detailed in Stepanchuk and Wong, *Mooncakes,* 61–80.

184. Wah is not a Chinese surname.

185. For more details, see Zhu, *A Chinaman's Chance,* 117–118; and Siu, *Chinese Laundryman.*

186. *Eureka Daily Sentinel,* November 28, 1878.

187. *GCN,* June 10 and 24, 1897.

188. Three-page printout of population totals, 1900–90, Elko County Recorder's Office, Miscellaneous Records.

Conclusion

1. Zhu, *A Chinaman's Chance.* See also Wikoff, "Chinese in Idaho County."

2. Zhu, *A Chinaman's Chance,* 99.

3. Ibid., 133.

4. Ibid., 110, 194.

5. Stapp, "Historic Ethnography," details the Chinese involvement in Pierce. See also Trull, "History."

6. Article 14 of the state constitution of Idaho, adopted January 5, 1861, prohibited the Chinese from mining, but because of economic necessity, an amendment was adopted on October 18, 1864, so that "leftover" claims could be sold to the Chinese; cited in Stapp, "Historic Ethnography," 57–58.

7. See University of California–Hastings College of the Law's study of anti-Chinese laws, "All Persons Born or Naturalized," compiled in 2001.

8. Stapp, "Historic Ethnography," 332–33.

9. *Daily Bulletin* (San Francisco), May 19, 1865; and Stapp, "Historic Ethnography," 376.

10. Stapp, "Historic Ethnography," 114, table 13.

11. Wegars, "History and Archaeology," chapter 4.

12. United States Bureau of the Census, *Ninth Census,* 1870.

13. Raymond, Statistics of Mines, 198.

14. United States Bureau of the Census, *Tenth Census,* 1880.

15. Stapp, "Historic Ethnography," 358367.

16. "The Territory of Montana," 487–99.

17. Stapp, "Historic Ethnography," 62.

18. Couch, "Topophilia," 4.

19. Ronald L. James, "'Why No Chinamen'" 14–24.

20. Zhu, *A Chinaman's Chance,* 184–85.

21. Wegars, "History and Archaeology."

22. Ying-ying Chen, "In the Colonies."

23. Lyman, Willmott, and Ho, "Rules," 530–39.

24. Ying-ying Chen, "In the Colonies," 163–164.

25. McGowan, "Typology," 34–45; McGowan, " Archaeology," 11–17; and McGowan, "Ringbarkers," 31–46. See also Ritchie, "Archaeology" on the Chinese experiences.

26. Ying-ying Chen, "In the Colonies," 118–122.

27. Inglis, "Chinese in Australia," 266–81. The figures do not include those who were part Chinese, who brought the total of Chinese and part-Chinese to 78 percent of the total population.

28. The South African experience is detailed in Richardson, "Recruiting," 85–108.

29. Kynoch, "Controlling," 309.

30. See the *Cuba Commission Report.*

31. "Chinese Are Getting Rich" and "Celestials to Operate Mine," *Los Angeles Times,* March 27, 1910, and July 18, 1915. On the Chinese in Dutch Flat, see Christopher, "Placer County," 50–67.

32. "America's Richest Chinese Divides Fortune with Sheriff Hammel . . ." *San Jose Mercury News,* March 28, 1912.

33. "Sam Yet Sells Gold Estate," *Los Angeles Times,* January 2, 1928.

34. Chung and Mary K Rusco, oral interview with Frank Chang (son of James Chang On); Census manuscripts, 1900, 1910, 1920, Nevada, Humboldt, and Pershing counties, Winnemucca and Lovelock.

35. "Acknowledging Nevada's Chinatowns," online.

36. Zhu, *A Chinaman's Chance,* 191–93.

37. Chinn, *Bridging,* 71–75.

38. Sung, *Survey,* 75.

Bibliography

Archival Materials

1906 Donation Letter, Northeastern Nevada Museum, Elko.
Chinese Merchants of San Francisco. Message to Governor Bigler dated January 30, 1855, in "Remarks of the Chinese Merchants of San Francisco upon Governor Bigler's Message and Some Common Objections . . ." 1855. San Francisco, CA. Found at Beinecke Library, Yale University, New Haven, CT.
Ing Hay and Lung On. Papers and Books. Kam Wah Chung and Company Museum. John Day, OR.
Kam Wah Chung Collection. Oregon Historical Society, Portland.
Kubli, Kasper. Papers. Special Collections Library, Box 12. University of Oregon–Eugene.
Lingenfelter, Richard. Papers. University of California, San Diego, Special Collections.
Penrod, Emanuel. "Letters and Writings." Manuscripts #1416. Nevada Historical Society, Reno.

Government Documents

California

California Reporter.

Nevada

Elko County Justice Court Records. Index to Criminal Docket.
Elko County Recorder's Office. Death Book and Death Records.
———. Deeds.
———. Government Land Office Plat Map, 1885, T. 39 N., 51 E.
———. Index to Bills of Sale, 1890–1937, and Bills of Sale.
———. Index to Marriages, 1869–1949.
———. Index to Miscellaneous Records, 1869–1941.
———. Miscellaneous Records.
———. Tax Assessment Rolls. Various years.
———. Writs of Attachments, 1869–99.

Nevada Historical Society, Reno. Chinese File.
Nevada Revised Statutes.
Nevada State Constitution.
Nevada State Historic Preservation Office. "Find People." http://nevadaculture.org/
Nevada State Legislature. *Appendix to Journals of the Assembly and Senate,* Seventh Session, 1875 and Eighth Session, 1877.
———. "Biennial Report of the State Mineralogist, 1877 and 1878." *Appendix to the State Legislature,* Ninth Session, 1879.
———. "Biennial Report of the Warden of the Nevada State Prison." *Appendix to Journals of the Senate and Assembly,* 1865–1904.
———. *Journal of the Assembly,* 1870–1900.
Nevada State Library and Archives. Carson City. Chinese File. Ormsby County Tax Assessment Rolls.
Statues of the State of Nevada, 8th Session.
Storey County Courthouse. *Arrest Records,* 1864–1890.
Storey County Recorder's Office. *Book of Deeds.*
Washoe County Recorder's Office. *Court Records* (on microfilm).
———. *Deeds* (on microfilm).

Oregon

Grant County Library. Chinese File.
Oregon Legislative Assembly. 1st sess., 1860, *Laws and Journals,* 49–52.
———. "An Act to Tax and Protect Chinamen Mining in Oregon." 4th sess., 1866, *Laws, 1866–1872.*
Oregon State Constitution.

Washington, DC

Immigration and Naturalization Service. Record Groups 85 and 86. National Archives and Records Administration, San Bruno, CA, and Washington, DC.
United States Bureau of the Census. *Ninth Census of the United States: Population and Social Statistics.* Washington, DC, 1872.
———. *Tenth Census of the United States: Population (1880).* Washington, DC.
———. *Eleventh Census of the United States: Population (1890).* Washington, DC, 1892.
———. *Compendium of the Eleventh Census: Part 1.* Vol. 50, part 3. Washington, DC, 1894.
———. *Twelfth Census of the United States: Population (1900).* Washington, DC.
———. *Thirteenth Census of the United States: Population (1910).* Washington, DC.
———. *Fourteenth Census of the United States: Population (1920).* Washington, DC.
———. *Fifteenth Census of the United States: Population (1930).* Washington, DC.
United States Congress. *Congressional Record,* 1882, 1892, 1950.

United States Consulate General, Control Unit. Index of Clan Names by Villages for Hoiping [Kaiping] District, Chunghsn [Zhongshan] District, and Toishan [Taishan] District, Hong Kong, 1965. At NARA, San Bruno, CA, Research Room.

United States Department of Agriculture, Census Office. *Statistical View of the United States: Compendium.* Washington, DC, 1854.

United States House of Representatives. *Congressional Record,* 59 Cong., 1 sess. (1906), Doc. 847 "Facts Concerning the Enforcement of the Chinese Exclusion Laws." A Report from the Bureau of Immigration, 162 pp. Electronically available in the U.S. Congressional Serial Set, v. 4990 Session v. 50.

United States National Archives and Records Administration. Washington, DC. *Census Manuscript.* Microfilm for years 1850–1930. Available at University of Nevada–Las Vegas Lied Library.

Newspapers, Directories, and Bulletins

Baker City Herald (Baker City, OR)

Daily Free Press (Elko, NV)

Daily Silver State (Winnemucca, NV)

Dutch Flat (CA) Historical Society and Museum, 1999

Elko Free Press (Elko, NV)

Elko Post (Elko, NV)

Eureka Daily Sentinel (Eureka, NV)

Gold Creek News (Gold Creek, NV)

Grant County Express (Grant County, OR)

Humboldt Star (Winnemucca, NV)

Idaho Statesman (Lewiston and Boise, ID)

International Chinese Business Directory. Ed. Kin Wong. San Francisco, 1913.

Mining and Scientific Press (San Francisco, CA)

Nevada State Journal (Reno, NV)

Oregonian (Portland, OR)

Owyhee Avalanche (Boise, ID)

Polk's Nevada Gazetteer and Business Directory. Salt Lake City, UT: R. L. Polk, 1907–8, 1912–13, 1914–15.

San Francisco Bulletin (San Francisco, CA)

San Joaquin Republican (Stockton, CA)

Territorial Enterprise (Virginia City, NV)

Tonopah Bonanza (Tonopah, NV)

Tuscarora Times and Mining Review (Tuscarora, NV)

Tuscarora Times-Review (Tuscarora, NV)

Weekly Elko Independent (Elko, NV)

Weekly Oregonian (Portland, OR)

Online Sources

All accessed between 2005 and 2008.

On Nevada:

"Acknowledging Nevada's Chinatowns." Chinese Genealogy, posting dated May 2006. http://siyigenealogy.proboards28.com/index.cgi?board=news&action
"China Ditch: Osino to Elko." http://www.elkorose.com/chinaditch.html
"History of the Sierra County Sheriff's Gallows," http://www.sierracounty.ws/index.php?module+pagemaster&PAGE
"Howard Hickson's Histories." www.outbacknevada.us/howh/
Nevada State Historic Preservation Office, census data, 1860–1920. http://nevadaculture.org/
"Online Nevada Encyclopedia." www.onlinenevada.org
"Sierra County History, Sierra County Government." http://www.sierracounty.ws/index.php?module=pagemaster&PAGE_user_op=view_page&PAGE_id=27&MMN_position=142:142

On Oregon:

1870 Oregon census compilation. http://www.rootsweb.ancestry.com/~cenfiles/or
Oregon Historical Society. http://www.ohs.org/education/focus

On Baker County, OR:

"Chinese Cemetery, Baker City, Baker County, Oregon." http://www.oregongenealogy.com/baker/baker/chinese.htm
"Chinese Heritage, Baker County, Oregon." http://www.oregongenealogy.com/baker/chinese_heritage.htm
"The Chinese in Baker County, Oregon." http://www.oregongenealogy.com/baker/chinese.htm
"Kam Wah Chung & Co. Museum." http://oregonstateparkstrust.org/OurWork/EasternOR/kamwahchung
"Sparta, Baker County, Oregon." www.oregongenealogy.com/baker/sparta

On Grant County, OR:

1870 Federal Census Grant County, Oregon (Camp Harney). usgwcensus.org/cenfiles/or/grant/1870/sh374b.txt
1870 Federal Census Grant County, Oregon (Index N–Z). files.usgwarchives.org/or/grant/census/1870/indx-n-z.txt
Grant County 1870 Census. gesswhoto.com/grantcensus.html
"Grant County Census, USGenWeb Census Project." http://www.rootsweb.ancestry.com/~cenfiles/or

"Grant County History, Oregon State Archives." http://arcweb.sos.state.or.us/county/cpgranthome.html
"Grant County in the Beginning." http://gesswhoto.com/beginning.html

Other:

"Central Pacific Railroad Photographic History Museum." http://www.cprr.org
Court cases on the Chinese and the determination of ownership of land. http://bulk.resource.org/courts.gov/c/F1/0104/001/00000192.txt

Articles, Books, Interviews, Archaeological and Government Reports, Master's Theses, and Doctoral Dissertations

Aarim-Heriot, Najia. *Chinese Immigrants, African Americans, and Racial Anxiety in the United States, 1848–82*. Urbana: University of Illinois Press, 2003.
Abraham, Terry. "Class, Gender, and Race: Chinese Servants in the North American West." A paper presented at the Joint Regional Conference Hawai'i/Pacific and Pacific Northwest Association for Asian American Studies, Honolulu, March 26, 1996. http://www.uidaho.edu/special-collections/papers/chservnt.htm
———. "Stepping Stones to Empowerment: Chinese Servants in the American West." http://www.uidaho.edu/special-collections/papers/stepping.htm
Ahmed, Diane L. *The Opium Debate and Chinese Exclusion Laws in the Nineteenth-Century American West*. Reno: University of Nevada Press, 2007.
Allerfeldt, Kristofer. "Race and Restriction: Anti-Asian Immigration Pressures in the Pacific North-west of America during the Progressive Era, 1885–1924." *History* 88, no. 289 (January 2003): 53–74.
Anderson, Kay J. *Vancouver's Chinatown: Racial Discourse in Canada, 1875–1980*. Montreal: McGill-Queen's University Press, 1991.
Angel, Myron, ed. *History of Nevada, with Illustrations and Biographical Sketches of Its Prominent Men and Pioneers*. Reprint of 1881 "Thompson and West." Berkeley: Howell-North Books, 1958.
Armentrout, L. Eve. "American Involvement in Chinese Revolutionary Activities, 1898–1913." Master's thesis, California State College, Hayward, 1972.
Armentrout-Ma, L. Eve. *Revolutionaries, Monarchists, and Chinatowns: Chinese Politics in the Americas and the 1911 Revolution*. Honolulu: University of Hawaii Press, 1990.
———. "Urban Chinese on the Sinitic Frontier: Social Organizations in United States Chinatowns, 1849–1898." *Modern Asian Studies* 17 (1983): 107–35.
Ary, T. S., Steven G. Barringer, Jerry L. Haggard, Brian R. Hanson, John C. Lacy, John D. Morgan, Clayton J. Parr, and Donald E. Smith. *Mining Law of 1872: A Legal and Historical Analysis.*, Washington, DC: National Legal Center for the Public Interest, 1989.

Ashbaugh, Don. *Nevada's Turbulent Yesterday: A Study in Ghost Towns.* Los Angeles: Westernlore Press, 1963.

Auerhahn, Kathleen. "The Split Labor Market and the Origins of Antidrug Legislation in the United States." *Law and Social Inquiry* 24, no. 2 (Spring 1999): 411–40.

Bain, David Haward. *Empire Express: Building the First Transcontinental Railroad.* New York: Viking, 1999.

Bancroft, Hubert Howe. *History of California, 1884–90.* Vol. 24. San Francisco: History Company, 1890.

———. *History of Nevada, 1540–1888.* San Francisco, 1890. Reprinted Reno: University of Nevada Press, 1981.

———. *History of Oregon, 1886–1888.* Vol. 31. San Francisco: History Co., 1890.

Barde, Robert Eric. *Immigration at the Golden Gate: Passenger Ships, Exclusion, and Angel Island.* Westport, CT: Praeger, 2008.

Barlow, Jeffrey, and Christine Richardson. *China Doctor of John Day,* Portland, OR: Binford & Mart, 1979.

Barnes, Linda Louise. "Alternative Pursuits: A History of Chinese Healing Practices in the Context of American Religions and Medicines with an Ethnographic Focus on the City of Boston." PhD diss., Harvard University, 1995.

Barth, Gunther. *Bitter Strength: A History of the Chinese in the United States, 1850–1870.* Cambridge: Harvard University Press, 1964.

Baumler, Alan. *The Chinese and Opium under the Republic: Worse Than Floods and Wild Beasts.* Albany: State University of New York Press, 2007.

BeDunnah, Gary. *History of the Chinese in Nevada, 1855–1904.* San Francisco: Arno Press, 1973.

Beggs, Jacqueline. *The Chinese Laborers of Lake Chabot, San Leandro, California: A History of Their Contributions to the Construction of Lake Chabot Dam, 1874–1892.* Oakland: Alameda County Historical Society, 1997.

Bentley, R. Alexander, Herbert D. G. Maschner, and Christopher Chippindale, ed. *Handbook of Archaeological Theories.* Lanham, MD: Altamira Press, 2007.

Bilheimer, Ruth K. "Pawns of Fate: Chinese/Paiute Intercultural Marriages, 1860–1920, Walker River." Master's thesis, University of Nevada, Las Vegas, 1998.

"Biography of Lee Chew." In Katzman and Tuttle, *Plain Folk,* 164–75.

Blackburn, George M., and Sherman L. Ricards. "The Chinese of Virginia City, Nevada: 1870." *Amerasia Journal* 7, no. 1 (1980): 51–72.

———. "The Prostitutes and Gamblers of Virginia City, Nevada: 1870." *Pacific Historical Review* 48, no. 2 (1979): 239–58.

———. "Unequal Opportunity on a Mining Frontier: The Role of Gender, Race, and Birthplace." *Pacific Historical Review* 62, no. 1 (February 1993): 19–38.

Blue, Verne. *Mining Laws of Jackson County, 1860–1876.* Portland: Oregon Historical Society, 1922.

Blythe, Wilfred. *The Impact of Chinese Secret Societies in Malaya: A Historical Study.* London: Kuala Lumpur Press, 1969.

Borthwick, John David. *The Gold Hunters: A First-Hand Picture of Life in California Mining Camps in the Early Fifties.* Oyster Bay, NY: Nelson Doubleday, 1917.

———. *Three Years in California.* Edinburgh: W. Blackwood, 1857. Reprinted, Oakland: Biobooks, 1948.

Boswell, Terry E. "A Split Labor Market Analysis of Discrimination Against Chinese Immigration, 1850–1882." *American Sociological Review* 51, no. 3 (June 1986): 352–71.

Bowles, Samuel. *Across the Continent: A Summer's Journey to the Rocky Mountains, the Mormons and the Pacific States.* Springfield, MA: S. Bowles and Company, 1866.

Brown, Martin, and Peter Philips. "Competition, Racism, and Hiring Practices Among California Manufacturers, 1860–1882." *Industrial and Labor Relations Review* 40, no. 1 (1986): 61–74.

Browne, John Ross. *Mineral Resources of the Pacific States and Territories.* San Francisco: n.p., 1868.

Browne, John Ross, and James W. Taylor. "Reports upon the Mineral Resources of the United States." Report for the U.S. Treasury Department, 1867–68.

Bulmer, M. I. A. "Sociological Models of the Mining Community." *Sociological Review* 23, no. 1 (February 1975): 61–92.

Burgess, J. S. "The Guilds and Trade Associations of China." *Annals of the American Academy of Political and Social Science* 152 (November 1930): 72–80.

Cai Shaoqing. "On the Origin of the Gelaohui." *Modern China* 10, no. 4 (October 1984): 481–508.

Calavita, Kitty. "Chinese Exclusion and the Open Door with China: Structural Contradictions and the 'Chaos' of Law, 1882–1910." *Social Legal Studies* 10, no. 2 (2001): 203–26.

———. "Collisions at the Intersection of Gender, Race, and Class: Enforcing the Chinese Exclusion Laws." *Law & Society Review* 40, no. 2 (2006): 249–82.

———. "The Paradoxes of Race, Class, Identity, and 'Passing': Enforcing the Chinese Exclusion Acts, 1882–1910." *Law and Social Inquiry* 25 (January 2000): 1–40.

Cantor, Milton, ed. *American Workingclass Culture: Explorations in American Labor and Social History.* Westport, CT: Greenwood Press, 1979.

Carlson, Helen S. *Nevada Place Names: A Geographical Dictionary,* Reno: University of Nevada Press, 1974.

Carranco, Lynwood. "Chinese Expulsion from Humboldt County." *Pacific Historical Review* 30, no. 4 (November 1961): 328–40.

———. "The Chinese in Humboldt County, California: 'A Study in Prejudice,'" *Journal of the West* 12, no. 1 (1973): 139–62.

Carter, Gregg Lee. "Social Demography of the Chinese in Nevada: 1870–1880." *Nevada Historical Society Quarterly,* 18, no. 2 (Summer 1975): 73–89.

Cassel, Susie Lan. "To Inscribe the Self Daily: The Discovery of the Ah Quin Diary." In Cassel, *The Chinese in America,* 54–76.

Cassel, Susie Lan, ed. *The Chinese in America: A History from Gold Mountain to the New Millennium.* Walnut Creek, CA: AltaMira Press, 2002.

Chace, Paul G. "Returning Thanks: Chinese Rites in an American Community." PhD diss., University of California, Riverside, 1992.

Chan, Anthony. "The Myth of the Chinese Sojourner in Canada." In Ujimoto and Hirabayashi, *Visible Minorities and Multiculturalism.*

Chan, Loren B. "The Chinese in Nevada: An Historical Survey, 1856–1970." *Nevada Historical Society Quarterly* 24, no. 4 (Winter 1982): 266–314.

Chan, Sucheng. *Asian Americans: An Interpretative History.* Boston: Twayne, 1991.

———. "The Changing Contours of Asian-American Historiography." *Rethinking History: The Journal of Theory and Practice* 11, no. 1 (2007): 125–47.

———. "Chinese Livelihood in Rural California: The Impact of Economic Change, 1860–1880." *Pacific Historical Review* 53, no. 3 (August 1984): 273–307.

———. "Introduction. Chinese American Historiography: What Difference Has the Asian American Movement Made?" In Chan and Hsu, *Chinese Americans and the Politics of Race and Culture,* 1–61.

———. *This Bittersweet Soil: The Chinese in California Agriculture, 1860–1910.* Berkeley: University of California Press, 1986.

Chan, Sucheng, and Madeline Y. Hsu, ed. *Chinese Americans and the Politics of Race and Culture.* Philadelphia: Temple University Press, 2007.

Chang, Iris. *The Chinese in America: A Narrative History.* New York: Penguin Books, 2004.

Chen, Chia-lin. "A Gold Dream in the Blue Mountains: A Study of the Chinese Immigrants in the John Day Area, Oregon, 1870–1910." Master's thesis, Portland State University, 1972.

Chen, Shehong. *Being Chinese, Becoming Chinese American.* Urbana: University of Illinois Press, 2002.

Chen, Ying-ying. "In the Colonies of Tang: Historical Archaeology of Chinese Communities in the North Cariboo District, British Columbia (1860s-1940s)." PhD diss., Simon Fraser University, 2001.

Chen, Yong. "The Internal Origins of Chinese Emigration to California Reconsidered." *Western History Quarterly* 28 (Winter 1997): 521–46.

Cheng, Lucie, and Edna Bonacich, ed. *Labor Immigration Under Capitalism: Asian Workers in the United States before World War II.* Berkeley: University of California Press, 1984.

Chin, Art. *Golden Tassels: A History of the Chinese in Washington, 1857–1977.* Seattle: n.p., 1977.

Chinese Consolidated Benevolent Association. *Dreams of the West: A History of the Chinese in Oregon, 1850–1950.* Portland: Ooligan Press, 2007.

Chinn, Thomas W. *Bridging the Pacific: San Francisco Chinatown and Its People.* San Francisco: Chinese Historical Society of America, 1989.

Chiu, Herman B. "Power of the Press: How Newspapers in Four Communities Erased Thousands of Chinese from Oregon History." *Journal of Media History* 16, no. 1 (Winter 1999): 65.

Chiu, Ping. *Chinese Labor in California, 1850–1880: An Economic Study.* Madison: State Historical Society of Wisconsin, 1963.

Chopp, Henry N. *United States Mineral Lands: Laws Governing Their Occupancy and Disposal,* 2nd ed., 1882. Reprinted, New York: Arno Press, 1979.

Choy, Philip P., Lorraine Dong, and Marlon K. Hom. *Coming Man: 19th Century American Perceptions of the Chinese,* Seattle: University of Washington Press, 1995.
Christman, Lanelle E. "Women Zhonghua Huiguan: Chinese Transnationalism and the Creation of a Liberal Public Sphere." Master's thesis, University of Nevada, Las Vegas, 2009.
Christopher, Paul. "Placer County in 1874: The Letters of Duncan McKenzie." *Pacific Historian* 19, no. 1 (1975): 50–67.
Chung, Sue Fawn. "Ah Cum Kee (1876–1929) and Loy Lee Ford (1882–1921): Between Two Worlds." In Lindenmeyer, *Ordinary Women, Extraordinary Lives,* 179–95.
———. "Between Two Worlds: The Zhigongtang and Chinese American Funerary Rituals." In Cassel, *Chinese in America,* 217–38.
———. "Destination: Nevada, the Silver Mountain." In "Origins and Destinations," 111–39.
———. "Gue Gim Wah: A Pioneering Chinese American Woman of Nevada." In Hartigan, *History and Humanities,* 45–79.
———. Interview with Maxine Chan of Seattle, WA,1999–2001.
———. Interview with Fred P. Frampton of Elko and Reno, NV, 1999–2002.
———. Interview with Anna Kwock of San Francisco, CA, 1970.
———. Interview with Juanita Pontoon of Schurz, NV, 1991.
———. Interview with Antoine Primeaux of Elko, NV, 1999.
———. Interview with Penny Rucks of Reno, NV, 1999.
———. "I've Been Workin' on the Railroad." *World and I* (August 1991): 420–31.
———. "Their Changing World: Chinese Women on the Comstock, 1860–1910." In James and Raymond, *Comstock Women,* 203–28.
———. "The Zhigongtang in the United States, 1860–1949." In Yeh and Esherick, *Empire, Nation, and Beyond,* 231–49.
Chung, Sue Fawn, and Elmer P. Rusco. "The Anti-Chinese Movement in Tonopah, Nevada." In *Chinese America: History and Perspectives 2003* (January 2003): 35–45.
Chung, Sue Fawn, and Mary K. Rusco. Interview with Frank Chang of Lovelock, NV, 1980s.
Chung, Sue Fawn, and Priscilla Wegars, ed. *Chinese American Death Rituals: Respecting the Ancestors.* Walnut Creek, CA: AltaMira Press, 2005.
Chung, Sue Fawn, Fred P. Frampton, and Timothy Murphy. "Venerate These Bones: Chinese American Burial Practices as Seen in Carlin, Nevada." In Chung and Wegars, *Chinese American Death Rituals,* 107–46.
Cohen, Lucy M. "George W. Gift, Chinese Labor Agent in the Post-Civil War South." *Chinese America: History and Perspectives* (1995): 157–78.
Colby, William E. "Mining Laws in Recent Years." *California Law Review* 33, no. 3 (September 1945): 368–87.
Cole, Richard P., and Gabriel J. Chin. "Emerging from the Margins of Historical Consciousness: Chinese Immigrants and the History of American Law." *Law and History Review* 17, no. 2 (Summer 1999): 325–64.
Conlin, Joseph Robert. *Bacon, Beans, and Galantines: Food and Foodways on the Western Mining Frontier.* Reno: University of Nevada Press, 1986.

Coolidge, Mary Roberts. *Chinese Immigration.* New York: Henry Holt & Co., 1909.

Couch, Samuel L. "Topophilia and Chinese Miners: Place Attachment in North Central Idaho." PhD diss., University of Idaho, 1996.

Craddock, Paul T. *Early Metal Mining and Production.* Washington, DC: Smithsonian Institution Press, 1995.

Crouch, Craig E. "Hydraulic Mining in California." In "Hydraulic Gold Mining in California's Sierra Nevada Mountains." http://cprr.org/Museum/Hydraulic_Mining/

Crowder, Linda Sun. "The Chinese Mortuary Tradition in San Francisco Chinatown." In Chung and Wegars, *Chinese American Death Rituals,* 195–240.

Cuba Commission Report: A Hidden History of the Chinese in Cuba. Introduction by Denise Helly. Baltimore: Johns Hopkins University Press, 1993. Reprint of 1876 Shanghai publication.

Culin, Stewart. "Chinese Secret Societies in the United States." *Journal of American Folk-Lore* 3, no. 1 (1890): 42–43.

———. "The Practice of Medicine by the Chinese in America." *Medical and Surgical Reporter* (March 19, 1887): 1–3. Bancroft Library, University of California–Berkeley.

Currier, Viola Noon. "The Chinese Web in Oregon History." Master's thesis, University of Oregon, 1928.

Dancing with the Dragon: A Study of Ritual and Inter-ethnic Community Relations. n.p., 1994.

Daniels, Roger. *Anti-Chinese Violence in North America.* New York: Arno Press, 1978.

———. *Asian America: Chinese and Japanese in the United States since 1850.* Seattle: University of Washington Press, 1988.

———. *Coming to America: A History of Immigration and Ethnicity in American Life,* 2nd ed. New York: Perennial, 2002.

Davis, Bancroft G. "Fifty Years of Mining Law." *Harvard Law Review* 50, no. 6 (April 1937): 897–908.

del Mar, David Peterson. *Oregon's Promise: An Interpretative History.* Corvallis: Oregon State University Press, 2003.

Dickman, Diana L. "Living with Exclusion: Chinese Merchants in Baker City, Oregon, 1899–1915." Paper presented to the Oregon Heritage Commission, 2008.

Dillingham, Eric. "Tuscarora Greenstrip Cultural Resources Survey, T. 39 and 40 N., R. 51., Elko County, Nevada." Report for the Bureau of Land Management, August 23, 2001. Paper provided by Dr. William Fawcett, archaeologist, Bureau of Land Management, Elko District, NV.

Dirlik, Arif, ed. *Chinese on the American Frontier.* Lanham, MD: Rowman & Littlefield, 2001.

Donner, P. *The Last Days of the Republic.* San Francisco: Alta California Publishing House, 1880.

Doo, Leigh-Wai. "Dispute Settlement in Chinese-American Communities." *American Journal of Comparative Law* 21, no. 4 (Autumn 1973): 627–63.

Dorian, James P. *Minerals, Energy and Economic Development in China.* Oxford: Clarendon Press, 1994.

Edson, Christopher Howard. *The Chinese in Eastern Oregon, 1860–1890.* San Francisco: R & E Research Associates, 1974.

Emmons, S. F., and G. F. Becker. *Statistics and Technology of the Precious Metals.* Washington, DC, 1885, part of a twenty-two volume work sponsored by the United States Department of the Interior, Census Office, Tenth Census, 1880.

Faire, David. "The Plight of Farmers: A Study of the Rural Economy of Jiangnan and the Pearl River Delta, 1870–1937." *Modern China* 11, no. 1 (January 1985): 3–37.

Farnham, Wallace D. "The Development of an Oregon County, 1852–1890: Mines, Farms, and a Railroad." *Pacific Historical Review* 25, no. 1 (February 1956): 29–45.

Fee, Jeffrey M. "Idaho's Chinese Mountain Gardens." In Wegars, *Hidden Heritage,* 65–96.

Feuerwerker, Albert, Rhoads Murphey, and Mary C. Wright, ed. *Approaches to Modern Chinese History.* Berkeley: University of California Press, 1967.

Flaherty, Stacy A. "Boycott in Butte: Organized Labor and the Chinese Community, 1896–1897." *Montana* 37, no. 1 (1987): 34–47.

Fong, Eric W., and William T. Markham. "Anti-Chinese Politics in California in the 1870s: An Intercounty Analysis." *Sociological Perspectives* 45, no. 2 (Summer 2002): 183–210.

Fong, Mak Lau. *The Sociology of Secret Societies: A Study of Chinese Secret Societies in Singapore and Peninsular Malaysia.* Kuala Lumpur: Oxford University Press, 1981.

Fong, Timothy P., and Larry H. Shinagawa, ed. *Asian Americans: Experiences and Perspectives.* Upper Saddle River, NJ: Prentice Hall, 2000.

Fong, Walter N. "Chinese Labor Unions in America." *The Chautauquan: A Weekly News Magazine* (July 1896): 23–27.

Frampton, Fred P. Interview with Dave McKinney of Gold Creek, NV, 1993. National Forest Service.

Frampton, Fred P. et al. Interview with Della Baker Johns, 1999, typed transcript at National Forest Service, Humboldt–Toiyabe Office, Elko, NV.

Frampton, Fred P., Roger D. Johnson, Suzan Rose, and Phil Stevens. "A Class III Cultural Resources Inventory of the Proposed BHP Poorman Creek Minerals Development Project and the Proposed AUR Coleman Canyon Minerals Development Project, Elko County, Nevada." Paper on file at the United States Department of Agriculture Forest Service Office, Humboldt–Toiyabe National Forest, Elko, NV.

Frederick, David. *Rugged Justice: The Ninth Circuit Court of Appeals and the American West, 1891–1941.* Berkeley: University of California Press, 1994.

Fredlund, Lynn, Dale Decco, Gene Munson, and Dave Ferguson. "Archaeological Investigations in the German Gulch Historic District (24SB212): A Historic Chinese and Euroamerican Placer Mining Area in Southwestern Montana." Vol. 1. Report prepared by GCM Services Inc. (1991): Butte, MT.

Freedman, Maruice. "Immigrants and Associations: Chinese in Nineteenth-Century

Singapore." *Comparative Studies in Society and History* 3, no. 1 (October 1960): 25–48.

Fritz, Christian G. "A Nineteenth Century *Habeus Corpus* Mill: Chinese Before the Federal Courts in California." *American Journal of Legal History* 32 (October 1988): 347–72.

Geer, William P. "Salvage Excavation of BS-780: An Early Boise Basin Chinese Placer Mining Site." A Report for the National Forest Service, Boise National Forest, Department of Agriculture (1985): Boise, ID.

Geertz, Clifford. *The Interpretation of Cultures*. New York: Basic Books, 1973.

Giacomazzi, Sharon. *Trails and Tales of Yosemite and the Central Sierra*. Mendocino, CA: Bored Feet Press, 2001.

Glick, Clarence. *Sojourners and Settlers: Chinese Migrants in Hawaii*. Honolulu: University Press of Hawaii, 1980.

Golas, Peter J. *Joseph Needham's Science and Civilisation in China*, Vol. 5: Chemistry and Chemical Technology, Part 13: Mining. Cambridge: Cambridge University Press, 1999.

Golove, David M. "Treaty-Making and the Nation: The Historical Foundations of the Nationalist Conception of Treaty Power." *Michigan Law Review* 98, no. 5 (March 2000): 1075–1319.

Gompers, Samuel. *Meat vs. Rice* (1902). Bancroft Library, University of California–Berkeley.

Goss, Helen Rocca. *The Life and Death of a Quicksilver Mine*. Los Angeles: Historical Society of Southern California, 1958.

Granger, A. E., M. M. Bell, G. C. Simmons, and F. Lee. "Geology and Mineral Resources of Elko County." *Nevada Bulletin* 54 (1957): Reno, NV.

Greenland, Powell. *Hydraulic Mining in California: A Tarnished Legacy*. Spokane, WA: Arthur H. Clark Company, 2001.

Grimwade, Gordon. "Gold, Gardens, Temples and Feasts: Chinese Temple, Croydon, Queensland." *Australasian Historical Archaeology: Archaeology of the Overseas Chinese* 21 (2003): 50–57.

Gust, Sherri M. "Animal Bones from Historic Urban Chinese Sites: A Comparison of Sacramento, Woodland, Tucson, Ventura, and Lovelock." In Wegars, *Hidden Heritage*, 177–214.

Gyory, Andrew. *Closing the Gate: Race, Politics, and the Chinese Exclusion Act*. Chapel Hill: University of North Carolina Press, 1998.

Hall, Shawn. *Connecting the West: Historic Railroad Stops and Stage Stations of Elko County, Nevada*. Reno: University of Nevada Press, 2002.

———. *Old Heart of Nevada: Ghost Towns and Mining Camps of Elko County*. Reno: University of Nevada Press, 1998.

Hallmark, Bruce. "Chinese Health Hazards and Traditional Chinese Medicine in the Frontier Northwest." *Pacific Northwest Forum*, 6, no. 1 (1992): 60–79.

Hagaman, Wally, and Hank Meals. "The Nevada City, California Chinese Quarter." HistoricHwy49.com. http://www.historichwy49.com/ethnic/chinese.html.

Handlin, Oscar. *The Uprooted: The Epic Story of the Great Migrations That Made the American People.* Boston: Little, Brown and Company, 1951.

Hansen, Lawrence Douglas. "The Chinese: Six Companies of San Francisco and the Smuggling of Chinese Immigrants Across the U.S.-Mexican Border, 1882–1930." *Journal of the Southwest* 48, no. 1 (2006): 37–61.

Hansen, Marcus Lee. *The Immigrant in American History.* Boston: Harvard University Press, 1940.

Hardesty, Donald. *The Archaeology of Mining and Miners: A View from the Silver State.* Pleasant Hill, CA: Society for Historical Archaeology, 1988.

Hardesty, Donald L., and Eugene M. Hattori. "Archaeological Studies in the Cortez Mining District, 1981 and 1982." Technological Reports No. 8 and No. 12 (1982, 1983): Reno, NV.

Hardesty, Donald, Steven Mehls, Edward Stone, and Monique Kimball. *Riepetown: A Data Recovery Report from the Historic Townsite of Riepetown, White Pine County, Nevada.* Sparks, NV: n.p., 1994.

Hartigan, Francis X., ed. *History and Humanities.* Reno: University of Nevada Press, 1989.

Hazlett, Francis G. "Historical Sketches and Reminiscences of Dayton, Nevada." *Nevada Historical Society Paper* 3 (1932): 21–22.

Hershatter, Gail. *Dangerous Pleasures: Prostitution and Modernity in Twentieth Century Shanghai.* Berkeley: University of California Press, 1997.

Higham, John. *Strangers in the Land: Patterns of American Nativism, 1860–1928,* 2nd ed. Brunswick, NJ: Rutgers University Press, 1988.

Highberger, Mark. "Snake River Massacre." *Old West* (Winter 1997): 4.

Hillinger, Charles. "The Saga of Tuscarora: Chinese Fulfill Last Duty to Their Dead." *Los Angeles Times,* Section C, June 18, 1972.

Hing, Bill Ong. *Making and Remaking Asian America Through Immigration Policy, 1850–1990.* Stanford: Stanford University Press, 1993.

Hirata, Lucie Cheng. "Free, Indentured, Enslaved: Chinese Prostitutes in Nineteenth-Century America." *Signs: Journal of Women in Culture and Society* 5, no. 1 (Autumn, 1979): 3–29.

Hittel, John S. *The Resources of California: Comprising Agriculture, Mining, Geography, Climate, Commerce, Etc. Etc., and the Past and Future Development of the State.* San Francisco: A. Roman & Co., 1863.

Hittel, John S., James W Marshall, and Edwin G Waite. *The Discovery of Gold in California.* Palo Alto: Lewis Osborne, 1968.

Hom, Marlon K. "'Fallen Leaves' Homecoming: Notes on the 1893 Gold Mountain Charity Cemetery in Xinhui." *Chinese America: History and Perspectives* (2002): 36–50.

———. *Songs of Gold Mountain: Cantonese Rhymes from San Francisco Chinatown.* Berkeley: University of California Press, 1987.

Hoy, William. *The Chinese Six Companies: A Short, General Historical Resumé of Its Origin, Function, and Importance in the Life of the California Chinese.* San Francisco: Chinese Consolidated Benevolent Association, 1942.

———. "Native Festivals of the California Chinese." *Western Folklore* 7, no. 3 (July 1948): 240–50.

Hsu, Madeline. *Dreaming of Gold, Dreaming of Home : Transnationalism and Migration between the United States and South China, 1882–1943*. Stanford: Stanford University Press, 2000.

———. "Gold Mountain Dreams and Paper Son Schemes: Chinese Immigration Under Exclusion." *Chinese America: History and Perspectives* (1997): 46–60.

———. "Migration and Native Place: Qiaokan and the Imagined Community of Taishan County, Guangdong, 1893–1993." *Journal of Asian Studies* 59, no. 2 (May 2000): 307–31.

Huang, Steven Shih-chao. "Chinese in the United States and the Revolutionary Movement in China, 1898–1911." Master's thesis, San Jose State University, 1961.

Hune, Shirley. "Politics of Chinese Exclusion: Legislative Executive Conflict, 1876–1882." *Amerasia Journal* 9, no. 1 (1982): 5–28.

———. "Rethinking Race: Paradigms and Policy Formation." In Fong and Shinagawa, *Asian Americans*, 79–85.

Hunt-Jones, Patricia. "The Heart of a Community: An Archaeological and Historical Study of Island Mountain's Chinese General Store." Master's thesis, University of Nevada, Reno, 2006.

Hutcheson, Austin E. "Early Mining Districts of Nevada's Comstock Lode." *Historian* 8, no. 1 (1945): 5–18.

Hutchinson, E. P. *Legislative History of Immigration Policy 1789–1965*. Philadelphia: University of Pennsylvania Press, 1981.

An Illustrated History of Baker, Grant, Malheur, and Harney Counties. Portland: n.p., 1902.

Inglis, Christine. "Chinese in Australia." *International Migration Review* 6, no. 3 (Autumn 1972): 266–81.

Irick, Robert L. *Ch'ing Policy Toward the Coolie Trade, 1847–1878*. Taipei: Chinese Materials Center, 1982.

Ispisua, Wendy. "Island Mountain District Chinese Settlement." 1993. Unpublished ms. Lied Library Special Collections, University of Nevada–Las Vegas. Including transcript of interview with Della Johns.

Jackson, Alfred T. *The Diary of a Forty-Niner*. Ed. Chauncey L. Canfield. Boston: Houghton Mifflin Co., 1920.

Jackson, James C. *Chinese in the West Borneo Goldfields: A Study in Cultural Geography*. Hull, England: University of Hull, 1970.

James, Ronald L. "'Why No Chinamen are Found in Twin Falls.'" *Idaho Yesterdays* 36, no. 4 (1993): 14–24.

James, Ronald L., and John C. Lytle. "Ruins of a World: Chinese Gold Mining at the Mon-Tung Site in the Snake River Canyon." *Idaho Cultural Resource Series IV* (1995): Boise, ID.

James, Ronald M. *The Roar and the Silence: A History of Virginia City and the Comstock Lode*. Reno: University of Nevada Press, 1998.

James, Ronald M., and Elizabeth C. Raymond, *Comstock Women: The Making of a Mining Community.* Reno: University of Nevada Press, 1998.

James, Walter. "Walter James: Reminiscences of My Younger Days," ed. Marlon K. Hom. In *Chinese America: History and Perspectives* (1995): 75–86

Janisch, Hudson. "The Chinese, the Courts, and the Constitution: A Study of the Legal Issues Raised by Chinese Immigrants in the United States, 1850–1902." JD diss., University of Chicago, 1971.

Johnson, Andrew. "Quicksilver Landscapes: The Mercury Mining Boom, Chinese Labor, and the California Constitution of 1879." *Journal of the West* 43, no. 1 (Winter 2004): 21–29.

Johnson, Maureen. *Placer Gold Deposits of Nevada.* Pico Rivera, n.d. Reprint of *Geological Survey Bulletin* 1356.

Jones, Edward Gardner. *The Oregonian's Handbook of the Pacific Northwest,* chap. 2, n88. Portland: The Oregonian Publishing Co., 1894.

Jue, Willard G. "Chin Gee-hee, Chinese Pioneer Entrepreneur in Seattle and Toishan." *Annals of the Chinese Historical Society of the Pacific Northwest* (1983): 31–38

Jung, Maureen A. "Capitalism Comes to the Diggings: From Gold-Rush Adventure to Corporate Enterprise." In Rawls and Orsi, *A Golden State,* 31–34.

Kanazawa, Mark. "Immigration, Exclusion, and Taxation: Anti-Chinese Legislation in Gold Rush California." *Journal of Economic History* 65, no. 3 (September 2005): 779–805.

Karlin, Jules Alexander. "The Anti-Chinese Outbreak in Tacoma, 1885." *Pacific Historical Review* 23, no. 3 (May 1954): 271–83.

Karthikeyan, Hrishi, and Gabriel J. Chin. "Preserving Racial Identity: Population Patterns and the Application of Anti-miscegnation Statues to Asian Americans, 1910–1950." *Asian Law Journal* 9 (2002): 1–39.

Katzman, David M., and William M. Tuttle Jr., ed. *Plain Folk: The Life Stories of Undistinguished Americans,* Urbana: University of Illinois Press, 1982.

Kelley, Robert L. "Forgotten Giant: The Hydraulic Gold Mining Industry in California." *Pacific Historical Review* 23, no. 4 (November 1954): 343–56.

Kersten, Earl W. Jr. "The Early Settlement of Aurora, Nevada, and Nearby Mining Camps." *Annals of the Association of American Geographers* 54, no. 2 (December 1964): 490–507.

Keys, John. *Chinese Herbs, Their Botany, Chemistry, and Pharmacodynamics.* Rutland, VT: Charles E. Tuttle and Company, 1976.

Kim, Hyung-chan, ed. *Asian Americans and the Supreme Court: A Documentary History.* New York: Greenwood Press, 1992.

Kim, S. S. "Burlingame and the Inauguration of the Co-Operative Policy." *Modern Asian Studies* 5, no. 4 (1971): 337–54.

King, Haitung, and Frances B. Locke. "Chinese in the United States: A Century of Occupational Transition." *International Migration Review* 14, no. 1 (Spring 1980): 15–42.

Kingsleynews.com. "Unlike Most Chinese Immigrants of His Time, Gin Lin Found

Respect and a Mountain of Gold." www.kingsleynews.com/applegate.good, March 23, 2009.

Knapp, A. Bernard, and Vincent Pigott. "The Archaeology and Anthropology of Mining: Social Approaches to an Industrial Past." *Current Anthropology* 38, no. 2 (April 1997): 300–304.

Kraus, George. *High Road to Promontory: Building the Central Pacific (now Southern Pacific) Across the High Sierra.* Palo Alto, CA: American West Publishing Company, 1969.

Kwong, Peter and Dusanka Miscevic. *Chinese America: The Untold Story of America's Oldest New Community.* New York: New Press, 2005.

Kynoch, Gary. "Controlling the Coolies: Chinese Mineworkers and the Struggle for Labor in South Africa, 1904–1910." *International Journal of African Historical Studies* 36, no. 2 (2003): 309–29.

Lai, Him Mark. *Becoming Chinese American: A History of Communities and Institutions.* Walnut Creek, CA: AltaMira Press, 2003.

———. "Chinese Regional Solidarity: Case Study of the Hua Xian (Fah Yuen) Community in California." *Chinese America: History and Perspectives* (1994): 19–60.

———. "Historical Development of the Chinese Consolidated Benevolent Association/*Huiguan* System." *Chinese America: History and Perspectives* (1987). Reprinted and updated in *Becoming Chinese American: A History of Communities and Institutions,* Walnut Creek, CA: AltaMira Press, 2004. 39–76.

Lake, Holly. "Construction of the CPRR: Chinese Immigrant Contribution." *Northeastern Nevada Historical Society Quarterly* 94, no. 4 (1994).

LaLande, Jeffrey. "'Celestials' in the Oregon Siskiyous: Diet, Dress, and Drug Use of the Chinese Miners in Jackson County, ca. 1860–1900." *Northwest Anthropological Research Notes* 16, no. 1 (1982): 1–61.

———. "Sojourners in the Oregon Siskiyous: Adaptation and Acculturation of the Chinese Miners in the Applegate Valley, California 1855–1900." Master's thesis, Oregon State University, 1981.

Lammers, John C. "The Accommodation of Chinese Immigrants in Early California Courts." *Sociological Perspectives* 31, no. 4 (October 1988): 446–65.

LaPointe, Daphane D., Joseph V. Tingley, and Richard B. Jones. *Mineral Resources of Elko County, Nevada.* Reno: University of Nevada–Reno MacKay School of Mines, 1991.

Lau, Estelle T. *Paper Families: Identity, Immigration Administration, and Chinese Exclusion.* Durham, NC: Duke University Press, 2006.

Lee, En-Han. "China's Response to Foreign Investment in Her Mining Industry (1902–1911)." *Journal of Asian Studies* 28, no. 1 (November 1968): 55–76.

Lee, Erika. *At America's Gates: Chinese Immigration during the Exclusion Era, 1882–1943.* Chapel Hill: University of North Carolina Press, 2003.

Lee, Murray K. "Ah Quin: One of San Diego's Founding Fathers." In Cassel, *Chinese in America,* 308–28.

Lee, Robert. "The Origins of Chinese Immigration to the United States 1848–1882." In *The Life, Influence and the Role of the Chinese in the United States.*

Lee, Rose Hum. *Growth and Decline of Chinese Communities in the Rocky Mountain Region.* New York: Arno Press, 1978.

Leong, Sow-Theng. *Migration and Ethnicity in Chinese History: Hakkas, Pengmin, and Their Neighbors,* ed. Tim Wright. Stanford: Stanford University Press, 1997.

Leshy, John D. *The Mining Law: A Study in Perpetual Motion.* Washington, DC: Resources for the Future, Inc., 1987.

Lettieri, Michelle. "Maximize Our Missions! *Mu-tsai,* Missionaries, and Material Representation." Master's thesis, University of Nevada, Las Vegas, 2007.

Libecap, Gary D. "Government Support of Private Claims to Public Minerals: Western Mineral Rights." *Business History Review* 5 (Autumn 1979): 354–85.

Li Enhan, *Wan Qing ti shouhui Kuangchuan yuntong* [The Late Qing Movement for the Restoration of Mining Rights]. Taipei: Zhong yang yanjiuyuan jindai shiyan jiu suo, 1963.

Liestman, Daniel. "Horizontal Inter-ethnic Relations: Chinese and American Indians in the Nineteenth-Century American West." *Western Historical Quarterly* 30, no. 3 (Autumn 1999): 327–50.

———. "Nineteenth-Century Chinese and the Environment of the Pacific Northwest." *Pacific Northwest Quarterly* 90, no. 1 (1998–1999): 17–29.

———. "'The Various Celestials among Our Town:' Euro-American Response to Port Townsend's Chinese Colony." *Pacific Northwest Quarterly* 85, no. 3 (July 1994): 93–104.

The Life, Influence and the Role of the Chinese in the United States, 1776–1960. San Francisco: Chinese Historical Society of America, 1976.

Limbaugh, Ronald, and Willard P. Fuller. *Calaveras Gold: The Impact of Mining on a Mother Lode County.* Reno: University of Nevada Press, 2004.

Lincoln, Francis Church. *Mining Districts and Mineral Resources of Nevada.* Reno: Nevada Newsletter Publishing Co., 1923.

Lindenmeyer, Kriste, ed. *Ordinary Women, Extraordinary Lives: Women in American History.* Wilmington, DE: SR Books, 2000.

Ling, Huping. "Family and Marriage of Late-Nineteenth and Early-Twentieth Century Chinese Immigrant Women." *Journal of American Ethnic History* 19, no. 2 (Winter 2000): 43–63.

———. *Surviving on the Gold Mountain: A History of Chinese American Women and Their Lives.* Albany: State University of New York Press, 1998.

Lingenfelter, Richard E. *The Hardrock Miners: A History of the Mining Labor Movement in the American West, 1863–1893.* Berkeley: University of California Press, 1974.

Lister, Florence C. and Robert H. Lister. *The Chinese of Early Tucson: Historic Archaeology from the Tucson Urban Renewal Project.* Tucson: University of Arizona Press, 1989.

Liu Bojo. *Meiguo huajiao shi* [The History of the Chinese in America] Taipei: Zhongyang yanjiu yuan, 1977.

Liu, Haiming. "The Resilience of Ethnic Culture: Chinese Herbalists in the American Medical Profession." *Journal of Asian American Studies* 1, no. 2 (1998): 173–91.

———. *A Transnational History of a Chinese Family: Immigrant Letters, Family Business, and Reverse Migration.* New Brunswick, NJ: Rutgers University Press, 2005.
Liu, Hong. "Old Linkages, New Networks: The Globalization of Overseas Chinese Voluntary Associations and Its Implications." *China Quarterly* 155 (September 1998): 582–609.
Liu, Kwang-ching. "Chinese Merchant Guilds: An Historical Inquiry." *Pacific Historical Review* 57, no. 1 (February 1988): 1–23.
Longenecker, Julia G., and Darby C. Stapp. "The Study of Faunal Remains from an Overseas Chinese Mining Camp in Northern Idaho." In Wegars, *Hidden Heritage,* 97–124.
Loomis, A. W. "Medical Arts in the Chinese Quarter." *Overland Monthly* 2 (June 1869): 496.
Louie, Emma Woo. *Chinese American Names: Tradition and Transition.* Jefferson, NC: McFarland, 1998.
———. "A New Perspective on Surnames Among Chinese Americans." *Amerasia* 12, no. 1 (1985–86): 1–22.
Lowe, Sharon. "Pipe Dreams and Reality: Opium in Comstock Society, 1860–1887." *Nevada Historical Society Quarterly* 36, no. 3 (1993): 178–93.
Lydon, Sandy. *Chinese Gold: The Chinese in the Monterey Bay Region.* Capitola, CA: Capitola Book Co., 1985.
Lyman, Stanford M. *Chinese Americans.* New York: Random House, 1974.
———. "Marriage and the Family Among Chinese Immigrants to America, 1850–960." *Phylon* 29, no. 4 (Winger 1968): 321–30.
Lyman, Stanford M., W. E. Willmott, and Berching Ho. "Rules of a Chinese Secret Society in British Columbia." *Bulletin of the School of Oriental and African Studies* 27, no. 3 (1964): 530–39.
McElrath, Jean. *Aged in Sage.* Wells, NV: Recorder, 1964.
Magnaghi, Russell M. "Virginia City's Chinese Community, 1860–1880." *Nevada Historical Society Quarterly* 24, no. 2 (Summer 1981): 130–57.
Mann, Ralph. *After the Gold Rush: Society in Grass Valley and Nevada City, California, 1849–1870.* Stanford: Stanford University Press, 1982.
———. "Community Change and Caucasian Attitudes Toward the Chinese: The Case of Two California Mining Towns, 1850–1870." In Cantor, *American Workingclass Culture,* 397–422.
———. "The Decade after the Gold Rush: Social Structure in Grass Valley and Nevada City, California, 1850–1860." *Pacific Historical Review* 41, no. 4 (November 1972): 484–504.
Mao Shaoyu, ed. *Tang Song Ci* [Tang and Song Poems], Jiangxi, China: n.p., 1995.
Mark, Gregory Yee. "Opium in America and the Chinese." *Chinese America: History and Perspectives* (1997): 61–74.
Marmor, Jason. "Overseas Chinese Placer Mining Sites in the Santa Clara River Watershed: Documentary Evidence, Archaeological Implications, and Significance." *Pacific Coast Archaeological Society Quarterly* 34, no. 1 (Winter 1998): 1–24.

Mayer, Carl J. "The 1872 Mining Law: Historical Origins of the Discovery Rule." *University of Chicago Law Review* 53, no. 2 (Spring 1986): 624–53.

McClain, Charles J. "The Chinese Struggle for Civil Rights in Nineteenth Century America: The First Phase, 1850–1870." *California Law Review* 72, no. 4 (July 1984): 529–68.

———. "The Chinese Struggle for Civil Rights in 19th-Century America: The Unusual Case of Baldwin v. Franks." *Law and History Review* 3, no. 2 (Autumn 1985): 349–73.

———. *In Search of Equality: The Chinese Struggle Against Discrimination in Nineteenth-Century America.* Berkeley: University of California Press, 1994.

McConnell, Gregory Clark. "An Historical Geography of the Chinese in Oregon." Master's thesis, University of Oregon, 1979.

McCunn, Ruthanne Lum. *Chinese American Portraits: Personal Histories, 1828–1988.* San Francisco: Chronicle Books, 1988.

McGowan, Barry. "The Archaeology of Chinese Alluvial Mining in Australia." *Australasian Historical Archaeology* 21 (2003): 11–17.

———. "Ringbarkers and Market Gardeners: A Comparison of the Rural Chinese of New South Wales and California." *Chinese America: History and Perspective* (2006): 31–46.

———. "The Typology and Techniques of Alluvial Mining: The Example of the Shoalhaven and Mangarlowe Goldfields in Southern New South Wales." *Australasian Historical Archaeology* 14 (1996): 34–45.

McGrath, Roger D. "The Heritage of the Trans-Sierra Frontier." In *Gunfighters, Highwaymen, and Vigilantes: Violence on the Frontier.* Berkeley: University of California Press, 1984. 247–60.

McKanna, Clare V. Jr. "Enclaves of Violence in Nineteenth-Century California." *Pacific Historical Review* 73, no. 3 (August 2004): 391–423.

McKeown, Adam. *Chinese Migrant Networks and Cultural Change: Peru, Chicago, Hawaii, 1900–1936.* Chicago: University of Chicago Press, 2001.

———. "Conceptualizing Chinese Diasporas, 1842–1949," *Journal of Asian Studies* 58, no. 2 (May 1999), 306–37.

Meade, Edward Sherwood. "The Production of Gold Since 1850." *Journal of Political Economy* 6, no. 1 (December 1897): 1–2.

Mears, Eliot Grinnell. *Resident Orientals on the American Pacific Coast.* New York: Arno Press, 1978.

Mei, June. "Socioeconomic Origins of Emigration: Guangdong to California, 1850–1882." In Cheng and Bonachich, *Labor Immigration Under Capitalism,* 219–47.

Mendershausen, Ralph. *Treasures of the South Fork: Trails and History Along the South Fork of the Merced River at Yosemite's Front Door.* Fresno, CA: Book Publishers, 1983.

Miller, Stuart Creighton. *The Unwelcome Immigrant: The American Image of the Chinese, 1875–1882.* Berkeley: University of California Press, 1969.

Mills, Lester W. *A Sagebrush Saga.* Springville, UT: Art City Publishing Co., 1956.

Minke, Pauline. *Chinese in the Mother Lode, 1850–1870*. San Francisco: R and E Research Associates, [1960] 1974.
Minnick, Sylvia Sun. *Samfow: The San Joaquin Chinese Legacy*. Fresno, CA: Panorama West, 1988.
Murbarger, Nell. Interview with Hugh Martin, 1963. Transcript at Northeastern Nevada Museum, Elko.
———. "Sidewalk to Nowhere." *True West* (December 1963): 1, 21.
———. *Sovereigns of the Sage: True Stories of People and Places in the Great Sagebrush Kingdom of the Western United States*. Palm Desert, CA: Desert Magazine Press, 1958.
Murray, Dian H. *The Origins of the Tiandihui: The Chinese Triads in Legend and History*. Stanford: Stanford University Press, 1994.
Myrick, David. *Railroads of Nevada and Eastern California*. Berkeley: Howell-North Books, 1962.
Naruta, Anna Noel. "'Creating Whiteness' in California: Racialization Processes, Land, and Policy in the Context of California's Chinese Exclusion Movements, 1850 to 1910." PhD diss., University of California, Berkeley, 2006.
Ngai, Mae M. "History as Law and Life: *Tape v. Hurley* and the Origins of Chinese American Middle Class." In Chan and Hsu, *Chinese Americans and the Politics of Race and Culture*, 62–90.
Nelson, Judy. "The Final Journey Home: Chinese Burial Practices in Spokane." *Pacific Northwest Forum* 6, no. 1 (1992): 70–76.
Nicolini, Delores Yescas, Richard Yescas, and Roberta McDow. "Chinese Camp." *Pacific Historian* 16, no. 2 (Summer, 1972): 47–64.
Nokes, R. Gregory. "'A Most Daring Outrage': Murders at Chinese Massacre Cove, 1887." *Oregon Historical Quarterly* 107, no. 3 (Fall 2006): 326–53.
———. *Masscred for Gold: The Chinese in Hells Canyon*, Corvallis, OR: Oregon State University Press, 2009.
Okihiro, Gary. *Columbia Guide to Asian American History*. New York: Columbia University Press, 2001.
"Origins and Destinations." 1992 Conference on Chinese Americans. Los Angeles: Chinese Historical Society of Southern California and UCLA Asian American Studies Center, 1994.
Ownby, David. *Brotherhoods and Secret Societies in Early and Mid-Qing China: The Formation of a Tradition*. Stanford: Standford University Press, 1996.
Ownby, David, and Mary Somers Heidhues, ed. *"Secret Societies" Reconsidered: Perspectives on the Social History of Modern South China and Southeast Asia*. Armonk, NY: M.E. Sharpe, 1993.
Pan, Lynn, ed. *The Encyclopedia of the Chinese Overseas*. Singapore: Landmark Books, 1998.
Pascoe, Peggy. "Miscegenation Law, Court Cases, and Ideologies of 'Race' in Twentieth Century America." *Journal of American History* 83, no.1 (June 1996): 44–69.
Patterson, Edna, Louise A. Ulph, and Victor Goodwin. *Nevada's Northeast Frontier*. Reno: University of Nevada Press, 1991.

Paul, Rodman W. "After the Gold Rush: San Francisco and Portland." *Pacific Historical Review* 51, no. 1 (February 1982): 1–21.

———. *California Gold: The Beginning of Mining in the Far West.* Lincoln: University of Nebraska Press, 1965.

———. *Mining Frontiers of the Far West, 1848–1880.* Albuquerque: University of New Mexico Press, [1963] 1980.

———. "The Origin of the Chinese Issue in California." *Mississippi Valley Historical Review* 25, no. 2 (September 1938): 181–96.

Peffer, George Anthony. *If They Don't Bring Their Women Here: Chinese Female Immigration Before Exclusion.* Urbana: University of Illinois Press, 1999.

Pfaelzer, Jean. *Driven Out: The Forgotten War Against Chinese Americans.* New York: Random House, 2007.

Pitt, Leonard M. "The Beginnings of Nativism in California." *Pacific Historical Review* 30, no. 1 (February 1961): 23–38.

———. "The Foreign Miners' Tax of 1850: A Study of Nativism and Antinativism in Gold Rush California." Master's thesis, University of California, Los Angeles, 1955.

Qin, Yucheng. *The Diplomacy of Nationailsm: The Six Companies and China's Policy Toward Exclusion.* Honolulu: University of Hawaii Press, 2009.

———. "Six Companies Diplomacy: Chinese Merchants and Late Qing Policy Toward Exclusion, 1848–1911." PhD diss., University of Iowa, 2002.

Rawls, James, and Richard J. Orsi. *A Golden State: Mining and Economic Development in Gold Rush California.* Berkeley: University of California Press, 1999.

Raymond, Rossiter W. Statistics of Mines and Mining in the States and Territories West of the Rocky Mountains. U.S. House Exec. Doc. 210, 42nd Cong., 3rd Sess., 1872.

Renner, George T. "Chinese Influence in the Development of Western United States." *Annals of the American Academy of Political and Social Science* 152 (November 1930): 356–69.

Reynolds, C. N. "The Chinese Tongs." *American Journal of Sociology* 40, no. 5 (March 1935): 612–23.

Rich, Burdett A., and Henry P. Farnham, ed. *The Lawyers Reports Annotated,* New Series Book 7 (Rochester, NY, 1907), 813–87. http://bulk.resource.org/courts.gov/c/F1/0104/001/00000192.txt

Richardson, Peter. "The Recruiting of Chinese Indentured Labour for the South African Gold-Mines, 1903–1908." *Journal of African History* 18, no. 1 (1977): 85–108.

Ritchie, Neville A. "Archaeology and History of the Chinese in Southern New Zealand During the Nineteenth Century: A Study of Acculturation, Adaptation, and Change." PhD diss., University of Otago, Dunedin, New Zealand, 1986.

———. "Form and Adaptation: Nineteenth Century Chinese Miners' Dwellings in Southern New Zealand." In Wegars, *Hidden Heritage,* 335–74.

Robbins, William G. "Opportunity and Persistence in the Pacific Northwest: A Quantitative Study of Early Roseburg, Oregon." *Pacific Historical Review* 39, no. 3 (August 1970): 279–96.

Roediger, David R. *Working Toward Whiteness: How America's Immigrants Became White.* New York: Basic Books, 2005.

Rohe, Randall E. "After the Gold Rush: Chinese Mining in the Far West, 1850–1890." In Dirlik, *Chinese on the American Frontier,* 3–26. Originally published in *Montana: Magazine of Western History* 32, no. 4 (1982): 2–19.

———. "The Chinese and Hydraulic Mining in the Far West." *Mining History Association Annual* 1 (1994): 73–91.

———. "Chinese River Mining in the West." *Montana: Magazine of Western History* 46, no. 3 (1996): 14–29.

———. "Origins and Diffusion of Traditional Placer Mining in the West." *Material Culture* 18, no. 3 (1986): 127–66.

Rohwer, August. "Paper on the Gold Creek Area of Northern Elko County." n.p., 1940. Paper on file at the United States Department of Agriculture Forest Service Office, Humboldt–Toiyabe National Forest, Elko, NV.

Romeo, Jacqueline. "Irony Lost: Bret Harte's Heathen Chinee and the Popularization of the Comic Coolie as Trickster in Frontier Melodrama." *Theatre History Studies* 26 (2006): 108–36.

Ross, Marion. "Jacksonville, an Oregon Gold Rush Town." *Journal of the Society of Architectural Historians* 12, no. 4 (December 1853): 19–25.

Ruitenbeek, Klaas. "Mazu, the Patroness of Sailors, in Chinese Pictorial Art." *Artibus Asiae* 58, no. 3/4 (1999): 281–329.

Rusco, Elmer. "The Chinese Massacres of 1866." *Nevada Historical Society Quarterly* 45, no. 1 (2002): 3–30.

Rusco, Mary K. "Chinese in Lovelock, Nevada: History and Archaeology." *Halcyon* (1981): 141–51.

———. "Counting the Lovelock Chinese." *Nevada Historical Society Quarterly* 24, no. 4 (1981): 319–28.

Ryan, Edward. Annual Report of the [Nevada] State Inspector of the Mines, 1910. Carson City, 1911.

Sandmeyer, Elmer Clarence. *The Anti-Chinese Movement in California.* Urbana: University of Illinois Press, 1973.

Sando, Ruth Ann, and David L. Felton. "Inventory Records of Ceramics and Opium from a Nineteenth Century Chinese Store in California." In Wegars, *Hidden Heritage,* 151–76.

Sangren, P. Steven. "Traditional Chinese Corporations: Beyond Kinship." *Journal of Asian Studies* 43, no. 3 (May 1984): 391–415.

Sarvis, Will. "Gifted Healer: Ing Hay and the Chinese Medical Tradition in Eastern Oregon, 1888–1948." *Journal of the West* 44, no. 3 (2005): 62–69.

Sawin, Herbert A. "One Hundred Years of California Placer Mining." *Scientific Monthly* 9, no. 1 (July 1949): 56–62.

Saxton, Alexander. *The Indispensable Enemy: Labor and the Anti-Chinese Movement in California.* Berkeley: University of California Press, 1971.

Sayler, Lucy E. *Laws Harsh as Tigers: Chinese Immigrants and the Shaping of Modern Immigration Law.* Chapel Hill: University of North Carolina Press, 1995.

Schmidt, Ryan. "The Forgotten Chinese Cemetery of Carlin, Nevada: A Bioanthropological Assessment." Master's thesis, University of Nevada, Las Vegas, 2006.

Schwantes, Carlos A. "Protest in a Promised Land: Unemployment, Disinheritance, and the Origin of Labor Militancy in the Pacific Northwest, 1855–1886." *Western Historical Quarterly* 13, no. 4 (1982): 373–90.

Scott, Irving M. "Hydraulic Mining Illustrated, Part I." *Overland Monthly* 12, no. 72 (December 1888): 576–85.

Seiwert, Hubert with Ma Xisha. *Popular Religious Movements and Heterodox Sects in Chinese History.* Leiden: Brill, 2003.

Sharley-Hubbard, Ann. "'Buildings Realize Culture': Chinese Vernacular Architecture in the Pacific Northwest, 1860–1910." Master's thesis, Goucher College, 2009.

Simmel, Georg. *Conflict: The Web of Group-Affiliations.* Trans. Kurt H. Worlff and Reinhard Bendix. Glencoe, IL: Free Press, [1955] 1964.

Sinn, Elizabeth, "Xin Xi Guxiang: A Study of Regional Associations as a Bonding Mechanism in the Chinese Diaspora: The Hong Kong Experience." *Modern Asian Studies* 31, no. 2 (May 1997): 375–97.

Siu, Paul. *The Chinese Laundryman: A Study of Social Isolation.* New York: New York University Press, 1987.

———. "The Sojourner." *American Journal of Sociology* 58 (July 1952–May 1953): 34–44.

Smith, Amanda M. "Choosing Chinese Medicine: Idaho's C. K. Ah Fong and the Turn of the Century Apothecaries in the American West." *Journal of the West* 46, no. 3 (2007): 24–31.

Smith, Carl T. *Chinese Christians: Elites, Middlemen, and the Church in Hong Kong.* Hong Kong: Oxford University Press, 2006.

Smith, Duane A. "Comstock Miseries: Medicine and Mining in the 1860s." *Nevada Historical Society Quarterly,* 36, no. 1 (Spring 1993): 1–12.

Smith, Lindsay M. "Identifying Chinese Ethnicity Through Material Culture: Archaeological Excavations at Kiandra, NSW." *Australasian Historical Archaeology: Archaeology of Overseas Chinese* 21 (2003): 18–29.

Smith, Roxann Gess. "Grant County in the Beginning." http://gesswhoto.com/beginning.html

So, Alvin Yiu-Cheong. "Ethnic Doctors in Los Angeles's Chinatown." *Journal of Ethnic Studies* 11, no. 4 (Winter 1984): 75–82.

Sohn, Anton. *The Healers of 19th Century Nevada: A Compendium of Medical Practitioners.* Reno: University of Nevada Press, 1997.

Sohoni, Deenesh. "Unsuitable Suitors: Anti-Miscegenation Laws, Naturalization Laws, and the Construction of Asian Identities." *Law and Society Review* 41, no. 2 (2007): 587–618.

Speer, William. *The Oldest and Newest Empire, or China and the United States.* Hartford, CT: S. S. Scranton, 1870.

Spence, Jonathan D. *The Search for Modern China.* New York: Norton, 1990.

Spier, Robert F. G. "Food Habits of Nineteenth-Century California Chinese." *California Historical Society Quarterly* 37, no. 1–2 (1958): 79–84, 129–36.

Stahler, Michael L. "William Speer: Champion of California's Chinese, 1852–1857." *Journal of Presbyterian History* 48, no. 2 (1970): 113–29.

Stanton, William. *The Triad Society, or the Heaven and Earth Society.* Shanghai: Kelly and Walsh, 1900.

Stapp, Darby Campbell. "The Documentary Record of an Overseas Chinese Mining Camp." In Wegars, *Hidden Heritage,* 3–32.

———. "The Historic Ethnography of a Chinese Mining Community in Idaho." PhD diss., University of Pennsylvania, 1990.

Steeves, Laban Richard. "Chinese Gold Miners of Northeastern Oregon, 1862–1900." Master's thesis, University of Oregon, 1984.

Stepanchuk, Carol, and Charles Wong. *Mooncakes and Hungry Ghosts: Festivals of China.* San Francisco: China Books & Periodicals, 1991.

Stevens, Sue Ann. "Midas: A 20th Century Gold Mining Camp." *Northeastern Nevada Historical Society Quarterly* 4 (1984): 110–20.

Stevens, Todd M. "Brokers Between Worlds: Chinese Merchants and Legal Culture in the Pacific Northwest, 1852–1925." PhD diss., Princeton University, 2003.

Stewart, William Morris. *The Mineral Resources of the Pacific States and Territories: A Lecture Delivered at the Cooper Institute, New York City, May 16, 1865,* New York: D. van Nostrand, 1865.

Stratton, David H. "The Snake River Massacre of Chinese Miners, 1887." In Dirlik, *Chinese on the American Frontier,* 115–30.

Stretch, Richard H. "Biennial Report of the State Minerologist to the Nevada State Legislature." Ninth Session, 1879.

Striker, Michael, and Roderick Sprague. "Excavations at the Warren Chinese Mining Camp Site, 1989–1992." *University of Idaho Anthropological Reports* 94 (1993): Moscow, ID.

Sun, E-tu Zen. "Mining Labor in the Ch'ing Period." In Feuerwerker, Murphey, and Wright, *Approaches to Modern Chinese History,* 45–67.

Sung, Betty Lee. *Mountain of Gold: The Story of the Chinese in America.* New York: Praeger, 1967.

———. *A Survey of Chinese-American Manpower and Employment.* New York: Praeger, 1976.

Supernowicz, Dana. "A Contextual History, Programmatic Agreement and Evaluation Plan for Historic Water Conveyance Systems on the Eldorado." n.p., 1990. Paper on file at the United States Department of Agriculture Forest Service Office files, Humboldt–Toiyabe National Forest, Elko, NV.

Takaki, Ronald. *Strangers from a Different Shore: A History of Asian Americans.* Boston: Little, Brown, 1989.

Tchudi, Stephen, ed. *Community in the American West.* Reno and Las Vegas: Nevada Humanities Committee, 1999.

"The Territory of Montana, Plaintiff and Respondent, v. 3000 Feet of Mining Ground, and Fouk Lee, Defendant and Appellant." *American Law Register* 22, no. 8 (1852–1891); new series 13 (August 1874): 487–99. http://www.jstor.org/stable/3303398.

Thornton, Brian. "Exceptions to the Rule: Chinese Merchants and the Exclusion Laws, 1890–1894." *Pacific Northwest Forum* 6, no. 1 (1992): 50–59.

Toepel, Kathryn Anne, William F. Willingham, and Rick Minor. *Cultural Resource Overview of BLM Lands in North-Central Oregon: Archaeology, Ethnography, History.* Eugene: Department of Anthropology, University of Oregon, 1980.

Tong, Benson. *The Chinese Americans.* Westport, CT: Greenwood Press, 2000.

Torok, John Hayakawa. "Reconstruction and Racial Nativism: Chinese Immigrants and the Debates on the Thirteenth, Fourteenth, and Fifteenth Amendments and Civil Rights Laws." *Asian Law Journal* (May 1996). Reprinted as "Asians and the Reconstruction Era Constitutional Amendments and Civil Rights Laws," in *Asian Americans and Congress: A Documentary History.* Ed. Hyung-Chan Kim, Wesport, CT: Greenwood Press, 1996.

Tow, Julius S. *The Real Chinese in America.* New York: Academy Press, 1923.

Trull, Fern Coble. "The History of the Chinese in Idaho from 1864 to 1910." Master's thesis, University of Oregon, Eugene, 1946.

Tsai, Shih-shan Henry. *China and the Overseas Chinese in the United States, 1868–1911.* Fayetteville: University of Arkansas Press, 1983.

———. *The Chinese Experience in America.* Bloomington: Indiana University Press, 1986.

Tsu, Cecilia. "'Independent of the Unskilled Chinaman': Race, Labor, and Family Farming in California's Santa Clara Valley." *Western Historical Society Quarterly* 37, no. 4 (Winter 2006): 474–95.

Ujimoto, K. V., and G. Hirabayashi, ed. *Visible Minorities and Multiculturalism: Asians in Canada.* Toronto: Butterworths, 1980.

Umbeck, John. "A Theory of Contract Choice and the California Gold Rush." *Journal of Law and Economics* 20, no. 2 (October 1977): 421–37.

University of California–Hastings College of Law. "All Persons Born or Naturalized . . . The Legacy of US v. Wong Kim Ark." http://holmes.uchastings.edu/library/topical-and-course-research-guides/wkadisplay/laws3.htm.

Valentine, David W. "American Canyon: A Chinese Village." In Tchudi, *Community in the American West,* 107–30.

———. "Chinese Placer Mining in the United States: An Example from American Canyon, Nevada." In Cassel, *Chinese in America,* 37–53.

———. "Historical and Archaeological Investigation of 26PE2137." Master's thesis, University of Nevada, Las Vegas, 1999.

Vanderburg, William O. "Placer Mining in Nevada." *University of Nevada Bulletin* 30, no. 4 (1936). Reissued as *Nevada Bureau of Mines and Geology Bulletin* 27 (1983).

Wakeman, Frederic E. Jr. *Strangers at the Gate: Social Disorder in South China, 1839–1861.* Berkeley: University of California Press, 1966.

Walker, Townsend. "Gold Mountain Guests: Chinese Migration to the United States, 1848–1882." *Journal of Economic History* 37, no. 1 (March 1977): 264–67.

Wang, Di. "Huaren shequ de chongtu, kongzhi yu zizhi: 'er zhan' qian Meiguo chengshi zhong de zhongguo chuanong shehui zuzhi [Conflict, control, and autonomy in Chinese communities: traditional Chinese social organizations in pre-World War II American cities]." *Shixue Yuekan* [Journal of Historical Science] 11 (2006): 93–101.

Wang, Guanhua. *In Search of Justice: The 1905–1906 Chinese Anti-American Boycott.* Cambridge: Harvard University Press, 2001.

Wang, Kung-Ping. "Mineral Resources of China: With Special Reference to the Nonferrous Metals." *Geographical Review* 34, no. 4 (October 1944): 621–35.

Wegars, Priscilla Spires. "Ah Hee Diggings: Final Report of Archaeological Investigations at OR_GR-16, the Granite, Oregon, Chinese Walls Site, 1992 through 1994." *Historical Archaeology* 30, no. 2 (1996): 119–20.

———. *Hidden Heritage: Historical Archaeology of the Overseas Chinese.* Amityville, NY: Baywood Publishing Co., 1993.

———. "The History and Archaeology of the Chinese in Northern Idaho, 1880 through 1910." PhD diss., University of Idaho, 1991.

Wells, Merle W. *Gold Camps and Silver Cities: Nineteenth-Century Mining in Central and Southern Idaho.* Moscow: University of Idaho Press, 2002.

Wen Zhengde, "Breaking Racial Barriers: Wo Kee Company: A Collaboration Between a Chinese Immigrant and White American in Nineteenth-Century America." Ed. Laurene Wu McClain. *Chinese America: History and Perspectives* (2005): 13–19.

Wikoff, Melvin D. "Chinese in the Idaho County Gold Fields: 1864–1933." Master's thesis, Texas A & M University, 1972.

Williams, Stephen. "The Chinese in the California Mines, 1848–1860." Master's thesis, Stanford University, 1930.

Wilson, Robert. "A History of the Chinese Question in Early Oregon, 1850–1886." Master's thesis, University of Washington, 1942.

Wong, Marie Rose. *Sweet Cakes, Long Journey: The Chinatowns of Portland, Oregon.* Seattle: University of Washington Press, 2004.

Wong, Siu-lun. "The Chinese Family Firm: A Model." *British Journal of Sociology* 36, no. 1 (March 1985): 58–72.

Woon, Yuen-fong. "Ethnic Identity and Ethnic Boundaries: The Sino-Vietnamese in Victoria, British Columbia." *Canadian Review of Sociology and Anthropology* 22, no. 4 (1986): 534–58.

———. "International Links and the Socioeconomic Development of Rural China: An Emigrant Community in Guangdong." *Modern China,* 16, no. 2 (April 1990): 139–72.

———. *Social Organization in South China, 1911–1949: The Case of the Kuan Lineage in K'ai-p'ing County.* Ann Arbor: Center for Chinese Studies, University of Michigan, 1984.

———. "The Voluntary Sojourner among the Overseas Chinese: Myth or Reality." *Pacific Affairs* 56 (1983): 673–90.

Wortman, Roy. "Denver's Anti-Chinese Riot, 1880." *Colorado Magazine* 42, no. 4 (1965): 275–91.

Wright, William [Dan de Quille]. *The Big Bonanza.* 1876. Reprint, New York: Alfred A. Knopf, 1947.

Wrobleski, David Eugene. "The Archaeology of Chinese Work Camps on the Virginia and Truckee Railroad." Master's thesis, University of Nevada, Reno, 1996.

Wu, David Y. Hu. "To Kill Three Birds with One Stone: The Rotating Credit Associations of the Papua New Guinea Chinese." *American Ethnologist* 1, no. 3 (August 1974): 565–84.
Wunder, John R. "The Chinese and the Courts in the Pacific Northwest: Justice Denied?" *Pacific Historical Review* 52, no. 2 (May 1983): 191–211.
———. "Chinese in Trouble: Criminal Law and Race on the Trans-Mississippi West Frontier." *Western Historical Quarterly* 17, no. 1 (January 1986): 25–41.
———. "What's Old about the New Western History: Race and Gender, Part 1," *Pacific Northwest Quarterly* 85, no. 2 (April 1994), 50–58.
Wylie, Jerry, and Richard E. Fike. "Chinese Opium Smoking Techniques and Paraphernalia." In Wegars, *Hidden Heritage*, 255–306.
Wyman, Mark. "Industrial Revolution in the West: Hard-Rock Miners and the New Technology." *Western Historical Quarterly* 5, no. 1 (January 1974): 39–57.
———. "Mining Law in Idaho." *Idaho Yesterdays* 25, no. 1 (1981): 14–22.
Wynne, Robert Edward. *Reaction to the Chinese in the Pacific Northwest and British Columbia, 1850–1910*. New York: Arno Press, 1978.
Xu Shi, "The Images of the Chinese in the Rocky Mountain Region: 1855–1882." PhD diss., Brigham Young University, 1996.
Yang, Philip Q. "The 'Sojourner Hypothesis' Revisited." *Diaspora* 9, no. 2 (Fall 2000): 235–58.
Yeh, Wen-hsin, and Joseph Esherick, ed. *Empire, Nation, and Beyond: Chinese History in Late Imperial and Modern Times*. Berkeley: University of California Press, 2006.
Yen Ching-Hwang, "Class Structure and Social Mobility in the Chinese Community in Singapore and Malaya, 1800–1911." *Modern Asian Studies* 21, no. 3 (1987): 417–45.
Yen, Tzy Kuei. "Chinese Workers and the First Transcontinental Railroad of the United States of America." PhD diss., St. John's University, 1977.
Yeung, Yue-man and David K. Y. Chu, eds. *Guangdong: Survey of Province Undergoing Rapid Change*. Hong Kong: Chinese University Press, 1994.
Yip, Christopher. "Association, Residence, and Shop: An Appropriation of Commercial Blocks in North American Chinatowns." *Perspectives in Vernacular Architecture* 5 (1995): 109–17.
Yu, Henry. *Thinking Orientals: Migration, Contract, and Exoticism in Modern America*. New York: Oxford University Press, 2001.
Yu, Ying-shih. "Han [Dynasty]." *Food in Chinese Culture: Anthropological and Historical Perspectives*. Ed. K. C. Chang. New Haven, CT: Yale University Press, 1977. 58–60.
Yung, Judy. *Unbound Feet: A Social History of Chinese Women in San Francisco*. Berkeley: University of California Press, 1995.
Zerbe, Richard O. Jr., and C. Leigh Anderson. "Culture and Fairness in the Development of Institutions in the California Gold Fields." *Journal of Economic History* 61, no. 1 (March 2001): 114–43.
Zhou Nanjing, ed. *Huaqiao Huaren baike quanshu* [Encyclopedia of the Chinese Overseas and Chinese People]. Beijing: Zhongguo huaqiao chubanshe, 2001.

Zhu, Liping. *A Chinaman's Chance: The Chinese on the Rocky Mountain Mining Frontier.* Niwot; University Press of Colorado, 1997.

———. "Ethnic Oasis: Chinese Immigrants in the Frontier Black Hills." In Zhu and Fosha, *Ethnic Oasis,* 3–43.

———. "How the Other Half Lived: Chinese Daily Life in Boise Basin Mining Camps." *Idaho Yesterdays* 38, no. 4 (1995): 20–28.

———. "No Need to Rush: The Chinese, Placer Mining, and the Western Environment." *Montana* 49, no. 3 (Autumn 1999): 42–57.

Zhu, Liping, and Rose Estep Fosha. *Ethnic Oasis: The Chinese in the Black Hills.* Pierre: South Dakota State Historical Society Press, 2004.

Zo, Kil Young. "Chinese Emigration into the United States, 1850–1880, PhD diss., Columbia University, 1971.

———. "Chinese Emigration: The Means of Obtaining Passage to America." *Journal of Asian Studies* (Korea) 28, no. 2 (1975): 215–29.

Index

Some Chinese names are not separated by a comma because the last name may be any of the words listed in accordance to the Chinese word order.

THE ASIAN AMERICAN EXPERIENCE

The Hood River Issei: An Oral History of Japanese Settlers in Oregon's Hood River Valley *Linda Tamura*

Americanization, Acculturation, and Ethnic Identity: The Nisei Generation in Hawaii *Eileen H. Tamura*

Sui Sin Far/Edith Maude Eaton: A Literary Biography *Annette White-Parks*

Mrs. Spring Fragrance and Other Writings *Sui Sin Far; edited by Amy Ling and Annette White-Parks*

The Golden Mountain: The Autobiography of a Korean Immigrant, 1895–1960 *Easurk Emsen Charr; edited and with an introduction by Wayne Patterson*

Race and Politics: Asian Americans, Latinos, and Whites in a Los Angeles Suburb *Leland T. Saito*

Achieving the Impossible Dream: How Japanese Americans Obtained Redress *Mitchell T. Maki, Harry H. L. Kitano, and S. Megan Berthold*

If They Don't Bring Their Women Here: Chinese Female Immigration before Exclusion *George Anthony Peffer*

Growing Up Nisei: Race, Generation, and Culture among Japanese Americans of California, 1924–49 *David K. Yoo*

Chinese American Literature since the 1850s *Xiao-huang Yin*

Pacific Pioneers: Japanese Journeys to America and Hawaii, 1850–80 *John E. Van Sant*

Holding Up More Than Half the Sky: Chinese Women Garment Workers in New York City, 1948–92 *Xiaolan Bao*

Onoto Watanna: The Story of Winnifred Eaton *Diana Birchall*

Edith and Winnifred Eaton: Chinatown Missions and Japanese Romances *Dominika Ferens*

Being Chinese, Becoming Chinese American *Shehong Chen*

"A Half Caste" and Other Writings *Onoto Watanna; edited by Linda Trinh Moser and Elizabeth Rooney*

Chinese Immigrants, African Americans, and Racial Anxiety in the United States, 1848–82 *Najia Aarim-Heriot*

Not Just Victims: Conversations with Cambodian Community Leaders in the United States *Edited and with an introduction by Sucheng Chan; interviews conducted by Audrey U. Kim*

The Japanese in Latin America *Daniel M. Masterson with Sayaka Funada-Classen*

Survivors: Cambodian Refugees in the United States *Sucheng Chan*

From Concentration Camp to Campus: Japanese American Students and World War II *Allan W. Austin*

Japanese American Midwives: Culture, Community, and Health Politics *Susan L. Smith*

In Defense of Asian American Studies: The Politics of Teaching and Program Building *Sucheng Chan*

Lost and Found: Reclaiming the Japanese American Incarceration *Karen L. Ishizuka*

Religion and Spirituality in Korean America *Edited by David Yoo and Ruth H. Chung*

Moving Images: Photography and the Japanese American Incarceration *Jasmine Alinder*

Camp Harmony: Seattle's Japanese Americans and the Puyallup Assembly Center *Louis Fiset*

Chinese American Transnational Politics *Him Mark Lai, edited and with an introduction by Madeline Y. Hsu*

Issei Buddhism in the Americas *Edited by Duncan Ryûken Williams and Tomoe Moriya*

Hmong America: Reconstructing Community in Diaspora *Chia Youyee Vang*

In Pursuit of Gold: Chinese American Miners and Merchants in the American West *Sue Fawn Chung*

SUE FAWN CHUNG is a professor of history at the University of Nevada, Las Vegas, and coeditor of *Chinese American Death Rituals: Respecting the Ancestors.*

The University of Illinois Press
is a founding member of the
Association of American University Presses.

University of Illinois Press
1325 South Oak Street
Champaign, IL 61820-6903
www.press.uillinois.edu